BR

BR LOCOMOTIVE NUMBERING

COLIN J. MARSDEN

LONDON
IAN ALLAN LTD

First published 1984

ISBN 0 7110 1445 0

Published by Ian Allan Ltd, Shepperton, Surrey; and printed by Ian Allan Printing Ltd at their works at Coombelands in Runnymede, England.

Class 50 No 50002 *Superb* starts the descent of Hemerdon Bank on 25 June 1981 with a short airbraked freight bound for Plymouth.
Colin J. Marsden

Introduction

For probably more than a century the numbers and names carried by railway locomotives have caused much interest from casual railway observers and ardent enthusiasts alike. This product, the first of its type undertaken by the publishers, traces *all* diesel, electric and gas turbine locomotives to operate on BR and its constituent companies from the early 1900s to the present day.

This volume has been prepared in numerical order with private company built types first, followed by experimental and prototype machines, BR standard numbered locomotives and finally BR TOPS (Total Operations Processing System) numbered locomotives divided into two parts electric and diesel.

For space reasons and clarity all diesel and electric classes are listed under 1957 numbers with their appropriate TOPS number following, and in the case of locomotives which carried pre-1957 numbers these are given directly after the 1957 standard number under the relevant column heading. Locomotives that have been renumbered within the TOPS system are listed with the final number or present number given in the right-hand number column. Names are listed with the month and year of fixture to the locomotive where known; those allocated names, but with no plates at the time of going to press are marked N/F. Works numbers together with the builder are quoted but only where works numbers were or are carried on the locomotive. Works/construction numbers of other locomotives are not included as no identification could be gained from their numbers after locomotives departed from the builders' works.

The column marked 'Date or period introduced' gives the month or allocation period (13 per year) of introduction into capital stock (a note should be made that this could often be a month or more after the locomotive was actually completed). The column headed 'Date withdrawn' gives the actual date (by month) the machine was removed from the capital stock fleet. Where only a year is quoted in the introduced/withdrawn column the months/period were not quoted on the official allocation lists. The 'Disposal code' column gives a letter code (the key appears after the Introduction) and informs the reader of the fate of a locomotive after withdrawal from the running fleet, the 'Disposal details' column gives either the scrapping location and date if known, the present user of the machine or its eventual fate. The latest industrial number or identification carried is also included where known. The 'Notes' column gives additional information that the author thought would be of interest to the reader.

Following the heading of each different class a brief description is given with some basic technical details, and *all* class numbers/codes known to be allocated to the type.

The present classes and those allocated TOPS five-figured numbers are cross-referenced with the 1957 number section for ease in identification of modern classes. The present TOPS five-figured numbers give the observer far more information than just an identification number. The first two digits identify the locomotive class, normally the higher the number the higher powered the locomotive, the third digit can be one of two things, either it can be the start of the individual identification number of the machine, or the sub-class number, ie: 08 399 is the 399th member of Class 08, while 33 101 is the first of sub-section one of the Class 33s. The final two digits are always identification numbers.

It should be emphasised that enthusiasts should not attempt to visit locomotives in industrial use unless specific permission is sought from the owners, also access should never be attempted to any railway premises unless the correct permission has been granted, for the presence of casual observers may not be welcome and could indeed be the cause of an accident and may well result in legal action against offenders, thereby rendering it difficult for officially booked visits.

I would like to record my thanks to a number of people who have assisted with information for this product, especially Mr J. N. Faulkner and Mr D. Porter. My thanks also goes to Sandra Fenn for invaluable assistance with the production of the manuscript and the unenviable task of numerically listing the locomotives.

For further technical detail of current types reference should be made to the 'Motive Power Recognition' volume dealing with Locomotives.

The author would be pleased to receive a note of any errors or omissions found in this product, to keep the records up-to-date, so that any future editions can be accurate in all respects. Information should be addressed to Mr C. J. Marsden, c/o Ian Allan Ltd, Terminal House, Shepperton, Middlesex TW17 8AS.

Colin J. Marsden
Surbiton
August 1984

This book is correct to 1 August 1984.

Front cover:
Class 55 'Deltic' No D9010 *The Kings Own Scottish Borderer* poses outside Haymarket depot. *GEC Traction Ltd*

Front cover, inset:
Number area on side of Class 33 No 33014. The locomotive's former number 6522 can be seen through the paintwork. Beneath the number a standard locomotive information panel is attached. *Colin J. Marsden*

Back cover, top:
Two Class 73/1s both in revised livery stand outside Stewarts Lane depot in May 1984. No 73105 is painted in blue with wrap round yellow ends, grey roof and has large sized numbers and logo, while No 73123 *Gatwick Express* displays the BR Executive colours. *Colin J. Marsden*

Back cover, bottom:
WR IC125 set No 253029 approaches Box Tunnel in the summer of 1980 with a Paddington-Bristol service. *Colin J. Marsden*

Abbreviation Codes used in Disposal Listings

A	—	Awaiting removal or scrapping
C	—	Cut up
D	—	To departmental stock
E	—	Exported
I	—	To internal user fleet or returned to capital stock from departmental stock
P	—	Preserved
R	—	Rebuilt
S	—	Sold for further use

The following codes are also used at various locations throughout the book:

A/Barclay	—	Andrew Barclay
A/Whitworth	—	Armstrong Whitworth
B/Boveri	—	Brown Boveri
BR	—	British Railways
BRB	—	British Railways Board
BRCW	—	Birmingham Railway Carriage & Wagon Company
BREL	—	British Railways Engineering Ltd
B/Peacock	—	Beyer Peacock Ltd
BSC	—	British Steel Corporation
BTH	—	British Thomson Houston
CCD	—	Coal Concentration Depot
CEGB	—	Central Electricity Generating Board
DTG	—	Diesel Traction Group
DVR	—	Dart Valley Railway
EE	—	English Electric
EE(DK)	—	English Electric Dick Kerr Ltd
EE(VF)	—	English Electric Vulcan Foundry
GEC	—	General Electric Company
GWR	—	Great Western Railway
H/Clarke	—	Hudswell Clarke
H/Leslie	—	Hawthorn & Leslie
H/Wolfe	—	Harland & Wolfe
KWVR	—	Keighley & Worth Valley Railway
LMSR	—	London Midland & Scottish Railway
LNER	—	London & North Eastern Railway
MRPS	—	Midland Railway Preservation Society
M/Vickers	—	Metropolitan Vickers
NBL	—	North British Locomotive Company
NCB	—	National Coal Board
NSF	—	National Smokeless Fuels
R/Hornsby	—	Ruston & Hornsby
RPS	—	Railway Preservation Society
RSH	—	Robert Stephenson & Hawthorn Ltd
RTC	—	Railway Technical Centre
SR	—	Southern Railway (Region)
WD	—	War Department
WLA	—	Western Locomotive Association
YEC	—	Yorkshire Engine Company

Diesel/Gas Turbine Traction Part 1

Section 1
Pre-Nationalisation Numbers

Southern Railway

SR/English Electric 0-6-0 diesel-electric shunter developing 350hp built by Southern Railway at their Ashford Works to basically established EE design. Used for evaluation against steam traction mainly in Norwood yard.

Original No	*BR 1948 No*	*Built by*	*Works No*	*Date taken into stock*	*Date withdrawn*	*Disposal Code*
SR1	15201	SR Ashford	—	— 1937	December 1964	C
SR2	15202	SR Ashford	—	— 1937	December 1964	C
SR3	15203	SR Ashford	—	— 1937	December 1964	C

Great Western Railway

GWR/Hawthorne Leslie 0-6-0 diesel-electric shunter developing 350hp built as design alternative to steam traction for shunting yards.

Original No	*BR 1948 No*	*Built by*	*Works No*	*Date taken into stock*	*Date withdrawn*	*Disposal code*
GWR2	15100	H/Leslie	HL 3853	December 1935	April 1965	C

London & North Eastern Railway

LNER Shunter design using the 0-6-0 chassis, and the established 350hp English Electric 6K power unit. Evaluated against steam traction at a number of locations.

Original No	*BR 1948 No*	*Built by*	*Works No*	*Date taken into stock*	*Date withdrawn*	*Disposal code*
8000	15000	LNER Doncaster	—	August 1944	August 1967	C
8001	15001	LNER Doncaster	—	August 1944	April 1967	C
8002	15002	LNER Doncaster	—	March 1945	August 1967	C
8003	15003	LNER Doncaster	—	April 1945	August 1967	C

Engine: EE 6K of 350hp
Weight: 55½ ton
Wheel dia: 54in
Max speed: 30mph
Class codes: D3/12, then 3/9A

Tractive effort: 30,000lb
Length: 30ft 3¼in
Height: 12ft 9in
Width: 8ft 5⅝in

Original No	*Disposal details*	*Notes*
SR1	G. Cohen & Co, Morriston, Swansea	
SR2	J. Cashmore Ltd, Great Bridge, Tipton	
SR3	Hayes Ltd, Bridgend	

Engine: EE 6K of 350hp
Weight: 51¾ ton
Wheel dia: 48½in
Max speed: 19mph
Class codes: D3/10, then 3/11A

Tractive effort: 30,000lb
Length: 29ft 0½in
Height: 12ft 5½in
Width: 9ft 0in

Original No	*Disposal detail*	*Notes*
GWR2	G. Cohen & Co, Kettering	

Engine: EE 6K of 350hp
Weight: 50 ton
Wheel dia: 48½in
Max speed: 20mph
Class codes: DEJ-1, D3/9, later 3/10

Tractive effort: 32,000lb
Length: 29ft 1in
Height: 12ft 6⅛in
Width: 9ft 0in

Original No	*Disposal details*	*Notes*
8000	A. King Ltd, Norwich	
8001	J. Cashmore Ltd, Great Bridge, Tipton	
8002	A. King Ltd, Norwich	
8003	Slag Reduction Co Ltd, Ickles, Rotherham	

London Midland & Scottish Railway

Various prototypes were built as an alternative to steam shunting traction in yards — eventually leading to the standard 0-6-0 design of today.

LMS No	*BR 1948 No*	*Built by*	*Works No*	*Date introduced*	*Date withdrawn*	*Disposal code*
1831	—	LMSR Derby	8071/31	May 1934	September 1939	C
7050	—	EE Preston	2047/34	November 1934	March 1943	P
7051	—	Hunslet	1697/32	May 1933	December 1945	P
7052	—	Hunslet	1721/33	January 1934	December 1943	C
7053	—	Hunslet	1723/34	November 1934	December 1942	C
7054	—	Hunslet	1724/34	November 1934	May 1943	C
7055	—	H/Clarke	D580/34	December 1934	April 1939	D
7056	—	H/Clarke	D581/35	October 1935	May 1939	D
7057	—	H/Wolff	—	February 1935	January 1944	S
7058	13000*	A/Whitworth	D20/33	February 1934	November 1949	C
7059	—	A/Whitworth	D54/36	May 1936	November 1944	S
7060	—	A/Whitworth	D55/36	May 1936	December 1942	S
7061	—	A/Whitworth	D56/36	June 1936	November 1944	S
7062	—	A/Whitworth	D57/36	June 1936	November 1944	S
7063	—	A/Whitworth	D58/36	July 1936	November 1944	S
7064	—	A/Whitworth	D59/36	July 1936	November 1944	S
7065	—	A/Whitworth	D60/36	July 1936	December 1942	S
7066	—	A/Whitworth	D61/36	August 1936	December 1942	S
7067	—	A/Whitworth	D62/36	September 1936	December 1944	S
7068	—	A/Whitworth	D63/36	October 1936	December 1942	S

No (range)	Engine type	Weight	Wheel dia	Max speed	T/effort	Length	Width	Height
1831	Davey Paxman	$46\frac{1}{8}$ ton	55in	25mph	21,000lb	30ft $3\frac{3}{4}$in	8ft $7\frac{1}{2}$in	12ft 9in
7050	W. Allan 8RS18	$28\frac{1}{2}$ ton	36in	12mph	11,200lb	23ft 10in	8ft 5in	12ft 8in
7051	MAN 6cyl	$21\frac{1}{2}$ ton	36in	30mph	11,312lb	23ft 2in	8ft 4in	12ft 0in
7052	McLaren/Benze 8MBD	$26\frac{3}{4}$ ton	40in	8mph	12,800lb	24ft $8\frac{1}{2}$in	8ft 3in	12ft 1in
7053	Brotherhood/Ricardo R25	26ton	40in	$13\frac{3}{4}$mph	13,680lb	24ft $8\frac{1}{2}$in	8ft 3in	12ft $7\frac{7}{8}$in
7054	Davey-Paxman 6V25	$30\frac{3}{4}$ ton	40in	13mph	18,600lb	24ft $8\frac{1}{2}$in	8ft 8in	12ft $8\frac{1}{2}$in
7055-6	Mirless Ricardo	30 ton	40in	19mph	12,500lb	26ft $10\frac{1}{2}$in	8ft 7in	12ft 0in
7057	TR4 Hydraulic	$27\frac{1}{2}$ ton	38in	10mph	11,200lb	25ft $4\frac{1}{2}$in	8ft 6in	12ft 0in
7058	Armstrong Whitworth 6LU22	$40\frac{1}{2}$ ton	42in	30mph	22,400lb	28ft 10in	8ft $6\frac{1}{2}$in	12ft $5\frac{3}{4}$in
7059-68	Armstrong Whitworth 6LTD22	52 ton	51in	20mph	30,000lb	31ft $4\frac{1}{2}$in	8ft 7in	12ft 6in
7069-78	EE6K	51 ton	$48\frac{1}{2}$in	30mph	30,000lb	28ft $6\frac{3}{4}$in	8ft 9in	12ft 4in
7079	EE6K	$51\frac{1}{2}$ ton	$48\frac{1}{2}$in	35mph	30,000lb	28ft 6in	8ft 9in	12ft 4in
7080-7119	EE6K	51-55 ton	$51\frac{1}{2}$in	20mph	33,000lb	31ft $4\frac{1}{2}$in 32ft $5\frac{1}{2}$in	8ft 7in	12ft 7in

*No not carried

LMS No	Disposal details	Notes	Original LMS No
1831	After use, converted to mobile power unit, and later scrapped by BR		—
7050	National Railway Museum, York	Sold to War Department after LMS use	7400*
7051	National Railway Museum, York	Sold back to makers December 1945 after LMS use	7401
7052	Birds, Long Marston	Sold to Admiralty December 1943, then to scrap November 1966	7402
7053	Hunslet Eng Co		7403
7054	NCB Hickleton Main Coll October 1974	Sold to Hunslet, then to NCB Yorkshire	7404*
7055	To departmental stock	Converted to mobile power unit No 953	7405*
7056	To departmental stock	Converted to mobile power unit No 954	7406*
7057	Northern Counties Committee as 22005		7407*
7058	BR Derby Works	*Allocated No — never carried	7408
7059	WD used in France/Belgium	Went to WD service August 1940. Sold to Belgian Railway — withdrawn March 1958	
7060	WD used in Egypt	Went to WD service January 1941, withdrawn 1945, scrapped in Suez	
7061	Used in France/Belgium	Went to WD service in October 1940. Sold to Belgian Railway, withdrawn February 1965	—
7062	WD used at various UK points	Went to WD service October 1940 and remained in WD service after war use	—
7063	WD used at various UK points	Went to WD service September 1940, lent to CEGB at Hams Hall, scrapped February 1966	
7064	WD used in France/Belgium	Went to WD service September 1940. Sold to Belgian Railway — withdrawn May 1961	
7065	WD used in Egypt	Went to WD service January 1941. Taken into Egyptian State Railway stock	
7066	WD used in Egypt	Went to WD service January 1941. Withdrawn in Egypt and scrapped 1952	
7067	WD used in France/Belgium	Went to WD service in July 1941. Sold to Belgian Railway — withdrawn January 1966	
7068	WD used in Egypt	Went to WD service January 1941. Taken into Egyptian State Railway stock	

LMS No	BR 1948 No	Built by	Works No	Date Introduced	Date Withdrawn	Disposal code
7069	—	H/Leslie	HL3841	January 1936	December 1940	S
7070	—	H/Leslie	HL3842	January 1936	December 1940	S
7071	—	H/Leslie	HL3843	February 1936	December 1940	S
7072	—	H/Leslie	HL3844	March 1936	December 1940	S
7073	—	H/Leslie	HL3845	April 1936	December 1940	S
7074	12000	H/Leslie	HL3846	April 1936	June 1961	C
7075	—	H/Leslie	HL3847	June 1936	December 1940	S
7076	12001	H/Leslie	HL3848	August 1936	February 1962	C
7077	—	H/Leslie	HL3849	September 1936	December 1940	S
7078	—	H/Leslie	HL3850	October 1936	December 1940	S
7079	12002	H/Leslie	HL3816	April 1934	June 1956	C
7080	12003	LMSR Derby	—	May 1939	November 1967	C
7081	12004	LMSR Derby	—	May 1939	December 1967	C
7082	12005	LMSR Derby	—	May 1939	September 1967	C
7083	12006	LMSR Derby	—	June 1939	September 1967	C
7084	12007	LMSR Derby	—	June 1939	October 1967	C
7085	12008	LMSR Derby	—	September 1939	July 1967	C
7086	12009	LMSR Derby	—	November 1939	September 1967	C
7087	12010	LMSR Derby	—	December 1939	September 1967	C
7088	12011	LMSR Derby	—	December 1939	September 1967	C
7089	12012	LMSR Derby	—	December 1939	March 1966	C
7090	12013	LMSR Derby	—	December 1939	December 1967	C
7091	12014	LMSR Derby	—	January 1940	November 1967	C
7092	12015	LMSR Derby	—	March 1940	October 1967	C
7092	12015	LMSR Derby	—	March 1940	October 1967	C
7093	12016	LMSR Derby	—	April 1940	September 1967	C
7094	12017	LMSR Derby	—	April 1940	October 1967	C
7095	12018	LMSR Derby	—	May 1940	September 1967	C
7096	12019	LMSR Derby	—	June 1940	September 1967	C
7097	12020	LMSR Derby	—	June 1940	November 1967	C
7098	12021	LMSR Derby	—	June 1940	September 1967	C
7099	12022	LMSR Derby	—	July 1940	December 1966	C
7100	—	LMSR Derby	—	December 1940	December 1942	S
7101	—	LMSR Derby	—	January 1941	December 1942	S
7102	—	LMSR Derby	—	April 1941	December 1942	S
7103	—	LMSR Derby	—	April 1941	December 1942	S
7104	—	LMSR Derby	—	April 1941	December 1942	S
7105	—	LMSR Derby	—	July 1941	December 1942	S
7106	—	LMSR Derby	—	July 1941	December 1942	S
7107	—	LMSR Derby	—	July 1941	December 1942	S
7108	—	LMSR Derby	—	October 1941	December 1942	S
7109	—	LMSR Derby	—	October 1941	December 1942	S
7110	12023	LMSR Derby	—	January 1942	December 1967	C
7111	12024	LMSR Derby	—	January 1942	December 1967	C
7112	12025	LMSR Derby	—	February 1942	November 1967	C
7113	12026	LMSR Derby	—	February 1942	October 1967	C
7114	12027	LMSR Derby	—	February 1942	October 1967	C
7115	12028	LMSR Derby	—	March 1942	June 1967	C
7116	12029	LMSR Derby	—	March 1942	May 1966	C
7117	12030	LMSR Derby	—	March 1942	August 1964	C
7118	12031	LMSR Derby	—	July 1942	December 1967	C
7119	12032	LMSR Derby	—	June 1942	December 1967	C

7120-7132 see Section 3 Nos 12033-12045

LMS No	*Disposal details*	*Notes*
7069	WD used in France	Used by GWR during late 1939, went to WD service June 1941
7070	WD used in France	Went to WD service January 1940
7071	WD used in France	Went to WD service June 1941
7072	WD used in France	Went to WD service June 1941
7073	WD used in France	Went to WD service January 1940
7074	BR Derby Works	
7075	WD used in France	Went to WD service January 1940
7076	BR Horwich Works	Went to WD service November 1939, returning to LMS in 1940
7077	WD used in France	Went to WD service November 1939
7078	WD used in France	Went to WD service January 1940
7079	BR Derby Works	Built at English Electric as demonstrator locomotive. Not taken into capital stock until 1936
7080	Slag Reduction Co, Ickles, Rotherham	
7081	J. Cashmore Ltd, Great Bridge, Tipton	
7082	C. F. Booth Ltd, Rotherham	
7083	Slag Reduction Co, Ickles, Rotherham	
7084	Slag Reduction Co, Ickles, Rotherham	
7085	C. F. Booth Ltd, Rotherham	
7086	Slag Reduction Co, Ickles, Rotherham	
7087	Slag Reduction Co, Ickles, Rotherham	
7088	BR Derby Works	
7089	W. Hatton Ltd, Bolton	
7090	Slag Reduction Co, Ickles, Rotherham	
7091	Slag Reduction Co, Ickles, Rotherham	
7092	Slag Reduction Co, Ickles, Rotherham	To WD service, August 1941, returning in 1943
7093	Slag Reduction Co, Ickles, Rotherham	
7094	Slag Reduction Co, Ickles, Rotherham	
7095	Slag Reduction Co, Ickles, Rotherham	
7096	Slag Reduction Co, Ickles, Rotherham	
7097	Slag Reduction Co, Ickles, Rotherham	
7098	Slag Reduction Co, Ickles, Rotherham	
7099	J. Cashmore Ltd, Great Bridge, Tipton	
7100	Taken into Egyptian State Railway stock	To WD used in Egypt
7101	Taken into Egyptian State Railway stock	To WD used in Egypt
7102	Taken into Egyptian State Railway stock	To WD used in Egypt, used by LMS prior to going to WD use
7103	Taken into Italian Railway stock	To WD used in Egypt and then Italy
7104	Taken into Egyptian State Railway stock	To WD used in Egypt
7105	Taken into Italian Railway stock	To WD used in Egypt and then Italy, used by LMS prior to going to WD use
7106	Taken into Italian Railway stock	To WD used in North Africa and then Italy, used by LMS prior to going to WD use
7107	Taken into Egyptian State Railway stock	To WD used in Egypt
7108	Taken into Egyptian State Railway stock	To WD used in Egypt
7109	Taken into Italian Railway stock	To WD used in North Africa and then Italy
7110	W. Hatton Ltd, Bolton	
7111	J. Cashmore Ltd, Great Bridge, Tipton	
7112	Slag Reduction Co, Ickles, Rotherham	
7113	Slag Reduction Co, Ickles, Rotherham	
7114	Slag Reduction Co, Ickles, Rotherham	
7115	C. F. Booth Ltd, Rotherham	
7116	BR Derby Works	
7117	BR Derby Works	
7118	J. Cashmore Ltd, Great Bridge, Tipton	
7119	J. Cashmore Ltd, Great Bridge, Tipton	

7400-7408 see 7050-7058

LMS Derby-built 0-6-0 diesel shunter under construction at Derby Works in 1931. *Author's collection*

Hawthorn Leslie/LMS No 7073 introduced during 1936. This locomotive went to WD service. *Author's collection*

Brush-built Type 4 prototype No D0280 *Falcon*, later to become BR Class 53 No D1200. *BR*

English Electric *Deltic* stands inside its builder's works at Preston before the name was applied. *GEC Traction Ltd*

Section 2
Experimental Locomotives

Over the years several prototype locomotives have operated on the BR system — giving private companies a full size traction test bed.

D0226/7

Two English Electric designed and built experimental 0-6-0 shunting locomotives were built during 1956, to evaluate the slightly higher power output of the 500hp installed engine. D0226 was fitted with a diesel-electric transmission, while D0227 had hydraulic transmission.

Running No	*Built by*	*Works No*	*Dates on loan*	*Date withdrawn*	*Disposal Code*
D0226	EE	EE D226	1956-57	October 1960	P
D0227	EE	EE D227	1956-57	September 1959	C

D0260

Prototype Type 4 main line loco, constructed by BRCW/Sulzer/AEI, during 1962, in the hopes that the railways board would adopt the design as the future standard Type 4.

Running No	*Name*	*Built by*	*Works No*	*Date on loan*	*Date withdrawn*	*Disposal Code*
D0260	*Lion*	BRCW, Smethwick	BRCW 260	April 1962	October 1963	C

D0280

Brush Traction designed and built Type 4 prototype, using two Maybach MD655 high speed engines, driving main generator units. Designed as possible 2nd generation main line motive power.

Original No	*BR 1957 No*	*Name*	*Built by*	*Works No*	*Date on loan*	*Date sold to BR*
D0280	D1200	*Falcon*	Brush	Brush 280	September 1961	December 1970

D9998

One of five demonstrator locos built by Brush at Beyer Peacock Works, Manchester, for active trials on BR.

Running No	*Built by*	*Works No*	*Dates on loan*	*Date withdrawn*	*Disposal code*
D9998	Brush	—	1961-62	—	—

Engine: EE 6RKT of 500hp
Weight: 48 ton
Wheel dia: 48in
Max speed: 35mph
Class codes: —

Tractive effort: 33,000lb
Length: 28ft 8in
Width: 8ft $9\frac{1}{2}$in
Height: 12ft 2in

Running No	*Disposal details*	*Notes*
D0226	KWVR at Haworth	When built carried No D226. Returned to English Electric prior to disposal
D0227	RSH Darlington Works c1964	When built carried No D227

Engine: Sulzer 12LDA28A of 2,750hp
Weight: 114 ton
Bogie type: Co-Co
Max speed: 100mph
Class codes: —

Tractive effort: 50,000lb
Length: 63ft 6in
Width: 8ft 10in
Height: 12ft $9\frac{1}{16}$in

Running No	*Disposal details*	*Notes*
D0260	BRCW Smethwick	

Engine: (2) Maybach MD655 units giving a total 2,700hp
Weight: 115 ton
Bogie type: Co-Co
Max speed: 100mph
Class code: BR Class 53

Tractive effort: 60,000lb
Length: 68ft 10in
Width: 8ft 9in
Height: 12ft $9\frac{7}{8}$in

Original No	*Date withdrawn*	*Disposal Code*	*Disposal detail*	*Notes*
D0280	October 1975	C	J. Cashmore Ltd, Newport	Taken into BR stock as Class 53

Engine: Petter-McLaren
Weight: $29\frac{3}{4}$ ton
Max speed: 18mph

Tractive effort: 19,200lb
Length: 21ft $10\frac{1}{2}$in
Width: 8ft 9in
Height: 11ft 6in

Running No	*Disposal details*	*Notes*
D9998	—	Returned to Brush Ltd after loan to BR

DP2

English Electric built prototype Type 4, based on Type 5 'Deltic' body shell, but using one large 16-cylinder engine as its prime mover. Loco later fitted with sophisticated electronic power/control equipments, later installed in Class 50 locomotives.

Running No	*Built by*	*Works No*	*Date on loan*	*Date withdrawn*	*Disposal code*
DP2	EE (VF)	D733/EE3205	February 1962	July 1967	C

GT3

Gas-turbine powered prototype based on a steam style 4-6-0 chassis, used at various LMR locations during early 1960s but design eventually dropped.

Running No	*Built by*	*Works No*	*Date on loan*	*Date withdrawn*	*Disposal Code*
GT3	EE (VF)	EE.D228	May 1961	October 1962	C

HS4000

Brush/Hawker Siddeley prototype Type 5 mixed traffic loco fitted with highly sophisticated electronic power/control principles used for Trials on ER and LMR on both passenger and freight duties, design not adopted and loco sold.

Running No	*Name*	*Built by*	*Works No*	*Date on loan*	*Date withdrawn*	*Disposal Code*
HS4000	*Kestrel*	Brush	Brush 711	January 1968	January 1971	S

DP1

English Electric designed/built Type 5 prototype utilising two high speed opposed piston engines, design eventually adopted for EE/BR Class 55 'Deltic' locomotives.

Running No	*Name*	*Built by*	*Works No*	*Date on loan*	*Date withdrawn*	*Disposal code*
DP1*	*Deltict*	EE (DK)	EE2003	December 1955	March 1961	P

Taurus/Janus

Two prototype shunters were produced by Yorkshire Engine Co of the centre cab design, as possible design for BR standard shunting loco, locomotives not favoured by BR.

Running No	*Name*	*Built by*	*Works No*	*Dates on loan*	*Date withdrawn*	*Disposal code*
—	*Taurus*	YEC	YEC2875	1961-62	March 1964	C
—	*Janus*	YEC	YEC2595	June 1956	August 1956	S

Engine: EE 16CSVT of 2,700hp
Weight: 105 ton
Bogie type: Co-Co
Max speed: 90mph
Class code: —

Tractive effort: 50,000lb
Length: 69ft 6in
Height: 12ft 10in
Width: 9ft 9½in

Running No	*Disposal details*	*Notes*
DP2	EE (VF) c1968	Following collision loco condemned and returned to EE

Power unit: EM27L gas turbine of 2,700hp
Weight: 85 ton
Wheel arr: 4-6-0
Max speed: 90mph
Class code: —

Tractive effort: 36,000lb
Length: 68ft 0½in
Height: 13ft 0in
Width: 8ft 10in

Running No	*Disposal details*	*Notes*
GT3	EE (VF)/Wards Ltd, Salford	Internal equipment removed by EE and body sold

Engine: Sulzer 16LVA24 of 4,000hp
Weight: 133 ton
Bogie type: Co-Co
Max speed: 100mph (designed for 130mph max)
Class code: —

Tractive effort: 70,000lb
Length: 66ft 6in
Height: 13ft 0½in
Width: 9ft 2in

Running No	*Disposal details*	*Notes*
HS4000	Sold to Soviet Railways	Used in USSR as test and trial locomotive

Engine: (2) Napier 18.25 units, giving 3,300hp
Weight: 106 ton
Bogie type: Co-Co
Max speed: 90mph

Tractive effort: 60,000lb
Length: 66ft 0in
Height: 12ft 10½in
Width: 8ft 9½in
Class code: —

Running No	*Disposal details*	*Notes*
DP1	On display at Science Museum	*Number allocated but not carried †Originally allocated name *Enterprise*

Taurus
Engine: (2) RRC8SFL giving total 622hp
Weight: 58 ton
Wheel dia: 44in
Max speed: 25mph
Tractive effort: 45,000lb
Length: —
Height: —
Width: —

Janus
Engine: (2) RRC6SFL giving total 400hp
Weight: 48 ton
Wheel dia: 44in
Max speed: 23mph
Tractive effort: 30,000lb
Length: —
Height: —
Width: —

Running No	*Disposal details*	*Notes*
—	YEC c1965	
—	BSC Scunthorpe No 3	

Section 3
British Railways 1948 Numbers

10000/1

Two prototype Co-Co main line locomotives were constructed in 1947-48 as the first move to oust steam traction from the main lines. The loco's were built by LMSR/BR and used in a number of areas. Many features of these locomotives were built into subsequent BR/private company designs.

BR 1948 No	*Built by*	*Works No*	*Date introduced*	*Date withdrawn*	*Disposal code*
10000	LMSR Derby	—	December 1947	March 1966	C
10001	BR Derby	—	July 1948	December 1963	C

10100

LMR/Fell experimental 4-8-4DM locomotive built by consortium including BR, Ricardo Co, and L. F. R. Fell, the latter had a special interest in the compression-ignition engine, the unit operated on various LMR lines until 1958.

BR 1948 No	*Built by*	*Works No*	*Date introduced*	*Date withdrawn*	*Disposal Code*
10100	BR Derby	—	January 1951	November 1958	C

10201-3

SR/BR designed and built diesel-electric prototypes, with the intention of a design to oust steam from the SR main lines. After use on SR, all transferred to LMR to work alongside LMSR/LMR prototypes, Nos 10000-10001.

BR 1948 No	*Built by*	*Works No*	*Date introduced*	*Date withdrawn*	*Disposal code*
10201	BR Ashford	—	November 1950	December 1963	C
10202	BR Ashford	—	May 1951	December 1963	C
10203	BR Brighton	—	March 1954	December 1963	C

Engine: EE 16SVT of 1,600hp
Weight: 127½ ton
Bogie type: Co-Co
Max speed: 93mph
Class code: D16/1, 16/8, 6P5F, later 5P5F

Tractive effort: 41,400lb
Length: 61ft 2in
Height: 12ft 11½in
Width: 9ft 3in

BR 1948 No	*Disposal details*	*Notes*
10000	J. Cashmore Ltd, Great Bridge, Tipton, c1968	
10001	Cox & Danks Ltd, Acton, London, c1968	

Engine: Four Paxman 12-cyl units of 500hp each
Weight: 120 tons
Wheel arr: 4-8-4 (4-(4-4)-4)
Max speed: 84mph
Class code: 6P5F

Tractive effort: 25,000lb
Length: 50ft 0in
Height: 13ft 0in
Width: 9ft 0in

BR 1948 No	*Disposal details*	*Notes*
10100	BR Derby Works, January 1960	

Engine: EE 16CSVT of 1,760/2,000hp*
Weight: 132-135 ton
Bogie type: 1Co-Co1
Max speed: 90mph
Class codes: D16/2, 16/9 (10201-2),
D20/3, 20/9 (10203) *10203

Tractive effort: 48,000lb/50,000lb*
Length: 63ft 9in
Height: 13ft 1in
Width: 9ft 3in

BR 1948 No	*Disposal details*	*Notes*
10201	J. Cashmore Ltd, Great Bridge, Tipton, c1968	Stored from December 1962
10202	J. Cashmore Ltd, Great Bridge, Tipton, c1968	Stored from December 1962
10203	J. Cashmore Ltd, Great Bridge, Tipton, c1968	Stored from December 1962

10800

LMSR/NBL Type 1 locomotive No 10800 was ordered by the LMSR late in 1947, with the intention of finding a replacement for steam on secondary and branch lines.

BR 1948 No	*Name*	*Built by*	*Works No*	*Date introduced*	*Date withdrawn*	*Disposal code*
10800	*Hawk**	NBL Glasgow	NBL 26413	May 1950	August 1959	C

11001

SR designed but BR built 0-6-0 diesel shunter for SR shunting yards, and local trip freight. Fitted with 'Box-Poc' wheels (Bulleid design).

BR 1948 No	*Built by*	*Works No*	*Date introduced*	*Date withdrawn*	*Disposal code*
11001	BR Ashford	—	1950	August 1959	C

11104

4-wheel diesel-mechanical shunting locomotive built by Hibberd for use in West Hartlepool P/way yards — taken into BR departmental stock.

BR 1948 No	*Built by*	*Works No*	*Date introduced*	*Date withdrawn*	*Disposal code*
11104	Hibberd	Planet 3466	1950	May 1953	D

11100-11115 see D2200-D2214
11116-11120 see D2500-D2504
11121-11135 see D2215-D2229
11136-11143 see D2550-D2557
11144-11148 see D2505-D2509
11149-11160 see D2230-D2241
11161-11176 see D2558-D2573
11177-11186 see D2400-D2409
11187-11211 see D2000-D2024

Engine: Paxman 16PHXL of 827hp
Weight: 69¾ ton
Bogie type: Bo-Bo
Max speed: 70mph
Class code: —
Tractive effort: 34,500lb
Length: 41ft 10½in
Height: 12ft 9½in
Width: 9ft 2in

BR 1948 No	*Disposal details*	*Notes*
10800	After withdrawal sold to Brush Ltd who used locomotive as test bed, and allocated Brush Works No 710. After being used as a mobile power unit in 1972, the locomotive was scrapped by Brush. Cut by February 1976	*Name never carried

Engine: Paxman Ricardo V12 of 500hp
Weight: 49½ ton
Wheel dia: 54in
Max speed: 43½mph
Class code: —
Tractive effort: 33,000lb
Length: 33ft 3in
Height: 12ft 11½in
Width: 8ft 7½in

BR 1948 No	*Disposal details*	*Notes*
11001	BR Ashford Works, December 1959	

Engine: English National DA4 of 52hp
Weight: 11 ton
Wheel dia: —
Max speed: 15mph
Tractive effort: —
Length: —
Height: —
Width: —

BR 1948 No	*Disposal details*	*Notes*
11104	To Departmental stock No 52	

11212-11229 see D2242-D2259
11500-11502 see D2950-D2952
11503-11506 see D2953-D2956
11507-11508 see D2957-D2958
11700-11707 see D2700-D2707
11708-11719 see D2708-D2719
12000/1/2 see LMS Nos 7074/6/9
12003-12032 see LMS Nos 7080-7119

Class 11

LMSR/BR diesel-electric shunter design, adopted as standard following various trials with prototype locomotives during the early 1940s. This design was the forerunner to the Class 08/09 locomotives.

BR 1948 No	*Previous LMS No*	*Built by*	*Works No*	*Date introduced*	*Date withdrawn*	*Disposal code*
12033	7120	LMSR Derby	—	April 1945	January 1969	C
12034	7121	LMSR Derby	—	May 1945	October 1968	C
12035	7122	LMSR Derby	—	June 1945	October 1968	C
12036	7123	LMSR Derby	—	August 1945	October 1968	C
12037	7124	LMSR Derby	—	October 1945	October 1968	C
12038	7125	LMSR Derby	—	December 1945	January 1969	C
12039	7126	LMSR Derby	—	August 1947	October 1968	C
12040	7127	LMSR Derby	—	September 1947	October 1968	C
12041	7128	LMSR Derby	—	October 1947	October 1968	C
12042	7129	LMSR Derby	—	November 1947	October 1968	C
12043	7130	BR Derby	—	February 1948	October 1968	C
12044	7131	BR Derby	—	March 1948	November 1968	C
12045	7132*	BR Derby	—	April 1948	January 1969	C
12046	7133*	BR Derby	—	May 1948	January 1969	C
12047	7134*	BR Derby	—	August 1948	January 1969	C
12048	7135*	BR Derby	—	December 1948	January 1969	C
12049	7136*	BR Derby	—	December 1948	October 1971	S
12050	7137*	BR Derby	—	January 1949	July 1970	C
12051	7138*	BR Derby	—	February 1949	October 1971	C
12052	7139*	BR Derby	—	March 1949	June 1971	S
12053	7140*	BR Derby	—	April 1949	April 1971	C
12054	7141*	BR Derby	—	May 1949	July 1970	C
12055	7142*	BR Derby	—	June 1949	June 1971	C
12056	7143*	BR Derby	—	July 1949	September 1971	C
12057	7144*	BR Derby	—	August 1949	January 1969	C
12058	7145*	BR Derby	—	October 1949	April 1971	C
12059	7146*	BR Derby	—	October 1949	January 1969	C
12060	7147*	BR Derby	—	November 1949	January 1971	S
12061	7148*	BR Derby	—	November 1949	October 1971	S
12062	7149*	BR Derby	—	December 1949	April 1970	C
12063	7150*	BR Derby	—	December 1949	January 1972	S
12064	7151*	BR Derby	—	December 1949	March 1969	C
12065	7152*	BR Derby	—	December 1949	May 1971	C
12066	7153*	BR Derby	—	December 1949	March 1969	C
12067	7154*	BR Derby	—	February 1950	January 1969	C
12068	7155*	BR Derby	—	March 1950	December 1967	C
12069	—	BR Derby	—	July 1950	March 1971	C
12070	—	BR Derby	—	August 1950	October 1969	C
12071	—	BR Derby	—	August 1950	October 1971	S
12072	—	BR Derby	—	August 1950	December 1968	C
12073	—	BR Derby	—	September 1950	November 1971	C
12074	—	BR Derby	—	September 1950	January 1972	S
12075	—	BR Derby	—	September 1950	November 1971	C
12076	—	BR Derby	—	October 1950	December 1971	C
12077	—	BR Derby	—	October 1950	October 1971	P
12078	—	BR Derby	—	October 1950	January 1971	C
12079	—	BR Derby	—	November 1950	August 1971	C
12080	—	BR Derby	—	November 1950	April 1971	C
12081	—	BR Derby	—	November 1950	June 1970	C
12082	—	BR Derby	—	November 1950	October 1971	S

Engine: EE 6K of 350hp
Weight: 47⅛ ton
Wheel dia: 48½in
Max speed: 20mph
Tractive effort: 35,000lb
Length: 29ft 1½in
Height: 12ft 5⅞in
Width: 8ft 7in

*No Not Carried

Class codes: DEJ3, D3/8, D3/8A and TOPS 11

BR 1948 No	*Disposal details*	*Notes*
12033	J. Cashmore Ltd, Great Bridge Tipton, August 1970	
12034	J. McWilliams, Shettleston, Glasgow	
12035	J. McWilliams, Shettleston, Glasgow	
12036	J. Cashmore Ltd, Great Bridge, Tipton, March 1970	
12037	J. Cashmore Ltd, Great Bridge, Tipton, July 1970	
12038	G. Cohen, Kettering, Northamptonshire, July 1971	
12039	J. Cashmore Ltd at Bescot MPD, January 1970	
12040	J. Cashmore Ltd, Great Bridge, Tipton, February 1970	
12041	J. Cashmore Ltd, Newport, Gwent	
12042	J. Cashmore Ltd, Newport, Gwent, November 1969	
12043	J. Cashmore Ltd, Great Bridge, Tipton	
12044	J. Cashmore Ltd, Great Bridge, Tipton	
12045	J. Cashmore Ltd, Great Bridge, Tipton	
12046	G. Cohen Ltd at Bletchley MPD	
12047	J. Cashmore Ltd, Great Bridge, Tipton	
12048	J. Cashmore Ltd, Great Bridge, Tipton, March 1970	
12049	Day & Sons, Brentford	
12050	NCB Philadelphia, Tyne & Wear	Used by NCB until 1972
12051	J. Cashmore Ltd, Great Bridge, Tipton	
12052	D. Crouch Ltd, Widdrington, Northumberland as MP228	
12053	Birds Ltd, Long Marston, Worcestershire	
12054	A. R. Adams, Newport, Gwent, February 1984	
12055	C. F. Booth, Rotherham, South Yorkshire, August 1972	
12056	G. Cohen, Kettering, Northamptonshire	
12057	J. Cashmore Ltd, Great Bridge, Tipton, February 1970	
12058	J. Cashmore Ltd, Newport, Gwent	
12059	J. Cashmore Ltd, Newport, Gwent	
12060	NCB Philadelphia, Tyne & Wear, No 512	
12061	NSF Nantgarw, Treforest, Glamorgan, No 4	
12062	BR Derby Works	
12063	NSF Nantgarw, Treforest, Glamorgan, No 5	
12064	J. Cashmore Ltd, Great Bridge, Tipton, January 1970	
12065	J. Cashmore Ltd, Great Bridge, Tipton	
12066	J. Cashmore Ltd, Great Bridge, Tipton, February 1970	
12067	G. Cohen, Kettering, Northamptonshire, February 1970	
12068	G. Cohen, Kettering, Northamptonshire, June 1968	
12069	Birds Ltd, Long Marston, Worcestershire	
12070	C. F. Booth, Rotherham, South Yorkshire	
12071	NSF Nantgarw, Treforest, Glamorgan, No 6	
12072	G. Cohen, Kettering, Northamptonshire, February 1970	
12073	C. F. Booth, Rotherham, South Yorkshire, August 1972	
12074	NCB Swalwell, Tyne & Wear	
12075	G. Cohen, Kettering, Northamptonshire, July 1973	
12076	G. Cohen, Kettering, Northamptonshire, July 1973	
12077	Midland Railway Centre, at Butterley	
12078	G. Cohen, Kettering, Northamptonshire, November 1971	
12079	C. F. Booth, Rotherham, South Yorkshire, August 1972	
12080	BR Doncaster Works	
12081	C. F. Booth, Rotherham, South Yorkshire, August 1972	
12082	UKF Fertilisers Ince & Elton, Cheshire	

BR 1948 No	Previous LMS No	Built by	Works No	Date introduced	Date withdrawn	Disposal code
12083	—	BR Derby	—	November 1950	October 1971	S
12084	—	BR Derby	—	December 1950	May 1971	S
12085	—	BR Derby	—	December 1950	May 1971	C
12086	—	BR Derby	—	December 1950	July 1969	C
12087	—	BR Derby	—	December 1950	June 1971	C
12088	—	BR Derby	—	June 1951	May 1971	S
12089	—	BR Derby	—	June 1951	September 1970	C
12090	—	BR Derby	—	June 1951	June 1971	C
12091	—	BR Derby	—	July 1951	June 1970	C
12092	—	BR Derby	—	August 1951	March 1969	C
12093	—	BR Derby	—	August 1951	May 1971	S
12094	—	BR Derby	—	September 1951	October 1971	C
12095	—	BR Derby	—	December 1951	March 1969	C
12096	—	BR Derby	—	December 1951	February 1969	C
12097	—	BR Derby	—	December 1951	May 1971	C
12098	—	BR Derby	—	February 1952	April 1971	S
12099	—	BR Derby	—	March 1952	May 1971	S
12100	—	BR Derby	—	April 1952	March 1969	C
12101	—	BR Derby	—	May 1952	August 1970	C
12102	—	BR Derby	—	June 1952	February 1971	C
12103	—	BR Darlington	—	March 1952	November 1971	C
12104	—	BR Darlington	—	April 1952	April 1967	C
12105	—	BR Darlington	—	April 1952	March 1967	C
12106	—	BR Darlington	—	April 1952	August 1970	C
12107	—	BR Darlington	—	May 1952	December 1967	C
12108	—	BR Darlington	—	May 1952	December 1971	C
12109	—	BR Darlington	—	June 1952	November 1972	C
12110	—	BR Darlington	—	June 1952	November 1972	C
12111	—	BR Darlington	—	July 1952	May 1971	C
12112	—	BR Darlington	—	July 1952	November 1969	C
12113	—	BR Darlington	—	July 1952	April 1971	C
12114	—	BR Darlington	—	July 1952	May 1971	C
12115	—	BR Darlington	—	August 1952	October 1970	C
12116	—	BR Darlington	—	August 1952	September 1969	C
12117	—	BR Darlington	—	August 1952	February 1969	C
12118	—	BR Darlington	—	September 1952	May 1971	C
12119	—	BR Darlington	—	September 1952	December 1968	C
12120	—	BR Darlington	—	September 1952	January 1969	S
12121	—	BR Darlington	—	September 1952	May 1971	C
12122	—	BR Darlington	—	September 1952	June 1971	S
12123	—	BR Darlington	—	October 1952	July 1967	C
12124	—	BR Darlington	—	October 1952	December 1968	C
12125	—	BR Darlington	—	October 1952	June 1969	C
12126	—	BR Darlington	—	October 1952	November 1968	C
12127	—	BR Darlington	—	October 1952	October 1967	C
12128	—	BR Darlington	—	October 1952	July 1970	C
12129	—	BR Darlington	—	November 1952	September 1967	C
12130	—	BR Darlington	—	November 1952	July 1972	C
12131	—	BR Darlington	—	November 1952	April 1969	P
12132	—	BR Darlington	—	November 1952	June 1972	C
12133	—	BR Darlington	—	December 1952	January 1969	S
12134	—	BR Darlington	—	December 1952	October 1972	C
12135	—	BR Darlington	—	December 1952	June 1969	C
12136	—	BR Darlington	—	December 1952	December 1971	C
12137	—	BR Darlington	—	December 1952	November 1968	C
12138	—	BR Darlington	—	December 1952	November 1968	C

13000-13357 see D3000-D3357
13362-13366 see D3362-D3366

BR 1948 No	*Disposal details*	*Notes*
12083	Tilcon Ltd, Cracoe, Nr Skipton, Yorkshire	
12084	NCB Philadelphia Works, No 514	
12085	T. W. Ward, Barrow	
12086	J. Cashmore, Great Bridge, Tipton, February 1970	
12087	G. Cohen, Kettering, Northamptonshire	
12088	NCB Swalwell, Tyne & Wear	Out of use
12089	BR Derby Works	
12090	C. F. Booth, Rotherham, South Yorkshire, August 1970	
12091	BR Derby Works	
12092	J. Cashmore, Great Bridge, Tipton, January 1970	
12093	D. Crouch, Widdrington, Northumberland, MP229	
12094	C. F. Booth, Rotherham, South Yorkshire, August 1972	
12095	J. Cashmore, Great Bridge, Tipton, August 1970	
12096	G. Cohen, Kettering, Northamptonshire, February 1970	
12097	BR Doncaster Works	
12098	NCB Philadelphia, Tyne & Wear, No 513	
12099	NCB Bowers Row disposal point	
12100	J. Cashmore, Great Bridge, Tipton, January 1970	
12101	G. Cohen, Kettering, Northamptonshire, August 1971	
12102	G. Cohen, Kettering, Northamptonshire, October 1971	
12103	J. Cashmore, Newport, Gwent	
12104	G. Cohen Ltd at BR Depot, Stratford	
12105	BR Stratford Diesel Repair Shop	
12106	C. F. Booth, Rotherham, South Yorkshire	
12107	J. McWilliams, Shettleston, Glasgow, September 1968	
12108	T. W. Ward Ltd, Beighton, South Yorkshire, March 1977	
12109	Marple & Gillott, Attercliffe, South Yorkshire, August 1973	
12110	Marple & Gillott, Attercliffe, South Yorkshire, September 1973	
12111	BR Stratford Diesel Repair Shop	
12112	C. F. Booth, Rotherham, South Yorkshire	
12113	G. Cohen, Kettering, Northamptonshire, August 1971	
12114	BR Stratford Diesel Repair Shop	
12115	BR Stratford Diesel Repair Shop	
12116	G. Cohen, Kettering, Northamptonshire, January 1970	
12117	Arnott Young, Parkgate, Rotherham, Yorkshire	
12118	G. Cohen, Kettering, Northamptonshire	
12119	NCB Philadelphia, Tyne & Wear	
12120	NCB Philadelphia, Tyne & Wear, No 510	
12121	C. F. Booth, Rotherham, South Yorkshire, April 1972	
12122	NCB British Oak Disposal point	Out of use
12123	T. W. Ward, Beighton, South Yorkshire, March 1968	
12124	G. Cohen, Kettering, Northamptonshire, July 1969	
12125	J. McWilliams, Shettleston, Glasgow	
12126	Arnott Young, Parkgate, Rotherham, Yorkshire, August 1969	
12127	BR Doncaster Works	
12128	C. F. Booth, Rotherham, South Yorkshire	
12129	Steel-Breaking & Dismantling Co, Chesterfield	
12130	J. Cashmore, Newport, Gwent	
12131	North Norfolk Railway, Sheringham	Previously used by NCB at Snowdown colliery, Kent
12132	J. Cashmore, Newport, Gwent, March 1973	
12133	NCB Philadelphia, Tyne & Wear, No 511	
12134	G. Cohen, Kettering, Northamptonshire, March 1973	
12135	J. McWilliams, Shettleston, Glasgow	
12136	T. W. Ward, Beighton, South Yorkshire, March 1977	
12137	J. E. McMurray, Greenford at BR Depot, Stratford	
12138	G. Cohen, Kettering, Northamptonshire, October 1969	

15000-15003 see LNER No 8000-8003

15004

Brush Ltd/LNER Doncaster 0-6-0 shunting locomotive, built to the established EE design. Built as a Brush demonstrator and not taken into railway stock until 1949. Fitted for compressed air starting.

BR 1948 No	*Built by*	*Works No*	*Date introduced*	*Date withdrawn*	*Disposal code*
15004	BR Doncaster	—	1949	September 1962	C

15097-9

LNER Motor Rail & Tram Car 'Simplex' 4-wheel petrol shunters used as engineers department pilots.

BR 1948 No	*Built by*	*Works No*	*Date introduced*	*Date withdrawn*	Disposal code
15097	Simplex	MR2126	1922	June 1950	C
15098	Simplex	MR1931	1919	September 1956	C
15099	Simplex	MR2037	1920	December 1956	C

15100 see GWR No 2

15101-6

EE/GWR Standard 0-6-0 diesel-electric shunter, built soon after nationalisation at Swindon, as replacement for steam in selected shunting yards.

BR 1948 No	*Built by*	*Works No*	*Date introduced*	*Date withdrawn*	*Disposal code*
15101	BR Swindon	—	April 1948	August 1967	C
15102	BR Swindon	—	April 1948	July 1967	C
15103	BR Swindon	—	May 1948	August 1967	C
15104	BR Swindon	—	May 1948	July 1967	C
15105	BR Swindon	—	July 1948	August 1967	C
15106	BR Swindon	—	July 1948	August 1967	C

15201-15203 see SR1-SR3

Class 12

EE/SR standard 0-6-0 diesel-electric shunter, planned prior to nationalisation, but built after, used in various SR yards on all three divisions alongside steam traction.

BR 1948 No	*Built by*	*Works No*	*Date introduced*	*Date withdrawn*	*Disposal code*
15211	BR Ashford	—	April 1949	December 1971	C
15212	BR Ashford	—	April 1949	December 1971	C
15213	BR Ashford	—	April 1949	November 1968	C

Engine: Brush/Petter SS4 of 350hp
Weight: $51\frac{1}{4}$ ton
Wheel dia: 48in
Max speed: 22mph
Class codes: DEJ 2, D3/14, 3/2

Tractive effort: 32,000lb
Length: 29ft 1in
Height: 12ft $6\frac{1}{8}$in
Width: 9ft 0in

BR 1948 No	*Disposal details*	*Notes*
15004	BR Doncaster Works, c1963	

Engine: Dorman 2JO of 40hp
Weight: 8 ton
Wheel dia: 37in
Max speed: $7\frac{1}{2}$mph
Class code: Y11 (steam series)

Tractive effort: —
Length: —
Height: —
Width: —

BR 1948 No	*Disposal details*	*Notes*
15097		Introduced August 1925 to LNER Engineers Dept, later renumbered by BR to 15097
15098		Ex-GER owned, carried number 8430 (6/25), 7591 (1942), 8188 (6/46), 68188 (1/48), BR No from 1949
15099		Ex-NBR owned, carried number 8431 (7/30), 7592 (1942), 8189 (6/46), 68189 (1/48), BR No from 1949

Engine: EE 6K of 350hp
Weight: $46\frac{1}{2}$ ton
Wheel dia: $48\frac{1}{2}$in
Max speed: 20mph
Class codes: D3/11, later 3/11

Tractive effort: 35,000lb
Length: 29ft $1\frac{1}{2}$in
Height: 12ft $5\frac{5}{8}$in
Width: 9ft 0in

BR 1948 No	*Disposal details*	*Notes*
15101	G. Cohen, Kettering, Northamptonshire, January 1970	Carried No 502 when built but renumbered by April 1948
15102	Steelbreaking & Dismantling Co, Chesterfield September 1968	
15103	Steelbreaking & Dismantling Co, Chesterfield September 1968	
15104	Steelbreaking & Dismantling Co, Chesterfield September 1968	
15105	G. Cohen, Kettering, Northamptonshire, January 1970	
15106	G. Cohen, Kettering, Northamptonshire, c1970	

Engine: EE 6K of 350hp
Weight: 48 ton
Wheel dia: 54in
Max speed: $27\frac{1}{2}$mph
Class code: D3/13, later 3/9, and TOPS Class 12

Tractive effort: 24,600lb
Length: 29ft $5\frac{3}{4}$in
Height: 12ft $8\frac{5}{8}$in
Width: 9ft 0in

BR 1948 No	*Disposal details*	*Notes*
15211	J. Cashmore, Newport, Gwent, December 1972	
15212	J. Cashmore, Newport, Gwent, December 1972	
15213	BR Hither Green Diesel Depot, March 1970	

BR 1948 No	Built by	Works No	Date introduced	Date withdrawn	Disposal code
15214	BR Ashford	—	May 1949	October 1971	C
15215	BR Ashford	—	May 1949	March 1968	C
15216	BR Ashford	—	June 1949	March 1969	C
15217	BR Ashford	—	June 1949	August 1970	C
15218	BR Ashford	—	June 1949	January 1970	C
15219	BR Ashford	—	July 1949	October 1971	C
15220	BR Ashford	—	July 1949	October 1971	C
15221	BR Ashford	—	August 1949	October 1971	C
15222	BR Ashford	—	September 1949	October 1971	C
15223	BR Ashford	—	October 1949	June 1969	C
15224	BR Ashford	—	October 1949	October 1971	P
15225	BR Ashford	—	November 1949	October 1971	C
15226	BR Ashford	—	December 1950	April 1969	C
15227	BR Ashford	—	February 1951	April 1970	C
15228	BR Ashford	—	April 1951	February 1969	C
15229	BR Ashford	—	July 1951	October 1971	C
15230	BR Ashford	—	September 1951	October 1971	C
15231	BR Ashford	—	October 1951	October 1971	S
15232	BR Ashford	—	November 1951	April 1971	C
15233	BR Ashford	—	November 1951	May 1969	C
15234	BR Ashford	—	December 1951	December 1968	C
15235	BR Ashford	—	December 1951	May 1971	C
15236	BR Ashford	—	January 1952	December 1968	C

18000

Swiss design and built gas turbine powered locomotive with an electric transmission, ordered by the GWR, as an option to steam or diesel traction, after trials on BR loco sold to IUR.

BR 1948 No	Built by	Works No	Date introduced	Date withdrawn	Disposal code
18000	B/Boveri	BB4559	1950	December 1960	S

18100

Metropolitan-Vickers built gas turbine powered locomotive with an electric transmission, ordered by the GWR for comparison with No 18000 above — loco later rebuilt as first 25kV electric.

BR 1948 No	Built by	Date introduced	Date withdrawn	Disposal code
18100	M/Vickers	1952	December 1957	R

BR 1948 No	Disposal details	Notes
15214	J. Cashmore, Newport, Gwent, c1972	
15215	BR Swindon Works, August 1968	
15216	BREL Swindon Works, February 1970	
15217	BR Selhurst CM&EE Workshop, July 1971	
15218	C. F. Booth, Rotherham, South Yorkshire c1971	
15219	J. Cashmore, Newport, Gwent, c1972	
15220	J. Cashmore, Newport, Gwent, December 1972	
15221	J. Cashmore, Newport, Gwent, c1972	
15222	J. Williams, Bleanyfan Quarry, Kidwelly	First acquired by J. Cashmore, Newport, later sold as mobile generator, used until May 1968 then cut up
15223	C. F. Booth, Rotherham, South Yorkshire, c1971	
15224	Preserved by North Downs Railway project	After withdrawal used by NCB Betteshanger Colliery and numbered NCB 1802/B5
15225	J. Cashmore, Newport, Gwent, May 1972	
15226	J. Cashmore, Newport, Gwent, December 1969	
15227	BREL Eastleigh Works, June 1970	
15228	BR Swindon Works, July 1969	
15229	J. Cashmore, Newport, Gwent, c1972	
15230	J. Cashmore, Newport, Gwent, c1973	
15231	Tilcon Construction Ltd, Grassington, Skipton	
15232	BREL Swindon Works, February 1972	
15233	J. Cashmore, Newport, Gwent, December 1969	
15234	BREL Swindon Works, February 1970	
15235	J. Cashmore, Newport, Gwent, December 1972	
15236	BREL Swindon Works, February 1970	

Engine: Gas turbine of 2,500hp
Weight: 115 ton
Bogie type: A1A-A1A
Max speed: 90mph
Class code: 4P

Tractive effort: 60,000lb
Length: 63ft 0in
Height: 13ft 4in
Width: 9ft $2\frac{1}{4}$in

BR 1948 No	Disposal details	Notes
18000	Sold to International Union of Railways, SBB as trial and test locomotive. Now preserved	Arrived on BR late in 1949 from Swiss builders

Engine: Gas turbine of 3,000hp
Weight: $129\frac{1}{2}$ ton
Bogie type: Co-Co
Max speed: 90mph
Class code: 5P

Tractive effort: 60,000lb
Length: 66ft $9\frac{1}{4}$in
Height: 12ft 10in
Width: 9ft 0in

BR 1948 No	Disposal details	Notes
18100	After use on BR as gas turbine locomotive taken to GEC Stockton Works, and rebuilt to 25kV trial locomotive	Although withdrawn December 1957 18100 was returned to Stockton in mid-1954. After rebuilding as 25kV locomotive renumbered E1000

SECTION 4
BRITISH RAILWAYS 1957 NUMBERS

CLASS 44

These 10 locomotives were ordered in 1955 under the BR Modernisation plan, and were the first production run of main-line locomotives ordered to replace steam traction from the main lines.

BR 1957 No	*TOPS No*	*Name*	*Built by*	*Works No*	*Date introduced*	*Date withdrawn*
D1	44 001	*Scafell Pike*	BR Derby	—	September 1959	October 1976
D2	44 002	*Helvellyn*	BR Derby	—	October 1959	February 1979
D3	44 003	*Skiddaw*	BR Derby	—	October 1959	July 1976
D4	44 004	*Great Gable*	BR Derby	—	October 1959	November 1980
D5	44 005	*Cross Fell*	BR Derby	—	November 1959	April 1978
D6	44 006	*Whernside*	BR Derby	—	December 1959	January 1977
D7	44 007	*Ingleborough*	BR Derby	—	December 1959	November 1980
D8	44 008	*Penyghent*	BR Derby	—	December 1959	November 1980
D9	44 009	*Snowdon*	BR Derby	—	December 1959	March 1979
D10	44 010	*Tryfan*	BR Derby	—	February 1960	May 1977

Class 45

Subsequent fleet of Type 4 locomotives of same design as previous class, with detail mods, class later divided into two sub classes under TOPS 45/0 locomotives with steam heat, 45/1 locomotives with electric train supply equipment.

BR 1957 No	*TOPS No*	*Name*	*Built by*	*Works No*	*Period introduced*	*Date withdrawn*
D11	45 122	—	BR Derby	—	10/60	
D12	45 011	—	BR Derby	—	11/60	May 1981
D13	45 001	—	BR Derby	—	11/60	
D14	45 015	—	BR Derby	—	12/60	
D15	45 018	—	BR Derby	—	13/60	January 1981
D16	45 016	—	BR Derby	—	13/60	
D17	45 024	—	BR Derby	—	13/60	October 1980
D18	45 121	—	BR Derby	—	13/60	
D19	45 025	—	BR Derby	—	13/60	May 1981
D20	45 013	—	BR Derby	—	2/61	
D21	45 026	—	BR Derby	—	3/61	
D22	45 132	—	BR Derby	—	4/61	
D23	45 017	—	BR Derby	—	4/61	
D24	45 027	—	BR Derby	—	4/61	May 1981
D25	45 021	—	BR Derby	—	4/61	December 1980
D26	45 020	—	BR Derby	—	4/61	
D27	45 028	—	BR Derby	—	5/61	January 1981

Engine: Sulzer 12LDA28A of 2,300hp
Weight: 133 ton
Bogie type: 1Co-Co1
Max speed: 90mph
Class codes: D23/1, 23/1 later Class 44

Tractive effort: 70,000lb
Length: 67ft 11in
Height: 12ft 10⅛in
Width: 8ft 10⅝in

BR 1957 No	*Disposal code*	*Disposal details*	*Notes*
D1	C	BREL Derby Works, February 1977	
D2	C	BREL Derby Works, October 1979	
D3	C	BREL Derby Works, July 1976	
D4	P	Midland Railway Centre, Butterley	
D5	C	BREL Derby Works, December 1978	
D6	C	BREL Derby Works, February 1978	
D7	C	BREL Derby Works, November 1981	
D8	P	Strathspey Railway, Aviemore	
D9	C	BREL Derby Works, July 1980	
D10	C	BREL Derby Works, July 1978	Originally withdrawn September 1976 — reinstated October 1976

Engine: Sulzer 12LDA28B of 2,500hp
Weight: 136 ton
Bogie type: 1Co-Co1
Max speed: 90mph
Class code: D25/1, 25/1 later Class 45/0 and 45/1

Tractive effort: 70,000lb
Length: 67ft 11in
Height: 12ft 10⅛in
Width: 8ft 10⅝in

BR 1957 No	*Disposal code*	*Disposal details*	*Notes*
D11			
D12	C	BREL Derby Works	
D13			
D14			
D15	C	BREL Swindon Works, November 1982	
D16			
D17	C	BREL Swindon Works, September 1983	Stored from October 1980
D18			
D19	C	BREL Derby Works	
D20			
D21			
D22			
D23			
D24	C	BREL Swindon Works, September 1983	
D25	C	BREL Swindon Works, April 1983	Stored from October 1980
D26			
D27	C	BREL Swindon Works, March 1983	

BR 1957 No	TOPS No	Name	Built by	Works No	Period introduced	Date withdrawn
D28	45 124	—	BR Derby	—	5/61	
D29	45 002	—	BR Derby	—	5/61	
D30	45 029	—	BR Derby	—	5/61	
D31	45 030	—	BR Derby	—	6/61	November 1980
D32	45 126	—	BR Derby	—	6/61	
D33	45 019	—	BR Derby	—	7/61	
D34	45 119	—	BR Derby	—	7/61	
D35	45 117	—	BR Derby	—	7/61	
D36	45 031	—	BR Derby	—	7/61	May 1981
D37	45 009	—	BR Derby	—	7/61	
D38	45 032	—	BR Derby	—	7/61	December 1980
D39	45 033	—	BR Derby	—	8/61	
D40	45 133	—	BR Derby	—	8/61	
D41	45 147	—	BR Derby	—	8/61	
D42	45 034	—	BR Derby	—	9/61	
D43	45 107	—	BR Derby	—	9/61	
D44	45 035	—	BR Derby	—	9/61	May 1981
D45	45 036	—	BR Derby	—	9/61	
D46	45 037	—	BR Derby	—	10/61	
D47	45 116	—	BR Derby	—	10/61	
D48	45 038	—	BR Derby	—	10/61	
D49	45 039	*The Manchester Regt*, October 1965	BR Derby	—	10/61	December 1980
D50	45 040	*King's Shropshire Light Infantry*, June 1965	BR Crewe	—	6/62	
D51	45 102	—	BR Crewe	—	6/62	
D52	45 123	*The Lancashire Fusilier*, October 1963	BR Crewe	—	6/62	
D53	45 041	*Royal Tank Regt*, September 1964	BR Crewe	—	7/62	
D54	45 023	*The Royal Pioneer Corps*, November 1963	BR Crewe	—	8/62	
D55	45 144	*Royal Signals*, June 1965	BR Crewe	—	10/62	
D56	45 137	*The Bedfordshire & Hertfordshire Regt (TA)*, October 1963	BR Crewe	—	12/62	
D57	45 042	—	BR Crewe	—	7/63	
D58	45 043	*The Kings Own Royal Border Regt*, September 1963	BR Crewe	—	2/62	
D59	45 104	*The Royal Warwickshire Fusilier*, May 1964	BR Crewe	—	2/62	
D60	45 022	*Lytham St Annes*, May 1964	BR Crewe	—	2/62	
D61	45 112	*Royal Army Ordnance Corps*, September 1965	BR Crewe	—	3/62	
D62	45 143	*5th Royal Inniskilling Dragoon Guards*, November 1964	BR Crewe	—	3/62	
D63	45 044	*Royal Inniskilling Fusilier*, September 1965	BR Crewe	—	4/62	
D64	45 045	*Coldstream Guardsman*, April 1965	BR Crewe	—	4/62	May 1983
D65	45 111	*Grenadier Guardsman*, May 1964	BR Crewe	—	4/62	
D66	45 146	—	BR Crewe	—	4/62	

BR 1957 No	*Disposal code*	*Disposal details*	*Notes*
D28			Withdrawn January 1981, used as generator at Thorpe Marsh CEGB. Reinstated August 1982
D29			
D30			
D31	C	BREL Derby Works, April 1981	
D32			
D33			
D34			
D35			
D36	C	BREL Derby Works, October	
D37			
D38	C	BREL Swindon Works, September 1983	Stored from September 1980
D39			
D40			
D41			
D42			
D43			
D44	C	BREL Derby Works, November 1981	
D45			
D46			
D47			
D48			
D49	C	BREL Swindon Works, April 1983	Stored from November 1980
D50			
D51			
D52			
D53			
D54			
D55			
D56			
D57			
D58			
D59			
D60			
D61			
D62			
D63			
D64	A	BREL Derby Works	
D65			
D66			

BR 1957 No	*TOPS No*	*Name*	*Built by*	*Works No*	*Period introduced*	*Date withdrawn*
D67	45 118	*The Royal Artilleryman,* September 1965	BR Crewe	—	5/62	
D68	45 046	*Royal Fusilier,* January 1967	BR Crewe	—	10/60	
D69	45 047	—	BR Crewe	—	11/60	August 1980
D70	45 048	*The Royal Marines,* December 1964	BR Crewe	—	12/60	
D71	45 049	*The Staffordshire Regt (The Prince of Wales's Own),* May 1966	BR Crewe	—	12/60	
D72	45 050	—	BR Crewe	—	12/60	
D73	45 110	—	BR Crewe	—	12/60	
D74	45 051	—	BR Crewe	—	13/60	
D75	45 052	—	BR Crewe	—	12/60	
D76	45 053	—	BR Crewe	—	12/60	November 1983
D77	45 004	*Royal Irish Fusilier,* September 1965	BR Crewe	—	13/60	
D78	45 150	—	BR Crewe	—	13/60	
D79	45 005	—	BR Crewe	—	13/60	
D80	45 113	—	BR Crewe	—	13/60	
D81	45 115	—	BR Crewe	—	13/60	
D82	45 141	—	BR Crewe	—	13/60	
D83	45 142	—	BR Crewe	—	13/60	
D84	45 055	*Royal Corps of Transport,* June 1966	BR Crewe	—	13/60	
D85	45 109	—	BR Crewe	—	2/61	
D86	45 105	—	BR Crewe	—	3/61	
D87	45 127	—	BR Crewe	—	2/61	
D88	45 136	—	BR Crewe	—	3/61	
D89	45 006	*Honourable Artillery Company,* June 1965	BR Crewe	—	3/61	
D90	45 008	—	BR Crewe	—	3/61	December 1980
D91	45 056	—	BR Crewe	—	3/61	
D92	45 138	—	BR Crewe	—	3/61	
D93	45 057	—	BR Crewe	—	4/61	
D94	45 114	—	BR Crewe	—	4/61	
D95	45 054	—	BR Crewe	—	4/61	
D96	45 101	—	BR Crewe	—	4/61	
D97	45 058	—	BR Crewe	—	4/61	
D98	45 059	*Royal Engineer,* December 1968	BR Crewe	—	5/61	
D99	45 135	*3rd Carabinier,* December 1965	BR Crewe	—	5/61	
D100	45 060	*Sherwood Forester,* September 1961	BR Crewe	—	5/61	
D101	45 061	—	BR Crewe	—	5/61	August 1981
D102	45 140	—	BR Crewe	—	5/61	
D103	45 062	—	BR Crewe	—	6/61	
D104	45 063	—	BR Crewe	—	6/61	
D105	45 064	—	BR Crewe	—	6/61	
D106	45 106	—	BR Crewe	—	6/61	
D107	45 120	—	BR Crewe	—	7/61	
D108	45 012	—	BR Crewe	—	8/61	
D109	45 139	—	BR Crewe	—	7/61	
D110	45 065	—	BR Crewe	—	8/61	
D111	45 129	—	BR Crewe	—	8/61	
D112	45 010	—	BR Crewe	—	8/61	
D113	45 128	—	BR Crewe	—	9/61	
D114	45 066	—	BR Crewe	—	9/61	
D115	45 067	—	BR Crewe	—	9/61	July 1977
D116	45 103	—	BR Crewe	—	9/61	
D117	45 130	—	BR Crewe	—	9/61	

BR 1957 No	*Disposal code*	*Disposal details*	*Notes*
D67			
D68			
D69	C	BREL Derby Works, April 1981	
D70			
D71			
D72			
D73			
D74			
D75			
D76	A	BREL Crewe Works	Stored 1980-1983
D77			
D78			
D79			
D80			
D81			
D82			
D83			
D84			
D85			
D86			
D87			
D88			
D89			
D90	C	BREL Swindon Works, September 1983	Stored from August 1980
D91			
D92			
D93			
D94			
D95			
D96			
D97			
D98			
D99			
D100			
D101	C	BREL Swindon Works, April 1982	
D102			
D103			
D104			
D105			
D106			
D107			
D108			
D109			
D110			
D111			
D112			
D113			
D114			
D115	C	BREL Derby Works, June 1980	
D116			
D117			

BR 1957 No	*TOPS No*	*Name*	*Built by*	*Works No*	*Period introduced*	*Date withdrawn*
D118	45 068	—	BR Crewe	—	10/61	
D119	45 007	—	BR Crewe	—	10/61	
D120	45 108	—	BR Crewe	—	10/61	
D121	45 069	—	BR Crewe	—	10/61	
D122	45 070	—	BR Crewe	—	11/61	
D123	45 125	—	BR Crewe	—	11/61	
D124	45 131	—	BR Crewe	—	11/61	
D125	45 071	—	BR Crewe	—	11/61	July 1981
D126	45 134	—	BR Crewe	—	12/61	
D127	45 072	—	BR Crewe	—	12/61	
D128	45 145	—	BR Crewe	—	12/61	
D129	45 073	—	BR Crewe	—	12/61	October 1981
D130	45 148	—	BR Crewe	—	13/61	
D131	45 074	—	BR Crewe	—	13/61	
D132	45 075	—	BR Crewe	—	13/61	
D133	45 003	—	BR Crewe	—	13/61	
D134	45 076	—	BR Crewe	—	13/61	
D135	45 149	—	BR Crewe	—	13/61	
D136	45 077	—	BR Crewe	—	13/61	
D137	45 014	*The Cheshire Regiment* June 1966	BR Crewe	—	13/61	

Class 46

This fleet of 56 locomotives were the final type based on the original 10 Class 44s ordered in 1955. This fleet were fitted with Brush Electrical equipment, and therefore formed a separate class from Class 45.

BR 1957 No	*TOPS No*	*Name*	*Built by*	*Works No*	*Period* Date introduced*	*Date 1st withdrawn*
D138	46 001	—	BR Derby	—	11/61*	December 1980
D139	46 002	—	BR Derby	—	11/61*	December 1980
D140	46 003	—	BR Derby	—	12/61*	October 1978
D141	46 004	—	BR Derby	—	12/61*	June 1983
D142	46 005	—	BR Derby	—	13/61*	December 1977
D143	46 006	—	BR Derby	—	12/61*	December 1980
D144	46 007	—	BR Derby	—	13/61*	December 1980
D145	46 008	—	BR Derby	—	13/61*	October 1981
D146	46 009	—	BR Derby	—	13/61*	October 1983
D147	46 010	—	BR Derby	—	13/61*	December 1980
D148	46 011	—	BR Derby	—	13/61*	
D149	46 012	—	BR Derby	—	13/61*	July 1980
D150	46 013	—	BR Derby	—	13/61*	August 1980
D151	46 014	—	BR Derby	—	1/62*	May 1984
D152	46 015	—	BR Derby	—	2/62*	December 1980
D153	46 016	—	BR Derby	—	1/62*	December 1983
D154	46 017	—	BR Derby	—	2/62*	December 1980
D155	46 018	—	BR Derby	—	2/62*	December 1980

BR 1957 No	*Disposal code*	*Disposal details*	*Notes*
D118			
D119			
D120			
D121			
D122			
D123			
D124			
D125	C	BREL Swindon July 1983	
D126			
D127			
D128			
D129	C	BREL Derby October 1982	
D130			
D131			
D132			
D133			
D134			
D135			
D136			
D137			

Engine: Sulzer 12LDA28B of 2,500hp
Weight: 138 ton
Bogie type: 1Co-Co1
Max speed: 90mph
Class code: 25/1A later Class 46

Tractive effort: 70,000lb
Length: 67ft 11in
Height: 12ft 10⅛in
Width: 8ft 10⅝in

BR 1957 No	*Date reinstated*	*Date 2nd withdrawal*	*Disposal code*	*Disposal details*	*Notes*
D138	September 1981	December 1981	C	BREL Swindon July 1982	Store from October 1980
D139	February 1981	September 1981	A	BREL Swindon	Store from November 1980
D140			C	BREL Derby March 1980	
D141			A	BREL Swindon	
D142			C	BREL Derby March 1978	
D143	November 1981	January 1982	A	BREL Swindon	Store from October 1980
D144	November 1981	February 1982	A	BREL Swindon	Store from November 1980
D145			C	BREL Swindon December 1982	
D146			D	To Departmental Stock—97401	
D147	November 1981				Store from October 1980
D148					
D149			C	BREL Swindon October 1980	
D150			A	BREL Swindon	
D151			A	BREL Swindon	
D152			A	BREL Swindon	Store from November 1980
D153			C	BREL Swindon 8/84	
D154	November 1981	April 1984	A	BREL Swindon	Store from November 1980
D155	November 1981	December 1983	A	BREL Swindon	Store from November 1980

BR 1957 No	TOPS No	Name	Built by	Works No	Period* Date introduced	Date withdrawn
D156	46 019	—	BR Derby	—	2/62*	December 1980
D157	46 020	—	BR Derby	—	3/62*	December 1980
D158	46 021	—	BR Derby	—	3/62*	December 1980
D159	46 022	—	BR Derby	—	3/62*	December 1980
D160	46 023	—	BR Derby	—	4/62*	December 1983
D161	46 024	—	BR Derby	—	4/62*	April 1978
D162	46 025	—	BR Derby	—	4/62*	December 1980
D163	46 026	*Leicestershire & Derbyshire Yeomanry*, April 1962	BR Derby	—	4/62*	
D164	46 027	—	BR Derby	—	4/62*	
D165	46 028	—	BR Derby	—	5/62*	May 1984
D166	46 029	—	BR Derby	—	May 1962	January 1983
D167	46 030	—	BR Derby	—	May 1962	December 1980
D168	46 031	—	BR Derby	—	May 1962	April 1983
D169	46 032	—	BR Derby	—	June 1962	October 1981
D170	46 033	—	BR Derby	—	June 1962	May 1981
D171	46 034	—	BR Derby	—	July 1962	December 1980
D172	46 035	—	BR Derby	—	July 1962	
D173	46 036	—	BR Derby	—	July 1962	May 1982
D174	46 037	—	BR Derby	—	July 1962	December 1980
D175	46 038	—	BR Derby	—	August 1962	December 1980
D176	46 039	—	BR Derby	—	August 1962	October 1983
D177	46 040	—	BR Derby	—	August 1962	December 1980
D178	46 041	—	BR Derby	—	September 1962	December 1980
D179	46 042	—	BR Derby	—	September 1962	December 1980
D180	46 043	—	BR Derby	—	September 1962	December 1980
D181	46 044	—	BR Derby	—	September 1962	April 1984
D182	46 045	—	BR Derby	—	September 1962	
D183	46 046	—	BR Derby	—	October 1962	May 1984
D184	46 047	—	BR Derby	—	October 1962	September 1984
D185	46 048	—	BR Derby	—	October 1962	September 1981
D186	46 049	—	BR Derby	—	November 1962	December 1982
D187	46 050	—	BR Derby	—	November 1962	December 1980
D188	46 051	—	BR Derby	—	December 1962	December 1983
D189	46 052	—	BR Derby	—	January 1963	
D190	46 053	—	BR Derby	—	January 1963	February 1981
D191	46 054	—	BR Derby	—	January 1963	December 1980
D192	46 055	—	BR Derby	—	January 1963	May 1981
D193	46 056	—	BR Derby	—	January 1963	October 1982

BR 1957 No	*Date reinstated*	*Date 2nd withdrawal*	*Disposal Code*	*Disposal details*	*Notes*
D156			C	BREL Swindon August 1983	Store from November 1980
D157			A	BREL Swindon	Store from October 1980
D158	November 1981	January 1983	A	BREL Swindon	Store from October 1980
D159	November 1981	March 1982	C	BREL Swindon September 1983	Store from October 1980
D160			D	To Departmental Stock — 97402	
D161			C	BREL Derby October 1978	
D162	November 1981				Store from September 1980
D163					
D164			A	BR Gateshead depot	
D165					
D166			A	BREL Swindon	
D167			C	BREL Swindon November 1982	Store from October 1980
D168			C	BREL Swindon August 1983	
D169	January 1982	April 1984	A	BR Stratford depot	
D170	January 1982	June 1983	A	BREL Swindon	
D171			C	BREL Swindon October 1982	Store from November 1980
D172					
D173			C	BREL Swindon January 1983	
D174	December 1981	June 1984			Store from November 1980
D175	November 1981	March 1982	C	BREL Swindon January 1984	Store from November 1980
D176			A	BREL Swindon	
D177			C	BREL Derby April 1982	Store from October 1980
D178			C	BREL Swindon August 1983	Store from October 1980
D179			C	BREL Swindon November 1982	Store from October 1980
D180			C	BREL Swindon May 1984	Store from October 1980
D181			A	BREL Swindon	
D182					
D183			A	BR Gateshead depot	
D184					
D185			C	BREL Swindon September 1983	
D186			A	BREL Swindon	
D187	November 1981	October 1982	A	BREL Swindon	Store from October 1980
D188			C	BREL Swindon April 1984	
D189					
D190			C	BREL Derby July 1981	
D191	November 1981	January 1982	C	BREL Swindon July 1983	Store from October 1980
D192	January 1982	October 1982	A	BREL Swindon	
D193			A	BREL Swindon	

North British-built Bo-Bo No 10800, painted in black livery with white bogies. This locomotive was later sold to Brush for research purposes.
Author's collection

LMS designed, BR-built 0-6-0 diesel-electric No 12100, introduced in April 1952. *BR*

No D201 hauls an up express between Hatfield and Brookmans Park on 9 July 1958 when the locomotive was only three months old. *BR*

Under TOPS the 'Westerns' became Class 52 but only ever carried their 1957 style numbers. No D1010 *Western Campaigner* stands at Paddington at the head of a railtour.
Colin J. Marsden

Class 40

The first order under the Modernisation Plan placed with an outside contractor was in 1955 when the first of several orders for Type 4 2,000hp locomotives was placed with English Electric powered by the EE16SVT unit developing 2,000hp.

BR 1957 No	*TOPS No*	*Name*	*Built by*	*Works No*	**Period Date introduced*
D200	40 122	—	EE(VF)	EE2367/D395	March 1958
D201	40 001	—	EE(VF)	EE2368/D396	April 1958
D202	40 002	—	EE(VF)	EE2369/D397	April 1958
D203	40 003	—	EE(VF)	EE2370/D398	May 1958
D204	40 004	—	EE(VF)	EE2371/D399	May 1958
D205	40 005	—	EE(VF)	EE2372/D400	June 1958
D206	40 006	—	EE(VF)	EE2373/D401	July 1958
D207	40 007	—	EE(VF)	EE2374/D402	July 1958
D208	40 008	—	EE(VF)	EE2375/D403	August 1958
D209	40 009	—	EE(VF)	EE2376/D404	September 1958
D210	40 010	*Empress of Britain,* May 1960	EE(VF)	EE2666/D427	5/59*
D211	40 011	*Mauretania,* September *1960*	EE(VF)	EE2667/D428	6/59*
D212	40 012	*Aureol,* September 1960	EE(VF)	E2667/D429	6/59*
D213	40 013	*Andania,* June 1962	EE(VF)	E2668/D430	6/59*
D214	40 014	*Antonia,* May 1961	EE(VF)	E2669/D431	6/59*
D215	40 015	*Aquitania,* May 1962	EE(VF)	E2670/D432	7/59*
D216	40 016	*Campania,* May 1962	EE(VF)	E2671/D433	7/59*
D217	40 017	*Carinthia,* May 1962	EE(VF)	E2672/D434	7/59*
D218	40 018	*Carmania,* July 1961	EE(VF)	E2673/D435	7/59*
D219	40 019	*Caronia,* June 1962	EE(VF)	E2674/D436	7/59*
D220	40 020	*Franconia,* February 1963	EE(VF)	E2675/D437	8/59*
D221	40 021	*Ivernia,* March 1961	EE(VF)	E2676/D438	8/59*
D222	40 022	*Laconia,* October 1962	EE(VF)	E2677/D439	8/59*
D223	40 023	*Lancastria,* May 1961	EE(VF)	E2678/D440	8/59*
D224	40 024	*Lucania,* August 1962	EE(VF)	E2679/D441	9/59*
D225	40 025	*Lusitania,* March 1962	EE(VF)	E2680/D442	9/59*
D226	40 026	—	EE(VF)	E2681/D443	9/59*
D227	40 027	*Parthia,* June 1962	EE(VF)	E2682/D444	9/59*
D228	40 028	*Samaria,* September 1962	EE(VF)	E2683/D445	9/59*
D229	40 029	*Saxonia,* March 1963	EE(VF)	E2684/D446	9/59*
D230	40 030	*Scythia,* April 1961	EE(VF)	E2685/D447	10/59*
D231	40 031	*Sylvania,* May 1962	EE(VF)	E2686/D448	10/59*
D232	40 032	*Empress of Canada,* March 1961	EE(VF)	E2687/D449	10/59*
D233	40 033	*Empress of England,* September 1961	EE(VF)	E2688/D450	10/59*
D234	40 034	*Accra,* May 1962	EE(VF)	E2689/D451	10/59*
D235	40 035	*Apapa,* May 1962	EE(VF)	E2690/D452	10/59*
D236	40 036	—	EE(VF)	E2691/D453	11/59*
D237	40 037	—	EE(VF)	E2692/D454	October 1959
D238	40 038	—	EE(VF)	E2693/D455	October 1959
D239	40 039	—	EE(VF)	E2694/D456	October 1959
D240	40 040	—	EE(VF)	E2695/D457	October 1959
D241	40 041	—	EE(VF)	E2715/D458	October 1959
D242	40 042	—	EE(VF)	E2716/D459	November 1959
D243	40 043	—	EE(VF)	E2717/D460	November 1959
D244	40 044	—	EE(VF)	E2718/D461	November 1959
D245	40 045	—	EE(VF)	E2719/D462	November 1959

Engine: EE16SVT of 2,000hp
Weight: 133 ton
Bogie type: 1Co-Co1
Max speed: 90mph
Class code: D20/1, 20/3 later Class 40

Tractive effort: 52,000lb
Length: 69ft 6in
Height: 12ft 10in
Width: 9ft 0in

BR 1957 No	*Date withdrawn*	*Disposal code*	*Disposal details*	*Notes*
D200				Withdrawn August 1981 Reinstated April 1983 for BR Preservation
D201	July 1984	A	BR Carlisle depot	
D202	May 1984	A	BR Carlisle depot	
D203	September 1982	C	BREL Doncaster, January 1984	
D204				
D205	January 1976	C	BREL Crewe, February 1977	
D206	March 1983	A	BREL Crewe	
D207	February 1983	C	BREL Doncaster, February 1984	
D208	November 1982	A	BREL Crewe	
D209				
D210	July 1981	C	BREL Swindon, August 1983	
D211	October 1980	C	BREL Swindon	
D212				
D213				
D214	November 1981	C	BREL Swindon, December 1983	
D215				
D216	May 1981	C	BREL Swindon, December 1983	
D217	February 1981	C	BREL Swindon, August 1981	
D218	September 1981	C	BREL Crewe, August 1983	
D219	December 1981	C	BREL Doncaster, February 1984	
D220	August 1982	A	BREL Crewe	
D221	July 1976	C	BREL Crewe, May 1977	
D222	March 1984	A	BR Longsight depot	
D223	May 1981	A	BREL Crewe	
D224	June 1984			
D225	October 1982	A	BR Healey Mills depot	
D226	August 1980	C	BREL Swindon, June 1983	Planned name *Media* — never carried
D227	April 1983	C	BREL Crewe, April 1984	
D228				
D229	April 1984	A	BR Crewe depot	
D230	April 1983	C	BREL Crewe, May 1984	
D231	May 1981	C	BREL Crewe, May 1983	
D232	February 1981	C	BREL Swindon, April 1983	
D233				
D234	January 1984	C	BREL Doncaster, April 1984	
D235				
D236	January 1982	C	BREL Swindon, August 1982	
D237	August 1981	C	BREL Swindon, October 1983	
D238	December 1980	C	BREL Swindon, March 1982	
D239	January 1976	C	BREL Crewe, October 1976	
D240	July 1980	C	BREL Doncaster, November 1980	
D241	July 1976	C	BREL Crewe, July 1978	
D242	December 1980	C	BREL Derby, February 1981	
D243	January 1976	C	BREL Crewe, April 1977	
D244				
D245	August 1976	C	BREL Derby, March 1977	

BR 1957 No	TOPS No	Name	Built by	Works No	*Period Date introduced
D246	40 046	—	EE(VF)	E2720/D463	November 1959
D247	40 047	—	EE(VF)	E2721/D464	November 1959
D248	40 048	—	EE(VF)	E2722/D465	November 1959
D249	40 049	—	EE(VF)	E2723/D466	November 1959
D250	40 050	—	EE(VF)	E2724/D467	December 1959
D251	40 051	—	EE(VF)	E2772/D468	December 1959
D252	40 052	—	EE(VF)	E2773/D469	December 1959
D253	40 053	—	EE(VF)	E2775/D470	January 1960
D254	40 054	—	EE(VF)	E2774/D471	December 1959
D255	40 055	—	EE(VF)	E2777/D472	1/60*
D256	40 056	—	EE(VF)	E2778/D473	January 1960
D257	40 057	—	EE(VF)	E2779/D474	February 1960
D258	40 058	—	EE(VF)	E2780/D475	February 1960
D259	40 059	—	EE(VF)	E2781/D476	February 1960
D260	40 060	—	EE(VF)	E2782/D497	2/60*
D261	40 061	—	EE(VF)	E2783/D498	2/60*
D262	40 062	—	EE(VF)	E2784/D499	9/60*
D263	40 063	—	EE(VF)	E2785/D500	3/60*
D264	40 064	—	EE(VF)	E2786/D501	3/60*
D265	40 065	—	EE(VF)	E2787/D502	3/60*
D266	40 066	—	EE(VF)	E2788/D503	3/60*
D267	40 067	—	EE(VF)	E2789/D504	3/60*
D268	40 068	—	EE(VF)	E2790/D505	4/60*
D269	40 069	—	EE(VF)	E2791/D506	4/60*
D270	40 070	—	EE(VF)	E2792/D507	April 1960
D271	40 071	—	EE(VF)	E2793/D508	April 1960
D272	40 072	—	EE(VF)	E2794/D509	April 1960
D273	40 073	—	EE(VF)	E2795/D510	May 1960
D274	40 074	—	EE(VF)	E2796/D511	May 1960
D275	40 075	—	EE(VF)	E2797/D512	May 1960
D276	40 076	—	EE(VF)	E2798/D513	May 1960
D277	40 077	—	EE(VF)	E2799/D514	May 1960
D278	40 078	—	EE(VF)	E2800/D515	June 1960
D279	40 079	—	EE(VF)	E2801/D516	June 1960
D280	40 080	—	EE(VF)	E2802/D517	June 1960
D281	40 081	—	EE(VF)	E2803/D518	June 1960
D282	40 082	—	EE(VF)	E2804/D519	June 1960
D283	40 083	—	EE(VF)	E2805/D520	July 1960
D284	40 084	—	EE(VF)	E2806/D521	July 1960
D285	40 085	—	EE(VF)	E2807/D522	July 1960
D286	40 086	—	EE(VF)	E2808/D523	July 1960
D287	40 087	—	EE(VF)	E2809/D524	8/60*
D288	40 088	—	EE(VF)	E2811/D526	8/60*
D289	40 089	—	EE(VF)	E2810/D525	9/60*
D290	40 090	—	EE(VF)	E2812/D527	9/60*
D291	40 091	—	EE(VF)	E2813/D528	9/60*
D292	40 092	—	EE(VF)	E2814/D529	9/60*
D293	40 093	—	EE(VF)	E2815/D530	10/60*
D294	40 094	—	EE(VF)	E2816/D531	10/60*
D295	40 095	—	EE(VF)	E2817/D532	10/60*
D296	40 096	—	EE(VF)	E2818/D533	10/60*
D297	40 097	—	EE(VF)	E2819/D534	11/60*
D298	40 098	—	EE(VF)	E2820/D535	11/60*
D299	40 099	—	EE(VF)	E2821/D536	11/60*
D300	40 100	—	EE(VF)	E2822/D537	11/60*
D301	40 101	—	EE(VF)	E2823/D538	11/60*
D302	40 102	—	EE(VF)	E2824/D539	12/60*
D303	40 103	—	EE(VF)	E2825/D540	12/60*
D304	40 104	—	EE(VF)	E2826/D541	12/60*

BR 1957 No	*Date withdrawn*	*Disposal code*	*Disposal details*	*Notes*
D246	February 1983	S	HM Govt Moreton-on-Lugg	
D247				
D248	October 1977	C	BREL Doncaster, July 1980	
D249	January 1983	A	BREL Crewe	
D250	August 1983	C	BREL Doncaster, November 1983	
D251	January 1978	C	BREL Doncaster, December 1978	
D252	June 1983	C	BREL Crewe, November 1983	
D253	August 1976	C	BREL Crewe, April 1977	
D254	December 1977	C	BREL Crewe, December 1978	
D255	November 1982	C	BREL Doncaster, May 1983	
D256				
D257	July 1984	A	BR Crewe depot	
D258				
D259	August 1977	C	BREL Doncaster, October 1978	
D260				
D261	June 1983	C	BREL Crewe, April 1984	
D262	November 1981	C	BREL Swindon, June 1983	
D263	April 1984	A	BR Bescot depot	
D264	April 1982	C	BREL Crewe, December 1983	
D265	November 1981	A	BREL Crewe	
D266	April 1981	C	BREL Swindon, October 1981	
D267	July 1981	C	BREL Doncaster, April 1982	
D268	July 1983	C	BREL Doncaster, October 1983	
D269	September 1983	C	BREL Doncaster June 1984	
D270	June 1981	C	BREL Doncaster, March 1982	
D271	December 1980	C	BREL Swindon, October 1981	In store from September 1980
D272	August 1977	C	BREL Glasgow, June 1978	
D273	June 1983	A	BREL Crewe	
D274	March 1984	A	BR Crewe depot	
D275	December 1981	A	BREL Derby	
D276	April 1983	C	BREL Doncaster, November 1983	
D277	June 1983	C	BREL Doncaster, April 1984	
D278	August 1981	C	BREL Swindon, November 1983	
D279				
D280	September 1983	C	BREL Doncaster July 1984	
D281	February 1983	C	BREL Doncaster, August 1983	
D282				
D283	November 1981	A	BREL Swindon	
D284	May 1983	C	BREL Crewe May 1984	
D285	March 1984	A	BR Crewe depot	
D286				
D287	August 1982	A	BR Healey Mills depot	
D288	February 1982	A	BREL Crewe	
D289	July 1976	C	BREL Crewe, November 1978	
D290	November 1983	A	BR Carlisle depot	
D291				
D292	November 1982	A	BREL Swindon	
D293	December 1983	C	BREL Doncaster, May 1984	
D294	October 1982	A	BR Healey Mills depot	
D295	September 1981	C	BREL Swindon, October 1983	
D296	December 1983	C	BREL Doncaster, May 1984	
D297	June 1983	C	BREL Doncaster, April 1984	
D298	April 1981	C	BREL Swindon, April 1983	
D299				
D300	December 1980	C	BREL Swindon, June 1981	Stored from October 1980
D301	August 1982	A	BREL Crewe	
D302	January 1976	C	BREL Crewe, January 1977	
D303	February 1982	C	BREL Crewe, June 1983	
D304				

BR 1957 No	TOPS No	Name	Built by	Works No	*Period Date introduced
D305	40 105	—	RSH	E2725/RSH8135	10/60*
D306	40 106	—	RSH	E2726/RSH8136	11/60*
D307	40 107	—	RSH	E2727/RSH8137	11/60*
D308	40 108	—	RSH	E2728/RSH8138	12/60*
D309	40 109	—	RSH	E2729/RSH8139	12/60*
D310	40 110	—	RSH	E2730/RSH8140	12/60*
D311	40 111	—	RSH	E2731/RSH8141	13/60*
D312	40 112	—	RSH	E2732/RSH8142	13/60*
D313	40 113	—	RSH	E2733/RSH8143	13/60*
D314	40 114	—	RSH	E2734/RSH8144	13/60*
D315	40 115	—	RSH	E2850/RSH8145	1/61*
D316	40 116	—	RSH	E2851/RSH8146	1/61*
D317	40 117	—	RSH	E2852/RSH8147	2/61*
D318	40 118	—	RSH	E2853/RSH8148	2/61*
D319	40 119	—	RSH	E2854/RSH8149	3/61*
D320	40 120	—	RSH	E2855/RSH8150	3/61*
D321	40 121	—	RSH	E2856/RSH8151	4/61*
D322	—	—	RSH	E2857/RSH8152	4/61*
D323	40 123	—	RSH	E2858/RSH8153	5/61*
D324	40 124	—	RSH	E2859/RSH8154	7/61*
D325	40 125	—	EE(VF)	E3071/D621	13/60*
D326	40 126	—	EE(VF)	E3072/D622	13/60*
D327	40 127	—	EE(VF)	E3073/D623	13/60*
D328	40 128	—	EE(VF)	E3074/D624	1/61*
D329	40 129	—	EE(VF)	E3075/D625	1/61*
D330	40 130	—	EE(VF)	E3076/D626	2/61*
D331	40 131	—	EE(VF)	E3077/D627	2/61*
D332	40 132	—	EE(VF)	E3078/D628	2/61*
D333	40 133	—	EE(VF)	E3079/D629	2/61*
D334	40 134	—	EE(VF)	E3080/D630	3/61*
D335	40 135	—	EE(VF)	E3081/D631	3/61*
D336	40 136	—	EE(VF)	E3082/D632	3/61*
D337	40 137	—	EE(VF)	E3083/D633	3/61*
D338	40 138	—	EE(VF)	E3084/D634	4/61*
D339	40 139	—	EE(VF)	E3085/D635	4/61*
D340	40 140	—	EE(VF)	E3086/D636	4/61*
D341	40 141	—	EE(VF)	E3087/D637	5/61*
D342	40 142	—	EE(VF)	E3088/D638	5/61*
D343	40 143	—	EE(VF)	E3089/D639	5/61*
D344	40 144	—	EE(VF)	E3090/D640	5/61*
D345	40 145	—	EE(VF)	E3091/D641	May 1961
D346	40 146	—	EE(VF)	E3092/D642	May 1961
D347	40 147	—	EE(VF)	E3093/D643	May 1961
D348	40 148	—	EE(VF)	E3094/D644	June 1961
D349	40 149	—	EE(VF)	E3095/D645	June 1961
D350	40 150	—	EE(VF)	E3096/D646	June 1961
D351	40 151	—	EE(VF)	E3097/D647	June 1961
D352	40 152	—	EE(VF)	E3098/D648	July 1961
D353	40 153	—	EE(VF)	E3099/D649	July 1961
D354	40 154	—	EE(VF)	E3100/D650	July 1961
D355	40 155	—	EE(VF)	E3101/D651	August 1961
D356	40 156	—	EE(VF)	E3102/D652	August 1961
D357	40 157	—	EE(VF)	E3103/D653	9/61*
D358	40 158	—	EE(VF)	E3104/D654	9/61*
D359	40 159	—	EE(VF)	E3105/D655	10/61*
D360	40 160	—	EE(VF)	E3106/D656	10/61*
D361	40 161	—	EE(VF)	E3107/D657	10/61*

BR 1957 No	*Date withdrawn*	*Disposal code*	*Disposal details*	*Notes*
D305	December 1980	C	BREL Swindon, March 1981	Stored from November 1980
D306	April 1983	P	Great Central Railway, Loughborough	
D307	December 1981	A	BREL Crewe	
D308	August 1980	C	BREL Swindon, December 1980	
D309	December 1980	C	BREL Swindon, February 1984	Stored from November 1980
D310	December 1980	C	BREL Swindon, August 1983	
D311	May 1981	C	BREL Swindon, February 1982	
D312	December 1980	A	BREL Swindon	
D313	October 1981	C	BREL Swindon, January 1984	
D314	December 1980	C	BREL Swindon, August 1982	Stored from October 1980
D315	March 1982	A	BREL Crewe	
D316	February 1981	C	BREL Swindon, July 1981	
D317	September 1981	C	BREL Swindon, October 1983	
D318				
D319	December 1980	C	BREL Swindon, October 1982	
D320	May 1981	C	BREL Swindon, October 1983	
D321	March 1983	C	BREL Crewe, January 1984	
D322	September 1967	C	BR Crewe, November 1967	
D323	July 1980	A	BREL Doncaster	
D324	January 1984	C	BREL Doncaster, April 1984	
D325	May 1981	C	BREL Swindon, December 1983	
D326	February 1984	C	BREL Doncaster, April 1984	
D327	February 1982	C	BREL Swindon, December 1983	
D328	September 1982	C	BREL Doncaster, August 1983	
D329	May 1984	A	BREL Doncaster	
D330	March 1982	C	BREL Swindon, April 1983	
D331	October 1983	A	BREL Crewe	
D332	March 1982	A	BREL Derby	
D333	January 1984	C	BREL Doncaster, May 1984	
D334	May 1981	C	BREL Swindon, December 1983	
D335				
D336	May 1982	C	BREL Crewe, December 1983	
D337	January 1981	C	BREL Swindon, November 1981	
D338	August 1982	C	BREL Crewe, March 1984	
D339	February 1982	A	BREL Crewe	
D340	March 1982	C	BREL Crewe, December 1983	
D341	September 1982	C	BREL Doncaster July 1984	
D342	April 1980	C	BREL Crewe, September 1983	
D343				
D344	May 1981	C	BREL Swindon, September 1983	
D345	June 1983	P	Bury Transport Museum	Owned by Class 40 PS
D346	December 1980	C	BREL Swindon, December 1983	Stored from October 1980
D347	September 1980	C	BREL Swindon, July 1983	
D348	August 1982	A	BR Healey Mills depot	
D349	August 1981	A	BREL Swindon	
D350				
D351	February 1981	C	BREL Swindon, September 1982	
D352				
D353	October 1983	C	BREL Crewe June 1984	
D354	January 1982	A	BREL Swindon	
D355				
D356	July 1980	C	BREL Swindon, December 1980	
D357	July 1983	C	BREL Doncaster, October 1983	
D358	December 1983	A	BREL Doncaster	
D359	March 1982	C	BREL Swindon, March 1984	
D360				
D361	December 1980	C	BREL Swindon, June 1981	

BR 1957 No	TOPS No	Name	Built by	Works No	*Period Date introduced
D362	40 162	—	EE(VF)	E3108/D658	11/61*
D363	40 163	—	EE(VF)	E3109/D659	11/61*
D364	40 164	—	EE(VF)	E3110/D660	11/61*
D365	40 165	—	EE(VF)	E3111/D661	11/61*
D366	40 166	—	EE(VF)	E3112/D662	12/61*
D367	40 167	—	EE(VF)	E3113/D663	12/61*
D368	40 168	—	EE(VF)	E3114/D664	12/61*
D369	40 169	—	EE(VF)	E3115/D665	13/61*
D370	40 170	—	EE(VF)	E3116/D666	13/61*
D371	40 171	—	EE(VF)	E3117/D667	13/61*
D372	40 172	—	EE(VF)	E3118/D668	1/62*
D373	40 173	—	EE(VF)	E3119/D669	1/62*
D374	40 174	—	EE(VF)	E3120/D670	1/62*
D375	40 175	—	EE(VF)	E3121/D671	2/62*
D376	40 176	—	EE(VF)	E3122/D672	2/62*
D377	40 177	—	EE(VF)	E3123/D673	2/62*
D378	40 178	—	EE(VF)	E3124/D674	2/62*
D379	40 179	—	EE(VF)	E3125/D675	2/62*
D380	40 180	—	EE(VF)	E3126/D676	3/62*
D381	40 181	—	EE(VF)	E3127/D677	3/62*
D382	40 182	—	EE(VF)	E3128/D678	3/62*
D383	40 183	—	EE(VF)	E3129/D679	3/62*
D384	40 184	—	EE(VF)	E3130/D680	4/62*
D385	40 185	—	EE(VF)	E3131/D681	March 1962
D386	40 186	—	EE(VF)	E3132/D682	April 1962
D387	40 187	—	EE(VF)	E3133/D683	April 1962
D388	40 188	—	EE(VF)	E3134/D684	April 1962
D389	40 189	—	EE(VF)	E3135/D685	May 1962
D390	40 190	—	EE(VF)	E3136/D686	May 1962
D391	40 191	—	EE(VF)	E3137/D687	May 1962
D392	40 192	—	EE(VF)	E3138/D688	May 1962
D393	40 193	—	EE(VF)	E3139/D689	June 1962
D394	40 194	—	EE(VF)	E3140/D690	June 1962
D395	40 195	—	EE(VF)	E3141/D691	June 1962
D396	40 196	—	EE(VF)	E3142/D692	July 1962
D397	40 197	—	EE(VF)	E3143/D693	July 1962
D398	40 198	—	EE(VF)	E3144/D694	August 1962
D399	40 199	—	EE(VF)	E3145/D695	September 1962

Class 50

This fleet of 50 Type 4 locomotives, later classified as Class 50 were built by English Electric from information and traction experience gained from their prototype No DP2. The locomotives were built to a BR design panel specification, but remained the property of English Electric being leased to BR. The locomotives were eventually sold to BR. The complete fleet has now been refurbished.

BR 1957 No	TOPS No	Name	Built by	Works No	Date introduced
D400	50 050	*Fearless,* August 1978	EE(VF)	E3770/D1141	October 1967
D401	50 001	*Dreadnought,* April 1978	EE(VF)	E3772/D1143	December 1967
D402	50 002	*Superb,* March 1978	EE(VF)	E3771/D1142	December 1967
D403	50 003	*Temeraire,* May 1978	EE(VF)	E3773/D1144	January 1968
D404	50 004	*St Vincent,* May 1978	EE(VF)	E3774/D1145	December 1967
D405	50 005	*Collingwood,* April 1978	EE(VF)	E3775/D1146	January 1968
D406	50 006	*Neptune,* September 1979	EE(VF)	E3776/D1147	April 1968
D407	50 007	*Sir Edward Elgar,* February 1984	EE(VF)	E3777/D1148	March 1968

BR 1957 No	Date withdrawn	Disposal code	Disposal details	Notes
D362	December 1982	A	BR Haymarket depot	
D363	June 1982	A	BREL Derby	
D364	July 1983	C	BREL Doncaster, January 1984	
D365	July 1981	C	BREL Doncaster, May 1983	
D366	February 1982	C	BREL Crewe, May 1983	
D367	February 1984	C	BREL Doncaster May 1984	
D368				
D369	December 1983	A	BREL Doncaster	
D370	December 1983	A	BREL Doncaster	
D371	December 1981	C	BREL Swindon, November 1982	
D372	September 1983	C	BREL Doncaster, February 1984	
D373	August 1981	A	BR Perth Yard	
D374	May 1984	A	BR Longsight depot	
D375	May 1981	C	BREL Swindon, February 1983	
D376	August 1981	A	BREL Swindon	
D377	June 1984	A	BR Newton Heath depot	
D378	June 1981	C	BREL Swindon, September 1983	
D379	February 1981	C	BREL Swindon, March 1982	
D380	May 1983	C	BREL Crewe, January 1984	
D381				
D382	June 1982	C	BREL Crewe, March 1984	
D383	May 1983	A	BREL Crewe	
D384	December 1982	C	BREL Doncaster, December 1983	
D385	August 1983	C	BREL Doncaster, December 1983	
D386	December 1982	C	BREL Doncaster, May 1983	
D387	August 1982	A	BR Healey Mills depot	
D388	August 1983	C	BREL Crewe June 1984	
D389	January 1976	C	BREL Crewe, April 1976	
D390	January 1976	C	BREL Crewe, May 1976	
D391	September 1983	C	BREL Crewe June 1984	
D392				
D393	October 1981	A	BREL Swindon	
D394				
D395	June 1984			
D396	May 1984	C	BREL Doncaster June 1984	
D397	September 1983	C	BREL Doncaster May 1984	
D398	January 1983	C	BREL Doncaster, March 1984	
D399	June 1982	C	BREL Doncaster, May 1983	

Engine: EE 16CSVT of 2,700hp
Weight: 115 ton
Bogie type: Co-Co
Max speed: 100mph
Class code: 27/3 later Class 50

Tractive effort: 48,500lb
Length: 68ft 6in
Height: 12ft 11$\frac{3}{4}$in
Width: 9ft 1$\frac{1}{4}$in

BR 1957 No	Date withdrawn	Disposal code	Disposal details	Notes
D400				
D401				
D402				
D403				
D404				
D405				
D406				
D407				Formerly named *Hercules* April 1978

BR 1957 No	TOPS No	Name	Built by	Works No	*Period Date introduced
D408	50 008	*Thunderer,* September 1978	EE(VF)	E3778/D1149	March 1968
D409	50 009	*Conqueror,* May 1978	EE(VF)	E3779/D1150	March 1968
D410	50 010	*Monarch,* March 1978	EE(VF)	E3780/D1151	March 1968
D411	50 011	*Centurion,* August 1979	EE(VF)	E3781/D1152	April 1968
D412	50 012	*Benbow,* April 1978	EE(VF)	E3782/D1153	April 1968
D413	50 013	*Agincourt,* April 1978	EE(VF)	E3783/D1154	April 1968
D414	50 014	*Warspite,* May 1978	EE(VF)	E3784/D1155	May 1968
D415	50 015	*Valiant,* April 1978	EE(VF)	E3785/D1156	April 1968
D416	50 016	*Barham,* April 1978	EE(VF)	E3786/D1157	May 1968
D417	50 017	*Royal Oak,* April 1978	EE(VF)	E3787/D1158	April 1968
D418	50 018	*Resolution,* April 1978	EE(VF)	E3788/D1159	April 1968
D419	50 019	*Ramillies,* April 1978	EE(VF)	E3789/D1160	May 1968
D420	50 020	*Revenge,* July 1978	EE(VF)	E3790/D1161	May 1968
D421	50 021	*Rodney,* July 1978	EE(VF)	E3791/D1162	May 1968
D422	50 022	*Anson,* April 1978	EE(VF)	E3792/D1163	May 1968
D423	50 023	*Howe,* May 1978	EE(VF)	E3793/D1164	June 1968
D424	50 024	*Vanguard,* April 1978	EE(VF)	E3794/D1165	June 1968
D425	50 025	*Invincible,* June 1978	EE(VF)	E3795/D1166	June 1968
D426	50 026	*Indomitable,* March 1978	EE(VF)	E3796/D1167	July 1968
D427	50 027	*Lion,* April 1978	EE(VF)	E3797/D1168	June 1968
D428	50 028	*Tiger,* May 1978	EE(VF)	E3798/D1169	July 1968
D429	50 029	*Renown,* November 1978	EE(VF)	E3799/D1170	July 1968
D430	50 030	*Repulse,* April 1978	EE(VF)	E3800/D1171	July 1968
D431	50 031	*Hood,* June 1978	EE(VF)	E3801/D1172	July 1968
D432	50 032	*Courageous,* July 1978	EE(VF)	E3802/D1173	July 1968
D433	50 033	*Glorious,* June 1968	EE(VF)	E3803/D1174	August 1968
D434	50 034	*Furious,* April 1978	EE(VF)	E3804/D1175	August 1968
D435	50 035	*Ark Royal,* January 1978	EE(VF)	E3805/D1176	August 1968
D436	50 036	*Victorious,* May 1978	EE(VF)	E3806/D1177	September 1968
437	50 037	*Illustrious,* June 1978	EE(VF)	E3807/D1178	September 1968
438	50 038	*Formidable,* May 1978	EE(VF)	E3808/D1179	October 1968
439	50 039	*Implacable,* June 1978	EE(VF)	E3809/D1180	October 1968
440	50 040	*Leviathan,* September 1978	EE(VF)	E3810/D1181	October 1968
441	50 041	*Bulwark,* May 1978	EE(VF)	E3811/D1182	October 1968
442	50 042	*Triumph,* October 1978	EE(VF)	E3812/D1183	October 1968
443	50 043	*Eagle,* June 1978	EE(VF)	E3813/D1184	October 1968
444	50 044	*Exeter,* April 1978	EE(VF)	E3814/D1185	November 1968
445	50 045	*Achilles,* April 1978	EE(VF)	E3815/D1186	November 1968
446	50 046	*Ajax,* October 1978	EE(VF)	E3816/D1187	November 1968
447	50 047	*Swiftsure,* May 1978	EE(VF)	E3817/D1188	December 1968
448	50 048	*Dauntless,* March 1978	EE(VF)	E3818/D1189	December 1968
449	50 049	*Defiance,* May 1978	EE(VF)	E3819/D1190	December 1968

Class 41

Under the 1955 Modernisation Scheme the WR opted for diesel-hydraulic traction in preference to diesel-electric adopted on the other regions. Five prototype locomotives were constructed by NBL that later led the way to the sizeable fleet of 'Warship' locomotives.

BR 1957 No	Name	Built by	Works No	Date introduced	Date withdrawn
D600	*Active*	NBL	27660	January 1958	December 1967
D601	*Ark Royal*	NBL	27661	March 1958	December 1967
D602	*Bulldog*	NBL	27662	November 1958	December 1967
D603	*Conquest*	NBL	27663	November 1958	December 1967
D604	*Cossack*	NBL	27664	January 1959	December 1967

BR 1957 No	*Date withdrawn*	*Disposal code*	*Disposal details*	*Notes*
D408				
D409				
D410				
D411				
D412				
D413				
D414				
D415				
D416				
D417				
D418				
D419				
D420				
D421				
D422				
D423				
D424				
D425				
D426				
D427				
D428				
D429				
D430				
D431				
D432				
D433				
D434				
D435				
D436				
437				
438				
439				
440				
441				
442				
443				
444				
445				
446				
447				
448				
449				

Engine: (2) NBL L12V 18/21S unit giving 2,000hp
Weight: 117½ ton
Bogie type: C-C
Max speed: 90mph
Class code: D20/2, 20/4, allocated BR Class 41
Tractive effort: 50,000lb
Length: 65ft 0in
Height: 12ft 10in
Width: 8ft 8in

BR 1957 No	*Disposal Code*	*Disposal details*	*Notes*
D600	C	Woodham Bros, Barry, March 1970	
D601	C	Woodham Bros, Barry, July 1980	
D602	C	J. Cashmore, Newport, Gwent, October 1968	
D603	C	J. Cashmore, Newport, Gwent, October 1968	
D604	C	J. Cashmore, Newport, Gwent, August 1968	

Class 42

Based on the German V200 diesel-hydraulic locomotives, this fleet of 'Warship' locomotives were ordered in 1956 and built at Swindon Works, for use on the WR West of England route. All except D800 were named after naval ships or establishments.

BR 1957 No	*Name*	*Built by*	*Works No*	*Date introduced*	*Date withdrawn*
D800*	*Sir Brian Robertson*	BR Swindon	—	August 1958	October 1968
D801*	*Vanguard*	BR Swindon	—	November 1958	August 1968
D802*	*Formidable*	BR Swindon	—	December 1958	October 1968
D803	*Albion*	BR Swindon	—	March 1959	January 1972
D804	*Avenger*	BR Swindon	—	April 1959	October 1971
D805	*Benbow*	BR Swindon	—	May 1959	October 1972
D806	*Cambrian*	BR Swindon	—	June 1959	November 1972
D807	*Caradoc*	BR Swindon	—	June 1959	September 1972
D808	*Centaur*	BR Swindon	—	July 1959	October 1971
D809	*Champion*	BR Swindon	—	August 1959	October 1971
D810	*Cockade*	BR Swindon	—	September 1959	December 1972
D811	*Daring*	BR Swindon	—	October 1959	January 1972
D812	*Royal Naval Reserve 1859-1959*	BR Swindon	—	November 1959	December 1972
D813	*Diadem*	BR Swindon	—	December 1959	January 1972
D814	*Dragon*	BR Swindon	—	January 1960	November 1972
D815	*Druid*	BR Swindon	—	January 1960	October 1971
D816	*Eclipse*	BR Swindon	—	February 1960	January 1972
D817	*Foxhound*	BR Swindon	—	March 1960	October 1971
D818	*Glory*	BR Swindon	—	March 1960	November 1972
D819	*Goliath*	BR Swindon	—	April 1960	October 1971
D820	*Grenville*	BR Swindon	—	May 1960	November 1972
D821	*Greyhound*	BR Swindon	—	May 1960	December 1972
D822	*Hercules*	BR Swindon	—	June 1960	October 1971
D823	*Hermes*	BR Swindon	—	July 1960	October 1971
D824	*Highflyer*	BR Swindon	—	July 1960	December 1972
D825	*Intrepid*	BR Swindon	—	August 1960	August 1972
D826	*Jupiter*	BR Swindon	—	September 1960	October 1971
D827	*Kelly*	BR Swindon	—	October 1960	January 1972
D828	*Magnificent*	BR Swindon	—	October 1960	July 1971
D829	*Magpie*	BR Swindon	—	November 1960	August 1972
D830	*Majestic*	BR Swindon	—	January 1961	March 1969
D831	*Monarch*	BR Swindon	—	January 1961	October 1971
D832	*Onslaught*	BR Swindon	—	February 1961	December 1972

Class continued with D866

Class 43

The NBL company were contracted to build a fleet of B-B 'Warships' concurrent with Swindon, except that a different power and transmission type was fitted.

BR 1957 No	*Name*	*Built by*	*Works No*	*Date introduced*	*Date withdrawn*
D833	*Panther*	NBL	27962	July 1960	October 1971
D834	*Pathfinder*	NBL	27963	July 1960	October 1971
D835	*Pegasus*	NBL	27964	August 1960	October 1971
D836	*Powerful*	NBL	27965	September 1960	May 1971
D837	*Ramillies*	NBL	27966	November 1960	May 1971

Engine: (2) MD650 giving 2,200hp (*2,000hp)
Weight: 78 ton
Bogie type: B-B
Max speed: 90mph
Class code: D22/1, 22/1, D800-2, D20/1 later Class 42

Tractive effort: 48,200lb
Length: 60ft 0in
Height: 13ft 0¾in
Width: 8ft 10in

BR 1957 No	*Disposal Code*	*Disposal details*	*Notes*
D800	C	J. Cashmore Ltd, Newport, Gwent, July 1969	
D801	C	BR Swindon October 1970	
D802	C	BR Swindon October 1970	
D803	C	BREL Swindon October 1972	
D804	C	BREL Swindon March 1972	
D805	C	BREL Swindon May 1973	
D806	C	BREL Swindon April 1975	
D807	C	BREL Swindon November 1972	
D808	C	BREL Swindon February 1972	
D809	C	BREL Swindon October 1972	
D810	C	BREL Swindon September 1973	
D811	C	BREL Swindon October 1972	
D812	C	BREL Swindon June 1973	Allocated name *Despatch* (not carried)
D813	C	BREL Swindon September 1972	
D814	C	BREL Swindon February 1974	Withdrawn January 1972, reinstated May 1972
D815	C	BREL Swindon October 1972	
D816	C	BREL Swindon September 1972	
D817	C	BREL Swindon March 1972	
D818	P	BREL Swindon	
D819	C	BREL Swindon March 1972	
D820	C	BREL Swindon August 1973	
D821	P	DTG on North York Moors Railway	
D822	C	BREL Swindon February 1972	
D823	C	BREL Swindon May 1972	
D824	C	BREL Swindon May 1975	
D825	C	BREL Swindon October 1972	Withdrawn January 1972, reinstated May 1972
D826	C	BREL Swindon January 1972	
D827	C	BREL Swindon October 1972	
D828	C	BREL Swindon March 1972	
D829	C	BREL Swindon January 1974	Withdrawn January 1972, reinstated May 1972
D830	C	BREL Swindon October 1971	(2) Paxman 12YJXL engines (2,400hp)
D831	C	BREL Swindon June 1972	
D832	P	Bury Transport Museum	After withdrawal used by RTC Derby for test trains

Engine: (2) MAN L12V12/21B units giving 2,200hp
Weight: 79 ton
Bogie type: B-B
Max speed: 90mph
Class code: D22/2, 22/2 later Class 43

Tractive effort: 49,030lb
Length: 60ft 0in
Height: 13ft 0¾in
Width: 8ft 10in

BR 1957 No	*Disposal Code*	*Disposal details*	*Notes*
D833	C	BREL Swindon February 1972	
D834	C	BREL Swindon February 1972	
D835	C	BREL Swindon December 1971	
D836	C	BREL Swindon March 1972	
D837	C	BREL Swindon June 1972	

BR 1957 No	*Name*	*Built by*	*Works No*	*Date introduced*	*Date withdrawn*
D838	*Rapid*	NBL	27967	October 1960	March 1971
D839	*Relentless*	NBL	27968	November 1960	October 1971
D840	*Resistance*	NBL	27969	February 1961	April 1969
D841	*Roebuck*	NBL	27970	December 1960	October 1971
D842	*Royal Oak*	NBL	27971	December 1960	October 1971
D843	*Sharpshooter*	NBL	27972	January 1961	May 1971
D844	*Spartan*	NBL	27973	March 1961	October 1971
D845	*Sprightly*	NBL	27974	April 1961	October 1971
D846	*Steadfast*	NBL	27975	April 1961	May 1971
D847	*Strongbow*	NBL	27976	April 1961	March 1971
D848	*Sultan*	NBL	27977	April 1961	March 1969
D849	*Superb*	NBL	27978	May 1961	May 1971
D850	*Swift*	NBL	27979	June 1961	May 1971
D851	*Temeraire*	NBL	27980	July 1961	May 1971
D852	*Tenacious*	NBL	27981	July 1961	October 1971
D853	*Thruster*	NBL	27982	August 1961	October 1971
D854	*Tiger*	NBL	27983	September 1961	October 1971
D855	*Triumph*	NBL	27984	October 1961	October 1971
D856	*Trojan*	NBL	27985	November 1961	May 1971
D857	*Undaunted*	NBL	27986	December 1961	October 1971
D858	*Valorous*	NBL	27987	December 1961	October 1971
D859	*Vanquisher*	NBL	27988	January 1962	March 1971
D860	*Victorious*	NBL	27989	January 1962	March 1971
D861	*Vigilant*	NBL	27990	February 1962	October 1971
D862	*Viking*	NBL	27991	March 1962	October 1971
D863	*Warrior*	NBL	27992	April 1962	March 1969
D864	*Zambesi*	NBL	27993	May 1962	March 1971
D865	*Zealous*	NBL	27994	June 1962	May 1971

Class 42 — Continued from D832

D866	*Zebra*	BR Swindon	—	March 1961	January 1971
D867	*Zenith*	BR Swindon	—	April 1961	October 1971
D868	*Zephyr*	BR Swindon	—	May 1961	October 1971
D869	*Zest*	BR Swindon	—	July 1961	October 1971
D870	*Zulu*	BR Swindon	—	October 1961	August 1971

Class 52

The final development of the diesel-hydraulic traction principle was this fleet of 74 Type 4 'Western' locomotives, built by BR at Swindon and Crewe Works for use on the WR West of England main line, and general passenger/freight duties.

BR 1957 No	*Name*	*Built by*	*Works No*	*Date introduced*	*Date withdrawn*
D1000	*Western Enterprise*	BR Swindon	—	December 1961	February 1974
D1001	*Western Pathfinder*	BR Swindon	—	February 1962	October 1976
D1002	*Western Explorer*	BR Swindon	—	March 1962	January 1974
D1003	*Western Pioneer*	BR Swindon	—	April 1962	January 1975
D1004	*Western Crusader*	BR Swindon	—	May 1962	August 1973
D1005	*Western Venturer*	BR Swindon	—	June 1962	November 1976
D1006	*Western Stalwart*	BR Swindon	—	July 1962	April 1975
D1007	*Western Talisman*	BR Swindon	—	August 1962	January 1974
D1008	*Western Harrier*	BR Swindon	—	September 1962	October 1974

BR 1957 No	*Disposal Code*	*Disposal details*	*Notes*
D838	C	BREL Swindon June 1972	
D839	C	BREL Swindon August 1972	
D840	C	BREL Swindon July 1970	
D841	C	BREL Swindon February 1972	
D842	C	BREL Swindon March 1972	Withdrawn March 1969, reinstated July 1969
D843	C	BREL Swindon April 1972	
D844	C	BREL Swindon May 1972	
D845	C	BREL Swindon May 1972	
D846	C	BREL Swindon December 1971	
D847	C	BREL Swindon March 1972	
D848	C	BREL Swindon August 1970	
D849	C	BREL Swindon July 1972	
D850	C	BREL Swindon March 1972	
D851	C	BREL Swindon June 1972	
D852	C	BREL Swindon June 1972	
D853	C	BREL Swindon May 1972	
D854	C	BREL Swindon May 1972	
D855	C	BREL Swindon April 1972	
D856	C	BREL Swindon January 1972	
D857	C	BREL Swindon April 1972	
D858	C	BREL Swindon June 1972	Withdrawn April 1969, reinstated July 1969
D859	C	BREL Swindon June 1972	
D860	C	BREL Swindon December 1971	
D861	C	BREL Swindon July 1972	
D862	C	BREL Swindon May 1972	
D863	C	J. Cashmore Ltd, Newport, Gwent August 1969	
D864	C	BREL Swindon November 1971	
D865	C	BREL Swindon June 1972	
D866	C	BREL Swindon October 1972	
D867	C	BREL Swindon September 1972	
D868	C	BREL Swindon April 1972	
D869	C	BREL Swindon June 1972	
D870	C	BREL Swindon May 1972	

Engine: (2) MD655 giving 2,700hp
Weight: 108 ton
Bogie type: C-C
Max speed: 90mph
Class code: D27/1, 27/1 later BR Class 52
Tractive effort: 70,000lb
Length: 68ft 0in
Height: 12ft 11$\frac{7}{8}$in
Width: 9ft 0in

BR 1957 No	*Disposal code*	*Disposal details*	*Notes*
D1000	C	BREL Swindon July 1974	
D1001	C	BREL Swindon August 1977	
D1002	C	BREL Swindon June 1974	
D1003	C	BREL Swindon August 1977	
D1004	C	BREL Swindon September 1974	
D1005	C	BREL Swindon June 1977	
D1006	C	BREL Swindon March 1977	
D1007	C	BREL Swindon February 1975	
D1008	C	BREL Swindon October 1975	

BR 1957 No	Name	Built by	Works No	Date introduced	Date withdrawn
D1009	*Western Invader*	BR Swindon	—	September 1962	November 1976
D1010	*Western Campaigner*	BR Swindon	—	October 1962	February 1977
D1011	*Western Thunderer*	BR Swindon	—	October 1962	October 1975
D1012	*Western Firebrand*	BR Swindon	—	November 1962	November 1975
D1013	*Western Ranger*	BR Swindon	—	December 1962	February 1977
D1014	*Western Leviathan*	BR Swindon	—	December 1962	August 1974
D1015	*Western Champion*	BR Swindon	—	January 1963	December 1976
D1016	*Western Gladiator*	BR Swindon	—	February 1963	December 1975
D1017	*Western Warrior*	BR Swindon	—	March 1963	August 1973
D1018	*Western Buccaneer*	BR Swindon	—	April 1963	June 1973
D1019	*Western Challenger*	BR Swindon	—	May 1963	May 1973
D1020	*Western Hero*	BR Swindon	—	May 1963	June 1973
D1021	*Western Cavalier*	BR Swindon	—	June 1963	August 1976
D1022	*Western Sentinel*	BR Swindon	—	July 1963	January 1977
D1023	*Western Fusilier*	BR Swindon	—	September 1963	February 1977
D1024	*Western Huntsman*	BR Swindon	—	October 1963	November 1973
D1025	*Western Guardsman*	BR Swindon	—	November 1963	October 1975
D1026	*Western Centurion*	BR Swindon	—	December 1963	October 1975
D1027	*Western Lancer*	BR Swindon	—	January 1964	November 1975
D1028	*Western Hussar*	BR Swindon	—	February 1964	October 1976
D1029	*Western Legionnaire*	BR Swindon	—	July 1964	November 1974
D1030	*Western Musketeer*	BR Crewe	—	September 1963	April 1976
D1031	*Western Rifleman*	BR Crewe	—	December 1963	February 1975
D1032	*Western Marksman*	BR Crewe	—	December 1963	May 1973
D1033	*Western Trooper*	BR Crewe	—	January 1964	September 1976
D1034	*Western Dragoon*	BR Crewe	—	April 1964	October 1975
D1035	*Western Yeoman*	BR Crewe	—	July 1962	January 1975
D1036	*Western Emperor*	BR Crewe	—	August 1962	November 1976
D1037	*Western Empress*	BR Crewe	—	August 1962	May 1976
D1038	*Western Sovereign*	BR Crewe	—	September 1962	October 1973
D1039	*Western King*	BR Crewe	—	September 1962	July 1973
D1040	*Western Queen*	BR Crewe	—	September 1962	February 1976
D1041	*Western Prince*	BR Crewe	—	October 1962	February 1977
D1042	*Western Princess*	BR Crewe	—	October 1962	July 1973
D1043	*Western Duke*	BR Crewe	—	October 1962	April 1976
D1044	*Western Duchess*	BR Crewe	—	November 1962	February 1975
D1045	*Western Viscount*	BR Crewe	—	November 1962	April 1974
D1046	*Western Marquis*	BR Crewe	—	December 1962	December 1975
D1047	*Western Lord*	BR Crewe	—	February 1963	February 1976
D1048	*Western Lady*	BR Crewe	—	December 1962	February 1977
D1049	*Western Monarch*	BR Crewe	—	December 1962	April 1976
D1050	*Western Ruler*	BR Crewe	—	January 1963	April 1975
D1051	*Western Ambassador*	BR Crewe	—	January 1963	September 1976
D1052	*Western Viceroy*	BR Crewe	—	February 1963	October 1975
D1053	*Western Patriarch*	BR Crewe	—	February 1963	November 1976
D1054	*Western Governor*	BR Crewe	—	March 1963	November 1976
D1055	*Western Advocate*	BR Crewe	—	March 1963	January 1976
D1056	*Western Sultan*	BR Crewe	—	March 1963	December 1976
D1057	*Western Chieftain*	BR Crewe	—	April 1963	May 1976
D1058	*Western Nobleman*	BR Crewe	—	March 1963	January 1977
D1059	*Western Empire*	BR Crewe	—	April 1963	October 1975
D1060	*Western Dominion*	BR Crewe	—	April 1963	November 1973
D1061	*Western Envoy*	BR Crewe	—	April 1963	October 1974
D1062	*Western Courier*	BR Crewe	—	May 1963	August 1974
D1063	*Western Monitor*	BR Crewe	—	May 1963	April 1976
D1064	*Western Regent*	BR Crewe	—	May 1963	December 1975

BR 1957 No	*Disposal Code*	*Disposal details*	*Notes*
D1009	C	BREL Swindon November 1978	
D1010	P	Foster Yeoman Ltd, Merehead	Renamed *Western Yeoman* after Preservation
D1011	C	BREL Swindon January 1979	
D1012	C	BREL Swindon April 1979	
D1013	P	Severn Valley Railway	Owned by WLA
D1014	C	BREL Swindon February 1975	
D1015	P	DTG at Swindon	
D1016	C	BREL Swindon August 1977	
D1017	C	BREL Swindon March 1975	
D1018	C	BREL Swindon March 1974	
D1019	C	BREL Swindon October 1974	
D1020	C	BREL Swindon April 1974	
D1021	C	BREL Swindon March 1979	
D1022	C	BREL Swindon December 1978	
D1023	P	National Railway Museum, currently on DVR	
D1024	C	BREL Swindon August 1974	
D1025	C	BREL Swindon January 1979	
D1026	C	BREL Swindon August 1976	
D1027	C	BREL Swindon June 1976	
D1028	C	BREL Swindon June 1979	
D1029	C	BREL Swindon May 1975	
D1030	C	BREL Swindon September 1976	
D1031	C	BREL Swindon October 1976	
D1032	C	BREL Swindon December 1974	
D1033	C	BREL Swindon May 1979	Used after withdrawal as steam heat unit
D1034	C	BREL Swindon February 1979	Used after withdrawal as steam heat unit
D1035	C	BREL Swindon September 1976	
D1036	C	BREL Swindon February 1977	
D1037	C	BREL Swindon February 1977	
D1038	C	BREL Swindon November 1974	
D1039	C	BREL Swindon September 1974	
D1040	C	BREL Swindon August 1976	Withdrawn October 1975, and then reinstated
D1041	P	Bury Transport Museum	
D1042	C	BREL Swindon May 1974	
D1043	C	BREL Swindon February 1977	
D1044	C	BREL Swindon September 1975	
D1045	C	BREL Swindon August 1975	
D1046	C	BREL Swindon November 1976	
D1047	C	BREL Swindon September 1976	
D1048	P	Steamport, Southport	Owned by Plym Valley RPS
D1049	C	BREL Swindon February 1977	
D1050	C	BREL Swindon April 1976	
D1051	C	BREL Swindon August 1977	
D1052	C	BREL Swindon April 1976	
D1053	C	BREL Swindon June 1977	
D1054	C	BREL Swindon May 1977	
D1055	C	BREL Swindon June 1976	
D1056	C	BREL Swindon May 1979	
D1057	C	BREL Swindon June 1977	
D1058	C	BREL Swindon June 1979	
D1059	C	BREL Swindon July 1976	
D1060	C	BREL Swindon July 1974	
D1061	C	BREL Swindon August 1975	
D1062	P	Severn Valley Railway	Owned by WLA
D1063	C	BREL Swindon August 1977	
D1064	C	BREL Swindon July 1977	

BR 1957 No	Name	Built by	Works No	Date introduced	Date withdrawn
D1065	*Western Consort*	BR Crewe	—	June 1963	November 1976
D1066	*Western Prefect*	BR Crewe	—	June 1963	November 1974
D1067	*Western Druid*	BR Crewe	—	July 1963	January 1976
D1068	*Western Reliance*	BR Crewe	—	July 1963	October 1976
D1069	*Western Vanguard*	BR Crewe	—	October 1963	October 1975
D1070	*Western Gauntlet*	BR Crewe	—	October 1963	December 1975
D1071	*Western Renown*	BR Crewe	—	November 1963	December 1976
D1072	*Western Glory*	BR Crewe	—	November 1963	November 1976
D1073	*Western Bulwark*	BR Crewe	—	December 1963	August 1974

Class 47

The standard Type 4 medium powered main line locomotive adopted for mass introduction was this fleet of Brush/BR locomotives derived from various prototypes and previous design. A total of 512 locomotives of the same type were built. Five locomotives (Nos 1702-6) were originally built as Class 48, but all later reverted to Class 47 with standard engines.

BR 1957 No	TOPS No	TOPS re-numbering	Name	Built by	Works No	Date introduced
D1100	47 298	—	—	BR Crewe	—	July 1966
D1101	47 518	—	—	BR Crewe	—	August 1966
D1102	47 519	—	—	BR Crewe	—	September 1966
D1103	47 520	—	—	BR Crewe	—	October 1966
D1104	47 521	—	—	BR Crewe	—	October 1966
D1105	47 522	—	—	BR Crewe	—	November 1966
D1106	47 523	—	—	BR Crewe	—	November 1966
D1107	47 524	—	—	BR Crewe	—	December 1966
D1108	47 525	—	—	BR Crewe	—	January 1967
D1109	47 526	—	—	BR Crewe	—	January 1967
D1110	47 527	—	—	BR Crewe	—	January 1967
D1111	47 528	—	—	BR Crewe	—	February 1967

Class continued with D1500
D1200 See No D0280

Class 47 — Continued from D1111

BR 1957 No	TOPS No	TOPS re-numbering	Name	Built by	Works No	Date introduced
D1500	47 401	—	*North Eastern*, December 1981	Brush	342	November 1962
D1501	47 402	—	*Gateshead*, November 1981	Brush	343	November 1962
D1502	47 403	—	*The Geordie*, February 1982	Brush	344	November 1962
D1503	47 404	—	*Hadrian*, March 1982	Brush	345	December 1962
D1504	47 405	—	*Northumbria*, October 1982	Brush	346	January 1963
D1505	47 406	—	*Rail Riders*, December 1981	Brush	347	January 1963
D1506	47 407	—	—	Brush	348	January 1963
D1507	47 408	—	*Finsbury Park*, February 1984	Brush	349	January 1963

BR 1957 No	*Disposal Code*	*Disposal details*	*Notes*
D1065	C	BREL Swindon August 1977	
D1066	C	BREL Swindon May 1975	
D1067	C	BREL Swindon September 1976	
D1068	C	BREL Swindon August 1977	
D1069	C	BREL Swindon February 1977	
D1070	C	BREL Swindon May 1979	
D1071	C	BREL Swindon November 1978	
D1072	C	BREL Swindon April 1977	
D1073	C	BREL Swindon August 1975	

Engine: Sulzer 12LDA28C of 2,750hp†
Class 48: Sulzer 12 LVA 24 of 2,650hp
47 901: Ruston RP12RK3CT of 3,300hp
Weight: 111-123 ton
Bogie type: Co-Co
Max speed: 95mph (47/7 — 100mph)
Class code: 27/2 (26/2 for Class 48)

Tractive effort: 62,000lb
Length: 63ft 7in
Height: 12ft 9⅜in
Width: 9ft 2in

† Now rated at 2,580hp
‡ Number never carried

BR 1957 No	*Date withdrawn*	*Disposal code*	*Disposal details*	*Notes*
D1100				
D1101				
D1102				
D1103				
D1104				
D1105				
D1106				
D1107				
D1108				
D1109				
D1110				
D1111				

BR 1957 No	*Date withdrawn*	*Disposal code*	*Disposal details*	*Notes*
D1500				
D1501				
D1502				
D1503				
D1504				
D1505				
D1506				
D1507				

BR 1957 No	TOPS No	TOPS re-numbering	Name	Built by	Works No	Date introduced
D1508	47 409	—	—	Brush	350	January 1963
D1509	47 410	—	—	Brush	351	February 1963
D1510	47 411	—	—	Brush	352	February 1963
D1511	47 412	—	—	Brush	353	February 1963
D1512	47 413	—	—	Brush	354	March 1963
D1513	47 414	—	—	Brush	355	March 1963
D1514	47 415	—	—	Brush	357	March 1963
D1515	47 416	—	—	Brush	356	March 1963
D1516	47 417	—	—	Brush	358	April 1963
D1517	47 418	—	—	Brush	359	April 1963
D1518	47 419	—	—	Brush	413	May 1963
D1519	47 420	—	—	Brush	360	April 1963
D1520	47 421	—	—	Brush	414	June 1963
D1521	47 001	—	—	Brush	415	June 1963
D1522	47 002	—	—	Brush	417	June 1963
D1523	47 003	—	—	Brush	416	June 1963
D1524	47 004	—	—	Brush	419	June 1963
D1525	47 422	—	—	Brush	418	June 1963
D1526	47 005	—	—	Brush	420	June 1963
D1527	47 423	—	—	Brush	421	June 1963
D1528	47 006	—	—	Brush	422	June 1963
D1529	47 007	—	—	Brush	423	June 1963
D1530	47 008	—	—	Brush	424	June 1963
D1531	47 424	—	—	Brush	425	June 1963
D1532	47 009	—	—	Brush	426	June 1963
D1533	47 425	—	—	Brush	427	August 1963
D1534	47 426	—	—	Brush	428	August 1963
D1535	47 427	—	—	Brush	429	August 1963
D1536	47 428	—	—	Brush	430	August 1963
D1537	47 010	—	—	Brush	431	August 1963
D1538	47 011	—	—	Brush	432	September 1963
D1539	47 012	—	—	Brush	433	September 1963
D1540	47 013	—	—	Brush	434	September 1963
D1541	47 429	—	—	Brush	436	September 1963
D1542	47 430	—	—	Brush	435	September 1963
D1543	47 014	—	—	Brush	438	September 1963
D1544	47 015	—	—	Brush	437	October 1963
D1545	47 431	—	—	Brush	439	October 1963
D1546	47 016	—	—	Brush	440	October 1963
D1547	47 432	—	—	Brush	441	October 1963
D1548	47 433	—	—	Brush	442	October 1963
D1549	47 434	—	—	Brush	443	October 1963
D1550	47 435	—	—	BR Crewe	—	January 1964
D1551	47 529	—	—	BR Crewe	—	January 1964
D1552	47 436	—	—	BR Crewe	—	January 1964
D1553	47 437	—	—	BR Crewe	—	January 1964
D1554	47 438	—	—	BR Crewe	—	January 1964
D1555	47 439	—	—	BR Crewe	—	February 1964
D1556	47 440	—	—	BR Crewe	—	February 1964
D1557	47 441	—	—	BR Crewe	—	February 1964
D1558	47 442	—	—	BR Crewe	—	February 1964
D1559	47 443	—	—	BR Crewe	—	March 1964
D1560	47 444	—	*University of Nottingham,* May 1981	BR Crewe	—	March 1964
D1561	47 445	—	—	BR Crewe	—	March 1964
D1562	—	—	—	BR Crewe	—	March 1964
D1563	47 446	—	—	BR Crewe	—	April 1964
D1564	47 447	—	—	BR Crewe	—	March 1964
D1565	47 448	—	—	BR Crewe	—	March 1964
D1566	47 449	—	—	BR Crewe	—	March 1964
D1567	47 450	—	—	BR Crewe	—	March 1964

BR 1957 No	*Date withdrawn*	*Disposal code*	*Disposal details*	*Notes*
D1508				
D1509				
D1510				
D1511				
D1512				
D1513				
D1514				
D1515				
D1516				
D1517				
D1518				
D1519				
D1520				
D1521				
D1522				
D1523				
D1524				
D1525				
D1526				
D1527				
D1528				
D1529				
D1530				
D1531				
D1532				
D1533				
D1534				
D1535				
D1536				
D1537				
D1538				
D1539				
D1540				
D1541				
D1542				
D1543				
D1544				
D1545				
D1546				
D1547				
D1548				
D1549				
D1550				
D1551				
D1552				
D1553				
D1554				
D1555				
D1556				
D1557				
D1558				
D1559				
D1560				
D1561				
D1562	June 1971	C	BREL Crewe September 1971	
D1563				
D1564				
D1565				
D1566				
D1567				

BR 1957 No	TOPS No	TOPS re-numbering	Name	Built by	Works No	*Period Date introduced
D1568	47 451	—	—	BR Crewe	—	March 1964
D1569	47 452	—	—	BR Crewe	—	March 1964
D1570	47 017	—	—	BR Crewe	—	March 1964
D1571	47 453	—	—	BR Crewe	—	April 1964
D1572	47 018	—	—	BR Crewe	—	April 1964
D1573	47 019	—	—	BR Crewe	—	April 1964
D1574	47 454	—	—	BR Crewe	—	April 1964
D1575	47 455	—	—	BR Crewe	—	April 1964
D1576	47 456	—	—	BR Crewe	—	April 1964
D1577	47 457	—	—	BR Crewe	—	April 1964
D1578	47 458	—	—	BR Crewe	—	May 1964
D1579	47 459	—	—	BR Crewe	—	May 1964
D1580	47 460	—	—	BR Crewe	—	May 1964
D1581	47 461	—	*Charles Rennie Mackintosh*, March 1982	BR Crewe	—	May 1964
D1582	47 462	—	—	BR Crewe	—	May 1964
D1583	47 020	47 556	—	BR Crewe	—	May 1964
D1584	47 021‡	47 531	—	BR Crewe	—	May 1964
D1585	47 022‡	47 542	—	BR Crewe	—	May 1964
D1586	46 463	—	—	BR Crewe	—	May 1964
D1587	47 464	—	—	BR Crewe	—	May 1964
D1588	47 023	—	—	BR Crewe	—	May 1964
D1589	47 465	—	—	BR Crewe	—	May 1964
D1590	47 466	—	—	BR Crewe	—	May 1964
D1591	47 024	47 557	—	BR Crewe	—	June 1964
D1592	47 025‡	47 544	—	BR Crewe	—	June 1964
D1593	47 467	—	—	BR Crewe	—	June 1964
D1594	47 468	—	—	BR Crewe	—	June 1964
D1595	47 469	—	*Glasgow Chamber of Commerce*	BR Crewe	—	June 1964
D1596	47 470	—	*University of Edinburgh*, July 1983	BR Crewe	—	June 1964
D1597	47 026	47 597	—	BR Crewe	—	June 1964
D1598	47 471	—	*Norman Tunna GC*, November 1982	BR Crewe	—	June 1964
D1599	47 027	47 558	*Mayflower*	BR Crewe	—	June 1964
D1600	47 472	—	—	BR Crewe	—	June 1964
D1601	47 473	—	—	BR Crewe	—	July 1964
D1602	47 474	—	—	BR Crewe	—	July 1964
D1603	47 475	—	—	BR Crewe	—	July 1964
D1604	47 476	—	—	BR Crewe	—	July 1964
D1605	47 028	47 559	*Sir Joshua Reynolds*, April 1982	BR Crewe	—	July 1964
D1606	47 029	—	—	BR Crewe	—	July 1964
D1607	47 477	—	—	BR Crewe	—	July 1964
D1608	47 478	—	—	BR Crewe	—	July 1964
D1609	47 030	47 618	—	BR Crewe	—	August 1964
D1610	47 031	47 560	*Tamar*, April 1982	BR Crewe	—	August 1964
D1611	47 032	—	—	BR Crewe	—	August 1964
D1612	47 479	—	—	BR Crewe	—	August 1964
D1613	47 033	—	—	BR Crewe	—	August 1964
D1614	47 034	47 561	—	BR Crewe	—	August 1964
D1615	47 035	47 594	—	BR Crewe	—	August 1964
D1616	47 480	—	*Robin Hood*, November 1979	BR Crewe	—	9/64*
D1617	47 036	47 562	*Sir William Burrell*, September 1983	BR Crewe	—	9/64*
D1618	47 037	47 563	—	BR Crewe	—	9/64*
D1619	47 038	47 564	—	BR Crewe	—	10/64*
D1620	47 039	47 565	—	BR Crewe	—	10/64*
D1621	47 040	—	—	BR Crewe	—	10/64*

BR 1957 No	*Date withdrawn*	*Disposal code*	*Disposal details*	*Notes*
D1568				
D1569				
D1570				
D1571				
D1572				
D1573				
D1574				
D1575				
D1576				
D1577				
D1578				
D1579				
D1580				
D1581				
D1582				
D1583				
D1584				
D1585				
D1586				
D1587				
D1588				
D1589				
D1590				
D1591				
D1592				
D1593				
D1594				
D1595				
D1596				
D1597				
D1598				
D1599				
D1600				
D1601				
D1602				
D1603				
D1604				
D1605				
D1606				
D1607				
D1608				
D1609				
D1610				
D1611				
D1612				
D1613				
D1614				
D1615				
D1616				
D1617				
D1618				
D1619				
D1620				
D1621				

BR 1957 No	TOPS No	TOPS re-numbering	Name	Built by	Works No	Period* Date introduced
D1622	47 041	—	—	BR Crewe	—	10/64*
D1623	47 042	47 586	—	BR Crewe	—	10/64*
D1624	47 043‡	47 566	—	BR Crewe	—	11/64*
D1625	47 044	47 567	—	BR Crewe	—	10/64*
D1626	47 045	47 568	—	BR Crewe	—	11/64*
D1627	47 481	—	—	BR Crewe	—	11/64*
D1628	47 046	See notes	—	BR Crewe	—	11/64*
D1629	47 047	47 569	—	BR Crewe	—	11/64*
D1630	47 048	47 570	—	BR Crewe	—	11/64*
D1631	47 049	—	—	BR Crewe	—	11/64*
D1632	47 050	—	—	BR Crewe	—	12/64*
D1633	47 051	—	—	BR Crewe	—	12/64*
D1634	47 052	—	—	BR Crewe	—	12/64*
D1635	47 053	—	—	BR Crewe	—	12/64*
D1636	47 482	—	—	BR Crewe	—	December 1964
D1637	47 483	—	—	BR Crewe	—	December 1964
D1638	47 054	—	—	BR Crewe	—	December 1964
D1639	47 055	—	—	BR Crewe	—	December 1964
D1640	47 056	—	—	BR Crewe	—	December 1964
D1641	47 057‡	47 532	—	BR Crewe	—	December 1964
D1642	47 058‡	47 547	—	BR Crewe	—	December 1964
D1643	47 059	—	—	BR Crewe	—	December 1964
D1644	47 060	—	—	BR Crewe	—	December 1964
D1645	47 061	—	—	BR Crewe	—	December 1964
D1646	47 062‡	47 545	—	BR Crewe	—	December 1964
D1647	47 063	—	—	BR Crewe	—	January 1965
D1648	47 064	—	—	BR Crewe	—	January 1965
D1649	47 065‡	47 535	*University of Leicester,* May 1982	BR Crewe	—	January 1965
D1650	47 066	—	—	BR Crewe	—	January 1965
D1651	47 067‡	47 533	—	BR Crewe	—	January 1965
D1652	47 068	—	—	BR Crewe	—	January 1965
D1653	47 069	—	—	BR Crewe	—	January 1965
D1654	47 070	47 620	—	BR Crewe	—	January 1965
D1655	47 071‡	47 536	—	BR Crewe	—	January 1965
D1656	47 072	47 609	—	BR Crewe	—	February 1965
D1657	47 073‡	47 537	*Sir Gwynedd — County of Gwynedd,* November 1982	BR Crewe	—	February 1965
D1658	47 074	—	—	BR Crewe	—	February 1965
D1659	47 075	—	—	BR Crewe	—	February 1965
D1660	47 076	—	*City of Truro*	BR Crewe	—	February 1965
D1661	47 077	47 613	*North Star*	BR Crewe	—	February 1965
D1662	47 484	—	*Isambard Kingdom Brunel*	BR Crewe	—	February 1965
D1663	47 078	—	*Sir Daniel Gooch*	BR Crewe	—	February 1965
D1664	47 079	—	*George Jackson Churchward*	BR Crewe	—	February 1965
D1665	47 080	47 612	*Titan*	BR Crewe	—	March 1965
D1666	47 081	47 606	*Odin*	BR Crewe	—	March 1965
D1667	47 082	—	*Atlas*	BR Crewe	—	March 1965
D1668	47 083	—	*Orion*	BR Crewe	—	March 1965
D1669	47 084	47 538	*Python*	BR Crewe	—	March 1965
D1670	47 085	—	*Mammoth*	BR Crewe	—	March 1965
D1671	—	—	*Thor*	BR Crewe	—	March 1965

BR 1957 No	*Date withdrawn*	*Disposal code*	*Disposal details*	*Notes*
D1622				
D1623				
D1624				
D1625				
D1626				
D1627				
D1628				Renumbered 47 601 from December 1975, rebuilt again and renumbered 47 901 from November 1979
D1629				
D1630				
D1631				
D1632				
D1633				
D1634				
D1635				
D1636				
D1637				
D1638				
D1639				
D1640				
D1641				
D1642				
D1643				
D1644				
D1645				
D1646				
D1647				
D1648				
D1649				
D1650				
D1651				
D1652				
D1653				
D1654				
D1655				
D1656				
D1657				
D1658				
D1659				
D1660				
D1661				
D1662				
D1663				
D1664				Nameplate altered to *G. J. Churchward*, March 1979
D1665				
D1666				
D1667				
D1668				
D1669				
D1670				
D1671	April 1966	C	R. S. Hayes Bridgend, June 1966	Name transferred to D1677 after withdrawal

BR 1957 No	TOPS No	TOPS re-numbering	Name	Built by	Works No	Date introduced
D1672	47 086	—	*Colossus*	BR Crewe	—	March 1965
D1673	47 087	—	*Cyclops*	BR Crewe	—	April 1965
D1674	47 088	—	*Samson*	BR Crewe	—	April 1965
D1675	47 089	—	*Amazon*	BR Crewe	—	April 1965
D1676	47 090	—	*Vulcan*	BR Crewe	—	April 1965
D1677	47 091	—	*Thor*	BR Crewe	—	April 1965
D1678	47 092	47 534	—	BR Crewe	—	April 1965
D1679	47 093	—	—	BR Crewe	—	May 1965
D1680	47 094	—	—	BR Crewe	—	May 1965
D1681	47 095	—	—	BR Crewe	—	May 1965
D1682	47 096	—	—	Brush	444	October 1963
D1683	47 485	—	—	Brush	445	October 1963
D1684	47 097	—	—	Brush	446	November 1963
D1685	47 098	—	—	Brush	447	November 1963
D1686	47 099	—	—	Brush	448	November 1963
D1687	47 100	—	—	Brush	449	November 1963
D1688	47 101	—	—	Brush	450	November 1963
D1689	47 486	—	—	Brush	451	November 1963
D1690	47 102	—	—	Brush	452	November 1963
D1691	47 103	—	—	Brush	453	November 1963
D1692	47 104	—	—	Brush	454	November 1963
D1693	47 105	—	—	Brush	455	December 1963
D1694	47 106	—	—	Brush	456	December 1963
D1695	47 107	—	—	Brush	457	December 1963
D1696	47 108	—	—	Brush	458	December 1963
D1697	47 109	—	—	Brush	460	December 1963
D1698	47 110	—	—	Brush	459	January 1964
D1699	47 111	—	—	Brush	461	December 1963
D1700	47 112	—	—	Brush	462	January 1964
D1701	47 113	—	—	Brush	463	January 1964
D1702	47 114	—	—	Brush	464	November 1965
D1703	47 115	—	—	Brush	465	September 1965
D1704	47 116	—	—	Brush	466	July 1966
D1705	47 117	—	—	Brush	467	November 1965
D1706	47 118	—	—	Brush	468	December 1965
D1707	47 487	—	—	Brush	469	January 1964
D1708	47 119	—	—	Brush	470	January 1964
D1709	47 120	—	—	Brush	471	January 1964
D1710	47 121	—	—	Brush	472	January 1964
D1711	47 122	—	—	Brush	473	January 1964
D1712	47 123	—	—	Brush	474	January 1964
D1713	47 488	—	—	Brush	475	January 1964
D1714	47 124	—	—	Brush	476	February 1964
D1715	47 125	—	—	Brush	477	February 1964
D1716	47 489	—	—	Brush	487	February 1964
D1717	47 126	—	—	Brush	488	February 1964
D1718	47 127	47 539	*Rochdale Pioneers,* November 1982	Brush	489	February 1964
D1719	47 128	—	—	Brush	490	February 1964
D1720	47 129	—	—	Brush	491	March 1964
D1721	47 130	—	—	Brush	492	March 1964
D1722	47 131	—	—	Brush	493	March 1964
D1723	47 132	47 540	—	Brush	494	March 1964
D1724	47 133	—	—	Brush	495	March 1964

BR 1957 No	*Date withdrawn*	*Disposal code*	*Disposal details*	*Notes*
D1672				
D1673				
D1674				
D1675				
D1676				
D1677				
D1678				
D1679				
D1680				
D1681				
D1682				
D1683				
D1684				
D1685				
D1686				
D1687				
D1688				
D1689				
D1690				
D1691				
D1692				
D1693				
D1694				
D1695				
D1696				
D1697				
D1698				
D1699				
D1700				
D1701				
D1702				Completed July 1964, under test until November 1965
D1703				Completed July 1964, under test until September 1965
D1704				Completed July 1964, under test until July 1966
D1705				Completed August 1964, under test until November 1965
D1706				Completed August 1964, under test until December 1965
D1707				
D1708				
D1709				
D1710				
D1711				
D1712				
D1713				
D1714				
D1715				
D1716				
D1717				
D1718				
D1719				
D1720				
D1721				
D1722				
D1723				
D1724				

BR 1957 No	TOPS No	TOPS re-numbering	Name	Built by	Works No	Date introduced
D1725	47 490	—	—	Brush	496	March 1964
D1726	47 134	47 622	—	Brush	497	March 1964
D1727	47 135	—	—	Brush	498	April 1964
D1728	47 136	—	—	Brush	499	April 1964
D1729	47 137	—	—	Brush	500	April 1964
D1730	47 138	47 607	—	Brush	501	April 1964
D1731	47 139‡	47 550	—	Brush	502	June 1964
D1732	47 140	—	—	Brush	503	April 1964
D1733	47 141	47 614	—	Brush	504	June 1964
D1734	—	—	—	Brush	505	May 1964
D1735	47 142	—	—	Brush	506	May 1964
D1736	47 143	—	—	Brush	508	April 1964
D1737	47 144	—	—	Brush	507	May 1964
D1738	47 145	—	—	Brush	509	May 1964
D1739	47 146	—	—	Brush	510	June 1964
D1740	47 147	—	—	Brush	511	June 1964
D1741	47 148	—	—	Brush	512	June 1964
D1742	47 149	47 617	—	Brush	513	May 1964
D1743	47 150	—	—	Brush	514	June 1964
D1744	47 151	—	—	Brush	515	June 1964
D1745	47 152	—	—	Brush	516	July 1964
D1746	47 153	47 551	—	Brush	517	July 1964
D1747	47 154	47 546	—	Brush	518	July 1964
D1748	47 155	—	—	Brush	519	July 1964
D1749	47 156	—	—	Brush	486	July 1964
D1750	47 157	—	—	Brush	478	July 1964
D1751	47 158	—	*Henry Ford,* July 1981	Brush	479	July 1964
D1752	47 159	—	—	Brush	480	July 1964
D1753	47 491	—	—	Brush	481	July 1964
D1754	47 160	47 605	—	Brush	482	August 1964
D1755	47 161	47 541	*The Queen Mother,* October 1982	Brush	483	August 1964
D1756	47 162	—	—	Brush	484	September 1964
D1757	47 163	47 610	—	Brush	485	September 1964
D1758	47 164	47 571	—	Brush	520	August 1964
D1759	47 165	47 590	*Thomas Telford*	Brush	521	August 1964
D1760	47 492	—	—	Brush	522	September 1964
D1761	47 166	47 611	—	Brush	523	September 1964
D1762	47 167	47 580	*County of Essex,* July 1979	Brush	524	September 1964
D1763	47 168	47 572	—	Brush	525	September 1964
D1764	47 169	47 581	*Great Eastern,* March 1979	Brush	526	September 1964
D1765	47 170	47 582	*County of Norfolk,* August 1979	Brush	527	September 1964
D1766	47 171	47 592	—	Brush	528	September 1964
D1767	47 172	47 583	*County of Hertfordshire* July 1979	Brush	529	October 1964
D1768	47 173	47 573	—	Brush	530	October 1964
D1769	47 174	47 574	—	Brush	531	October 1964
D1770	47 175	47 575	—	Brush	532	October 1964
D1771	47 176	47 576	—	Brush	533	October 1964
D1772	47 177	47 599	—	Brush	534	October 1964
D1773	47 178	47 588	—	Brush	535	September 1964
D1774	47 179	47 577	*Benjamin Gimbert GC,* September 1981	Brush	536	October 1964
D1775	47 180	47 584	*County of Suffolk,* June 1979	Brush	537	October 1964
D1776	47 181	47 578	—	Brush	538	October 1964
D1777	47 182	47 598	—	Brush	539	November 1964

BR 1957 No	*Date withdrawn*	*Disposal code*	*Disposal details*	*Notes*
D1725				
D1726				
D1727				
D1728				
D1729				
D1730				
D1731				
D1732				
D1733				
D1734	March 1965	C	BR Crewe April 1965	
D1735				
D1736				
D1737				
D1738				
D1739				
D1740				
D1741				
D1742				
D1743				
D1744				
D1745				
D1746				
D1747				
D1748				
D1749				
D1750				
D1751				
D1752				
D1753				
D1754				
D1755				
D1756				
D1757				
D1758				
D1759				
D1760				
D1761				
D1762				
D1763				
D1764				
D1765				
D1766				
D1767				
D1768				
D1769				
D1770				
D1771				
D1772				
D1773				
D1774				
D1775				
D1776				
D1777				

BR 1957 No	TOPS No	TOPS re-numbering	Name	Built by	Works No	Period* Date introduced
D1778	47 183	47 579	*James Nightall GC,* September 1981	Brush	540	October 1964
D1779	47 184	47 585	*County of Cambridge,* May 1979	Brush	541	October 1964
D1780	47 185	47 602	—	Brush	542	October 1964
D1781	47 186	—	—	Brush	543	November 1964
D1782	47 301	—	—	Brush	544	November 1964
D1783	47 302	—	—	Brush	545	November 1964
D1784	47 303	—	—	Brush	546	November 1964
D1785	47 304	—	—	Brush	547	December 1964
D1786	47 305	—	—	Brush	548	November 1964
D1787	47 306	—	—	Brush	549	November 1964
D1788	47 307	—	—	Brush	550	December 1964
D1789	47 308	—	—	Brush	551	November 1964
D1790	47 309	—	—	Brush	552	December 1964
D1791	47 310	—	—	Brush	553	December 1964
D1792	47 311	—	—	Brush	554	January 1965
D1793	47 312	—	—	Brush	555	December 1964
D1794	47 313	—	—	Brush	556	December 1964
D1795	47 314	—	—	Brush	557	January 1965
D1796	47 315	—	—	Brush	558	January 1965
D1797	47 316	—	—	Brush	559	January 1965
D1798	47 317	—	—	Brush	560	January 1965
D1799	47 318	—	—	Brush	561	January 1965
D1800	47 319	—	—	Brush	562	January 1965
D1801	47 320	—	—	Brush	563	January 1965
D1802	47 321	—	—	Brush	564	January 1965
D1803	47 322	—	—	Brush	565	January 1965
D1804	47 323	—	—	Brush	566	February 1965
D1805	47 324	—	—	Brush	567	January 1965
D1806	47 325	—	—	Brush	568	January 1965
D1807	47 326	—	—	Brush	569	1/65*
D1808	47 327	—	—	Brush	570	1/65*
D1809	47 328	—	—	Brush	571	1/65*
D1810	47 329	—	—	Brush	572	2/65*
D1811	47 330	—	—	Brush	573	2/65*
D1812	47 331	—	—	Brush	574	2/65*
D1813	47 332	—	—	Brush	575	2/65*
D1814	47 333	—	—	Brush	576	2/65*
D1815	47 334	—	—	Brush	577	2/65*
D1816	47 335	—	—	Brush	578	2/65*
D1817	47 336	—	—	Brush	579	3/65*
D1818	47 337	—	—	Brush	580	2/65*
D1819	47 338	—	—	Brush	581	2/65*
D1820	47 339	—	—	Brush	582	2/65*
D1821	47 340	—	—	Brush	583	3/65*
D1822	47 341	—	—	Brush	584	3/65*
D1823	47 342	—	—	Brush	585	3/65*
D1824	47 343	—	—	Brush	586	3/65*
D1825	47 344	—	—	Brush	587	3/65*
D1826	47 345	—	—	Brush	588	3/65*
D1827	47 346	—	—	Brush	589	3/65*
D1828	47 347	—	—	Brush	590	3/65*
D1829	47 348	—	—	Brush	591	3/65*
D1830	47 349	—	—	Brush	592	3/65*
D1831	47 350	—	—	Brush	593	5/65*
D1832	47 351	—	—	Brush	594	4/65*
D1833	47 352	—	—	Brush	595	5/65*
D1834	47 353	—	—	Brush	596	4/65*
D1835	47 354	—	—	Brush	597	5/65*

BR 1957 No	Date withdrawn	Disposal code	Disposal details	Notes
D1778				
D1779				
D1780				
D1781				
D1782				
D1783				
D1784				
D1785				
D1786				
D1787				
D1788				
D1789				
D1790				
D1791				
D1792				
D1793				
D1794				
D1795				
D1796				
D1797				
D1798				
D1799				
D1800				
D1801				
D1802				
D1803				
D1804				
D1805				
D1806				
D1807				
D1808				
D1809				
D1810				
D1811				
D1812				
D1813				
D1814				
D1815				
D1816				
D1817				
D1818				
D1819				
D1820				
D1821				
D1822				
D1823				
D1824				
D1825				
D1826				
D1827				
D1828				
D1829				
D1830				
D1831				
D1832				
D1833				
D1834				
D1835				

BR 1957 No	TOPS No	TOPS re-numbering	Name	Built by	Works No	Period* Date introduced
D1836	47 355	—	—	Brush	598	4/65*
D1837	47 187	—	—	Brush	599	5/65*
D1838	47 188	—	—	Brush	600	5/65*
D1839	47 189	—	—	Brush	601	4/65*
D1840	47 190	—	—	Brush	602	6/65*
D1841	47 191	—	—	Brush	603	5/65*
D1842	47 192	—	—	BR Crewe	—	5/65*
D1843	47 193	—	—	BR Crewe	—	5/65*
D1844	47 194	—	—	BR Crewe	—	5/65*
D1845	47 195	—	—	BR Crewe	—	6/65*
D1846	47 196	—	—	BR Crewe	—	6/65*
D1847	47 197	—	—	BR Crewe	—	6/65*
D1848	47 198	—	—	BR Crewe	—	6/65*
D1849	47 199	—	—	BR Crewe	—	6/65*
D1850	47 200	—	—	BR Crewe	—	6/65*
D1851	47 201	—	—	BR Crewe	—	6/65*
D1852	47 202	—	—	BR Crewe	—	7/65*
D1853	47 203	—	—	BR Crewe	—	7/65*
D1854	47 204	—	—	BR Crewe	—	7/65*
D1855	47 205	—	—	BR Crewe	—	8/65*
D1856	47 206	—	—	BR Crewe	—	8/65*
D1857	47 207	—	—	BR Crewe	—	8/65*
D1858	47 208	—	—	BR Crewe	—	8/65*
D1859	47 209	—	—	BR Crewe	—	9/65*
D1860	47 210	—	—	BR Crewe	—	9/65*
D1861	47 211	—	—	BR Crewe	—	9/65*
D1862	47 212	—	—	Brush	624	May 1965
D1863	47 213	—	—	Brush	625	May 1965
D1864	47 214	—	—	Brush	626	May 1965
D1865	47 215	—	—	Brush	627	May 1965
D1866	47 216	47 299	—	Brush	628	May 1965
D1867	47 217	—	—	Brush	629	May 1965
D1868	47 218	—	—	Brush	630	May 1965
D1869	47 219	—	—	Brush	631	June 1965
D1870	47 220	—	—	Brush	632	June 1965
D1871	47 221	—	—	Brush	633	June 1965
D1872	47 222	—	*Appleby Frodingham,* June 1982	Brush	634	June 1965
D1873	47 223	—	—	Brush	635	May 1965
D1874	47 224	—	—	Brush	636	June 1965
D1875	47 356	—	—	Brush	637	July 1965
D1876	47 357	—	—	Brush	638	June 1965
D1877	47 358	—	—	Brush	639	June 1965
D1878	47 359	—	—	Brush	640	June 1965
D1879	47 360	—	—	Brush	641	July 1965
D1880	47 361	—	*Wilton Endeavour,* July 1983	Brush	642	February 1966
D1881	47 362	—	—	Brush	643	June 1965
D1882	47 363	—	—	Brush	644	July 1965
D1883	47 364	—	—	Brush	645	July 1965
D1884	47 365	—	—	Brush	646	July 1965
D1885	47 366	—	—	Brush	647	July 1965
D1886	47 367	—	—	Brush	648	August 1965
D1887	47 368	—	—	Brush	649	August 1965
D1888	47 369	—	—	Brush	650	July 1965
D1889	47 370	—	—	Brush	651	July 1965
D1890	47 371	—	—	Brush	652	July 1965
D1891	47 372	—	—	Brush	653	August 1965
D1892	47 373	—	—	Brush	654	August 1965

BR 1957 No	*Date withdrawn*	*Disposal code*	*Disposal details*	*Notes*
D1836				
D1837				
D1838				
D1839				
D1840				
D1841				
D1842				
D1843				
D1844				
D1845				
D1846				
D1847				
D1848				
D1849				
D1850				
D1851				
D1852				
D1853				
D1854				
D1855				
D1856				
D1857				
D1858	January 1980	C	BR Dundee depot April 1980	
D1859				
D1860				
D1861				
D1862				
D1863				
D1864				
D1865				
D1866				Renumbered within sub class December 1981
D1867				
D1868				
D1869				
D1870				
D1871				
D1872				
D1873				
D1874				
D1875				
D1876				
D1877				
D1878				
D1879				
D1880				Completed July 1965
D1881				
D1882				
D1883				
D1884				
D1885				
D1886				
D1887				
D1888				
D1889				
D1890				
D1891				
D1892				

BR 1957 No	*TOPS No*	*TOPS re-numbering*	*Name*	*Built by*	*Works No*	*Period* Date introduced*
D1893	47 374	—	—	Brush	655	August 1965
D1894	47 375	—	—	Brush	656	December 1965
D1895	47 376	—	—	Brush	657	September 1965
D1896	47 377	—	—	Brush	658	September 1965
D1897	47 378	—	—	Brush	659	September 1965
D1898	47 379	—	—	Brush	660	August 1965
D1899	47 380	—	—	Brush	661	August 1965
D1900	47 381	—	—	Brush	662	September 1965
D1901	47 225	—	—	Brush	663	September 1965
D1902	47 226	—	—	Brush	664	October 1965
D1903	47 227	—	—	Brush	665	September 1965
D1904	47 228	—	—	Brush	666	September 1965
D1905	47 229	—	—	Brush	667	September 1965
D1906	47 230	—	—	Brush	668	October 1965
D1907	47 231	—	—	Brush	669	September 1965
D1908	—	—	—	Brush	670	October 1965
D1909	47 232	—	—	Brush	671	October 1965
D1910	47 233	—	—	Brush	672	October 1965
D1911	47 234	—	—	Brush	673	October 1965
D1912	47 235	—	—	Brush	674	October 1965
D1913	47 236	—	—	Brush	675	October 1965
D1914	47 237	—	—	Brush	676	November 1965
D1915	47 238	—	—	Brush	677	December 1965
D1916	47 239	—	—	Brush	678	November 1965
D1917	47 240	—	—	Brush	679	December 1965
D1918	47 241	—	—	Brush	680	November 1965
D1919	47 242	—	—	Brush	681	November 1965
D1920	47 243	—	—	Brush	682	November 1965
D1921	47 244	—	—	Brush	683	December 1965
D1922	47 245	—	—	Brush	684	December 1965
D1923	47 246	—	—	Brush	685	December 1965
D1924	47 247	—	—	Brush	686	December 1965
D1925	47 248	47 616	—	Brush	687	December 1965
D1926	47 249	—	—	Brush	688	January 1966
D1927	47 250	47 600	—	Brush	689	January 1966
D1928	47 251	47 589	—	Brush	690	January 1966
D1929	47 252	47 615	—	Brush	691	February 1966
D1930	47 253	—	—	Brush	692	February 1966
D1931	47 254	—	—	Brush	693	February 1966
D1932	47 493	47 701	*Saint Andrew,* January 1979	Brush	694	February 1966
D1933	47 255	47 596	*Aldeburgh Festival*	Brush	695	March 1966
D1934	47 256	—	—	Brush	696	March 1966
D1935	47 257	—	—	Brush	697	March 1966
D1936	47 494	47 706	*Strathclyde,* May 1979	Brush	698	March 1966
D1937	47 495	47 704	*Dunedin,* February 1979	Brush	699	April 1966
D1938	47 258	—	—	Brush	700	April 1966
D1939	47 496	47 710	*Sir Walter Scott,* October 1979	Brush	701	4/66*
D1940	47 497	—	—	Brush	702	6/66*
D1941	47 498	47 711	*Greyfriars Bobby,* April 1981	Brush	703	7/66*
D1942	47 499	47 709	*The Lord Provost,* September 1979	Brush	704	6/66*
D1943	47 500	—	*Great Western,* February 1979	Brush	705	7/66*
D1944	47 501	—	—	Brush	706	7/66*
D1945	47 502	—	—	Brush	707	7/66*
D1946	47 503	—	—	Brush	708	7/66*
D1947	47 504	47 702	*Saint Cuthbert,* March 1979	Brush	709	7/66*

BR 1957 No	*Date withdrawn*	*Disposal code*	*Disposal details*	*Notes*
D1893				
D1894				
D1895				
D1896				
D1897				
D1898				
D1899				
D1900				
D1901				
D1902				
D1903				
D1904				
D1905				
D1906				
D1907				
D1908	August 1969	C	BR Crewe October 1969	
D1909				
D1910				
D1911				
D1912				
D1913				
D1914				
D1915				
D1916				
D1917				
D1918				
D1919				
D1920				
D1921				
D1922				
D1923				
D1924				
D1925				
D1926				
D1927				
D1928				
D1929				
D1930				
D1931				
D1932				
D1933				
D1934				
D1935				
D1936				
D1937				
D1938				
D1939				
D1940				
D1941				
D1942				
D1943				
D1944				
D1945				
D1946				
D1947				

BR 1957 No	*TOPS No*	*TOPS re-numbering*	*Name*	*Built by*	*Works No*	*Period* Date introduced*
D1948	47 505	47 712	*Lady Diana Spencer,* April 1981	Brush	610	8/66*
D1949	47 506	47 707	*Holyrood,* May 1979	Brush	611	9/66*
D1950	47 259‡	47 552	—	Brush	612	9/66*
D1951	47 507	—	—	Brush	613	11/66*
D1952	47 508	—	*Great Britain,* March 1979	Brush	614	11/66*
D1953	47 509	—	*Albion,* March 1979	Brush	615	12/66*
D1954	47 510	—	*Fair Rosamund*, March 1979	Brush	616	12/66*
D1955	47 511		—	Brush	617	12/66*
D1956	47 260	47 553	—	Brush	618	13/66*
D1957	47 554	47 705	*Lothian,* April 1979	Brush	619	1/67*
D1958	47 512	—	—	Brush	620	2/67*
D1959	47 513	—	—	Brush	621	2/67*
D1960	47 514	47 703	*Saint Mungo*, March 1979	Brush	622	7/67*
D1961	47 515	—	—	Brush	623	5/68*
D1962	47 262	47 608	—	BR Crewe	—	September 1965
D1963	47 263	47 587	—	BR Crewe	—	September 1965
D1964	47 264	47 618	—	BR Crewe	—	September 1965
D1965	47 265	47 591	—	BR Crewe	—	October 1965
D1966	47 266	—	—	BR Crewe	—	October 1965
D1967	47 267	47 603	—	BR Crewe	—	October 1965
D1968	47 516	47 708	*Waverley,* June 1979	BR Crewe	—	11/65*
D1969	47 268	47 595	*Confederation of British Industry*	BR Crewe	—	11/65*
D1970	47 269	—	—	BR Crewe	—	11/65*
D1971	47 270	—	—	BR Crewe	—	11/65
D1972	47 271	47 604	—	BR Crewe	—	11/65*
D1973	47 272	47 593	*Galloway Princess,* September 1983	BR Crewe	—	12/65*
D1974	47 273	—	—	BR Crewe	—	12/65*
D1975	47 517	—	—	BR Crewe	—	12/65*
D1976	47 274	—	—	BR Crewe	—	12/65*
D1977	47 275	—	—	BR Crewe	—	December 1965
D1978	47 276	—	—	BR Crewe	—	December 1965
D1979	47 277	—	—	BR Crewe	—	December 1965
D1980	47 278	—	—	BR Crewe	—	December 1965
D1981	47 279	—	—	BR Crewe	—	December 1965
D1982	47 280	—	—	BR Crewe	—	December 1965
D1983	47 281	—	—	BR Crewe	—	December 1965
D1984	47 282	—	—	BR Crewe	—	January 1966
D1985	47 283	—	—	BR Crewe	—	January 1966
D1986	47 284	—	—	BR Crewe	—	January 1966
D1987	47 285	—	—	BR Crewe	—	January 1966
D1988	47 286	—	—	BR Crewe	—	February 1966
D1989	47 287	—	—	BR Crewe	—	February 1966
D1990	47 288	—	—	BR Crewe	—	February 1966
D1991	47 289	—	—	BR Crewe	—	March 1966
D1992	47 290	—	—	BR Crewe	—	March 1966
D1993	47 291	—	—	BR Crewe	—	March 1966
D1994	47 292	—	—	BR Crewe	—	April 1966
D1995	47 293	—	—	BR Crewe	—	April 1966
D1996	47 294	—	—	BR Crewe	—	May 1966
D1997	47 295	—	—	BR Crewe	—	June 1966
D1998	47 296	—	—	BR Crewe	—	June 1966
D1999	47 297	—	—	BR Crewe	—	June 1966

BR 1957 No	*Date withdrawn*	*Disposal code*	*Disposal details*	*Notes*
D1948				
D1949				
D1950				
D1951				
D1952				
D1953				
D1954				
D1955				
D1956				
D1957				Allocated No 47 261 as 47/0 — never carried
D1958				
D1959				
D1960				
D1961				
D1962				
D1963				
D1964				
D1965				
D1966				
D1967				
D1968				
D1969				
D1970				
D1971				
D1972				
D1973				
D1974				
D1975				
D1976				
D1977				
D1978				
D1979				
D1980				
D1981				
D1982				
D1983				
D1984				
D1985				
D1986				
D1987				
D1988				
D1989				
D1990				
D1991				
D1992				
D1993				
D1994				
D1995				
D1996				
D1997				
D1998				
D1999				

Class 03

BR designed and built diesel-mechanical 0-6-0 shunters for use in small yards, private sidings, dock lines, etc, and fitted with a 204hp power unit, all locomotives of similar design, but two different exhaust stacks exist.

BR 1957 No	*BR 1948 No*	*TOPS No*	*Built by*	*Works No*	*Date introduced*	*Date withdrawn*
D2000	11187	—	BR Swindon	—	December 1957	May 1969
D2001	11188	—	BR Swindon	—	December 1957	June 1969
D2002	11189	—	BR Swindon	—	December 1957	June 1969
D2003	11190	—	BR Swindon	—	December 1957	May 1969
D2004	11191	03 004	BR Swindon	—	January 1958	May 1976
D2005	11192	03 005	BR Swindon	—	January 1958	November 1976
D2006	11193	—	BR Swindon	—	January 1958	October 1972
D2007	11194	03 007	BR Swindon	—	January 1958	May 1976
D2008	11195	03 008	BR Swindon	—	February 1958	December 1978
D2009	11196	03 009	BR Swindon	—	February 1958	July 1976
D2010	11197	03 010	BR Swindon	—	February 1958	November 1974
D2011	11198	—	BR Swindon	—	February 1958	October 1972
D2012	11199	03 012	BR Swindon	—	March 1958	December 1975
D2013	11200	03 013	BR Swindon	—	March 1958	July 1976
D2014	11201	03 014	BR Swindon	—	March 1958	June 1974
D2015	11202	—	BR Swindon	—	March 1958	July 1971
D2016	11203	03 016	BR Swindon	—	April 1958	December 1978
D2017	11204	03 017	BR Swindon	—	April 1958	February 1982
D2018	11205	03 018	BR Swindon	—	April 1958	November 1975
D2019	11206	—	BR Swindon	—	May 1958	July 1971
D2020	11207	03 020	BR Swindon	—	June 1958	December 1975
D2021	11208	03 021	BR Swindon	—	July 1958	November 1982
D2022	11209	03 022	BR Swindon	—	July 1958	November 1982
D2023	11210	—	BR Swindon	—	August 1958	July 1971
D2024	11211	—	BR Swindon	—	August 1958	July 1971
D2025	—	03 025	BR Swindon	—	September 1958	September 1977
D2026	—	03 026	BR Swindon	—	September 1958	February 1983
D2027	—	03 027	BR Swindon	—	October 1958	January 1976
D2028	—	—	BR Swindon	—	October 1958	December 1969
D2029	—	03 029	BR Swindon	—	October 1958	September 1979
D2030	—	—	BR Swindon	—	October 1958	August 1969
D2031	—	—	BR Swindon	—	November 1958	May 1969
D2032	—	—	BR Swindon	—	November 1958	July 1971
D2033	—	—	BR Swindon	—	December 1958	December 1971
D2034	—	03 034	BR Swindon	—	January 1959	February 1983
D2035	—	03 035	BR Swindon	—	February 1959	July 1976
D2036	—	—	BR Swindon	—	February 1959	December 1971
D2037	—	03 037	BR Swindon	—	February 1959	September 1976
D2038	—	—	BR Swindon	—	February 1959	March 1972
D2039	—	—	BR Swindon	—	March 1959	February 1972
D2040	—	—	BR Swindon	—	March 1959	June 1969
D2041	—	—	BR Swindon	—	April 1959	February 1970

Engine: Gardner 8L3 of 204hp
Weight: 30$\frac{1}{4}$ ton
Wheel dia: 43in
Max speed: 28$\frac{1}{2}$mph
Class codes: DJ15, D2/2, then 2/1, later BR Class 03

Tractive effort: 15,300lb
Length: 26ft 0in
Height: 11ft 10in
Width: 8ft 6in

BR 1957 No	*Disposal code*	*Disposal details*	*Notes*
D2000	C	Garnham, Harris & Elton, Chesterfield	
D2001	C	C. F. Booth, Rotherham, South Yorkshire	
D2002	C	Ingot Metals Ltd at Kentish Town	
D2003	C	Ingot Metals Ltd at Kentish Town	
D2004	C	G. Cohen, Kettering, Northamptonshire	
D2005	C	BREL Doncaster March 1977	
D2006	C	BREL Swindon	
D2007	C	G. Cohen, Kettering, Northamptonshire	
D2008	C	BREL Swindon	
D2009	C	G. Cohen, Kettering, Northamptonshire	
D2010	E	Sold for re-use in Italy May 1976	After withdrawal went to P. Wood, Queenborough, Kent
D2011	C	BREL Swindon	
D2012	S	Meyer Newman, Snailwell, No F135L	
D2013	C	BREL Doncaster March 1977	
D2014	C	BREL Doncaster April 1976	
D2015	C	G. Cohen, Kettering, Northamptonshire July 1972	
D2016	C	BR Swindon May 1979	
D2017	C	BREL Swindon September 1982	
D2018	S	600 Fragmentisers, Willesden as 600/2	
D2019	E	Exported to Italy September 1972	After withdrawal went to P. Wood, Queenborough, Kent
D2020	C	Meyer Newman, Snailwell, No F134L	After withdrawal used by Meyer Newman
D2021	C	BREL Swindon March 1983	
D2022	P	Swindon & Cricklade Railway	
D2023	P	Kent & East Sussex Railway No 44	Formally at Tees and Hartlepool Docks
D2024	P	Kent & East Sussex Railway No 45	Formally at Tees and Hartlepool Docks
D2025	C	BREL Swindon March 1978	
D2026	C	C. F. Booth, Rotherham, South Yorkshire April 1984	Withdrawn November 1982, reinstated November 1982
D2027	S	P. Wood Shipbreakers, Queenborough, Kent	
D2028	C	BREL Doncaster March 1972	
D2029	C	BREL Doncaster October 1979	
D2030	C	C. F. Booth, Rotherham, South Yorkshire November 1970	
D2031	C	Pollock & Brown, Northam, Hants September 1969	
D2032	E	Exported to Italy August 1972	After withdrawal went to P. Wood, Queenborough, Kent
D2033	E	Exported to Italy August 1972	After withdrawal went to P. Wood, Queenborough, Kent
D2034	C	C. F. Booth, Rotherham, South Yorkshire August 1983	Withdrawn December 1976, reinstated July 1977
D2035	C	G. Cohen, Kettering, Northamptonshire September 1977	
D2036	E	Exported to Italy August 1972	After withdrawal went to P. Wood, Queenborough, Kent
D2037	S	NCB British Oak disposal point	Out of use
D2038	C	T. W. Ward Ltd, Beighton, Sheffield May 1973	
D2039	C	T. W. Ward Ltd, Beighton, Sheffield May 1977	
D2040	C	C. F. Booth, Rotherham, South Yorkshire January 1971	
D2041	P	Colne Valley Railway, Castle Hedingham	After withdrawal used by CEGB until 1981

BR 1957 No	BR 1948 No	TOPS No	Built by	Works No	Date introduced	Date withdrawn
D2042	—	—	BR Swindon	—	April 1959	June 1969
D2043	—	—	BR Swindon	—	May 1959	September 1971
D2044	—	03 044	BR Doncaster	—	November 1958	January 1976
D2045	—	03 045	BR Doncaster	—	December 1958	February 1979
D2046	—	—	BR Doncaster	—	December 1958	October 1971
D2047	—	03 047	BR Doncaster	—	December 1958	July 1979
D2048	—	—	BR Doncaster	—	December 1958	October 1972
D2049	—	—	BR Doncaster	—	January 1959	August 1971
D2050	—	03 050	BR Doncaster	—	January 1959	August 1978
D2051	—	—	BR Doncaster	—	January 1959	December 1972
D2052	—	—	BR Doncaster	—	February 1959	October 1973
D2053	—	—	BR Doncaster	—	April 1959	October 1973
D2054	—	—	BR Doncaster	—	April 1959	November 1972
D2055	—	03 055	BR Doncaster	—	April 1959	June 1974
D2056	—	03 056	BR Doncaster	—	May 1959	June 1980
D2057	—	—	BR Doncaster	—	May 1959	October 1971
D2058	—	03 058	BR Doncaster	—	May 1959	June 1975
D2059	—	03 059	BR Doncaster	—	June 1959	
D2060	—	03 060	BR Doncaster	—	June 1959	December 1982
D2061	—	03 061	BR Doncaster	—	June 1959	December 1980
D2062	—	03 062	BR Doncaster	—	July 1959	December 1980
D2063	—	03 063	BR Doncaster	—	July 1959	
D2064	—	03 064	BR Doncaster	—	July 1959	June 1981
D2065	—	—	BR Doncaster	—	August 1959	December 1972
D2066	—	03 066	BR Doncaster	—	August 1959	
D2067	—	03 067	BR Doncaster	—	September 1959	August 1981
D2068	—	03 068	BR Doncaster	—	September 1959	April 1976
D2069	—	03 069	BR Doncaster	—	September 1959	December 1983
D2070	—	—	BR Doncaster	—	October 1959	November 1971
D2071	—	—	BR Doncaster	—	October 1959	May 1972
D2072	—	03 072	BR Doncaster	—	October 1959	May 1981
D2073	—	03 073	BR Doncaster	—	November 1959	
D2074	—	—	BR Doncaster	—	November 1959	May 1972
D2075	—	03 075	BR Doncaster	—	November 1959	July 1976
D2076	—	03 076	BR Doncaster	—	December 1959	March 1976
D2077	—	—	BR Doncaster	—	December 1959	October 1972
D2078	—	03 078	BR Doncaster	—	December 1959	
D2079	—	03 079	BR Doncaster	—	January 1960	April 1984
D2080	—	03 080	BR Doncaster	—	January 1960	December 1980
D2081	—	03 081	BR Doncaster	—	January 1960	December 1980
D2082	—	—	BR Doncaster	—	February 1959	December 1969
D2083	—	—	BR Doncaster	—	March 1959	June 1969
D2084	—	03 084	BR Doncaster	—	March 1959	
D2085	—	—	BR Doncaster	—	April 1959	December 1969
D2086	—	03 086	BR Swindon	—	May 1959	November 1983
D2087	—	—	BR Swindon	—	June 1959	June 1971
D2088	—	—	BR Swindon	—	July 1959	June 1972
D2089	—	03 089	BR Doncaster	—	May 1960	
D2090	—	03 090	BR Doncaster	—	May 1960	July 1976

BR 1957 No	Disposal code	Disposal details	Notes
D2042	C	Ingot Metals at Kentish Town September 1969	
D2043	C	P. Wood, Queenborough, Kent June 1972	
D2044	C	G. Cohen, Kettering, Northamptonshire September 1976	
D2045	C	BREL Doncaster September 1979	
D2046	S	Gulf Oil Ltd at Milford Haven as No 2	Rebuilt by Hunslet
D2047	C	BREL Doncaster October 1979	Withdrawn June 1976, reinstated September 1976
D2048	C	BREL Swindon May 1973	
D2049	S	NCB, West Hallam disposal point	Out of use
D2050	C	C. F. Booth, Rotherham, South Yorkshire May 1979	Withdrawn June 1976, reinstated November 1976
D2051	S	Ford Motor Ltd, Dagenham as No 4	
D2052	C	A. Draper, Hull December 1973	
D2053	C	A. Draper, Hull November 1973	
D2054	S	British Industrial Sand, Middleton Towers as *Centa*	
D2055	C	BREL Doncaster November 1974	
D2056	C	BREL Doncaster March 1981	
D2057	S	NCB Grimethorpe as No 1	Rebuilt by Hunslet
D2058	C	BREL Doncaster February 1977	
D2059			
D2060	C	BREL Doncaster July 1983	
D2061	C	BREL Swindon February 1982	Stored from October 1980
D2062	P	Dean Forest Railway, Norchard	Withdrawn June 1976, resintated September 1976, stored October 1980
D2063			
D2064	C	BREL Doncaster August 1981	
D2065	C	C. F. Booth, Rotherham, South Yorkshire July 1973	
D2066			
D2067	C	BREL Doncaster August 1982	
D2068	C	G. Cohen, Kettering, Northamptonshire September 1976	
D2069	S	F. Berry, Braunston Gate, Leics	
D2070	C	P. Wood Shipbreakers, Queenborough, Kent	Stored
D2071	C	A. Draper, Hull November 1973	
D2072	P	Lakeside & Haverthwaite Railway	
D2073			
D2074	C	A. Draper, Hull November 1973	
D2075	C	BREL Doncaster January 1979	
D2076	C	G. Cohen, Kettering, Northamptonshire October 1976	
D2077	C	BREL Swindon May 1973	
D2078			
D2079	C	To Departmental stock — 97805	
D2080	C	BREL Swindon March 1981	Stored from November 1980
D2081	E	Exported to Belgium November 1981	Stored from November 1980
D2082	C	BREL Doncaster September 1971	
D2083	C	Pollock & Brown, Northam, Hants	
D2084			
D2085	C	BREL Doncaster March 1972	
D2086	C	BREL Doncaster April 1984	
D2087	C	Pounds Shipbreakers, Fratton, Hants August 1973	
D2088	C	C. F. Booth, Rotherham, South Yorkshire March 1973	
D2089			
D2090	P	National Railway Museum, York	

BR 1957 No	*BR 1948 No*	*TOPS No*	*Built by*	*Works No*	*Date introduced*	*Date withdrawn*
D2091	—	03 091	BR Doncaster	—	June 1960	March 1974
D2092	—	03 092	BR Doncaster	—	June 1960	August 1977
D2093	—	—	BR Doncaster	—	June 1960	October 1971
D2094	—	03 094	BR Doncaster	—	June 1960	
D2095	—	03 095	BR Doncaster	—	July 1960	December 1975
D2096	—	03 096	BR Doncaster	—	July 1960	December 1976
D2097	—	03 097	BR Doncaster	—	July 1960	June 1976
D2098	—	03 098	BR Doncaster	—	July 1960	November 1975
D2099	—	03 099	BR Doncaster	—	August 1960	June 1976
D2100	—	—	BR Doncaster	—	August 1960	November 1971
D2101	—	—	BR Doncaster	—	August 1960	November 1971
D2102	—	03 102	BR Doncaster	—	September 1960	February 1976
D2103	—	03 103	BR Doncaster	—	September 1960	February 1979
D2104	—	03 104	BR Doncaster	—	September 1960	June 1975
D2105	—	03 105	BR Doncaster	—	September 1960	February 1976
D2106	—	03 106	BR Doncaster	—	September 1960	September 1975
D2107	—	03 107	BR Doncaster	—	October 1960	July 1981
D2108	—	03 108	BR Doncaster	—	October 1960	November 1976
D2109	—	03 109	BR Doncaster	—	October 1960	July 1975
D2110	—	03 110	BR Doncaster	—	November 1960	February 1976
D2111	—	03 111	BR Doncaster	—	November 1960	July 1980
D2112	—	03 112	BR Doncaster	—	November 1960	
D2113	—	03 113	BR Doncaster	—	December 1960	August 1975
D2114	—	—	BR Swindon	—	July 1959	May 1968
D2115	—	—	BR Swindon	—	August 1959	May 1968
D2116	—	—	BR Swindon	—	August 1959	October 1971
D2117	—	—	BR Swindon	—	September 1959	October 1971
D2118	—	—	BR Swindon	—	September 1959	June 1972
D2119	—	03 119	BR Swindon	—	September 1959	
D2120	—	03 120	BR Swindon	—	October 1959	
D2121	—	03 121	BR Swindon	—	October 1959	May 1961
D2122	—	—	BR Swindon	—	October 1959	November 1972
D2123	—	—	BR Swindon	—	November 1959	November 1968
D2124	—	—	BR Swindon	—	December 1959	February 1970
D2125	—	—	BR Swindon	—	December 1959	November 1968
D2126	—	—	BR Swindon	—	December 1959	October 1971
D2127	—	—	BR Swindon	—	December 1959	May 1968
D2128	—	03 128	BR Swindon	—	January 1960	July 1976
D2129	—	03 129	BR Swindon	—	January 1960	December 1981
D2130	—	—	BR Swindon	—	January 1960	August 1972

BR 1957 No	*Disposal code*	*Disposal details*	*Notes*
D2091	C	BREL Doncaster March 1977	
D2092	C	BREL Doncaster January 1978	
D2093	S	NCB Grimethorpe as No 2	Rebuilt by Hunslet
D2094			
D2095	C	G. Cohen, Kettering, Northamptonshire October 1976	
D2096	C	BREL Doncaster March 1977	
D2097	C	BREL Doncaster March 1979	
D2098	E	Exported to Italy May 1976	After withdrawal went to P. Wood Queenborough, Kent
D2099	C	NCB Monkton c1981	
D2100	C	G. Cohen, Kettering, Northamptonshire July 1972	
D2101	C	T. W. Ward, Beighton, Sheffield June 1972	
D2102	C	G. Cohen, Kettering, Northamptonshire September 1976	
D2103	C	BREL Doncaster May 1979	
D2104	C	BREL Doncaster February 1976	
D2105	C	G. Cohen, Kettering, Northamptonshire September 1976	
D2106	C	W. Heselwood, Attercliffe, Sheffield May 1976	
D2107	C	BREL Doncaster November 1982	
D2108	C	BREL Doncaster March 1977	
D2109	C	BREL Doncaster April 1976	
D2110	C	G. Cohen, Kettering, Northamptonshire September 1976	
D2111	C	BREL Swindon February 1981	Withdrawn June 1976, reinstated November 1976
D2112			
D2113	S	Gulf Oil Milford Haven	
D2114	C	Birds, Long Marston April 1973	Used after withdrawal
D2115	C	G. Cohen, Kettering, Northamptonshire September 1968	
D2116	C	Marple & Gillott, Sheffield August 1973	
D2117	P	Lakeside & Haverthwaite Railway	
D2118	S	Anglia Building Products, Lenwade, Norfolk	
D2119			Withdrawn January 1970, reinstated December 1970
D2120	C	C. F. Booth, Rotherham, South Yorkshire	
D2121	A	BREL Swindon	
D2122	C	Cashmores at Duport Steel, Briton Ferry September 1975	
D2123	C	Birds, Bristol November 1978	Used as generator at various Birds sites
D2124	C	Slag Reduction Ltd, Barrow in Furness September 1970	
D2125	C	Birds, Cardiff June 1976	Used as loco/generator at various Birds sites
D2126	C	P. Wood, Queenborough, Kent September 1973	
D2127	C	G. Cohen, Kingsbury, West Midlands October 1968	
D2128	E	To the Continent for scrap January 1977	First withdrawn January 1970, reinstated April 1970
D2129	C	C. F. Booth, Rotherham, South Yorkshire March 1983	In use after withdrawal
D2130	C	C. F. Booth, Rotherham, South Yorkshire March 1973	Withdrawn June 1972, reinstated July 1972

BR 1957 No	*BR 1948 No*	*TOPS No*	*Built by*	*Works No*	*Date introduced*	*Date withdrawn*
D2131	—	—	BR Swindon	—	February 1960	June 1968
D2132	—	—	BR Swindon	—	February 1960	May 1969
D2133	—	—	BR Swindon	—	February 1960	July 1969
D2134	—	03 134	BR Swindon	—	February 1960	July 1976
D2135	—	03 135	BR Swindon	—	March 1960	January 1976
D2136	—	—	BR Swindon	—	March 1960	January 1972
D2137	—	03 137	BR Swindon	—	April 1960	July 1976
D2138	—	—	BR Swindon	—	April 1960	May 1969
D2139	—	—	BR Swindon	—	April 1960	May 1968
D2140	—	—	BR Swindon	—	April 1960	April 1970
D2141	—	03 141	BR Swindon	—	May 1960	
D2142	—	03 142	BR Swindon	—	May 1960	October 1983
D2143	—	—	BR Swindon	—	January 1961	June 1968
D2144	—	03 144	BR Swindon	—	January 1961	
D2145	—	03 145	BR Swindon	—	February 1961	
D2146	—	—	BR Swindon	—	February 1961	September 1968
D2147	—	03 147	BR Swindon	—	June 1960	September 1975
D2148	—	—	BR Swindon	—	June 1960	November 1972
D2149	—	03 149	BR Swindon	—	June 1960	November 1982
D2150	—	—	BR Swindon	—	June 1960	November 1972
D2151	—	03 151	BR Swindon	—	July 1960	
D2152	—	03 152	BR Swindon	—	July 1960	October 1983
D2153	—	03 153	BR Swindon	—	July 1960	November 1975
D2154	—	03 154	BR Swindon	—	July 1960	September 1983
D2155	—	03 155	BR Swindon	—	August 1960	June 1975
D2156	—	03 156	BR Swindon	—	August 1960	November 1975
D2157	—	03 157	BR Swindon	—	August 1960	December 1975
D2158	—	03 158	BR Swindon	—	September 1960	
D2159	—	03 159	BR Swindon	—	September 1960	October 1977
D2160	—	03 160	BR Swindon	—	September 1960	December 1981
D2161	—	03 161	BR Swindon	—	September 1960	December 1981
D2162	—	03 162	BR Swindon	—	October 1960	
D2163	—	03 163	BR Swindon	—	October 1960	January 1976
D2164	—	03 164	BR Swindon	—	October 1960	January 1976
D2165	—	03 165	BR Swindon	—	October 1960	August 1975
D2166	—	03 166	BR Swindon	—	October 1960	November 1975
D2167	—	03 167	BR Swindon	—	November 1960	July 1975
D2168	—	03 168	BR Swindon	—	November 1960	August 1981
D2169	—	03 169	BR Swindon	—	November 1960	November 1975
D2170	—	03 170	BR Swindon	—	November 1960	
D2171	—	03 171	BR Swindon	—	November 1960	October 1977
D2172	—	03 172	BR Swindon	—	November 1960	May 1976
D2173	—	—	BR Swindon	—	November 1960	November 1973
D2174	—	03 174	BR Swindon	—	December 1960	November 1975
D2175	—	03 175	BR Swindon	—	December 1961	May 1983
D2176	—	—	BR Swindon	—	December 1961	May 1978

BR 1957 No	*Disposal code*	*Disposal details*	*Notes*
D2131	C	G. Cohen, Kettering, Northamptonshire November 1968	
D2132	S	NCB Pye Hill, Ironville, Nottinghamshire as *Lesley*	Used at various NCB sites following withdrawal
D2133	S	British Cellophane Ltd, Bridgewater	
D2134	C	Birds, Long Marston October 1976	
D2135	E	To the Continent for scrap January 1977	Sold from P. Wood, Queenborough
D2136	C	Robinson & Hanon, Blaydon June 1972	
D2137	C	BREL Doncaster December 1977	
D2138	S	NCB Pye Hill, Ironville, Nottinghamshire No 2	
D2139	S	National Smokeless Fuels, Nantgarw No 1	Owned by R. Adams as hire loco, then sold
D2140	C	BREL Swindon February 1972	
D2141			
D2142	A	BREL Swindon	Store May 1983
D2143	C	J. Cashmores, Newport, Gwent December 1968	
D2144			
D2145			
D2146	C	Birds, Long Marston July 1978	Used by Birds
D2147	C	C. F. Booth Ltd, Doncaster April 1976	
D2148	S	NCB Bowers Row	Used at various NCB terminals
D2149	C	BREL Doncaster June 1983	
D2150	S	British Salt, Middlewich, Cheshire	
D2151			
D2152	A	BREL Swindon	
D2153	E	Exported to Italy May 1976	After withdrawal went to P. Wood, Queenborough, Kent
D2154	C	BREL Doncaster November 1983	
D2155	C	BREL Doncaster April 1976	
D2156	E	Exported to Italy May 1976	After withdrawal went to P. Wood, Queenborough, Kent
D2157	E	Exported to Italy March 1977	After withdrawal went to P. Wood, Queenborough, Kent
D2158			
D2159	C	BREL Swindon October 1978	
D2160	C	C. F. Booth, Rotherham, South Yorkshire April 1983	Stored from April 1981
D2161	C	C. F. Booth, Rotherham, South Yorkshire April 1983	Withdrawn September 1976, reinstated February 1977, stored April 1981
D2162			
D2163	C	J. Cohen, Kettering, Northamptonshire September 1976	
D2164	E	Exported to Italy March 1977	After withdrawal went to P. Wood, Queenborough, Kent
D2165	C	C. F. Booth, Doncaster March 1976	
D2166	C	C. F. Booth, Rotherham, South Yorkshire June 1976	
D2167	C	BREL Doncaster June 1976	
D2168	C	BREL Doncaster April 1982	
D2169	C	A. Draper, Hull June 1976	
D2170			
D2171	C	G. Cohen, Kettering, Northamptonshire April 1978	
D2172	C	G. Cohen, Kettering, Northamptonshire August 1977	
D2173	C	BREL Doncaster March 1977	
D2174	C	C. F. Booth, Doncaster May 1976	
D2175	C	BREL Doncaster November 1983	
D2176	C	G. Cohen, Kettering, Northamptonshire November 1981	In use by Cohen's

BR 1957 No	BR 1948 No	TOPS No	Built by	Works No	Date introduced	Date withdrawn
D2177	—	—	BR Swindon	—	December 1961	September 1968
D2178	—	—	BR Swindon	—	January 1962	September 1969
D2179	—	03 179	BR Swindon	—	January 1962	
D2180	—	03 180	BR Swindon	—	February 1962	March 1984
D2181	—	—	BR Swindon	—	February 1962	May 1968
D2182	—	—	BR Swindon	—	March 1962	May 1968
D2183	—	—	BR Swindon	—	March 1962	September 1968
D2184	—	—	BR Swindon	—	April 1962	December 1968
D2185	—	—	BR Swindon	—	May 1962	December 1968
D2186	—	—	BR Swindon	—	June 1962	September 1969
D2187	—	—	BR Swindon	—	March 1961	May 1968
D2188	—	—	BR Swindon	—	March 1961	May 1968
D2189	—	03 189	BR Swindon	—	March 1961	
D2190	—	—	BR Swindon	—	April 1961	December 1968
D2191	—	—	BR Swindon	—	April 1961	May 1968
D2192	—	—	BR Swindon	—	May 1961	January 1969
D2193	—	—	BR Swindon	—	May 1961	January 1969
D2194	—	—	BR Swindon	—	May 1961	September 1968
D2195	—	—	BR Swindon	—	June 1961	September 1968
D2196	—	03 196	BR Swindon	—	June 1961	June 1983
D2197	—	03 197	BR Swindon	—	June 1961	
D2198	—	—	BR Swindon	—	June 1961	November 1970
D2199	—	—	BR Swindon	—	June 1961	June 1972

Class Continued with D2370

Class 04

The first fleet of diesel-mechanical 0-6-0 diesel shunting locomotives, ordered in 1950 to replace steam traction, especially on dock lines, where restricted clearances existed. Allocated new number range 111xx for diesel shunting power.

BR 1957 No	BR 1948 No	Built by	Works No	Date introduced	Date withdrawn
D2200	11100	Drewry	2397/D142	May 1952	April 1968
D2201	11101	Drewry	2398/D143	May 1952	April 1968
D2202	11102	Drewry	2399/D144	May 1952	February 1968
D2203	11103	Drewry	2400/D145	June 1952	December 1967
D2204	11105	Drewry	2485/D211	March 1953	October 1969
D2205	11106	Drewry	2486/D212	March 1953	July 1969
D2206	11107	Drewry	2487/D213	March 1953	July 1969
D2207	11108	Drewry	2482/D208	February 1953	December 1967
D2208	11109	Drewry	2483/D209	February 1953	July 1968
D2209	11110	Drewry	2484/D210	March 1953	July 1968
D2210	11111	Drewry	2508/D242	September 1954	May 1970
D2211	11112	Drewry	2509/D243	September 1954	July 1970

BR 1957 No	*Disposal code*	*Disposal details*	*Notes*
D2177	C	Birds, Long Marston June 1970	
D2178	S	NCB Nantgarw	Owned by A. R. Adam as hire loco
D2179			
D2180	S	Mayer Newman, Snailwell	Works pilot
D2181	S	NCB Gwent Coal Centre, Newport, Gwent — *Pride of Gwent*	Owned by A. R. Adam as hire loco, then sold
D2182	S	NCB Hucclescote opencast site, Leicester	Owned by A. R. Adam as hire loco
D2183	C	Birds, Long Marston, March 1970	
D2184	C	Southend Coal depot	
D2185	C	Birds, Long Marston, June 1978	Used by Birds at various sites
D2186	C	A. R. Adam, Newport, Gwent January 1981	
D2187	C	Birds, Long Marston February 1978	Used by Birds
D2188	C	Birds, Long Marston June 1978	Used by Birds
D2189			
D2190	C	Birds, Long Marston June 1970	
D2191	C	G. Cohen, Kingsbury, West Midlands November 1968	
D2192	P	Dart Valley Railway	Used on Torbay & Dartmouth Railway on some occasions
D2193	C	A. R. Adam, Newport, Gwent January 1981	
D2194	C	Birds, Long Marston July 1978	Used by Birds
D2195	C	BSC Works, Llanelli September 1981	Used by BSC
D2196	S	Boddy Industries, Carnforth, No 40	
D2197			
D2198	C	BREL Doncaster March 1972	
D2199	S	NCB Royston Drift Mine as No 1	Out of use

Engine: Gardner 8L3 of 204hp
Weight: 30½ ton
Wheel dia: 39in
Max speed: 25-27mph
Class code: DMS1, DJ12 then DJ12A, later D2/4 and 2/13, and BR Class 04

Tractive effort: 16,850lb
Length: 26ft 0½in
Height: 12ft 1⅜in
Width: 8ft 6in

BR 1957 No	*Disposal code*	*Disposal details*	*Notes*
D2200	C	A. Finlay, Birdwell, Worsborough, Yorkshire, July 1968	Power unit exported
D2201	C	A. Finlay, Birdwell, Worsborough, Yorkshire, July 1968	Power unit exported
D2202	C	G. Cohen, Kettering, Northamptonshire June 1968	
D2203	P	Yorkshire Dales Railway, Embsay	Used by Hemelite after withdrawal
D2204	C	Duport Steel Llanelli September 1979	Used by Duport Steel
D2205	P	Kent & East Sussex Railway No 46	
D2206	C	Hughes, Bolckow, Blyth, Northumberland December 1969	
D2207	P	North Yorkshire Moors Railway	Previously used by Hemelite Ltd
D2208	C	NCB Silverwood Colliery July 1978	Used by NCB at various South Yorkshire sites
D2209	C	NCB Kiveton Park Colliery September 1981	Used by NCB at various South Yorkshire sites
D2210	C	A. King Ltd, Norwich September 1970	
D2211	S	Rees Industries, Saron Works, Llwynhendy	

BR 1957 No	BR 1948 No	Built by	Works No	Date introduced	Date withdrawn
D2212	11113	Drewry	2510/D244	September 1954	November 1970
D2213	11114	Drewry	2529/D257	October 1954	August 1968
D2214	11115	Drewry	2530/D258	October 1954	July 1968
D2215	11121	Drewry	2538/D264	July 1955	February 1969
D2216	11122	Drewry	2539/D265	July 1955	May 1971
D2217	11123	Drewry	2540/D266	August 1955	May 1972
D2218	11124	Drewry	2541/D267	August 1955	August 1968
D2219	11125	Drewry	2542/D268	August 1955	April 1968
D2220	11126	Drewry	2543/D269	September 1955	February 1968
D2221	11127	Drewry	2544/D270	September 1955	July 1968
D2222	11128	Drewry	2545/D271	September 1955	November 1968
D2223	11129	Drewry	2546/D272	October 1955	May 1971
D2224	11130	Drewry	2547/D273	October 1955	April 1968
D2225	11131	Drewry	2548/D274	October 1955	March 1969
D2226	11132	Drewry	2549/D275	November 1955	April 1968
D2227	11133	Drewry	2550/D276	November 1955	April 1968
D2228	11134	Drewry	2551/D277	November 1955	July 1968
D2229	11135	Drewry	2552/D278	November 1955	December 1969
D2230	11149	Drewry	2554/D280	January 1956	March 1968
D2231	11150	Drewry	2555/D281	January 1956	June 1969
D2232	11151	Drewry	2556/D282	January 1956	March 1968
D2233	11152	Drewry	2557/D283	February 1956	September 1968
D2234	11153	Drewry	2558/D284	February 1956	April 1968
D2235	11154	Drewry	2559/D285	March 1956	April 1968
D2236	11155	Drewry	2560/D286	March 1956	February 1968
D2237	11156	Drewry	2561/D287	April 1956	October 1969
D2238	11157	Drewry	2562/D288	May 1956	July 1968
D2239	11158	Drewry	2563/D289	May 1956	September 1971
D2240	11159	Drewry	2564/D290	June 1956	April 1968
D2241	11160	Drewry	2565/D291	June 1956	May 1971
D2242	11212	Drewry	2572/7858	October 1956	October 1969
D2243	11213	Drewry	2575/7862	October 1956	July 1969
D2244	11214	Drewry	2576/7863	November 1956	June 1970
D2245	11215	Drewry	2577/7864	November 1956	December 1968
D2246	11216	Drewry	2578/7865	December 1956	July 1968
D2247	11217	Drewry	2579/7866	December 1956	November 1969
D2248	11218	Drewry	2580/7867	January 1957	June 1970
D2249	11219	Drewry	2581/7868	January 1957	December 1970

BR 1957 No	*Disposal code*	*Disposal details*	*Notes*
D2212	C	C. F. Booth, Rotherham, South Yorkshire July 1972	
D2213	C	NCB Manvers Main (Spare Pool) February 1978	Used as Pool loco by NCB South Yorkshire
D2214	C	C. F. Booth, Rotherham, South Yorkshire August 1969	
D2215	C	Birds, Long Marston September 1969	
D2216	E	Exported to Italy	After withdrawal went to P. Wood Queenborough
D2217	C	C. F. Booth, Rotherham, South Yorkshire October 1973	Withdrawn December 1971, reinstated February 1972
D2218	C	Garnham, Harris & Elton Ltd, Chesterfield August 1969	
D2219	C	National Carbonising, Barrow, Barnsley May 1977	
D2220	C	G. Cohen, Kettering, Northamptonshire May 1968	
D2221	C	C. F. Booth, Rotherham, South Yorkshire August 1969	
D2222	C	C. F. Booth, Rotherham, South Yorkshire June 1969	
D2223	C	G. Cohen, Kettering, Northamptonshire September 1971	
D2224	C	A. Draper, Hull August 1968	
D2225	S	NCB Wath Colliery as *Debra*	stored
D2226	C	A. Draper, Hull August 1968	
D2227	C	A. Draper, Hull August 1968	
D2228	C	Bowaters, Sittingbourne March 1979	Used by Bowaters
D2229	S	NCB Manton Colliery as No 5	Also used at Orgreave
D2230	C	Garnham, Harris & Elton Ltd, Chesterfield January 1969	
D2231	C	Steelbreaking & Dismantling Co, Chesterfield May 1970	
D2232	E	Exported to Italy	After withdrawal went to P. Wood, Queenborough
D2233	C	Steelbreaking & Dismantling Co, Chesterfield August 1969	
D2234	C	A. Draper, Hull August 1968	
D2235	C	A. Finlay, Birdwell, Worsborough, Yorkshire July 1968	
D2236	C	G. Cohen, Kettering, Northamptonshire May 1968	
D2237	C	Hughes, Bolckow, Blyth, Northumberland March 1970	
D2238	C	NCB Manvers Main CCP Wath 1983	NCB Pool loco
D2239	S	NCB Dodworth Colliery, Barnsley	
D2240	C	A. King Ltd, Norwich October 1970	
D2241	C	G. Cohen, Kettering, Northamptonshire November 1976	Used by G. Cohen
D2242	C	C. F. Booth, Rotherham, South Yorkshire June 1970	
D2243	C	Middlesbrough & Hartlepool docks March 1973	
D2244	C	A. R. Adam, Newport, Gwent, January 1981	Used as hire loco
D2245	P	Market Bosworth Light Railway	
D2246	S	Coal Mechanisation, Tolworth CCD	
D2247	C	Duport Steel, Briton Ferry September 1979	
D2248	S	NCB Maltby Main Colliery No 18 *Sue*	NCB South Yorkshire pool loco
D2249	C	P. Wood, Queenborough, Kent August 1971	

BR 1957 No	*BR 1948 No*	*Built by*	*Works No*	*Date introduced*	*Date withdrawn*
D2250	11220	Drewry	2594/7871	May 1957	June 1968
D2251	11221	Drewry	2595/7872	May 1957	December 1968
D2252	11222	Drewry	2596/7873	May 1957	October 1968
D2253	11223	Drewry	2597/7874	May 1957	March 1969
D2254	11224	Drewry	2598/7875	June 1957	June 1967
D2255	11225	Drewry	2599/7876	June 1957	March 1968
D2256	11226	Drewry	2600/7877	October 1957	September 1968
D2257	11227	Drewry	2601/7878	October 1957	January 1968
D2258	11228	Drewry	2602/7879	October 1957	September 1970
D2259	11229	Drewry	2603/7889	October 1957	December 1968
D2260	—	Drewry	2604/7890	December 1957	October 1970
D2261	—	Drewry	2605/7891	December 1957	March 1970
D2262	—	Drewry	2606/7892	December 1957	June 1968
D2263	—	Drewry	2607/7893	December 1957	November 1967
D2264	—	Drewry	2608/7894	December 1957	October 1969
D2265	—	Drewry	2609/7895	December 1957	March 1970
D2266	—	Drewry	2610/7896	January 1958	November 1967
D2267	—	Drewry	2611/7897	January 1958	December 1969
D2268	—	Drewry	2612/7898	February 1958	June 1968
D2269	—	Drewry	2613/7911	February 1958	August 1968
D2270	—	Drewry	2614/7912	March 1958	February 1968
D2271	—	Drewry	2615/7913	March 1958	October 1979
D2272	—	Drewry	2616/7914	March 1958	October 1970
D2273	—	Drewry	2617/7915	April 1958	October 1967
D2274	—	Drewry	2620/7918	July 1959	May 1969
D2275	—	Drewry	2619/7917	July 1959	October 1967
D2276	—	Drewry	2622/7920	August 1959	August 1969
D2277	—	Drewry	2621/7919	September 1959	May 1969
D2278	—	Drewry	2618/7916	November 1959	April 1970
D2279	—	Drewry	2656/8097	February 1960	May 1971
D2280	—	Drewry	2657/8098	February 1960	March 1971
D2281	—	Drewry	2658/8099	February 1960	October 1968
D2282	—	Drewry	2659/8100	February 1960	December 1970
D2283	—	Drewry	2660/8101	March 1960	November 1969
D2284	—	Drewry	2661/8102	March 1960	April 1971
D2285	—	Drewry	2662/8103	March 1960	August 1969

BR 1957 No	*Dispoal code*	*Disposal details*	*Notes*
D2250	C	Pounds Shipbreakers, Fratton, Hampshire June 1969	
D2251	C	Pollock & Brown, Southampton, Hants September 1969	
D2252	C	Pollock & Brown, Southampton, Hants November 1969	
D2253	C	G. Cohen, Kettering, Northamptonshire December 1969	
D2254	C	BR Selhurst depot July 1967	
D2255	C	Pollock & Brown, Southampton, Hants August 1968	
D2256	C	Pollock & Brown, Southampton, Hants August 1969	
D2257	C	Pollock & Brown, Southampton, Hants July 1968	
D2258	S	NCB Ilkeston disposal point	
D2259	C	Bowaters, Sittingbourne January 1978	Used by Bowaters
D2260	S	NCB Coed Bach, Kidwelly, *Thomas Harling*	
D2261	C	C. F. Booth, Rotherham, South Yorkshire August 1970	
D2262	C	Ford Motors, Dagenham July 1978	Used by Ford until July 1973
D2263	C	Pollock & Brown, Southampton, Hants December 1968	
D2264	C	C. F. Booth, Rotherham, South Yorkshire June 1970	
D2265	C	C. F. Booth, Rotherham, South Yorkshire September 1970	
D2266	C	C. F. Booth, Rotherham, South Yorkshire April 1968	
D2267	S	Ford Motors, Dagenham No 6	
D2268	C	T. W. Ward, Beighton, Sheffield November 1968	
D2269	C	Pounds Shipbreakers, Fratton, Hants June 1969	
D2270	C	Duport Steel, Briton Ferry September 1979	
D2271	P	West Somerset Railway, Minehead	After withdrawal to C. F. Booth, then preserved
D2272	S	British Fuels, Blackburn, Lancashire, named *Alfie*	
D2273	C	C. F. Booth, Rotherham, South Yorkshire November 1968	
D2274	C	NCB Maltby Main Colliery September 1980	
D2275	C	BR Swindon February 1968	
D2276	C	A. R. Adam, Newport, Gwent May 1977	Used as hire loco July 1970-March 1977
D2277	C	Braham's, Bury St Edmunds December 1969	
D2278	C	Pounds Shipbreakers at Stratford depot February 1971	
D2279	C	Stour Valley Railway	After withdrawal used by CEGB Rye House until October 1971
D2280	S	Ford Motors, Dagenham as No1	Out of use
D2281	C	Duport Steel, Briton Ferry August 1971	Used as spares loco since February 1969
D2282	C	P. Wood, Queenborough, Kent August 1971	
D2283	C	Hartwood Finance Co at Stratford depot August 1970	
D2284	S	Woolley Colliery, Barnsley	
D2285	C	Braham's, Bury St Edmunds March 1970	

BR 1957 No	*BR 1948 No*	*Built by*	*Works No*	*Date introduced*	*Date withdrawn*
D2286	—	Drewry	2663/8104	March 1960	May 1968
D2287	—	Drewry	2667/8120	April 1960	June 1968
D2288	—	Drewry	2668/8121	April 1960	December 1967
D2289	—	Drewry	2669/8122	April 1960	September 1971
D2290	—	Drewry	2670/8123	April 1960	November 1967
D2291	—	Drewry	2671/8124	June 1960	December 1967
D2292	—	Drewry	2672/8125	June 1960	December 1967
D2293	—	Drewry	2673/8126	June 1960	April 1971
D2294	—	Drewry	2674/8127	June 1960	February 1971
D2295	—	Drewry	2675/8128	June 1960	April 1971
D2296	—	Drewry	2677/8155	September 1960	November 1969
D2297	—	Drewry	2678/8156	September 1960	July 1970
D2298	—	Drewry	2679/8157	September 1960	December 1968
D2299	—	Drewry	2680/8158	September 1960	January 1970
D2300	—	Drewry	2681/8159	October 1960	May 1969
D2301	—	Drewry	2682/8160	October 1960	September 1968
D2302	—	Drewry	2683/8161	October 1960	June 1969
D2303	—	Drewry	2684/8162	November 1960	November 1967
D2304	—	Drewry	2685/8163	November 1960	February 1968
D2305	—	Drewry	2686/8164	November 1960	February 1968
D2306	—	Drewry	2687/8165	November 1960	February 1968
D2307	—	Drewry	2688/8166	November 1960	February 1968
D2308	—	Drewry	2689/8167	November 1960	February 1968
D2309	—	Drewry	2690/8168	November 1960	July 1968
D2310	—	Drewry	2691/8169	December 1960	January 1969
D2311	—	Drewry	2692/8170	December 1960	February 1968
D2312	—	Drewry	2693/8171	January 1961	February 1968
D2313	—	Drewry	2694/8172	January 1961	February 1968
D2314	—	Drewry	2695/8173	January 1961	February 1968
D2315	—	Drewry	2696/8174	February 1961	February 1968
D2316	—	Drewry	2697/8175	February 1961	February 1968
D2317	—	Drewry	2698/8176	February 1961	August 1969
D2318	—	Drewry	2699/8177	February 1961	February 1968
D2319	—	Drewry	2700/8178	February 1961	February 1968
D2320	—	Drewry	2701/8179	March 1961	February 1968
D2321	—	Drewry	2702/8180	March 1961	July 1968
D2322	—	Drewry	2703/8181	March 1961	August 1968

BR 1957 No	*Disposal code*	*Disposal details*	*Notes*
D2286	C	Pounds Shipbreakers, Fratton, Hants June 1969	
D2287	C	Pounds Shipbreakers, Fratton, Hants August 1969	
D2288	C	Pollock & Brown, Southampton, Hants August 1968	
D2289	E	Exported to Italy	After withdrawal went to P. Wood Queenborough
D2290	C	Pollock & Brown, Southampton, Hants August 1968	
D2291	C	Pollock & Brown, Southampton, Hants July 1968	
D2292	C	Pollock & Brown, Southampton, Hants September 1968	
D2293	C	P. Wood, Queenborough, Kent October 1972	
D2294	S	P. Wood, Queenborough, Kent as No 01	Yard pilot
D2295	E	Exported to Italy	After withdrawal went to P. Wood, Queenborough
D2296	C	Braham's, Bury St Edmunds April 1970	
D2297	C	Braham's, Bury St Edmunds September 1970	
D2298	P	Quainton Railway Centre	
D2299	C	C. F. Booth, Rotherham, South Yorkshire February 1984	Used by various NCB South Notts sites
D2300	S	NCB Manton	stored out of use
D2301	C	Steelbreaking & Dismantling, Chesterfield January 1970	
D2302	S	British Sugar Corporation, Ely	
D2303	C	BR Doncaster January 1969	
D2304	C	Duport Steel, Llanelli May 1977	
D2305	C	Duport Steel, Llanelli September 1981	
D2306	C	Duport Steel, Llanelli September 1981	
D2307	C	Duport Steel, Llanelli October 1979	
D2308	C	Duport Steel, Llanelli May 1980	Also used at Briton Ferry
D2309	C	C. F. Booth, Rotherham, South Yorkshire May 1969	
D2310	S	Coal Mechanisation, Tolworth CCD	
D2311	C	Slag Reduction, Rotherham, Yorkshire September 1968	
D2312	C	Slag Reduction, Rotherham, Yorkshire September 1968	
D2313	C	Slag Reduction, Rotherham, Yorkshire September 1968	
D2314	C	Slag Reduction, Rotherham, Yorkshire September 1968	
D2315	C	Hughes, Bolckow, Blyth, Northumberland August 1968	
D2316	C	C. F. Booth, Rotherham, South Yorkshire January 1969	
D2317	S	NCB Cortonwood Colliery, Wombwell	Also used at New Stubbin Colliery
D2318	C	Hughes, Bolckow, Blyth, Northumberland July 1968	
D2319	C	Arnott Young, Dinsdale December 1968	
D2320	C	C. F. Booth, Rotherham, South Yorkshire April 1969	
D2321	C	G. Cohen Ltd, Middlesbrough March 1969	
D2322	S	NCB Kiveton Colliery as No 24	Used in various South Yorkshire NCB sites

BR 1957 No	BR 1948 No	Built by	Works No	Date introduced	Date withdrawn
D2323	—	Drewry	2704/8182	March 1961	July 1968
D2324	—	Drewry	2705/8183	April 1961	July 1968
D2325	—	Drewry	2706/8184	April 1961	July 1968
D2326	—	Drewry	2707/8185	May 1961	August 1968
D2327	—	Drewry	2708/8186	May 1961	August 1968
D2328	—	Drewry	2709/8187	May 1961	September 1968
D2329	—	Drewry	2710/8188	June 1961	July 1968
D2330	—	Drewry	2711/8189	June 1961	July 1968
D2331	—	Drewry	2712/8190	June 1961	July 1968
D2332	—	Drewry	2713/8191	June 1961	June 1969
D2333	—	Drewry	2714/8192	July 1961	September 1969
D2334	—	Drewry	2715/8193	July 1961	July 1968
D2335	—	Drewry	2716/8194	August 1961	July 1968
D2336	—	Drewry	2717/8195	August 1961	July 1968
D2337	—	Drewry	2718/8196	August 1961	July 1968
D2338	—	Drewry	2719/8197	September 1961	July 1968
D2339	—	Drewry	2720/8198	October 1961	October 1967
D2340	—	Drewry	2593/7870	February 1961	October 1968
D2341	DS 1173	Drewry	2217/D46	March 1967†	December 1968

Class 03 — continued from D2199

BR 1957 No	TOPS No	Built by	Works No	Date introduced	Date withdrawn	Disposal code
D2370	03 370	BR Swindon	—	1967†	December 1982	C
D2371	03 371	BR Swindon	—	1967†		
D2372	—	BR Swindon	—	July 1961	November 1970	C
D2373	—	BR Swindon	—	August 1961	May 1968	S
D2374	—	BR Swindon	—	August 1961	May 1968	C
D2375	—	BR Swindon	—	August 1961	May 1968	C
D2376	—	BR Swindon	—	August 1961	May 1968	C
D2377	—	BR Swindon	—	September 1961	May 1968	C
D2378	—	BR Swindon	—	September 1961	June 1971	C
D2379	—	BR Swindon	—	October 1961	May 1968	C
D2380	—	BR Swindon	—	October 1961	May 1968	C
D2381	—	BR Swindon	—	October 1961	June 1972	P
D2382	03 382	BR Swindon	—	November 1961	October 1983	A
D2383	—	BR Swindon	—	November 1961	April 1971	C
D2384	—	BR Swindon	—	November 1961	May 1968	C
D2385	—	BR Doncaster	—	March 1961	February 1970	C

BR 1957 No	*Disposal code*	*Disposal details*	*Notes*
D2323	C	C. F. Booth, Rotherham, South Yorkshire May 1969	
D2324	S	Southern Developments, Aylesbury	
D2325	S	NCB Norwich CCD	
D2326	C	NCB Manvers Main Colliery February 1976	Spare pool loco
D2327	C	Coopers Metals, Attercliffe, Sheffield	Formerly used by NCB at Dinnington as No 12
D2328	S	NCB Kiveton Colliery as No 31	
D2329	C	Derwent Valley Light Railway	Acquired for spares
D2330	C	Turnbull Ltd, Thornaby August 1970	Formerly used by Ford Ltd, Dagenham
D2331	C	T. W. Ward, Beighton, Sheffield, January 1969	
D2332	S	NCB Thurcroft Colliery as *Lloyd*	Used at various NCB sites. Carries No D2238
D2333	S	Ford Motors, Dagenham as No 8	
D2334	S	NCB Thurcroft Colliery as No 33	NCB pool loco
D2335	C	NCB Maltby Main Colliery February 1980	NCB pool loco
D2336	C	NCB Manvers Main Colliery February 1978	NCB pool spares loco
D2337	S	NCB Manvers Main as *Dorothy*	NCB pool loco
D2338	C	T. W. Ward, Beighton, Sheffield January 1969	
D2339	C	Hughes, Bolckow, Blyth, Northumberland June 1968	
D2340	C	Duport Steel, Briton Ferry September 1979	Built 1956, loaned to BR from 1960
D2341	C	Pollock & Brown, Southampton October 1969	

†From Departmental fleet

BR 1957 No	*Disposal details*	*Notes*
D2370	BREL Doncaster July 1983	Departmental No 91 until 1967
D2371		Departmental No 92 until 1967
D2372	G. Cohen, Kettering, Northamptonshire December 1971	
D2373	NCB Manvers Main Colliery in store as No1	
D2374	G. Cohen, Kettering, Nothamptonshire December 1968	
D2375	G. Cohen, Kettering, Northamptonshire November 1968	
D2376	G. Cohen, Kettering, Northamptonshire November 1968	
D2377	BREL Swindon February 1970	
D2378	BREL Swindon October 1972	
D2379	BREL Swindon February 1970	
D2380	G. Cohen, Kettering, Northamptonshire December 1968	
D2381	Steamtown Carnforth	After withdrawal went to J. Gretton, Market Overton
D2382	BR Landore depot	Withdrawn June 1972, reinstated August 1972, stored May 1983
D2383	T. W. Ward, Beighton, Sheffield June 1972	
D2384	G. Cohen, Kettering, Northamptonshire November 1968	
D2385	C. F. Booth, Rotherham, South Yorkshire October 1970	

BR 1957 No	*TOPS No*	*Built by*	*Works No*	*Date introduced*	*Date withdrawn*	*Disposal code*
D2386	03 386	BR Doncaster	—	March 1961	March 1976	C
D2387	—	BR Doncaster	—	April 1961	December 1972	C
D2388	—	BR Doncaster	—	April 1961	July 1972	C
D2389	03 389	BR Doncaster	—	May 1961	February 1983	C
D2390	—	BR Doncaster	—	June 1961	May 1968	C
D2391	—	BR Doncaster	—	June 1961	November 1970	C
D2392	—	BR Doncaster	—	June 1961	June 1971	C
D2393	—	BR Doncaster	—	July 1961	December 1969	C
D2394	—	BR Doncaster	—	August 1961	November 1968	C
D2395	—	BR Doncaster	—	August 1961	May 1968	C
D2396	—	BR Doncaster	—	August 1961	May 1968	C
D2397	03 397	BR Doncaster	—	September 1961		
D2398	—	BR Doncaster	—	September 1961	October 1971	C
D2399	03 399	BR Doncaster	—	September 1961		

Unclassified

One of several small fleets of diesel-mechanical 0-6-0 locomotives built during the late 1950s, early 1960s, using the Gardner 8L3 engine. Built for use on the ER.

BR 1957 No	*BR 1957 No*	*Built by*	*Works No*	*Date introduced*	*Date withdrawn*	*Disposal code*
D2400	11177	A/Barclay	402	July 1956	October 1967	C
D2401	11178	A/Barclay	403	July 1956	December 1968	C
D2402	11179	A/Barclay	404	September 1956	September 1967	C
D2403	11180	A/Barclay	405	October 1956	January 1969	C
D2404	11181	A/Barclay	406	November 1956	January 1969	C
D2405	11182	A/Barclay	407	December 1956	December 1968	C
D2406	11183	A/Barclay	408	December 1956	May 1967	C
D2407	11184	A/Barclay	409	January 1957	January 1969	C
D2408	11185	A/Barclay	410	February 1957	May 1967	C
D2409	11186	A/Barclay	411	March 1957	December 1968	C

BR 1957 No	*Disposal details*	*Notes*
D2386	G. Cohen, Kettering, Northamptonshire December 1976	
D2387	C. F. Booth, Rotherham, South Yorkshire August 1973	
D2388	C. F. Booth, Rotherham, South Yorkshire July 1973	
D2389	C. F. Booth, Rotherham, South Yorkshire July 1983	
D2390	G. Cohen, Kettering, Northamptonshire November 1968	
D2391	G. Cohen, Kettering, Northamptonshire December 1971	
D2392	C. F. Booth, Rotherham, South Yorkshire March 1972	
D2393	C. F. Booth, Rotherham, South Yorkshire June 1971	
D2394	C. F. Booth, Rotherham, South Yorkshire September 1969	
D2395	G. Cohen, Kettering, Northamptonshire December 1968	
D2396	G. Cohen, Kettering, Northamptonshire November 1968	
D2397		Withdrawn May 1971, reinstated October 1971
D2398	Pounds Shipbreakers, Fratton, Hants October 1972	
D2399		

† From departmental fleet

Engine: Gardner 8L3 of 204hp
Weight: 32 ton
Wheel dia: 42in
Max speed: 17¾mph
Class code: DJ14, later D2/5, 2/12A

Tractive effort: 15,650lb
Length: 26ft 6¾in
Height: 12ft 0in
Width: 8ft 0in

BR 1957 No	*Disposal details*	*Notes*
D2400	Slag Reduction, Ickles, Rotherham, April 1968	
D2401	C. F. Booth, Rotherham, South Yorkshire January 1970	
D2402	C. F. Booth, Rotherham, South Yorkshire April 1968	
D2403	C. F. Booth, Rotherham, South Yorkshire January 1970	
D2404	C. F. Booth, Rotherham, South Yorkshire January 1970	
D2405	W. Heselwood, Attercliffe, Sheffield May 1969	
D2406	T. W. Ward, Beighton, Sheffield April 1968	
D2407	C. F. Booth, Rotherham, South Yorkshire August 1970	
D2408	T. W. Ward, Beighton, Sheffield April 1968	
D2409	C. F. Booth, Rotherham, South Yorkshire March 1970	

Class 06

Andrew Barclay designed and built 0-4-0 diesel-mechanical shunter fleet, introduced for use on the ScR. Some detail differences on cab design existed.

BR 1957 No	*TOPS No*	*Built by*	*Works No*	*Date introduced*	*Date withdrawn*	*Disposal code*
D2410	—	A/Barclay	425	June 1958	January 1969	C
D2411	—	A/Barclay	426	July 1958	June 1968	C
D2412	—	A/Barclay	427	September 1958	June 1968	C
D2413	06 001	A/Barclay	428	October 1958	September 1976	C
D2414	06 002	A/Barclay	429	October 1958	September 1981	C
D2415	—	A/Barclay	430	November 1958	June 1968	C
D2416	—	A/Barclay	431	November 1958	November 1972	C
D2417	—	A/Barclay	432	December 1958	June 1968	C
D2418	—	A/Barclay	433	January 1959	December 1968	C
D2419	—	A/Barclay	434	January 1959	January 1969	C
D2420	06 003	A/Barclay	435	February 1959	February 1981	D
D2421	06 004	A/Barclay	436	February 1959	March 1979	C
D2422	06 005	A/Barclay	437	March 1959	October 1980	C
D2423	06 006	A/Barclay	438	April 1959	June 1980	C
D2424	—	A/Barclay	439	April 1959	November 1972	C
D2425	—	A/Barclay	452	November 1959	June 1968	C
D2426	06 007	A/Barclay	453	November 1959	September 1977	C
D2427	—	A/Barclay	454	December 1959	September 1969	C
D2428	—	A/Barclay	455	January 1960	June 1968	C
D2429	—	A/Barclay	456	January 1960	April 1969	C
D2430	—	A/Barclay	457	January 1960	June 1968	C
D2431	—	A/Barclay	458	February 1960	November 1971	C
D2432	—	A/Barclay	459	February 1960	December 1968	E
D2433	—	A/Barclay	460	February 1960	June 1972	C
D2434	—	A/Barclay	461	March 1960	July 1969	C
D2435	—	A/Barclay	462	March 1960	November 1971	C
D2436	—	A/Barclay	463	April 1960	November 1971	C
D2437	06 008	A/Barclay	464	April 1960	October 1980	C
D2438	—	A/Barclay	465	May 1960	November 1972	C
D2439	—	A/Barclay	466	July 1960	November 1971	C
D2440	06 009	A/Barclay	467	August 1960	August 1975	C
D2441	—	A/Barclay	468	August 1960	March 1967	C
D2442	—	A/Barclay	469	September 1960	November 1972	C
D2443	—	A/Barclay	470	October 1960	June 1972	C
D2444	06 010	A/Barclay	471	October 1960	June 1975	C

Unclassified

Another of the early design of shunter powered by the Gardner 8L3 engine was this fleet of 10 Hudswell Clarke locomotives. Introduced for LMR use, mainly on dock lines.

BR 1957 No	*BR 1948 No*	*Built by*	*Works No*	*Date introduced*	*Date withdrawn*	*Disposal code*
D2500	11116	H/Clarke	D898	December 1955	May 1967	C
D2501	11117	H/Clarke	D899	January 1956	February 1967	C

Engine: Gardner 8L3 of 204hp
Weight: 36¾ ton
Wheel dia: 43in
Max speed: 22¾mph
Class code: D2/6, later 2/12 and BR Class 06

Tractive effort: 19,800lb
Length: 25ft 11in
Height: 11ft 10¼in
Width: 8ft 5in

BR 1957 No	*Disposal details*	*Notes*
D2410	G. H. Campbell, Airdrie c1969	
D2411	G. H. Campbell, Airdrie c1969	
D2412	G. H. Campbell, Airdrie c1969	
D2413	G. H. Campbell, Airdrie c1977	
D2414	BREL Swindon April 1982	Sent to Reading for spares to 97 804
D2415	G. H. Campbell, Airdrie c1969	
D2416	BREL Glasgow November 1973	
D2417	G. H. Campbell, Airdrie c1969	
D2418	G. H. Campbell, Airdrie c1969	
D2419	G. H. Campbell, Airdrie c1969	
D2420	To Departmental Stock 97 804	
D2421	BREL Glasgow February 1980	
D2422	BR Dundee depot July 1983	
D2423	BR Dundee depot July 1983	
D2424	BREL Glasgow January 1974	
D2425	G. H. Campbell, Airdrie c1969	
D2426	BREL Glasgow August 1979	Withdrawn January 1969, reinstated March 1969
D2427	J. McWilliam, Shettlestone, Glasgow January 1972	
D2428	G. H. Campbell, Airdrie February 1969	
D2429	J. McWilliam, Shettlestone, Glasgow April 1971	
D2430	G. H. Campbell, Airdrie c1969	
D2431	BREL Glasgow March 1972	
D2432	Exported to Italy in 1977	After withdrawal to P. Wood, Queenborough
D2433	BREL Glasgow June 1973	
D2434	J. McWilliam, Shettlestone, Glasgow October 1971	
D2435	G. H. Campbell, Airdrie c1974	
D2436	BREL Glasgow December 1973	
D2437	BR Polmadie depot August 1983	
D2438	G. H. Campbell, Airdrie c1974	
D2439	BREL Glasgow March 1973	
D2440	G. H. Campbell, Airdrie c1977	
D2441	Slag Reduction, Ickles, Rotherham August 1967	
D2442	G. H. Campbell, Airdrie c1974	
D2443	BREL Glasgow c1973	
D2444	BREL Glasgow c1979	

Engine: Gardner 8L3 of 204hp
Weight: 36¼ ton
Wheel dia: 42in
Max speed: 14mph
Class code: D2/7 later 2/14

Tractive effort: 16,100lb
Length: 26ft 3in
Height: 11ft 1in
Width: 8ft 6in

BR 1957 No	*Disposal details*	*Notes*
D2500	C. F. Booth, Rotherham, South Yorkshire April 1968	
D2501	Slag Reduction, Ickles, Rotherham August 1967	

BR 1957 No	*BR 1948 No*	*Built by*	*Works No*	*Date introduced*	*Date withdrawn*	*Disposal code*
D2502	11118	H/Clarke	D900	January 1956	October 1967	C
D2503	11119	H/Clarke	D901	February 1956	August 1967	C
D2504	11120	H/Clarke	D902	February 1956	March 1967	C
D2505	11144	H/Clarke	D938	April 1956	August 1967	C
D2506	11145	H/Clarke	D939	April 1956	November 1967	C
D2507	11146	H/Clarke	D940	May 1956	March 1967	C
D2508	11147	H/Clarke	D941	June 1956	May 1967	C
D2509	11148	H/Clarke	D942	July 1956	August 1967	C

Unclassified

A further development of the Hudswell Clarke 0-6-0 diesel-mechanical shunter powered by the Gardner 8L3 unit came in 1961 when 10 off-centre cab locos were introduced for the LMR.

BR 1957 No	*Built by*	*Works No*	*Date introduced*	*Date withdrawn*	*Disposal code*
D2510	H/Clarke	D1201	August 1961	August 1967	C
D2511	H/Clarke	D1202	August 1961	December 1967	P
D2512	H/Clarke	D1203	September 1961	May 1967	C
D2513	H/Clarke	D1204	October 1961	August 1967	C
D2514	H/Clarke	D1205	October 1961	August 1967	C
D2515	H/Clarke	D1206	October 1961	August 1967	C
D2516	H/Clarke	D1207	November 1961	August 1967	C
D2517	H/Clarke	D1208	November 1961	February 1967	C
D2518	H/Clarke	D1209	November 1961	February 1967	C
D2519	H/Clarke	D1210	November 1961	July 1967	P

Class 05

One of the largest fleets of 'small' shunters, were built by Hunslet from 1955, for ER, and ScR allocation, using a 0-6-0 chassis and the Gardner 8L3 power unit. Some detail differences existed.

BR 1957 No	*BR 1948 No*	*Built by*	*Works No*	*Date introduced*	*Date withdrawn*	*Disposal code*
D2550	11136	Hunslet	4866	October 1955	October 1966	C
D2551	11137	Hunslet	4867	October 1955	January 1968	C
D2552	11138	Hunslet	4868	February 1956	June 1967	C
D2553	11139	Hunslet	4869	February 1956	January 1968	C

BR 1957 No	*Disposal details*	*Notes*
D2502	C. F. Booth, Rotherham, South Yorkshire June 1968	
D2503	C. F. Booth, Rotherham, South Yorkshire April 1968	
D2504	C. F. Booth, Rotherham, South Yorkshire April 1968	
D2505	C. F. Booth, Rotherham, South Yorkshire April 1968	
D2506	Steelbreaking & Dismantling Co, Chesterfield June 1969	
D2507	Slag Reduction, Ickles, Rotherham August 1967	
D2508	C. F. Booth, Rotherham, South Yorkshire April 1968	
D2509	C. F. Booth, Rotherham, South Yorkshire April 1968	

Engine: Gardner 8L3 of 204hp
Weight: 34½ ton
Wheel dia: 42in
Max speed: 24mph
Class code: D2/12 later 2/14A

Tractive effort: 16,100lb
Length: 26ft 3¼in
Height: 12ft 0in
Width: 8ft 9in

BR 1957 No	*Disposal details*	*Notes*
D2510	C. F. Booth, Rotherham, South Yorkshire April 1968	
D2511	KWVR, Haworth, Yorkshire	Prior to preservation used by NCB Doncaster Area
D2512	C. F. Booth, Rotherham, South Yorkshire February 1968	
D2513	NCB Cadeby Colliery, Conisbrough October 1975	
D2514	C. F. Booth, Rotherham, South Yorkshire April 1968	
D2515	BR Bolton depot by W. Hatton May 1968	
D2516	BR Bolton depot by W. Hatton May 1968	
D2517	Slag Reduction, Ickles, Rotherham August 1967	
D2518	NCB Hatfield Colliery, Yorkshire June 1973	
D2519	KWVR, Haworth, Yorkshire	Prior to preservation used by NCB Doncaster Area

Engine: Gardner 8L3 of 204hp
Weight: 30¾ ton
Wheel dia: 40in
Max speed: 17¾mph
Class code: DJ13, later D2/8, 2/15A, 2/9, later BR Class 05

Tractive effort: 14,500lb
Length: 25ft 4in
Height: 11ft 0in
Width: 8ft 3in

BR 1957 No	*Disposal details*	*Notes*
D2550	BR Doncaster c1967	
D2551	C. F. Booth, Rotherham, South Yorkshire c1968	
D2552	C. F. Booth, Rotherham, South Yorkshire c1968	
D2553	C. F. Booth, Rotherham, South Yorkshire c1968	

BR 1957 No	*BR 1948 No*	*Built by*	*Works No*	*Date introduced*	*Date withdrawn*	*Disposal code*
D2554	11140	Hunslet	4870	March 1956	January 1981	D
D2555	11141	Hunslet	4871	June 1956	January 1968	C
D2556	11142	Hunslet	4872	July 1956	August 1967	C
D2557	11143	Hunslet	4873	August 1956	April 1967	C
D2558	11161	Hunslet	4896	October 1956	July 1967	C
D2559	11162	Hunslet	4897	October 1956	August 1967	C
D2560	11163	Hunslet	4998	February 1957	November 1967	C
D2561	11164	Hunslet	4999	March 1957	August 1967	C
D2562	11165	Hunslet	5000	March 1957	January 1968	C
D2563	11166	Hunslet	5001	June 1957	August 1967	C
D2564	11167	Hunslet	5002	June 1957	August 1967	C
D2565	11168	Hunslet	5003	June 1957	March 1967	C
D2566	11169	Hunslet	5004	August 1957	January 1968	C
D2567	11170	Hunslet	5005	August 1957	November 1967	C
D2568	11171	Hunslet	5006	September 1957	August 1967	C
D2569	11172	Hunslet	5007	September 1957	August 1967	C
D2570	11173	Hunslet	5008	October 1957	July 1967	C
D2571	11174	Hunslet	5009	October 1957	January 1968	C
D2572	11175	Hunslet	5010	December 1957	February 1967	C
D2573	11176	Hunslet	5011	January 1958	January 1968	C
D2574	—	Hunslet	5456	July 1958	June 1968	C
D2575	—	Hunslet	5457	July 1958	June 1968	C
D2576	—	Hunslet	5458	July 1958	June 1968	C
D2577	—	Hunslet	5459	July 1958	June 1968	C
D2578	—	Hunslet	5460	November 1958	July 1967	P
D2579	—	Hunslet	5461	December 1958	June 1968	C
D2580	—	Hunslet	5462	December 1958	June 1968	C
D2581	—	Hunslet	5463	December 1958	June 1968	C
D2582	—	Hunslet	5464	January 1959	June 1968	C
D2583	—	Hunslet	5465	January 1959	June 1968	C
D2584	—	Hunslet	5466	February 1959	July 1967	C
D2585	—	Hunslet	5467	April 1959	June 1968	C
D2586	—	Hunslet	5635	November 1959	March 1967	C
D2587	—	Hunslet	5636	November 1959	December 1967	P
D2588	—	Hunslet	5637	November 1959	March 1967	C
D2589	—	Hunslet	5638	November 1959	December 1967	C
D2590	—	Hunslet	5639	December 1959	June 1968	C
D2591	—	Hunslet	5640	December 1959	March 1967	C
D2592	—	Hunslet	5641	December 1959	March 1968	C
D2593	—	Hunslet	5642	December 1959	December 1967	P
D2594	—	Hunslet	5643	January 1960	March 1967	C
D2595	—	Hunslet	5644	January 1960	June 1968	C
D2596	—	Hunslet	5645	February 1960	June 1968	C
D2597	—	Hunslet	5646	June 1960	December 1967	C
D2598	—	Hunslet	5647	June 1960	December 1967	C

BR 1957 No	*Disposal details*	*Notes*
D2554	To Departmental Stock as 97803	
D2555	C. F. Booth, Rotherham, South Yorkshire c1968	
D2556	G. H. Campbell, Airdrie c1968	
D2557	C. F. Booth, Rotherham, South Yorkshire April 1968	
D2558	C. F. Booth, Rotherham, South Yorkshire March 1968	
D2559	G. H. Campbell, Airdrie c1968	
D2560	Slag Reduction, Ickles, Rotherham July 1968	
D2561	Duport Steel, Llanelli October 1972	Previous used at steel works
D2562	Slag Reduction, Ickles, Rotherham c1968	
D2563	C. F. Booth, Rotherham, South Yorkshire April 1968	
D2564	C. F. Booth, Rotherham, South Yorkshire March 1968	
D2565	C. F. Booth, Rotherham, South Yorkshire March 1968	
D2566	C. F. Booth, Rotherham, South Yorkshire c1968	
D2567	Slag Reduction, Ickles, Rotherham September 1968	
D2568	Duport Steel, Briton Ferry May 1969	Previously used at steel works
D2569	Duport Steel, Briton Ferry May 1969	Previously used at steel works
D2570	Duport Steel, Briton Ferry June 1971	Previously used at steel works
D2571	BR Glasgow c1969	
D2572	Slag Reduction, Ickles, Rotherham August 1967	
D2573	J. McWilliam, Shettleston, Glasgow	
D2574	G. H. Campbell, Airdrie February 1969	
D2575	G. H. Campbell, Airdrie February 1969	
D2576	Motherwell Machinery & Scrap Co	
D2577	Motherwell Machinery & Scrap Co December 1967	
D2578	Bulmer Railway Centre, Hereford	
D2579	G. H. Campbell, Airdrie	
D2580	G. H. Campbell, Airdrie	
D2581	G. H. Campbell, Airdrie	
D2582	G. H. Campbell, Airdrie	
D2583	G. H. Campbell, Airdrie	
D2584	Hunslet Co, Leeds August 1968	Used by Hunslet to provide spares
D2585	G. H. Campbell, Airdrie	
D2586	Slag Reduction, Ickles, Rotherham October 1967	
D2587	Privately in Wigan area	Rebuilt by Hunslet in 1969 Works No 7180
D2588	Slag Reduction, Ickles, Rotherham November 1967	
D2589	G. H. Campbell, Airdrie December 1965	
D2590	G. H. Campbell, Airdrie	
D2591	Slag Reduction, Ickles, Rotherham October 1967	
D2592	G. H. Campbell, Airdrie	
D2593	Bury Transport Museum	Rebuilt by Hunslet in 1969 Works No 7179
D2594	Slag Reduction, Ickles, Rotherham December 1967	
D2595	Hunslet Co, Leeds c1970	Used by Hunslet to provide spares
D2596	G. H. Campbell, Airdrie	
D2597	G. H. Campbell, Airdrie c1969	Previously used by NCB Scottish Area
D2598	NCB North East Area	Also used in NCB South Yorkshire Area

BR 1957 No	BR 1948 No	Built by	Works No	Date introduced	Date withdrawn	Disposal code
D2599	—	Hunslet	5648	June 1960	December 1967	C
D2600	—	Hunslet	5649	June 1960	December 1967	C
D2601	—	Hunslet	5650	August 1960	December 1967	C
D2602	—	Hunslet	5651	August 1960	July 1967	C
D2603	—	Hunslet	5652	September 1960	July 1967	C
D2604	—	Hunslet	5653	September 1960	December 1967	C
D2605	—	Hunslet	5654	September 1960	December 1967	C
D2606	—	Hunslet	5655	September 1960	February 1967	C
D2607	—	Hunslet	5656	October 1960	December 1967	C
D2608	—	Hunslet	5657	November 1960	December 1967	C
D2609	—	Hunslet	5658	November 1960	December 1967	C
D2610	—	Hunslet	5659	December 1960	December 1967	C
D2611	—	Hunslet	5660	January 1961	December 1967	C
D2612	—	Hunslet	5661	January 1961	February 1961	D
D2613	—	Hunslet	5662	February 1961	December 1967	C
D2614	—	Hunslet	5663	February 1961	March 1967	C
D2615	—	Hunslet	5664	February 1961	December 1967	C
D2616	—	Hunslet	5665	March 1961	December 1967	C
D2617	—	Hunslet	5666	March 1961	December 1967	C
D2618	—	Hunslet	5667	March 1961	June 1968	C

Unclassified

The North British Locomotive Co produced two fleets of 0-4-0 diesel-hydraulic shunting locomotives for use on the ScR. Of this first batch two different designs were constructed — all being built with no train brake equipment.

BR 1957 No	BR 1948 No	Built by	Works No	Date introduced	Date withdrawn	Disposal code
D2700	11700	NBL	27100	July 1953	November 1963	C
D2701	11701	NBL	27101	November 1953	March 1967	C
D2702	11702	NBL	27102	August 1954	March 1967	C
D2703	11703	NBL	27431	August 1955	February 1968	C
D2704	11704	NBL	27432	September 1955	June 1967	C
D2705	11705	NBL	27433	September 1955	August 1967	C
D2706	11706	NBL	27434	December 1955	March 1967	C
D2707	11707	NBL	27435	February 1956	March 1967	C

Unclassified

The second, larger fleet of NBL 0-4-0 diesel-hydraulic shunters commenced introduction from autumn 1957 being powered by a larger 225hp engine, and not being so bulky in appearance. All were built for Scotland, but some later operated south of the border.

BR 1957 No	BR 1948 No	Built by	Works No	Date introduced	Date withdrawn	Disposal code
D2708	11708	NBL	27703	August 1957	February 1967	C
D2709	11709	NBL	27704	September 1957	February 1967	C

BR 1957 No	Disposal details	Notes
D2599	NCB Askern Colliery May 1981	Also used in other NCB South Yorkshire collieries
D2600	Duport Steel, Briton Ferry June 1971	Previously used in Works
D2601	Duport Steel, Llanelli July 1979	Previously used in Works
D2602	Slag Reduction, Ickles, Rotherham	
D2603	C. F. Booth, Rotherham, South Yorkshire April 1968	Used after withdrawal at Menai Bridge
D2604	G. Cohen, Morriston, Swansea August 1968	
D2605	G. Cohen, Morriston, Swansea August 1968	
D2606	Slag Reduction, Ickles, Rotherham December 1967	
D2607	NCB South Yorkshire Area, Steetley Colliery July 1984	Has been used at various South Yorkshire sites
D2608	G. H. Campbell, Airdrie	
D2609	C. F. Booth, Rotherham, South Yorkshire	
D2610	C. F. Booth, Rotherham, South Yorkshire	
D2611	NCB Yorkshire Main Colliery December 1976	Previously used at colliery
D2612	To Departmental fleet as No 88	
D2613	NCB Bentley Colliery, Doncaster	Cut-up by Hazlewood Ltd
D2614	A. Draper, Hull November 1967	
D2615	C. F. Booth, Rotherham, South Yorkshire	As Departmental No 89 from January 1964 until November 1967 used at Dinsdale
D2616	NCB Hatfield Main Colliery June 1973	Previously used at Colliery
D2617	Hunslet Co, Leeds	Used by Hunslet to provide spares
D2618	G. H. Campbell, Airdrie February 1969	

Engine: Paxman 6RPH of 200hp
Weight: 32 ton
Wheel dia: 42in
Max speed: 14½mph
Class code: DY11, later D2/1, 2/4A
Tractive effort: 21,500lb
Length: 22ft 11½in
Height: 11ft 6in
Width: 8ft 6in

BR 1957 No	Disposal details	Notes
D2700	BR Darlington September 1964	Carried No D2600 for a few weeks in early 1958
D2701	A. Draper, Hull November 1967	
D2702	A. Draper, Hull November 1967	
D2703	Shipbreaking Industries, Faslane c1968	
D2704	Arnott Young Ltd, Carmyle, Glasgow October 1967	
D2705	J. N. Connel, Coatbridge, Lanark c1968	
D2706	Slag Reduction, Ickles, Rotherham August 1967	
D2707	Slag Reduction, Ickles, Rotherham August 1967	

Engine: MAN W6V17 of 225hp
Weight: 30 or 36 ton*
Wheel dia: 42in or 45in*
Max speed: 15 or 17mph*
Class code: DY11, later D2/10, 2/4 and 2/4B
*Dependent on build
Tractive effort: 20,080lb
Length: 23ft 2in or 24ft 5½in*
Height: 11ft 0in or 11ft 2¾in*
Width: 8ft 6in or 8ft 5in*

BR 1957 No	Disposal details	Notes
D2708	Slag Reduction, Ickles, Rotherham December 1967	
D2709	Slag Reduction, Ickles, Rotherham December 1967	

BR 1957 No	*BR 1948 No*	*Built by*	*Works No*	*Date introduced*	*Date withdrawn*	*Disposal code*
D2710	11710	NBL	27705	September 1957	March 1967	C
D2711	11711	NBL	27706	September 1957	February 1967	C
D2712	11712	NBL	27707	September 1957	March 1967	C
D2713	11713	NBL	27708	September 1957	March 1967	C
D2714	11714	NBL	27709	September 1957	March 1967	C
D2715	11715	NBL	27710	October 1957	March 1967	C
D2716	11716	NBL	27711	October 1957	March 1967	C
D2717	11717	NBL	27712	October 1957	July 1967	C
D2718	11718	NBL	27713	October 1957	July 1967	C
D2719	11719	NBL	27714	November 1957	February 1967	C
D2720	—	NBL	27815	June 1958	July 1967	C
D2721	—	NBL	27816	June 1958	July 1967	C
D2722	—	NBL	27817	July 1958	February 1967	C
D2723	—	NBL	27818	June 1958	July 1967	C
D2724	—	NBL	27819	July 1958	March 1967	C
D2725	—	NBL	27820	July 1958	June 1967	C
D2726	—	NBL	27821	July 1958	February 1967	C
D2727	—	NBL	27822	August 1958	March 1967	C
D2728	—	NBL	27823	August 1958	July 1967	C
D2729	—	NBL	27824	September 1958	March 1967	C
D2730	—	NBL	27825	September 1958	October 1967	C
D2731	—	NBL	27826	September 1958	October 1967	C
D2732	—	NBL	27827	October 1958	February 1967	C
D2733	—	NBL	27828	October 1958	February 1967	C
D2734	—	NBL	27829	October 1958	September 1967	C
D2735	—	NBL	27830	November 1958	March 1967	C
D2736	—	NBL	27831	November 1958	March 1967	C
D2737	—	NBL	27832	November 1958	March 1967	C
D2738	—	NBL	27833	November 1958	June 1967	C
D2739	—	NBL	27834	December 1958	March 1967	C
D2740	—	NBL	27835	December 1958	March 1967	C
D2741	—	NBL	27836	January 1959	February 1967	C
D2742	—	NBL	27837	January 1959	February 1967	C
D2743	—	NBL	27838	March 1959	February 1967	C
D2744	—	NBL	27839	April 1959	July 1967	C
D2745	—	NBL	27998	January 1960	April 1967	C
D2746	—	NBL	27999	February 1960	March 1967	C
D2747	—	NBL	28000	February 1960	July 1967	C
D2748	—	NBL	28001	February 1960	July 1967	C

BR 1957 No	Disposal details	Notes
D2710	Slag Reduction, Ickles, Rotherham August 1967	
D2711	Slag Reduction, Ickles, Rotherham November 1967	
D2712	Slag Reduction, Ickles, Rotherham November 1967	
D2713	Slag Reduction, Ickles, Rotherham September 1967	
D2714	Slag Reduction, Ickles, Rotherham September 1967	
D2715	Slag Reduction, Ickles, Rotherham September 1967	
D2716	Slag Reduction, Ickles, Rotherham August 1967	
D2717	Argosy Salvage, Shettleston, Glasgow c1967	
D2718	Argosy Salvage, Shettleston, Glasgow c1967	
D2719	Slag Reduction, Ickles, Rotherham November 1967	
D2720	J. N. Connel, Coatbridge, Lanark c1971	
D2721	Argosy Salvage, Shettleston, Glasgow c1967	
D2722	Slag Reduction, Ickles, Rotherham November 1967	
D2723	J. N. Connel, Coatbridge, Lanark c1967	
D2724	Slag Reduction, Ickles, Rotherham August 1967	
D2725	Motherwell Machinery & Scrap Co September 1967	
D2726	P. Wood, Queenborough, Kent October 1971	Used by P. Wood after withdrawal
D2727	Slag Reduction, Ickles Rotherham August 1967	
D2728	Argosy Salvage, Shettleston, Glasgow c1967	
D2729	Slag Reduction, Ickles, Rotherham August 1967	
D2730	Argosy Salvage, Shettleston, Glasgow June 1968	
D2731	Argosy Salvage, Shettleston, Glasgow June 1968	
D2732	Slag Reduction, Ickles, Rotherham October 1967	
D2733	Slag Reduction, Ickles, Rotherham November 1967	
D2734	Argosy Salvage, Shettleston, Glasgow c1968	
D2735	Slag Reduction, Ickles, Rotherham August 1967	
D2736	Birds, Cardiff July 1969	Used at various Birds sites
D2737	Slag Reduction, Ickles, Rotherham c1967	
D2738	Alex Smith Metals, Ayr January 1980	Rebuilt by A/Barclay used by NCB Scotland
D2739	Birds, Long Marston September 1969	
D2740	Slag Reduction, Ickles, Rotherham August 1967	
D2741	Slag Reduction, Ickles, Rotherham c1967	
D2742	Slag Reduction, Ickles, Rotherham c1967	
D2743	Slag Reduction, Ickles, Rotherham November 1967	
D2744	Argosy Salvage, Shettleston, Glasgow c1967	
D2745	Slag Reduction, Ickles, Rotherham August 1967	
D2746	Slag Reduction, Ickles, Rotherham August 1967	
D2747	Argosy Salvage, Shettleston, Glasgow c1967	
D2748	Argosy Salvage, Shettleston, Glasgow c1967	

BR 1957 No	BR 1948 No	Built by	Works No	Date introduced	Date withdrawn	Disposal code
D2749	—	NBL	28002	February 1960	July 1967	C
D2750	—	NBL	28003	February 1960	July 1967	C
D2751	—	NBL	28004	March 1960	July 1967	C
D2752	—	NBL	28005	March 1960	March 1967	C
D2753	—	NBL	28006	April 1960	June 1967	C
D2754	—	NBL	28007	April 1960	July 1967	C
D2755	—	NBL	28008	May 1960	July 1967	C
D2756	—	NBL	28009	May 1960	February 1968	C
D2757	—	NBL	28010	May 1960	June 1967	C
D2758	—	NBL	28011	May 1960	February 1968	C
D2759	—	NBL	28012	June 1960	October 1967	C
D2760	—	NBL	28013	June 1960	February 1968	C
D2761	—	NBL	28014	June 1960	October 1967	C
D2762	—	NBL	28015	June 1960	March 1967	C
D2763	—	NBL	28016	July 1960	June 1967	C
D2764	—	NBL	28017	July 1960	February 1968	C
D2765	—	NBL	28018	July 1960	March 1967	C
D2766	—	NBL	28019	July 1960	March 1967	C
D2767	—	NBL	28020	August 1960	June 1967	P
D2768	—	NBL	28021	August 1960	February 1968	C
D2769	—	NBL	28022	September 1960	February 1968	C
D2770	—	NBL	28023	September 1960	February 1968	C
D2771	—	NBL	28024	September 1960	March 1967	C
D2772	—	NBL	28025	September 1960	March 1967	C
D2773	—	NBL	28026	October 1960	February 1968	C
D2774	—	NBL	28027	October 1960	June 1967	S
D2775	—	NBL	28028	October 1960	February 1968	C
D2776	—	NBL	28029	October 1960	October 1967	C
D2777	—	NBL	28030	October 1960	March 1967	C
D2778	—	NBL	28031	November 1960	March 1967	C
D2779	—	NBL	28032	February 1961	February 1968	C
D2780	—	NBL	28033	March 1961	February 1968	C

Class 02

These 20 Yorkshire Engine Co-built locomotives, are the only machines constructed with a verandah. Built mainly for docks or areas with restricted loading gauge.

BR 1957 No	TOPS No	Built by	Works No	Date introduced	Date withdrawn	Disposal code
D2850	—	YEC	2809	September 1960	June 1970	C
D2851	02 001	YEC	2810	October 1960	June 1975	C
D2852	—	YEC	2811	October 1960	October 1973	C
D2853	02 003	YEC	2812	October 1960	June 1975	S
D2854	—	YEC	2813	November 1960	February 1970	S
D2855	—	YEC	2814	November 1960	October 1970	C
D2856	02 004	YEC	2815	November 1960	June 1975	C
D2857	—	YEC	2816	December 1960	April 1971	S
D2858	—	YEC	2817	December 1960	February 1970	S

BR 1957 No	*Disposal details*	*Notes*
D2749	Argosy Salvage, Shettleston, Glasgow c1967	
D2750	J. N. Connel, Coatbridge, Lanark c1967	
D2751	J. N. Connel, Coatbridge, Lanark c1967	
D2752	Slag Reduction, Ickles, Rotherham c1967	
D2753	Motherwell Machinery & Scrap Co October 1967	
D2754	J. N. Connel, Coatbridge, Lanark c1967	
D2755	Argosy Salvage, Shettleston, Glasgow c1967	
D2756	G. H. Campbell, Airdrie November 1968	
D2757	Birds, Cardiff October 1970	Used at various Birds sites
D2758	G. H. Campbell, Airdrie November 1968	
D2759	Argosy Salvage, Shettleston, Glasgow c1967	
D2760	G. H. Campbell, Airdrie November 1968	
D2761	Argosy Salvage, Shettleston, Glasgow c1967	
D2762	Slag Reduction, Ickles, Rotherham August 1967	
D2763	BSC Landore, Swansea April 1977	
D2764	Barnes & Bell, Coatbridge, Lanark	
D2765	Slag Reduction, Ickles, Rotherham September 1967	
D2766	Slag Reduction, Ickles, Rotherham August 1967	
D2767	Bury Transport Museum	After withdrawal used by Burmah Oil, Stanlow
D2768	Shipbreaking Industries, Faslane c1968	
D2769	G. H. Campbell, Airdrie November 1968	
D2770	G. H. Campbell, Airdrie November 1968	
D2771	Slag Reduction, Ickles, Rotherham August 1967	
D2772	Slag Reduction, Ickles, Rotherham August 1967	
D2773	Barnes & Bell, Coatbridge, Lanark c1968	
D2774	NCB Celynen South Colliery	Rebuilt by A/Barclay in 1968
D2775	G. H. Campbell, Airdrie c1968	
D2776	Argosy Salvage, Shettleston, Glasgow c1968	
D2777	Birds, Risca September 1968	Used at various Birds sites
D2778	Slag Reduction, Ickles, Rotherham September 1967	
D2779	G. H. Campbell, Airdrie November 1968	
D2780	Barnes & Bell, Coatbridge, Lanark c1968	

Engine: Rolls-Royce C6NFL176 of 170hp
Weight: 28¼ ton
Wheel dia: 40in
Max speed: 19½mph
Class code: D1/4, later 1/17 and BR Class 02
Tractive effort: 15,000lb
Length: 21ft 11⅞in
Height: 11ft 5¼in
Width: 8ft 6in

BR 1957 No	*Disposal details*	*Notes*
D2850	W. Heselwood, Attercliffe, Sheffield	
D2851	Arnott Young, Dudley Hill March 1976	Used after withdrawal
D2852	BR Allerton depot March 1976	Allocated No 02 002 but never carried
D2853	Lunt, Comley & Pitt, Shutt End, Staffs, as *Peter*	
D2854	C. F. Booth, Rotherham, South Yorkshire	Used as Booth's Works pilot
D2855	W. Heselwood, Attercliffe, Sheffield	
D2856	Redland Roadstone, Mountsorrel October 1978	Spares loco
D2857	Birds, Long Marston, as *Sir Alfred*	Used as Birds Works pilot
D2858	Lowton Metals, Newton-le-Willows	

BR 1957 No	BR 1948 No	Built by	Works No	Date introduced	Date withdrawn	Disposal code
D2859	—	YEC	2818	December 1960	March 1970	C
D2860	—	YEC	2843	September 1961	December 1970	P
D2861	—	YEC	2844	October 1961	December 1969	C
D2862	—	YEC	2845	October 1961	December 1969	C
D2863	—	YEC	2846	October 1961	December 1969	C
D2864	—	YEC	2847	October 1961	February 1970	C
D2865	—	YEC	2848	November 1961	March 1970	S
D2866	—	YEC	2849	November 1961	February 1970	S
D2867	—	YEC	2850	November 1961	September 1970	S
D2868	—	YEC	2851	November 1961	December 1969	S
D2869	—	YEC	2852	December 1961	December 1969	C

Unclassified

A small fleet of medium powered 0-4-0 diesel-hydraulic yard shunters introduced from 1958 mainly for use on the LMR, often being used as depot pilots.

BR 1957 No	Built by	Works No	Date introduced	Date withdrawn	Disposal code
D2900	NBL	27751	April 1958	February 1967	C
D2901	NBL	27752	April 1958	February 1967	C
D2902	NBL	27753	May 1958	February 1967	C
D2903	NBL	27754	May 1958	February 1967	C
D2904	NBL	27755	June 1958	February 1967	C
D2905	NBL	27756	June 1958	February 1967	C
D2906	NBL	27757	July 1958	February 1967	C
D2907	NBL	27758	September 1958	February 1967	C
D2908	NBL	27759	September 1958	February 1967	C
D2909	NBL	27760	October 1958	February 1967	C
D2910	NBL	27761	October 1958	February 1967	C
D2911	NBL	27995	December 1959	February 1967	C
D2912	NBL	27996	December 1959	February 1967	C
D2913	NBL	27997	December 1959	February 1967	C

Unclassified

These three 0-4-0 locomotives are a smaller version of the D2550 fleet, and were introduced for areas where unavoidably tight curves existed.

BR 1957 No	BR 1948 No	Built by	Works No	Date introduced	Date withdrawn	Disposal code
D2950	11500	Hunslet	4625	November 1954	December 1967	P
D2951	11501	Hunslet	4626	November 1955	December 1967	C
D2952	11502	Hunslet	4627	January 1955	December 1966	C

BR 1957 No	*Disposal details*	*Notes*
D2859	Birds, Long Marston April 1971	
D2860	National Railway Museum as museum pilot	Rebuilt in 1978 by Thomas Hill Ltd
D2861	C. F. Booth, Rotherham, South Yorkshire	
D2862	NCB Norton Colliery, Staffs April 1979	
D2863	T. W. Ward, Beighton, Sheffield August 1971	
D2864	W. Heselwood, Attercliffe, Sheffield April 1971	
D2865	APCM Beeston	Out of use
D2866	Arnott Young, Dalmuir, as AY1021	Used as pilot
D2867	Redland Roadstone, Barrow-on-Soar as *Dianne*	
D2868	Lunt, Comley & Pitt, Shutt End, Staffs as *Sam*	
D2869	T. W. Ward, Beighton, Sheffield August 1971	

Engine: MAN 6V17 of 330hp
Weight: 36 ton
Wheel dia: 45in
Max speed: 20mph
Class code: D3/1, later 3/4
*Depending on build

Tractive effort: 20,160lb
Length: 24ft 0½in or 23ft 11½in*
Height: 12ft 7in
Width: 8ft 9in

BR 1957 No	*Disposal details*	*Notes*
D2900	Slag Reduction, Ickles, Rotherham October 1967	
D2901	Slag Reduction, Ickles, Rotherham October 1967	
D2902	Slag Reduction, Ickles, Rotherham October 1967	
D2903	Slag Reduction, Ickles, Rotherham November 1967	
D2904	Slag Reduction, Ickles, Rotherham November 1967	
D2905	Slag Reduction, Ickles, Rotherham November 1967	
D2906	Slag Reduction, Ickles, Rotherham November 1967	
D2907	Slag Reduction, Ickles, Rotherham November 1967	
D2908	Slag Reduction, Ickles, Rotherham December 1967	
D2909	Slag Reduction, Ickles, Rotherham October 1967	
D2910	Slag Reduction, Ickles, Rotherham November 1967	
D2911	Slag Reduction, Ickles, Rotherham November 1967	
D2912	Slag Reduction, Ickles, Rotherham November 1967	
D2913	Slag Reduction, Ickles, Rotherham November 1967	

Engine: Gardner 6L3 of 153hp
Weight: 22½ ton
Wheel dia: 40in
Max speed: 14mph
Class code: DY1, later D1/1, 1/15

Tractive effort: 10,800lb
Length: 20ft 10in
Height: 11ft 10in
Width: 8ft 8in

BR 1957 No	*Disposal details*	*Notes*
D2950	Presently stored at Thyssen, Llanelli	Used by Llanelli Steel from 1967-1980
D2951	C. F. Booth, Rotherham, South Yorkshire c1969	
D2952	Slag Reduction, Ickles, Rotherham c1967	

Class 01

Another of the short wheelbase designs, for limited clearance operation. The final two locomotives becoming Class 01, and used on the Holyhead Breakwater System.

BR 1957 No	*BR 1948 No*	*TOPS No*	*Built by*	*Works No*	*Date introduced*	*Date withdrawn*
D2953	11503	—	A/Barclay	395	January 1956	June 1966
D2954	11504	01 001	A/Barclay	396	January 1956	September 1979
D2955	11505	01 002	A/Barclay	397	February 1956	March 1981
D2956	11506	—	A/Barclay	398	March 1956	May 1966
No 81	D2956*	—	A/Barclay	424	July 1967†	November 1967

Unclassified

This fleet of only two 0-4-0 diesel-mechanical locomotives was constructed by Ruston & Hornsby in 1956 to a design dating from the 1940s. Both were allocated to the ER from new.

BR 1957 No	*BR 1948 No*	*Built by*	*Works No*	*Date introduced*	*Date withdrawn*	*Disposal code*
D2957	11507	R/Hornsby	390774	March 1956	March 1967	C
D2958	11508	R/Hornsby	390777	May 1956	January 1968	S

Class 07

This fleet of off-centre cab diesel-electric locomotives was introduced for use in Southampton Docks, to replace steam traction. After withdrawal from BR service several passed to industrial use.

BR 1957 No	*TOPS No*	*Built by*	*Works No*	*Date introduced*	*Date withdrawn*	*Disposal code*
D2985	07 001	R/Hornsby	480686	June 1962	July 1977	S
D2986	07 002	R/Hornsby	480687	June 1962	July 1977	S
D2987	07 003	R/Hornsby	480688	June 1962	October 1976	S
D2988	—	R/Hornsby	480689	June 1962	May 1973	C
D2989	07 005	R/Hornsby	480690	June 1962	July 1977	S
D2990	07 006	R/Hornsby	480691	July 1962	July 1977	S
D2991	—	R/Hornsby	480692	July 1962	May 1973	D
D2992	—	R/Hornsby	480693	September 1962	May 1973	C
D2993	07 009	R/Hornsby	480694	September 1962	October 1976	E
D2994	07 010	R/Hornsby	480695	September 1962	October 1976	P
D2995	07 011	R/Hornsby	480696	October 1962	July 1977	S
D2996	07 012	R/Hornsby	480697	October 1962	July 1977	S
D2997	07 013	R/Hornsby	480698	November 1962	July 1977	S
D2998	—	R/Hornsby	480699	November 1962	May 1973	C

Engine: Gardner 6L3 of 153hp
Weight: 25 ton
Wheel dia: 38in
Max speed: 14¼mph
Class code: DY2, later D1/2, 1/2 and BR Class 01
*BR 1957 number
†From Departmental fleet

Tractive effort: 12,750lb
Length: 23ft 8in
Height: 11ft 10½in
Width: 8ft 5½in

BR 1957 No	*Disposal code*	*Disposal details*	*Notes*
D2953	S	Thames Matex, West Thurrock, Essex	Out of use
D2954	C	BR Holyhead Breakwater February 1982	
D2955	C	BR Holyhead Breakwater February 1982	
D2956	S	Mayer Newman, Snailwell, Norwich as A48L	Yard pilot loco (stored)
No 81	C	Duport Steel, Briton Ferry August 1969	2nd loco to carry No D2956

Engine: Ruston 6VPHL of 165hp
Weight: 28 ton
Wheel dia: 38½in
Max speed: 15mph
Class code: DY5, later D1/3 and 1/16

Tractive effort: 14,350lb
Length: 22ft 1¼in
Height: 11ft 0in
Width: 8ft 5½in

BR 1957 No	*Disposal details*	*Notes*
D2957	Slag Reduction, Ickles, Rotherham c1967	
D2958	C. F. Booth, Rotherham, South Yorkshire	Used as yard pilot. Stored from late 1981

Engine: Ruston 6RPHL of 275hp
Weight: 42½ ton
Wheel dia: 42in
Max speed: 20mph
Class code: 2/16 later Class 07

Tractive effort: 28,240lb
Length: 26ft 9½in
Height: 12ft 10in
Width: 8ft 6in

BR 1957 No	*Disposal details*	*Notes*
D2985	Peakstone, Peak Dale, Derbyshire	
D2986	NCB Coed Bach, Kidwelly	
D2987	British Industrial Sand, Oakamoor	
D2988	BREL Eastleigh by M. Claydon Ltd	
D2989	ICI Wilton, Middlesbrough as *Langbaurgh*	Rebuilt by Resco
D2990	NCB Coed Bach, Kidwelly	
D2991	Departmental — D2991	
D2992	BREL Eastleigh July 1976	
D2993	Exported to Italy March 1977	
D2994	West Somerset Railway, Minehead	
D2995	ICI Wilton, Middlesbrough as *Cleveland*	Rebuilt by Resco
D2996	NCB Cwmmawr, Kidwelly	
D2997	Dow Chemicals, Kings Lynn	Rebuilt by Resco
D2998	BREL Eastleigh July 1976	

Two of the pioneer diesel shunter classes stand side by side at Ipswich docks. On the left is No 11136 later No D2550 built by Hunslet, while on the right is No 11500, later No D2950, also built by Hunslet. *Author's collection*

No D2852 built by Yorkshire Engine Co is one of a class of 20 0-4-0 locomotives, built for dock line use. This locomotive was cut up by BR at Allerton during March 1976. *BR*

North British 0-4-0 diesel-hydraulic No D2903 in original condition. This example carried works number 27754 and was withdrawn in February 1967 and cut up by Slag Reduction at Ickles in common with the rest of the class. *Colin J. Marsden collection*

Four Class 08s were rebuilt in 1974/75 for Lamco Mining Co of Liberia, and fitted with buckeye couplers and air brake equipment. No D3092 is seen here after completion at Derby Works. *BR*

Unclassified

One of five Brush demonstrator locomotives constructed by Beyer Peacock Ltd of Gorton and loaned to BR for trial operation, used mainly on ER.

BR 1957 No	*TOPS No*	*Built by*	*Works No*	*Date introduced*	*Date withdrawn*	*Disposal code*
D2999	—	B/Peacock	100/7861	September 1960	October 1967	C

Class 08, 09, 10 and unclassified

The largest fleet of BR locomotives is the 0-6-0 diesel-electric shunter based on various LMSR prototype designs, built during both pre- and postwar years. Although the same basic body design has been used for well over 1,000 locomotives, various technical differences exist within the type. These standard design 0-6-0 diesel-electric shunters can be seen at almost any location on the BR system as they are allocated to all five operating regions.

Class 08/09. English Electric power unit and traction equipment.
D3000-D3116
D3127-D3136
D3167-D3438
D3454-D3472
D3503-D3511
D3652-D4048
D4095-D4192

Unclassified. Crossley power unit and Crompton Parkinson electrical equipment.
D3117-D3126

Unclassified. Lister-Blackstone power unit and BTH traction equipment.
D3152-D3166

Class 10. Lister-Blackstone power unit and GEC traction equipment.
D3137-D3151
D3439-D3453
D3473-D3502
D3512-D3651
D4049-D4094

BR 1957 No	*BR 1948 No*	*TOPS No*	*Built by*	*Works No*	*Date introduced*	*Date withdrawn*
D3000	13000	—	BR Derby	—	October 1952	November 1972
D3001	13001	—	BR Derby	—	October 1952	November 1972
D3002	13002	—	BR Derby	—	October 1952	July 1972
D3003	13003	—	BR Derby	—	October 1952	July 1972
D3004	13004	08 001	BR Derby	—	November 1952	June 1978
D3005	13005	08 002	BR Derby	—	November 1952	September 1977
D3006	13006	—	BR Derby	—	December 1952	November 1972
D3007	13007	08 003	BR Derby	—	December 1952	December 1977
D3008	13008	08 004	BR Derby	—	December 1952	August 1983
D3009	13009	08 005	BR Derby	—	December 1952	October 1978
D3010	13010	08 006	BR Derby	—	December 1952	February 1980
D3011	13011	—	BR Derby	—	December 1952	October 1972
D3012	13012	08 007	BR Derby	—	December 1952	January 1973
D3013	13013	—	BR Derby	—	December 1952	October 1972
D3014	13014	—	BR Derby	—	December 1952	October 1972
D3015	13015	08 008	BR Derby	—	January 1953	November 1983
D3016	13016	08 009	BR Derby	—	January 1953	November 1975
D3017	13017	08 010	BR Derby	—	January 1953	December 1977
D3018	13018	08 011	BR Derby	—	February 1953	

Engine: Petter McLaren MLE6 of 180hp
Weight: 29¾ ton
Wheel dia: 42in
Max speed: 18mph
Class code: None allocated
Tractive effort: 19,200lb
Length: 21ft 10½in
Height: 11ft 6in
Width: 8ft 9in

BR 1957 No	*Disposal details*	*Notes*
D2999	C. F. Booth, Rotherham, South Yorkshire October 1970	

English Electric/English Electric — Class 08/09

Engine: EE6K of 350hp
Weight: 48 ton
Wheel dia: 54in
Max speed: 15mph, 27mph*
Tractive effort: 35,000lb
Length: 29ft 3in
Height: 12ft 8⅝in
Width: 8ft 6in
Class code: DEJ 4, later D3/2. 3/1, then BR Class 08/09
*Class 09s only

Crossley/Crompton Parkinson — unclassified

Engine: Crossley ESNT6 of 350hp
Weight: 47½ ton
Wheel dia: 54in
Max speed: 20mph
Tractive effort: 35,000lb
Length: 29ft 3in
Height: 12ft 8⅝in
Width: 8ft 6in
Class code: D3/3, later 3/1B

Blackstone/BTH — unclassified

Engine: Blackstone ER6T of 350hp
Weight: 47½ ton
Wheel diameter: 54in
Max speed: 20mph
Tractive effort: 35,000lb
Length: 29ft 3in
Height: 12ft 8⅝in
Width: 8ft 6in
Class code: DEJ6, later D3/5, 3/1D

Blackstone/GEC — Class 10

Engine: Blackstone ER6T of 350hp
Weight: 47 ton
Wheel dia: 54in
Max speed: 20mph
Tractive effort: 35,000lb
Length: 29ft 3in
Height: 12ft 8⅝in
Width: 8ft 6in
Class code: DEJ 5, later D3/4, 3/1C

BR 1957 No	*Disposal code*	*Disposal details*	*Notes*
D3000	S	NCB Mardy Colliery	Used at various South Wales sites
D3001	C	BREL Doncaster November 1975	
D3002	P	Plym Valley Railway, Plymouth	Previously used by F. Yeoman Ltd
D3003	P	In children's playground, Wanstrow, Somerset	
D3004	C	BREL Swindon March 1979	
D3005	C	BREL Swindon January 1978	
D3006	D	To Departmental Stock — 966507	
D3007	C	BREL Glasgow July 1979	
D3008	A	BR Thornaby depot	
D3009	C	BREL Doncaster c1979	
D3010	C	BREL Swindon April 1980	
D3011	S	British Leyland, Longbridge as *Lickey*	
D3012	C	BREL Swindon October 1973	
D3013	C	J. Cashmore, Newport c1973	
D3014	S	NCB Merthyr Vale Colliery, Aberfan	
D3015	A	BR Gateshead depot	
D3016	C	BREL Swindon June 1976	
D3017	C	BREL Eastleigh February 1978	
D3018	A	BR Depot Bletchley	

BR 1957 No	*BR 1948 No*	*TOPS No*	*Built by*	*Works No*	**Period Date introduced*	*Date withdrawn*
D3019	13019	08 012	BR Derby	—	February 1953	June 1973
D3020	13020	08 013	BR Derby	—	April 1953	December 1973
D3021	13021	08 014	BR Derby	—	April 1953	May 1980
D3022	13022	08 015	BR Derby	—	May 1953	September 1980
D3023	13023	08 016	BR Derby	—	May 1953	May 1980
D3024	13024	08 017	BR Derby	—	June 1953	August 1973
D3025	13025	08 018	BR Derby	—	July 1953	July 1983
D3026	13026	—	BR Derby	—	October 1953	November 1972
D3027	13027	08 019	BR Derby	—	October 1953	September 1983
D3028	13028	08 020	BR Derby	—	October 1953	August 1973
D3029	13029	08 021	BR Derby	—	October 1953	
D3030	13030	08 022	BR Derby	—	October 1953	
D3031	13031	08 023	BR Derby	—	November 1953	September 1983
D3032	13032	08 024	BR Derby	—	November 1953	December 1982
D3033	13033	08 025	BR Derby	—	November 1953	December 1977
D3034	13034	—	BR Derby	—	December 1953	November 1972
D3035	13035	—	BR Derby	—	December 1953	December 1972
D3036	13036	08 026	BR Derby	—	December 1953	July 1982
D3037	13037	—	BR Derby	—	December 1953	December 1972
D3038	13038	—	BR Derby	—	December 1953	December 1972
D3039	13039	08 027	BR Derby	—	December 1953	November 1980
D3040	13040	08 028	BR Derby	—	January 1954	April 1981
D3041	13041	08 029	BR Derby	—	January 1954	March 1978
D3042	13042	08 030	BR Derby	—	February 1954	July 1982
D3043	13043	08 031	BR Derby	—	February 1954	July 1982
D3044	13044	08 032	BR Derby	—	March 1954	August 1974
D3045	13045	—	BR Derby	—	March 1954	November 1972
D3046	13046	08 033	BR Derby	—	April 1954	
D3047	13047	08 034	BR Derby	—	April 1954	July 1973
D3048	13048	08 035	BR Derby	—	April 1954	September 1979
D3049	13049	08 036	BR Derby	—	April 1954	September 1981
D3050	13050	08 037	BR Derby	—	May 1954	February 1980
D3051	13051	08 038	BR Derby	—	May 1954	June 1973
D3052	13052	08 039	BR Derby	—	May 1954	December 1973
D3053	13053	08 040	BR Derby	—	May 1954	June 1973
D3054	13054	08 041	BR Derby	—	June 1954	August 1978
D3055	13055	08 042	BR Derby	—	June 1954	March 1979
D3056	13056	08 043	BR Derby	—	8/54*	December 1977
D3057	13057	08 044	BR Derby	—	8/54*	January 1978
D3058	13058	08 045	BR Derby	—	9/54*	July 1982
D3059	13059	08 046	BR Derby	—	9/54*	May 1980
D3060	13060	08 047	BR Darlington	—	August 1953	October 1979
D3061	13061	08 048	BR Darlington	—	August 1953	December 1977
D3062	13062	08 049	BR Darlington	—	August 1953	May 1981
D3063	13063	08 050	BR Darlington	—	September 1953	October 1980
D3064	13064	08 051	BR Darlington	—	September 1953	July 1982
D3065	13065	08 052	BR Darlington	—	October 1953	January 1981
D3066	13066	08 053	BR Darlington	—	October 1953	March 1981
D3067	13067	08 054	BR Darlington	—	October 1953	February 1980
D3068	13068	08 055	BR Darlington	—	October 1953	November 1980
D3069	13069	—	BR Darlington	—	November 1953	January 1973
D3070	13070	08 056	BR Darlington	—	November 1953	
D3071	13071	08 057	BR Darlington	—	November 1953	July 1976
D3072	13072	08 058	BR Darlington	—	December 1953	April 1982
D3073	13073	08 059	BR Darlington	—	December 1953	September 1980

BR 1957 No	*Disposal code*	*Disposal details*	*Notes*
D3019	S	NCB Gwaun-Cae-Gurwen, Glamorgan as *Gwineth*	
D3020	C	BREL Doncaster April 1975	
D3021	C	C. F. Booth, Rotherham, South Yorkshire November 1981	
D3022	P	Severn Valley Railway	
D3023	S	NCB British Oak disposal point	Out of use
D3024	C	BREL Doncaster October 1975	
D3025	A	BR Allerton depot	
D3026	C	BREL Swindon April 1973	
D3027	A	BR Toton depot	
D3028	C	BREL Doncaster November 1975	
D3029			
D3030			Withdrawn July 1982, reinstated July 1982
D3031	A	BR Chester depot	Seen working after withdrawal
D3032	C	BREL Doncaster September 1983	
D3033	C	BREL Swindon March 1978	
D3034	C	BREL Derby November 1973	
D3035	D	To Departmental Stock — 966508	
D3036	A	BREL Swindon	
D3037	D	To Departmental Stock — 966510	
D3038	C	NCB Bates Colliery, Blyth June 1980	Previously used at various Northumberland NCB sites
D3039	C	BREL Swindon April 1982	
D3040	C	BREL Swindon April 1982	
D3041	C	BREL Swindon May 1978	
D3042	A	BREL Swindon	
D3043	A	BR Immingham depot	Withdrawn December 1981, reinstated July 1982
D3044	S	Foster Yeoman, Merehead, Somerset as No 33 *Mendip*	
D3045	C	BREL Glasgow April 1976	
D3046			
D3047	E	Lamco Mining Co, Liberia February 1975	Rebuilt at Derby before export
D3048	C	BREL Swindon January 1980	
D3049	C	BREL Swindon March 1983	
D3050	C	BREL Swindon October 1980	
D3051	C	BREL Derby August 1973	
D3052	C	J. Cashmore Ltd, Newport August 1974	
D3053	C	BREL Doncaster October 1975	
D3054	C	BREL Swindon April 1979	
D3055	C	BREL Doncaster May 1979	
D3056	C	BREL Swindon April 1978	
D3057	C	BREL Doncaster January 1979	
D3058	A	BREL Swindon	
D3059	S	Associated British Maltsters, Airdrie	
D3060	C	BREL Swindon July 1980	
D3061	C	BREL Doncaster May 1978	
D3062	C	BREL Swindon May 1983	
D3063	C	BREL Swindon January 1983	
D3064	A	BR Tinsley depot	
D3065	C	BR March depot by C. F. Booth January 1982	
D3066	C	BREL Swindon	
D3067	S	Tilcon Ltd, Grassington	
D3068	C	BREL Swindon April 1983	
D3069	D	To Departmental Stock — 966509	
D3070			
D3071	C	BREL Doncaster May 1977	
D3072	C	BREL Doncaster May 1983	
D3073	A	BREL Swindon	

BR 1957 No	BR 1948 No	TOPS No	Built by	Works No	*Period Date introduced	Date withdrawn
D3074	13074	08 060	BR Darlington	—	December 1953	June 1984
D3075	13075	08 061	BR Darlington	—	December 1953	May 1984
D3076	13076	08 062	BR Darlington	—	December 1953	
D3077	13077	08 063	BR Darlington	—	January 1954	July 1984
D3078	13078	—	BR Darlington	—	January 1954	November 1972
D3079	13079	08 064	BR Darlington	—	January 1954	
D3080	13080	08 065	BR Darlington	—	January 1954	September 1977
D3081	13081	08 066	BR Darlington	—	February 1954	September 1977
D3082	13082	08 067	BR Derby	—	10/54*	July 1983
D3083	13083	08 068	BR Derby	—	10/54*	July 1983
D3084	13084	08 069	BR Derby	—	10/54*	February 1983
D3085	13085	08 070	BR Derby	—	11/54*	December 1977
D3086	13086	08 071	BR Derby	—	11/54*	February 1978
D3087	13087	08 072	BR Derby	—	October 1954	June 1973
D3088	13088	08 073	BR Derby	—	October 1954	December 1973
D3089	13089	08 074	BR Derby	—	October 1954	December 1973
D3090	13090	08 075	BR Derby	—	October 1954	December 1981
D3091	13091	08 076	BR Derby	—	November 1954	September 1980
D3092	13092	—	BR Derby	—	November 1954	October 1972
D3093	13093	—	BR Derby	—	December 1954	May 1972
D3094	13094	—	BR Derby	—	December 1954	October 1972
D3095	13095	—	BR Derby	—	December 1954	May 1972
D3096	13096	—	BR Derby	—	December 1954	May 1972
D3097	13097	—	BR Derby	—	January 1955	May 1972
D3098	13098	—	BR Derby	—	January 1955	October 1972
D3099	13099	—	BR Derby	—	January 1955	October 1972
D3100	13100	—	BR Derby	—	January 1955	October 1972
D3101	13101	—	BR Derby	—	February 1955	May 1972
D3102	13102	08 077	BR Derby	—	February 1955	November 1977
D3103	13103	08 078	BR Derby	—	February 1955	August 1983
D3104	13104	08 079	BR Derby	—	February 1955	December 1983
D3105	13105	08 080	BR Derby	—	February 1955	November 1980
D3106	13106	08 081	BR Derby	—	March 1955	April 1980
D3107	13107	08 082	BR Derby	—	March 1955	November 1980
D3108	13108	08 083	BR Derby	—	March 1955	July 1984
D3109	13109	08 084	BR Derby	—	March 1955	November 1980
D3110	13110	08 085	BR Derby	—	March 1955	
D3111	13111	08 086	BR Derby	—	March 1955	August 1980
D3112	13112	08 087	BR Derby	—	April 1955	November 1979
D3113	13113	08 088	BR Derby	—	April 1955	September 1983
D3114	13114	08 089	BR Derby	—	April 1955	September 1980
D3115	13115	08 090	BR Derby	—	April 1955	November 1977
D3116	13116	08 091	BR Derby	—	April 1955	November 1982
D3117	13117	—	BR Derby	—	June 1955	July 1967
D3118	13118	—	BR Derby	—	June 1955	July 1967
D3119	13119	—	BR Derby	—	June 1955	July 1967
D3120	13120	—	BR Derby	—	July 1955	July 1967
D3121	13121	—	BR Derby	—	August 1955	April 1967
D3122	13122	—	BR Derby	—	September 1955	December 1966
D3123	13123	—	BR Derby	—	September 1955	December 1966
D3124	13124	—	BR Derby	—	September 1955	December 1966
D3125	13125	—	BR Derby	—	July 1957	July 1967
D3126	13126	—	BR Derby	—	July 1957	December 1966
D3127	13127	08 092	BR Darlington	—	July 1954	November 1978

BR 1957 No	*Disposal code*	*Disposal details*	*Notes*
D3074			
D3075			
D3076			
D3077			
D3078	D	To Departmental Stock — 966506	
D3079			
D3080	C	BREL Doncaster November 1978	
D3081	C	BREL Doncaster November 1978	
D3082	A	BR Tyseley depot	
D3083	A	BR Tyseley depot	Carried *Tyseley No 1*
D3084	C	BREL Doncaster March 1984	
D3085	D	To Departmental Stock — 97802	
D3086	C	BREL Doncaster July 1978	
D3087	S	T. W. Ward, Adderley Park, Birmingham	Previously used by CEGB at Birchills PS
D3088	S	NCB Bates Colliery, Blyth as 2100/526	Previously used at various Northumberland NCB sites (out of use)
D3089	C	BREL Derby June 1977	
D3090	C	BREL Swindon April 1982	
D3091	C	BREL Swindon April 1982	
D3092	E	Lamco Mining Co, Liberia May 1974	Rebuilt Derby before export
D3093	C	G. Cohen, Kettering, Northamptonshire January 1974	
D3094	E	Lamco Mining Co, Liberia May 1974	Rebuilt Derby before export
D3095	C	BREL Swindon December 1973	
D3096	C	BR Selhurst depot September 1972	
D3097	C	BREL Swindon December 1973	
D3098	E	Lamco Mining Co, Liberia May 1974	Rebuilt Derby before export
D3099	C	P. Wood, Queenborough, Kent April 1980	
D3100	E	Lamco, Mining Co, Liberia May 1974	Rebuilt Derby before export
D3101	S	Amey Roadstone, Loughborough	Out of use
D3102	S	Wiggins Teape Ltd, Fort William	
D3103	A	BR Carlisle depot	
D3104	A	BR Chester depot	
D3105	C	BREL Swindon May 1981	
D3106	C	BREL Swindon July 1980	
D3107	C	BREL Swindon February 1982	
D3108			
D3109	C	BREL Swindon February 1982	
D3110			
D3111	C	BREL Swindon January 1981	Prior to withdrawl stored unserviceable
D3112	C	BREL Swindon May 1980	
D3113	A	BR Crewe depot	
D3114	C	BREL Swindon December 1980	
D3115	C	BREL Swindon January 1979	
D3116	C	BREL Doncaster February 1984	
D3117	C	J. Cashmore, Great Bridge, Tipton February 1968	
D3118	C	J. Cashmore, Great Bridge, Tipton February 1968	
D3119	C	J. Cashmore, Great Bridge, Tipton February 1968	
D3120	C	G. Cohen, Kettering, Northamptonshire June 1968	
D3121	C	BR Workshops, Derby May 1968	
D3122	C	Garnham, Harris & Elton, Chesterfield July 1967	
D3123	C	J. Cashmore, Great Bridge, Tipton	
D3124	C	J. Cashmore, Great Bridge, Tipton	
D3125	C	G. Cohen, Kettering, Northamptonshire	
D3126	C	J. Cashmore, Great Bridge, Tipton	
D3127	C	BREL Doncaster February 1979	

BR 1957 No	*BR 1948 No*	*TOPS No*	*Built by*	*Works No*	**Period Date introduced*	*Date withdrawn*
D3128	13128	08 093	BR Darlington	—	August 1954	July 1981
D3129	13129	08 094	BR Darlington	—	August 1954	June 1983
D3130	13130	08 095	BR Darlington	—	August 1954	February 1983
D3131	13131	08 096	BR Darlington	—	August 1954	September 1984
D3132	13132	08 097	BR Darlington	—	October 1954	March 1981
D3133	13133	08 098	BR Darlington	—	October 1954	November 1980
D3134	13134	08 099	BR Darlington	—	October 1954	September 1982
D3135	13135	08 100	BR Darlington	—	November 1954	December 1982
D3136	13136	08 101	BR Darlington	—	December 1954	July 1983
D3137	13137	—	BR Darlington	—	March 1955	July 1970
D3138	13138	—	BR Darlington	—	March 1955	April 1972
D3139	13139	—	BR Darlington	—	March 1955	June 1968
D3140	13140	—	BR Darlington	—	April 1955	June 1968
D3141	13141	—	BR Darlington	—	May 1955	July 1971
D3142	13142	—	BR Darlington	—	June 1955	June 1968
D3143	13143	—	BR Darlington	—	June 1955	August 1969
D3144	13144	—	BR Darlington	—	June 1955	July 1969
D3145	13145	—	BR Darlington	—	June 1955	April 1972
D3146	13146	—	BR Darlington	—	July 1955	February 1968
D3147	13147	—	BR Darlington	—	July 1955	May 1968
D3148	13148	—	BR Darlington	—	July 1955	March 1968
D3149	13149	—	BR Darlington	—	July 1955	July 1970
D3150	13150	—	BR Darlington	—	July 1955	June 1968
D3151	13151	—	BR Darlington	—	August 1955	December 1967
D3152	13152	—	BR Darlington	—	February 1955	October 1967
D3153	13153	—	BR Darlington	—	February 1955	April 1972
D3154	13154	—	BR Darlington	—	February 1955	June 1968
D3155	13155	—	BR Darlington	—	February 1955	September 1967
D3156	13156	—	BR Darlington	—	March 1955	July 1967
D3157	13157	—	BR Darlington	—	March 1955	October 1967
D3158	13158	—	BR Darlington	—	March 1955	February 1967
D3159	13159	—	BR Darlington	—	August 1955	September 1967
D3160	13160	—	BR Darlington	—	August 1955	November 1967
D3161	13161	—	BR Darlington	—	September 1955	September 1967
D3162	13162	—	BR Darlington	—	September 1955	December 1967
D3163	13163	—	BR Darlington	—	September 1955	September 1967
D3164	13164	—	BR Darlington	—	September 1955	December 1967
D3165	13165	—	BR Darlington	—	October 1955	July 1967
D3166	13166	—	BR Darlington	—	October 1955	July 1967
D3167	13167	08 102	BR Derby	—	9/55*	

BR 1957 No	*Disposal code*	*Disposal details*	*Notes*
D3128	C	BREL Swindon March 1982	
D3129	A	BR Cambridge depot	
D3130	A	BR March depot	
D3131			
D3132	C	BREL Swindon June 1981	
D3133	C	BREL Swindon January 1981	
D3134	C	BREL Doncaster October 1983	
D3135	A	BR Cambridge depot	
D3136	A	BR Lincoln depot	
D3137	C	C. F. Booth, Doncaster c1971	
D3138	C	C. F. Booth, Rotherham, South Yorkshire c1972	
D3139	C	C. F. Booth, Rotherham, South Yorkshire May 1969	
D3140	C	C. F. Booth, Rotherham, South Yorkshire April 1969	
D3141	C	C. F. Booth, Rotherham, South Yorkshire c1972	
D3142	C	C. F. Booth, Rotherham, South Yorkshire March 1969	
D3143	C	G. Cohen, Kettering, Northamptonshire c1970	
D3144	C	Hughes, Bolckow, Blyth c1970	
D3145	C	C. F. Booth, Rotherham, South Yorkshire March 1973	
D3146	C	Hughes, Bolckhow, Blyth c1968	
D3147	C	C. F. Booth, Rotherham, South Yorkshire c1968	
D3148	C	C. F. Booth, Rotherham, South Yorkshire May 1969	
D3149	C	C. F. Booth, Rotherham, South Yorkshire c1971	
D3150	C	C. F. Booth, Rotherham, South Yorkshire April 1969	
D3151	C	Hughes, Bolckow, Blyth c1968	
D3152	C	Slag Reduction, Ickles, Rotherham March 1968	
D3153	C	C. F. Booth, Rotherham, South Yorkshire March 1968	
D3154	C	C. F. Booth, Rotherham, South Yorkshire April 1968	
D3155	C	C. F. Booth, Rotherham, South Yorkshire c1968	
D3156	C	C. F. Booth, Rotherham, South Yorkshire c1967	
D3157	C	Slag Reduction, Ickles, Rotherham c1968	
D3158	C	Slag Reduction, Ickles, Rotherham c1967	
D3159	C	C. F. Booth, Rotherham, South Yorkshire c1968	
D3160	C	Slag Reduction, Ickles, Rotherham c1968	
D3161	C	C. F. Booth, Rotherham, South Yorkshire c1968	
D3162	C	Slag Reduction, Ickles, Rotherham c1968	
D3163	C	C. F. Booth, Rotherham, South Yorkshire c1968	
D3164	C	Slag Reduction, Ickles, Rotherham c1968	
D3165	C	C. F. Booth, Rotherham, South Yorkshire c1967	
D3166	C	C. F. Booth, Rotherham, South Yorkshire c1967	
D3167			Withdrawn June 1984, reinstated June 1984

BR 1957 No	*BR 1948 No*	*TOPS No*	*Built by*	*Works No*	**Period Date introduced*	*Date withdrawn*
D3168	13168	08 103	BR Derby	—	9/55*	September 1983
D3169	13169	08 104	BR Derby	—	9/55*	July 1982
D3170	13170	08 105	BR Derby	—	9/55*	July 1983
D3171	13171	08 106	BR Derby	—	9/55*	January 1982
D3172	13172	—	BR Derby	—	9/55*	May 1972
D3173	13173	08 107	BR Derby	—	10/55*	December 1982
D3174	13174	08 108	BR Derby	—	10/55*	July 1984
D3175	13175	08 109	BR Derby	—	10/55*	April 1981
D3176	13176	08 110	BR Derby	—	10/55*	October 1979
D3177	13177	08 111	BR Derby	—	10/55*	February 1977
D3178	13178	08 112	BR Derby	—	10/55*	July 1982
D3179	13179	08 113	BR Derby	—	10/55*	March 1984
D3180	13180	08 114	BR Derby	—	11/55*	November 1983
D3181	13181	08 115	BR Derby	—	11/55*	July 1984
D3182	13182	08 116	BR Derby	—	October 1955	August 1982
D3183	13183	—	BR Derby	—	September 1955	December 1972
D3184	13184	08 117	BR Derby	—	October 1955	February 1977
D3185	13185	08 118	BR Derby	—	November 1955	March 1980
D3186	13186	08 119	BR Derby	—	November 1955	February 1977
D3187	13187	08 120	BR Derby	—	November 1955	October 1981
D3188	13188	08 121	BR Derby	—	November 1955	June 1984
D3189	13189	08 122	BR Derby	—	November 1955	June 1977
D3190	13190	08 123	BR Derby	—	November 1955	March 1984
D3191	13191	08 124	BR Derby	—	November 1955	March 1981
D3192	13192	08 125	BR Derby	—	November 1955	December 1981
D3193	13193	—	BR Derby	—	November 1955	September 1967
D3194	13194	08 126	BR Derby	—	November 1955	November 1980
D3195	13195	08 127	BR Derby	—	November 1955	August 1980
D3196	13196	08 128	BR Derby	—	December 1955	August 1980
D3197	13197	08 129	BR Derby	—	December 1955	July 1983
D3198	13198	08 130	BR Derby	—	December 1955	December 1982
D3199	13199	08 131	BR Derby	—	December 1955	March 1981
D3200	13200	08 132	BR Derby	—	December 1955	
D3201	13201	08 133	BR Derby	—	December 1955	September 1980
D3202	13202	08 134	BR Derby	—	December 1955	September 1981
D3203	13203	08 135	BR Derby	—	December 1955	February 1977
D3204	13204	08 136	BR Derby	—	December 1955	August 1983
D3205	13205	08 137	BR Derby	—	December 1955	November 1982
D3206	13206	08 138	BR Derby	—	December 1955	January 1978
D3207	13207	08 139	BR Derby	—	January 1956	September 1980
D3208	13208	08 140	BR Derby	—	February 1956	June 1977
D3209	13209	08 141	BR Derby	—	February 1956	
D3210	13210	08 142	BR Derby	—	February 1956	November 1983
D3211	13211	08 143	BR Derby	—	February 1956	March 1976
D3212	13212	08 144	BR Derby	—	February 1956	December 1977
D3213	13213	08 145	BR Derby	—	March 1956	December 1977
D3214	13214	08 146	BR Derby	—	March 1956	December 1980
D3215	13215	08 147	BR Derby	—	March 1956	July 1983
D3216	13216	08 148	BR Derby	—	March 1956	March 1984
D3217	13217	08 149	BR Darlington	—	April 1955	April 1981
D3218	13218	08 150	BR Darlington	—	April 1955	
D3219	13219	08 151	BR Darlington	—	April 1955	January 1979
D3220	13220	08 152	BR Darlington	—	April 1955	July 1980
D3221	13221	08 153	BR Darlington	—	April 1955	December 1982
D3222	13222	08 154	BR Darlington	—	June 1955	October 1979
D3223	13223	08 155	BR Darlington	—	July 1955	January 1979
D3224	13224	08 156	BR Darlington	—	June 1955	January 1979
D3225	13225	08 157	BR Darlington	—	June 1955	April 1977
D3226	13226	08 158	BR Darlington	—	July 1955	March 1979
D3227	13227	08 159	BR Darlington	—	December 1955	
D3228	13228	08 160	BR Darlington	—	December 1955	

BR 1957 No	*Disposal code*	*Disposal details*	*Notes*
D3168	A	BR Derby depot	
D3169	C	BREL Doncaster March 1984	
D3170	A	BR Carlisle depot	
D3171	C	BREL Swindon January 1983	
D3172	C	BREL Derby July 1972	
D3173	C	BREL Doncaster March 1984	
D3174			
D3175	C	BREL Swindon October 1981	
D3176	C	BREL Swindon April 1980	
D3177	D	To Departmental Stock — 968012	
D3178	C	BREL Swindon April 1984	
D3179	S	Powell Duffryn, Annasford	
D3180	A	BREL Swindon	
D3181			
D3182	C	BREL Doncaster July 1983	
D3183	S	NCB Merthyr Vale Colliery, Aberfan	
D3184	D	To Departmental Stock — 968010	
D3185	C	BREL Swindon August 1980	
D3186	D	To Departmental Stock — 968011	
D3187	C	BREL Swindon August 1982	
D3188			
D3189	C	BREL Doncaster December 1977	
D3190	A	BR Crewe depot	
D3191	C	BREL Swindon February 1982	
D3192	C	BREL Swindon February 1984	
D3193	C	BR Workshops Derby September 1967	
D3194	C	BREL Swindon December 1981	
D3195	C	BREL Swindon December 1980	
D3196	C	BREL Swindon February 1984	
D3197	C	BREL Doncaster May 1984	
D3198	A	BREL Swindon	
D3199	C	BREL Swindon August 1981	
D3200			
D3201	S	Sheerness Steel Co	
D3202	A	BREL Swindon	
D3203	C	BREL Swindon May 1977	
D3204	A	BR Neville Hill depot	
D3205	A	BR Lincoln depot	
D3206	C	BREL Swindon May 1978	
D3207	C	BREL Swindon April 1982	
D3208	C	BREL Swindon September 1977	
D3209			
D3210	S	NCB Hickleton	
D3211	C	BREL Swindon February 1977	
D3212	C	BREL Glasgow February 1980	
D3213	C	BREL Glasgow July 1978	
D3214	C	BREL Swindon May 1981	Stored from October 1980
D3215	A	BR Gateshead depot	
D3216	A	BR Gateshead depot	
D3217	C	BREL Swindon February 1984	
D3218			
D3219	C	BREL Eastleigh May 1980	
D3220	C	BREL Swindon November 1980	
D3221	A	BREL Swindon	
D3222	C	BREL Swindon March 1980	
D3223	C	BREL Swindon March 1980	
D3224	C	BREL Swindon February 1980	
D3225	S	Independent Sea Terminals, Swale, Kent	Previously used by Bowaters Ltd
D3226	C	BREL Swindon October 1979	
D3227			
D3228			

BR 1957 No	*BR 1948 No*	*TOPS No*	*Built by*	*Works No*	**Period Date introduced*	*Date withdrawn*
D3229	13229	08 161	BR Darlington	—	December 1955	
D3230	13230	08 162	BR Darlington	—	December 1955	July 1980
D3231	13231	08 163	BR Darlington	—	December 1955	December 1982
D3232	13232	08 164	BR Darlington	—	January 1956	
D3233	13233	08 165	BR Darlington	—	January 1956	July 1980
D3234	13234	08 166	BR Darlington	—	January 1956	July 1982
D3235	13235	08 167	BR Darlington	—	February 1956	September 1977
D3236	13236	08 168	BR Darlington	—	February 1956	
D3237	13237	08 169	BR Darlington	—	February 1956	March 1981
D3238	13238	08 170	BR Darlington	—	February 1956	
D3239	13239	08 171	BR Darlington	—	February 1956	April 1983
D3240	13240	08 172	BR Darlington	—	February 1956	
D3241	13241	08 173	BR Darlington	—	March 1956	May 1978
D3242	13242	08 174	BR Darlington	—	March 1956	August 1981
D3243	13243	08 175	BR Darlington	—	March 1956	December 1978
D3244	13244	08 176	BR Darlington	—	March 1956	
D3245	13245	08 177	BR Derby	—	May 1956	
D3246	13246	08 178	BR Derby	—	May 1956	May 1982
D3247	13247	08 179	BR Derby	—	May 1956	June 1975
D3248	13248	08 180	BR Derby	—	May 1956	May 1981
D3249	13249	08 181	BR Derby	—	May 1956	July 1982
D3250	13250	08 182	BR Derby	—	June 1956	March 1981
D3251	13251	08 183	BR Derby	—	June 1956	March 1984
D3252	13252	08 184	BR Derby	—	June 1956	June 1981
D3253	13253	08 185	BR Derby	—	June 1956	February 1982
D3254	13254	08 186	BR Derby	—	June 1956	
D3255	13255	—	BR Derby	—	June 1956	December 1972
D3256	13256	08 187	BR Derby	—	June 1956	July 1983
D3257	13257	08 188	BR Derby	—	June 1956	April 1983
D3258	13258	08 189	BR Derby	—	June 1956	December 1981
D3259	13259	08 190	BR Derby	—	June 1956	October 1980
D3260	13260	08 191	BR Derby	—	June 1956	
D3261	13261	—	BR Derby	—	June 1956	December 1972
D3262	13262	08 192	BR Derby	—	July 1956	July 1982
D3263	13263	08 193	BR Derby	—	August 1956	July 1983
D3264	13264	08 194	BR Derby	—	August 1956	November 1980
D3265	13265	08 195	BR Derby	—	August 1956	September 1983
D3266	13266	08 196	BR Derby	—	August 1956	October 1983
D3267	13267	08 197	BR Derby	—	August 1956	April 1982
D3268	13268	08 198	BR Derby	—	September 1956	December 1980
D3269	13269	08 199	BR Derby	—	September 1956	January 1983
D3270	13270	08 200	BR Derby	—	September 1956	
D3271	13271	08 201	BR Derby	—	September 1956	December 1982
D3272	13272	08 202	BR Derby	—	October 1956	
D3273	13273	08 203	BR Derby	—	October 1956	July 1984
D3274	13274	08 204	BR Derby	—	October 1956	August 1983
D3275	13275	08 205	BR Derby	—	October 1956	November 1983
D3276	13276	08 206	BR Derby	—	October 1956	
D3277	13277	08 207	BR Derby	—	October 1956	September 1980
D3278	13278	08 208	BR Derby	—	November 1956	
D3279	13279	08 209	BR Derby	—	November 1956	February 1983
D3280	13280	08 210	BR Derby	—	November 1956	
D3281	13281	08 211	BR Derby	—	November 1956	
D3282	13282	08 212	BR Derby	—	November 1956	September 1981
D3283	13283	08 213	BR Derby	—	November 1956	November 1980
D3284	13284	08 214	BR Derby	—	November 1956	February 1984
D3285	13285	08 215	BR Derby	—	November 1956	September 1982
D3286	13286	08 216	BR Derby	—	November 1956	November 1980
D3287	13287	08 217	BR Derby	—	November 1956	April 1982
D3288	13288	08 218	BR Derby	—	13/56*	July 1980

BR 1957 No	*Disposal code*	*Disposal details*	*Notes*
D3229			
D3230	C	BREL Swindon January 1981	
D3231	C	BREL Doncaster February 1984	
D3232			
D3233	C	BREL Swindon October 1980	
D3234	C	BREL Doncaster October 1983	
D3235	C	BREL Glasgow July 1979	
D3236			
D3237	C	BREL Swindon October 1981	
D3238			
D3239	C	BREL Doncaster September 1983	
D3240			
D3241	D	Departmental Service at Polmadie	As No PO1
D3242	C	BREL Swindon March 1982	
D3243	A	BR Townhill Junction depot	
D3244			
D3245			
D3246	C	BREL Swindon March 1984	
D3247	C	BREL Swindon August 1976	
D3248	C	BREL Swindon August 1981	First withdrawn January 1979, reinstated February 1979
D3249	A	BREL Swindon	
D3250	C	BREL Swindon March 1982	
D3251	A	BR Lincoln depot	
D3252	C	BREL Swindon April 1982	
D3253	C	BREL Swindon October 1982	
D3254			
D3255	S	NCB Mardy Colliery	Also used at other NCB South Wales sites
D3256	A	BREL Swindon	
D3257	A	BREL Swindon	
D3258	C	BREL Swindon March 1984	
D3259	C	BREL Swindon December 1980	
D3260			
D3261	S	NCB Tower Colliery, Hirwaun, Glamorgan	
D3262	A	BREL Swindon	
D3263	A	BREL Swindon	
D3264	C	BREL Swindon November 1983	
D3265	A	BREL Swindon	
D3266	A	BR Grangemouth depot	Stored July 1983
D3267	C	BREL Doncaster February 1984	
D3268	C	BREL Swindon November 1981	Stored from July 1980
D3269	C	BREL Doncaster July 1984	
D3270			
D3271	C	BREL Doncaster May 1984	
D3272			
D3273			
D3274	A	BREL Swindon	
D3275	A	BR Norwich depot	
D3276	A		
D3277	C	BREL Swindon April 1983	
D3278			
D3279	C	BREL Doncaster August 1983	
D3280	C	BREL Doncaster August 1983	
D3281			
D3282	C	BREL Swindon February 1982	
D3283	C	BREL Swindon August 1981	
D3284			
D3285	C	BREL Doncaster May 1983	
D3286	S	Sheerness Steel Co	
D3287	C	BREL Doncaster May 1983	
D3288	C	BREL Swindon August 1981	

BR 1957 No	*BR 1948 No*	*TOPS No*	*Built by*	*Works No*	**Period Date introduced*	*Date withdrawn*
D3289	13289	08 219	BR Derby	—	13/56*	March 1983
D3290	13290	08 220	BR Derby	—	13/56*	
D3291	13291	08 221	BR Derby	—	13/56*	March 1981
D3292	13292	08 222	BR Derby	—	13/56*	
D3293	13293	08 223	BR Derby	—	13/56*	June 1979
D3294	13294	08 224	BR Derby	—	13/56*	
D3295	13295	08 225	BR Derby	—	January 1957	
D3296	13296	08 226	BR Derby	—	January 1957	
D3297	13297	08 227	BR Derby	—	February 1957	October 1983
D3298	13298	08 228	BR Darlington	—	March 1956	
D3299	13299	08 229	BR Darlington	—	April 1956	December 1977
D3300	13300	08 230	BR Darlington	—	April 1956	December 1980
D3301	13301	08 231	BR Darlington	—	April 1956	June 1981
D3302	13302	08 232	BR Darlington	—	April 1956	September 1982
D3303	13303	08 233	BR Darlington	—	April 1956	May 1981
D3304	13304	08 234	BR Darlington	—	April 1956	September 1982
D3305	13305	08 235	BR Darlington	—	May 1956	July 1983
D3306	13306	08 236	BR Darlington	—	May 1956	September 1975
D3307	13307	08 237	BR Darlington	—	May 1956	
D3308	13308	08 238	BR Darlington	—	May 1956	March 1984
D3309	13309	08 239	BR Darlington	—	May 1956	July 1984
D3310	13310	08 240	BR Darlington	—	June 1956	July 1982
D3311	13311	08 241	BR Darlington	—	June 1956	October 1981
D3312	13312	08 242	BR Darlington	—	June 1956	
D3313	13313	08 243	BR Darlington	—	June 1956	
D3314	13314	08 244	BR Darlington	—	July 1956	
D3315	13315	08 245	BR Darlington	—	July 1956	May 1984
D3316	13316	08 246	BR Darlington	—	September 1956	August 1982
D3317	13317	08 247	BR Darlington	—	September 1956	March 1981
D3318	13318	08 248	BR Darlington	—	October 1956	
D3319	13319	08 249	BR Darlington	—	October 1956	
D3320	13320	08 250	BR Darlington	—	October 1956	
D3321	13321	08 251	BR Darlington	—	October 1956	September 1980
D3322	13322	08 252	BR Darlington	—	November 1956	August 1981
D3323	13323	08 253	BR Darlington	—	November 1956	
D3324	13324	08 254	BR Darlington	—	November 1956	
D3325	13325	08 255	BR Darlington	—	November 1956	
D3326	13326	08 256	BR Darlington	—	November 1956	February 1984
D3327	13327	08 257	BR Darlington	—	December 1956	
D3328	13328	08 258	BR Darlington	—	December 1956	
D3329	13329	08 259	BR Darlington	—	December 1956	March 1984
D3330	13330	08 260	BR Darlington	—	December 1956	August 1983
D3331	13331	08 261	BR Darlington	—	December 1956	December 1983
D3332	13332	08 262	BR Darlington	—	January 1957	January 1984
D3333	13333	08 263	BR Darlington	—	January 1957	March 1984
D3334	13334	08 264	BR Darlington	—	January 1957	July 1984
D3335	13335	08 265	BR Darlington	—	January 1957	December 1981
D3336	13336	08 266	BR Darlington	—	February 1957	
D3337	13337	08 267	BR Derby	—	March 1957	December 1977
D3338	13338	08 268	BR Derby	—	March 1957	
D3339	13339	08 269	BR Derby	—	March 1957	July 1984
D3340	13340	08 270	BR Derby	—	March 1957	December 1982
D3341	13341	08 271	BR Derby	—	April 1957	September 1981
D3342	13342	08 272	BR Derby	—	April 1957	January 1984
D3343	13343	08 273	BR Derby	—	April 1957	December 1982
D3344	13344	08 274	BR Derby	—	April 1957	
D3345	13345	08 275	BR Derby	—	April 1957	February 1983
D3346	13346	08 276	BR Derby	—	April 1957	June 1977
D3347	13347	08 277	BR Derby	—	May 1957	November 1981

BR 1957 No	*Disposal code*	*Disposal details*	*Notes*
D3289	C	BREL Doncaster August 1983	
D3290			
D3291	C	BREL Swindon November 1981	
D3292			Stored September 1983
D3293	C	BREL Swindon November 1980	
D3294			
D3295			
D3296			
D3297	A	BR Townhill Junction depot	Stored July 1983
D3298			
D3299	C	BREL Doncaster December 1978	
D3300	C	BREL Swindon May 1983	Stored from September 1980
D3301	C	BREL Swindon October 1981	
D3302	C	BREL Doncaster June 1983	
D3303	C	BR Stratford depot by G. Morris Co January 1982	
D3304	C	BREL Swindon December 1982	
D3305	A	BR Bletchley depot	
D3306	C	BREL Swindon September 1976	
D3307			
D3308			
D3309			
D3310	A	BREL Swindon	
D3311	C	BREL Swindon May 1982	
D3312			
D3313			
D3314			
D3315			
D3316	A	BREL Glasgow	
D3317	C	BREL Swindon	As PO1 at Polmadie from August 1977 to May 1978
D3318			
D3319			
D3320			
D3321	C	BREL Swindon January 1981	
D3322	C	BREL Swindon March 1982	
D3323			
D3324			
D3325			
D3326	A	BR Stratford depot	
D3327			
D3328			
D3329	A	BR Landore depot	
D3330	C	BREL Doncaster October 1983	
D3331	A	BREL Swindon	
D3332	A	BREL Swindon	Withdrawn October 1983, reinstated October 1983
D3333	A	BR Gateshead depot	
D3334			
D3335	A	BREL Swindon	
D3336			
D3337	D	To Departmental Stock — 97801	
D3338			
D3339			
D3340	C	BREL Doncaster January 1984	
D3341	C	BREL Swindon April 1983	
D3342	C	BREL Doncaster February 1984	
D3343	C	BREL Doncaster March 1984	
D3344			
D3345	C	BREL Doncaster July 1984	
D3346	C	BREL Doncaster November 1977	
D3347	C	BREL Doncaster July 1983	

BR 1957 No	*BR 1948 No*	*TOPS No*	*Built by*	*Works No*	**Period Date introduced*	*Date withdrawn*
D3348	13348	08 278	BR Derby	—	May 1957	June 1977
D3349	13349	08 279	BR Derby	—	May 1957	April 1981
D3350	13350	08 280	BR Derby	—	May 1957	October 1980
D3351	13351	08 281	BR Derby	—	May 1957	December 1980
D3352	13352	08 282	BR Derby	—	June 1957	November 1980
D3353	13353	08 283	BR Derby	—	June 1957	
D3354	13354	08 284	BR Derby	—	June 1957	
D3355	13355	08 285	BR Derby	—	June 1957	
D3356	13356	08 286	BR Derby	—	June 1957	April 1982
D3357	13357	08 287	BR Derby	—	June 1957	February 1983
D3358	—	08 288	BR Derby	—	June 1957	January 1983
D3359	—	08 289	BR Derby	—	June 1957	
D3360	—	08 290	BR Derby	—	July 1957	April 1982
D3361	—	08 291	BR Derby	—	July 1957	January 1983
D3362	13362	08 292	BR Derby	—	May 1957	May 1984
D3363	13363	08 293	BR Derby	—	May 1957	
D3364	13364	08 294	BR Derby	—	May 1957	November 1980
D3365	13365	08 295	BR Derby	—	May 1957	
D3366	13366	08 296	BR Derby	—	May 1957	
D3367	—	08 297	BR Derby	—	7/57*	
D3368	—	08 298	BR Derby	—	7/57*	March 1981
D3369	—	08 299	BR Derby	—	8/57*	July 1981
D3370	—	08 300	BR Derby	—	8/57*	July 1983
D3371	—	08 301	BR Derby	—	8/57*	December 1981
D3372	—	08 302	BR Derby	—	8/57*	June 1981
D3373	—	08 303	BR Derby	—	9/57*	December 1981
D3374	—	08 304	BR Derby	—	8/57*	
D3375	—	08 305	BR Derby	—	August 1957	
D3376	—	08 306	BR Derby	—	August 1957	December 1977
D3377	—	08 307	BR Derby	—	August 1957	December 1977
D3378	—	08 308	BR Derby	—	August 1957	
D3379	—	08 309	BR Derby	—	September 1957	
D3380	—	08 310	BR Derby	—	September 1957	September 1977
D3381	—	08 311	BR Derby	—	September 1957	December 1982
D3382	—	08 312	BR Derby	—	September 1957	May 1983
D3383	—	08 313	BR Derby	—	September 1957	May 1982
D3384	—	08 314	BR Derby	—	September 1957	February 1981
D3385	—	08 315	BR Derby	—	September 1957	February 1979
D3386	—	08 316	BR Derby	—	September 1957	March 1976
D3387	—	08 317	BR Derby	—	October 1957	October 1982
D3388	—	08 318	BR Derby	—	October 1957	October 1976
D3389	—	08 319	BR Derby	—	October 1957	April 1983
D3390	—	08 320	BR Derby	—	October 1957	December 1982
D3391	—	08 321	BR Derby	—	October 1957	May 1984
D3392	—	08 322	BR Derby	—	October 1957	September 1983
D3393	—	08 323	BR Derby	—	October 1957	July 1981
D3394	—	08 324	BR Derby	—	October 1957	
D3395	—	08 325	BR Derby	—	November 1957	July 1984
D3396	—	08 326	BR Derby	—	November 1957	October 1983
D3397	—	08 327	BR Derby	—	November 1957	February 1983
D3398	—	08 328	BR Derby	—	November 1957	December 1981
D3399	—	08 329	BR Derby	—	November 1957	July 1984
D3400	—	08 330	BR Derby	—	November 1957	
D3401	—	08 331	BR Derby	—	November 1957	
D3402	—	08 332	BR Derby	—	November 1957	
D3403	—	08 333	BR Derby	—	November 1957	December 1982
D3404	—	08 334	BR Derby	—	December 1957	
D3405	—	08 335	BR Derby	—	December 1957	
D3406	—	08 336	BR Derby	—	December 1957	April 1981

BR 1957 No	*Disposal code*	*Disposal details*	*Notes*
D3348	C	BREL Glasgow October 1977	
D3349	C	BREL Swindon April 1983	
D3350	C	BREL Swindon March 1982	
D3351	A	BREL Swindon	
D3352	C	BREL Swindon August 1981	
D3353			
D3354			
D3355			
D3356	A	BR Polmadie depot	
D3357	C	BREL Doncaster September 1983	
D3358	P	Mid-Hants Railway	
D3359			
D3360	C	BREL Swindon March 1984	
D3361	C	BREL Doncaster January 1984	
D3362	S	Carntyne Transport, Glasgow	Stored October 1983, reinstated December 1983
D3363			
D3364	C	BREL Swindon December 1981	
D3365			
D3366			Stored September 1983, reinstated December 1983
D3367			Stored September 1983
D3368	C	BREL Swindon July 1981	
D3369	C	BREL Swindon October 1982	
D3370	C	BREL Doncaster April 1984	
D3371	A	BREL Swindon	
D3372	C	BREL Swindon March 1982	
D3373	A	BREL Swindon	
D3374			Stored September 1983
D3375			
D3376	C	BREL Swindon December 1977	
D3377	C	BREL Swindon June 1978	
D3378			
D3379			
D3380	C	BREL Doncaster October 1978	
D3381	C	BREL Doncaster February 1984	
D3382	A	BR Motherwell depot	
D3383	C	BREL Doncaster February 1983	
D3384	C	BREL Glasgow September 1981	Stored from October 1980
D3385	C	BREL Doncaster November 1979	
D3386	C	BREL Swindon March 1977	
D3387	C	BREL Doncaster October 1983	
D3388	C	BREL Eastleigh April 1977	
D3389	A	BR Motherwell depot	
D3390	A	BR Toton depot	Sold to industry
D3391	A	BR Motherwell depot	
D3392	A	BREL Swindon	
D3393	C	BREL Swindon February 1982	
D3394			
D3395			
D3396	A	BR Motherwell depot	Stored July 1983
D3397	A	BR Bescot depot	
D3398	A	BREL Swindon	
D3399			
D3400			
D3401			
D3402			
D3403	A	BR Derby depot	
D3404			
D3405			
D3406	C	BREL Swindon March 1982	

BR 1957 No	*BR 1948 No*	*TOPS No*	*Built by*	*Works No*	*Date introduced*	*Date withdrawn*
D3407	—	08 337	BR Derby	—	December 1957	
D3408	—	08 338	BR Derby	—	January 1958	
D3409	—	08 339	BR Derby	—	January 1958	
D3410	—	08 340	BR Derby	—	January 1958	August 1981
D3411	—	08 341	BR Derby	—	January 1958	October 1983
D3412	—	08 342	BR Derby	—	January 1958	July 1982
D3413	—	08 343	BR Derby	—	January 1958	October 1983
D3414	—	08 344	BR Derby	—	February 1958	May 1984
D3415	—	08 345	BR Derby	—	February 1958	October 1983
D3416	—	08 346	BR Derby	—	February 1958	March 1984
D3417	—	08 347	BR Derby	—	February 1958	October 1983
D3418	—	08 348	BR Derby	—	February 1958	July 1982
D3419	—	08 349	BR Crewe	—	November 1957	July 1983
D3420	—	08 350	BR Crewe	—	December 1957	January 1984
D3421	—	08 351	BR Crewe	—	December 1957	January 1984
D3422	—	08 352	BR Crewe	—	December 1957	July 1983
D3423	—	08 353	BR Crewe	—	January 1958	July 1981
D3424	—	08 354	BR Crewe	—	February 1958	
D3425	—	08 355	BR Crewe	—	February 1958	April 1983
D3426	—	08 356	BR Crewe	—	February 1958	November 1982
D3427	—	08 357	BR Crewe	—	March 1958	September 1977
D3428	—	08 358	BR Crewe	—	March 1958	October 1977
D3429	—	08 359	BR Crewe	—	March 1958	January 1984
D3430	—	08 360	BR Crewe	—	April 1958	January 1983
D3431	—	08 361	BR Crewe	—	April 1958	
D3432	—	08 362	BR Crewe	—	April 1958	March 1982
D3433	—	08 363	BR Crewe	—	April 1958	August 1982
D3434	—	08 364	BR Crewe	—	May 1958	January 1983
D3435	—	08 365	BR Crewe	—	May 1958	September 1980
D3436	—	08 366	BR Crewe	—	May 1958	December 1980
D3437	—	08 367	BR Crewe	—	June 1958	
D3438	—	08 368	BR Crewe	—	June 1958	December 1980
D3439	—	—	BR Darlington	—	September 1957	September 1968
D3440	—	—	BR Darlington	—	September 1957	December 1968
D3441	—	—	BR Darlington	—	October 1957	September 1968
D3442	—	—	BR Darlington	—	October 1957	July 1968
D3443	—	—	BR Darlington	—	October 1957	December 1968
D3444	—	—	BR Darlington	—	October 1957	December 1968
D3445	—	—	BR Darlington	—	October 1957	November 1968
D3446	—	—	BR Darlington	—	October 1957	June 1968
D3447	—	—	BR Darlington	—	October 1957	March 1968
D3448	—	—	BR Darlington	—	November 1957	June 1968
D3449	—	—	BR Darlington	—	November 1957	December 1967
D3450	—	—	BR Darlington	—	November 1957	July 1968
D3451	—	—	BR Darlington	—	November 1957	July 1968
D3452	—	—	BR Darlington	—	November 1957	July 1968
D3453	—	—	BR Darlington	—	November 1957	July 1968

BR 1957 No	*Disposal code*	*Disposal details*	*Notes*
D3407			Stored September 1983
D3408			
D3409			
D3410	C	BREL Swindon March 1982	
D3411	A	BR Townhill Junction depot	Stored July 1983
D3412	C	BREL Swindon November 1983	
D3413	A	BR Eastfield depot	Stored July 1983
D3414			
D3415	A	BR Ayr depot	Stored July 1983
D3416	A	BR Townhill depot	
D3417	A	BR Grangemouth depot	Stored July 1983
D3418	A	BR Eastfield depot	
D3419	A	BREL Swindon	
D3420	A	BREL Swindon	
D3421	A	BREL Swindon	
D3422	A	BREL Swindon	
D3423	C	BREL Swindon March 1982	
D3424			
D3425	C	BREL Doncaster February 1984	
D3426	C	BREL Swindon December 1983	
D3427	C	BREL Swindon April 1979	
D3428	C	BREL Doncaster November 1977	
D3429	A	BREL Swindon	
D3430	A	BREL Swindon	
D3431			
D3432	C	BREL Swindon April 1983	
D3433	C	BREL Swindon April 1983	
D3434	C	BREL Swindon November 1983	Withdrawn December 1981, reinstated January 1982
D3435	C	BREL Swindon April 1981	
D3436	C	BREL Swindon February 1982	
D3437			
D3438	A	BREL Swindon	
D3439	C	Garnham, Harris & Elton Ltd, Chesterfield January 1969	
D3440	C	G. Cohen, Kettering, Northamptonshire c1969	
D3441	C	G. Cohen, Kettering, Northamptonshire March 1969	
D3442	C	C. F. Booth, Rotherham, South Yorkshire c1969	
D3443	C	C. F. Booth, Rotherham, South Yorkshire c1969	
D3444	C	G. Cohen, Kettering, Northamptonshire November 1969	
D3445	C	Cox & Dank, Park Royal c1969	
D3446	C	Steelbreaking & Dismantling, Chesterfield c1969	
D3447	C	C. F. Booth, Rotherham, South Yorkshire c1969	
D3448	C	Steelbreaking & Dismantling, Chesterfield September 1969	
D3449	C	C. F. Booth, Rotherham, South Yorkshire c1968	
D3450	C	C. F. Booth, Rotherham, South Yorkshire June 1972	
D3451	C	C. F. Booth, Rotherham, South Yorkshire June 1969	
D3452	S	English China Clay Ltd, Fowey as 73601	
D3453	C	C. F. Booth, Rotherham, South Yorkshire c1969	

BR 1957 No	*BR 1948 No*	*TOPS No*	*Built by*	*Works No*	*Date introduced*	*Date withdrawn*
D3454	—	08 369	BR Darlington	—	May 1957	
D3455	—	08 370	BR Darlington	—	May 1957	March 1984
D3456	—	08 371	BR Darlington	—	May 1957	October 1983
D3457	—	08 372	BR Darlington	—	June 1957	
D3458	—	08 373	BR Darlington	—	June 1957	
D3459	—	08 374	BR Darlington	—	June 1957	December 1982
D3460	—	08 375	BR Darlington	—	June 1957	
D3461	—	08 376	BR Darlington	—	June 1957	July 1983
D3462	—	08 377	BR Darlington	—	June 1957	June 1983
D3463	—	08 378	BR Darlington	—	July 1957	July 1981
D3464	—	08 379	BR Darlington	—	July 1957	December 1980
D3465	—	08 380	BR Darlington	—	July 1957	August 1982
D3466	—	08 381	BR Darlington	—	July 1957	December 1982
D3467	—	08 382	BR Darlington	—	August 1957	
D3468	—	08 383	BR Darlington	—	August 1957	
D3469	—	08 384	BR Darlington	—	August 1957	
D3470	—	08 385	BR Darlington	—	August 1957	
D3471	—	08 386	BR Darlington	—	August 1957	
D3472	—	08 387	BR Darlington	—	August 1957	May 1982
D3473	—	—	BR Darlington	—	December 1957	August 1968
D3474	—	—	BR Darlington	—	December 1957	June 1968
D3475	—	—	BR Darlington	—	December 1957	July 1968
D3476	—	—	BR Darlington	—	December 1957	June 1968
D3477	—	—	BR Darlington	—	December 1957	July 1968
D3478	—	—	BR Darlington	—	January 1958	June 1968
D3479	—	—	BR Darlington	—	January 1958	April 1969
D3480	—	—	BR Darlington	—	January 1958	August 1968
D3481	—	—	BR Darlington	—	February 1958	December 1968
D3482	—	—	BR Darlington	—	February 1958	July 1968
D3483	—	—	BR Darlington	—	March 1958	March 1969
D3484	—	—	BR Darlington	—	March 1958	August 1968
D3485	—	—	BR Darlington	—	March 1958	December 1968
D3486	—	—	BR Darlington	—	March 1958	November 1970
D3487	—	—	BR Darlington	—	March 1958	July 1968
D3488	—	—	BR Darlington	—	March 1958	December 1968
D3489	—	—	BR Darlington	—	April 1958	April 1968
D3490	—	—	BR Darlington	—	April 1958	July 1968
D3491	—	—	BR Darlington	—	April 1958	December 1968
D3492	—	—	BR Darlington	—	April 1958	June 1969
D3493	—	—	BR Darlington	—	April 1958	July 1968

BR 1957 No	*Disposal code*	*Disposal details*	*Notes*
D3454			
D3455	A	BR Gateshead depot	
D3456	A	BR Healey Mills depot	
D3457			
D3458			
D3459	A	BR Bletchley depot	
D3460			Stored April 1983, reinstated October 1983
D3461	C	BREL Doncaster April 1984	
D3462	A	BREL Swindon	
D3463	C	BREL Swindon March 1982	
D3464	C	BREL Swindon March 1981	
D3465	C	BREL Swindon May 1983	
D3466	C	BREL Doncaster May 1984	
D3467			
D3468			
D3469			Stored September 1983
D3470			Stored September 1983, reinstated October 1983
D3471			
D3472	A	BREL Swindon	
D3473	C	C. F. Booth, Rotherham, South Yorkshire c1969	
D3474	C	C. F. Booth, Rotherham, South Yorkshire c1969	
D3475	C	C. F. Booth, Rotherham, South Yorkshire c1969	
D3476	S	English China Clay Ltd, Fowey as 73603	
D3477	C	G. Cohen, Kettering, Northamptonshire January 1969	
D3478	C	C. F. Booth, Rotherham, South Yorkshire c1969	
D3479	C	G. Cohen, Kettering, Northamptonshire July 1969	
D3480	C	Garnham, Harris & Elton Ltd, Chesterfield January 1969	
D3481	C	C. F. Booth, Rotherham, South Yorkshire c1969	
D3482	C	C. F. Booth, Rotherham, South Yorkshire c1969	
D3483	C	G. Cohen, Kettering, Northamptonshire c1970	
D3484	C	Garnham, Harris & Elton Ltd, Chesterfield January 1969	
D3485	C	G. Cohen, Kettering, Northamptonshire July 1969	
D3486	C	C. F. Booth, Rotherham, South Yorkshire August 1971	
D3487	C	C. F. Booth, Rotherham, South Yorkshire June 1969	
D3488	C	G. Cohen, Kettering, Northamptonshire November 1969	
D3489	S	Felixstowe Dock & Railway Co, Felixstowe	*Colonel Tomline*
D3490	C	C. F. Booth, Rotherham, South Yorkshire c1969	
D3491	C	G. Cohen, Kettering, Northamptonshire November 1969	
D3492	C	G. Cohen, Kettering, Northamptonshire c1970	
D3493	C	C. F. Booth, Rotherham, South Yorkshire c1969	

BR 1957 No	*BR 1948 No*	*TOPS No*	*Built by*	*Works No*	*Date introduced*	*Date withdrawn*
D3494	—	—	BR Darlington	—	May 1958	May 1968
D3495	—	—	BR Darlington	—	May 1958	July 1968
D3496	—	—	BR Darlington	—	June 1958	November 1967
D3497	—	—	BR Doncaster	—	December 1957	April 1968
D3498	—	—	BR Doncaster	—	December 1957	June 1968
D3499	—	—	BR Doncaster	—	December 1957	January 1968
D3500	—	—	BR Doncaster	—	January 1958	January 1968
D3501	—	—	BR Doncaster	—	January 1958	July 1968
D3502	—	—	BR Doncaster	—	January 1958	February 1968
D3503	—	08 388	BR Derby	—	April 1958	
D3504	—	08 389	BR Derby	—	April 1958	
D3505	—	08 390	BR Derby	—	April 1958	
D3506	—	08 391	BR Derby	—	April 1958	
D3507	—	08 392	BR Derby	—	April 1958	February 1984
D3508	—	08 393	BR Derby	—	April 1958	
D3509	—	08 394	BR Derby	—	May 1958	
D3510	—	08 395	BR Derby	—	May 1958	
D3511	—	08 396	BR Derby	—	May 1958	
D3512	—	08 397	BR Derby	—	May 1958	
D3513	—	08 398	BR Derby	—	May 1958	
D3514	—	08 399	BR Derby	—	May 1958	
D3515	—	08 400	BR Derby	—	May 1958	
D3516	—	08 401	BR Derby	—	May 1958	
D3517	—	08 402	BR Derby	—	May 1958	
D3518	—	08 403	BR Derby	—	May 1958	
D3519	—	08 404	BR Derby	—	May 1958	June 1978
D3520	—	08 405	BR Derby	—	June 1958	
D3521	—	08 406	BR Derby	—	June 1958	
D3522	—	08 407	BR Derby	—	June 1958	
D3523	—	08 408	BR Derby	—	June 1958	
D3524	—	08 409	BR Derby	—	June 1958	
D3525	—	08 410	BR Derby	—	June 1958	
D3526	—	08 411	BR Derby	—	June 1958	
D3527	—	08 412	BR Derby	—	June 1958	
D3528	—	08 413	BR Derby	—	June 1958	
D3529	—	08 414	BR Derby	—	June 1958	
D3530	—	08 415	BR Derby	—	July 1958	
D3531	—	08 416	BR Derby	—	July 1958	
D3532	—	08 417	BR Derby	—	July 1958	
D3533	—	08 418	BR Derby	—	July 1958	
D3534	—	08 419	BR Derby	—	July 1958	
D3535	—	08 420	BR Derby	—	July 1958	
D3536	—	08 421	BR Derby	—	August 1958	
D3537	—	08 422	BR Derby	—	August 1958	
D3538	—	08 423	BR Derby	—	August 1958	
D3539	—	08 424	BR Derby	—	August 1958	
D3540	—	08 425	BR Derby	—	August 1958	
D3541	—	08 426	BR Derby	—	August 1958	July 1976
D3542	—	08 427	BR Derby	—	August 1958	
D3543	—	08 428	BR Derby	—	August 1958	
D3544	—	08 429	BR Derby	—	September 1958	September 1983

BR 1957 No	*Disposal code*	*Disposal details*	*Notes*
D3494	C	G. Cohen, Kettering, Northamptonshire March 1969	
D3495	C	C. F. Booth, Rotherham, South Yorkshire c1969	
D3496	C	BR Workshops, Doncaster c1968	
D3497	S	English China Clay Ltd, Fowey as 73602	Spares loco
D3498	C	C. F. Booth, Rotherham, South Yorkshire c1969	
D3499	C	C. F. Booth, Rotherham, South Yorkshire c1969	
D3500	C	J. Cashmore, Great Bridge, Tipton c1968	
D3501	C	C. F. Booth, Rotherham, South Yorkshire c1969	
D3502	C	J. Cashmore, Great Bridge, Tipton c1968	
D3503			
D3504			
D3505			
D3506			
D3507			Withdrawn October 1980, reinstated October 1980
D3508			
D3509			
D3510			
D3511			
D3512			
D3513			
D3514			
D3515			
D3516			
D3517			
D3518			Withdrawn October 1981, reinstated (stored) January 1983
D3519	C	BREL Doncaster January 1979	
D3520			
D3521			
D3522			
D3523			
D3524			
D3525			
D3526			
D3527			
D3528			
D3529			
D3530			Withdrawn July 1981, reinstated (stored) January 1983
D3531			
D3532			Withdrawn March 1982, reinstated June 1982
D3533			
D3534			Withdrawn December 1981, reinstated April 1983
D3535			
D3536			
D3537			
D3538			
D3539			
D3540			Stored January 1984
D3541	C	BREL Doncaster May 1977	
D3542			
D3543			
D3544	C	BREL Doncaster November 1983	

BR 1957 No	BR 1948 No	TOPS No	Built by	Works No	*Period Date introduced	Date withdrawn
D3545	—	08 430	BR Derby	—	September 1958	
D3546	—	08 431	BR Derby	—	September 1958	
D3547	—	08 432	BR Derby	—	September 1958	October 1983
D3548	—	08 433	BR Derby	—	September 1958	
D3549	—	08 434	BR Derby	—	September 1958	
D3550	—	08 435	BR Derby	—	October 1958	November 1980
D3551	—	08 436	BR Derby	—	October 1958	
D3552	—	08 437	BR Derby	—	October 1958	
D3553	—	08 438	BR Derby	—	October 1958	
D3554	—	08 439	BR Derby	—	October 1958	
D3555	—	08 440	BR Derby	—	October 1958	
D3556	—	08 441	BR Derby	—	October 1958	
D3557	—	08 442	BR Derby	—	November 1958	
D3558	—	08 443	BR Derby	—	November 1958	
D3559	—	08 444	BR Derby	—	November 1958	
D3560	—	08 445	BR Derby	—	November 1958	
D3561	—	08 446	BR Derby	—	November 1958	
D3562	—	08 447	BR Derby	—	November 1958	
D3563	—	08 448	BR Derby	—	November 1958	
D3564	—	08 449	BR Derby	—	November 1958	
D3565	—	08 450	BR Derby	—	13/58*	
D3566	—	08 451	BR Derby	—	13/58*	
D3567	—	08 452	BR Derby	—	13/58*	
D3568	—	08 453	BR Derby	—	13/58*	October 1980
D3569	—	08 454	BR Derby	—	13/58*	
D3570	—	08 455	BR Derby	—	13/58*	
D3571	—	08 456	BR Derby	—	1/59*	
D3572	—	08 457	BR Derby	—	1/59*	
D3573	—	08 458	BR Crewe	—	7/58*	
D3574	—	08 459	BR Crewe	—	8/58*	
D3575	—	08 460	BR Crewe	—	9/58*	
D3576	—	08 461	BR Crewe	—	9/58*	
D3577	—	08 462	BR Crewe	—	9/58*	
D3578	—	08 463	BR Crewe	—	10/58*	
D3579	—	08 464	BR Crewe	—	10/58*	
D3580	—	08 465	BR Crewe	—	10/58*	
D3581	—	08 466	BR Crewe	—	11/58*	
D3582	—	08 467	BR Crewe	—	11/58*	November 1981
D3583	—	08 468	BR Crewe	—	12/58*	
D3584	—	08 469	BR Crewe	—	12/58*	December 1981
D3585	—	08 470	BR Crewe	—	12/58*	
D3586	—	08 471	BR Crewe	—	12/58*	
D3587	—	08 472	BR Crewe	—	12/58*	
D3588	—	08 473	BR Crewe	—	12/58*	
D3589	—	08 474	BR Crewe	—	13/58*	
D3590	—	08 475	BR Crewe	—	13/58*	
D3591	—	08 476	BR Crewe	—	13/58*	
D3592	—	08 477	BR Crewe	—	1/59*	
D3593	—	08 478	BR Horwich	—	August 1958	
D3594	—	08 479	BR Horwich	—	September 1958	
D3595	—	08 480	BR Horwich	—	September 1958	
D3596	—	08 481	BR Horwich	—	September 1958	
D3597	—	08 482	BR Horwich	—	September 1958	
D3598	—	08 483	BR Horwich	—	October 1958	
D3599	—	08 484	BR Horwich	—	October 1958	

BR 1957 No	Disposal code	Disposal details	Notes
D3545			Stored July 1984
D3546			
D3547	C	BREL Doncaster February 1984	
D3548			
D3549			
D3550	C	BREL Swindon May 1983	
D3551			
D3552			
D3553			
D3554			
D3555			
D3556			
D3557			
D3558			
D3559			
D3560			
D3561			
D3562			Stored June 1983
D3563			
D3564			
D3565			
D3566			Withdrawn September 1981, reinstated (stored) January 1983
D3567			
D3568	C	BREL Swindon August 1982	
D3569			Withdrawn October 1981, reinstated (stored) January 1983
D3570			Withdrawn December 1981, reinstated (stored) January 1983
D3571			
D3572			Withdrawn December 1981, reinstated (stored) January 1983
D3573			
D3574			
D3575			
D3576			
D3577			
D3578			
D3579			Withdrawn December 1981, reinstated (stored) January 1983
D3580			
D3581			Withdrawn December 1981, reinstated (stored) January 1983
D3582	C	BREL Swindon November 1982	
D3583			
D3584	A	BREL Swindon	
D3585			
D3586			Stored May 1983
D3587			
D3588			
D3589			
D3590			
D3591			Stored October 1983
D3592			
D3593			
D3594			
D3595			
D3596			
D3597			
D3598			
D3599			

BR 1957 No	*BR 1948 No*	*TOPS No*	*Built by*	*Works No*	*Date introduced*	*Date withdrawn*
D3600	—	08 485	BR Horwich	—	October 1958	
D3601	—	08 486	BR Horwich	—	October 1958	
D3602	—	08 487	BR Horwich	—	October 1958	
D3603	—	08 488	BR Horwich	—	October 1958	
D3604	—	08 489	BR Horwich	—	November 1958	
D3605	—	08 490	BR Horwich	—	November 1958	
D3606	—	08 491	BR Horwich	—	November 1958	
D3607	—	08 492	BR Horwich	—	November 1958	
D3608	—	08 493	BR Doncaster	—	February 1958	
D3609	—	08 494	BR Doncaster	—	March 1958	
D3610	—	08 495	BR Doncaster	—	March 1958	
D3611	—	08 496	BR Doncaster	—	March 1958	
D3612	—	—	BR Darlington	—	June 1958	March 1969
D3613	—	—	BR Darlington	—	June 1958	February 1969
D3614	—	—	BR Darlington	—	July 1958	February 1969
D3615	—	—	BR Darlington	—	July 1958	December 1968
D3616	—	—	BR Darlington	—	July 1958	July 1969
D3617	—	—	BR Darlington	—	August 1958	July 1969
D3618	—	—	BR Darlington	—	August 1958	April 1969
D3619	—	—	BR Darlington	—	August 1958	February 1969
D3620	—	—	BR Darlington	—	August 1958	February 1967
D3621	—	—	BR Darlington	—	September 1958	July 1969
D3622	—	—	BR Darlington	—	September 1958	February 1969
D3623	—	—	BR Darlington	—	September 1958	February 1969
D3624	—	—	BR Darlington	—	September 1958	November 1968
D3625	—	—	BR Darlington	—	October 1958	August 1968
D3626	—	—	BR Darlington	—	October 1958	August 1968
D3627	—	—	BR Darlington	—	October 1958	August 1968
D3628	—	—	BR Darlington	—	October 1958	December 1967
D3629	—	—	BR Darlington	—	October 1958	May 1969
D3630	—	—	BR Darlington	—	October 1958	December 1968
D3631	—	—	BR Darlington	—	October 1958	June 1967
D3632	—	—	BR Darlington	—	October 1958	August 1968
D3633	—	—	BR Darlington	—	October 1958	December 1968
D3634	—	—	BR Darlington	—	November 1958	November 1971
D3635	—	—	BR Darlington	—	November 1958	December 1968
D3636	—	—	BR Darlington	—	November 1958	April 1968
D3637	—	—	BR Darlington	—	November 1958	November 1968
D3638	—	—	BR Darlington	—	November 1958	November 1970

BR 1957 No	*Disposal code*	*Disposal details*	*Notes*
D3600			
D3601			
D3602			
D3603			
D3604			
D3605			
D3606			
D3607			
D3608			
D3609			
D3610			Withdrawn November 1981, reinstated (stored) January 1983
D3611			
D3612	C	G. Cohen, Kettering, Northamptonshire July 1969	
D3613	S	NCB Moor Green Colliery, as D14 (*David*)	Used at various South Notts NCB sites
D3614	C	Garnham, Harris & Elton, Chesterfield c1969	
D3615	C	G. Cohen, Kettering, Northamptonshire July 1969	
D3616	C	Steelbreaking & Dismantling Co, Chesterfield c1970	
D3617	C	Steelbreaking & Dismantling Co Chesterfield c1970	
D3618	S	NCB Moor Green, Colliery, as D16 (*Robin*)	Used at various NCB South Notts sites
D3619	S	NCB Moor Green, Colliery, as D15 (*Simon*)	Used at various NCB South Notts sites
D3620	C	Slag Reduction, Ickles, Rotherham August 1967	
D3621	C	C. F. Booth, Rotherham, South Yorkshire c1970	
D3622	C	C. F. Booth, Rotherham, South Yorkshire July 1967	
D3623	C	C. F. Booth, Rotherham, South Yorkshire September 1969	
D3624	C	C. F. Booth, Rotherham, South Yorkshire c1969	
D3625	C	C. F. Booth, Rotherham, South Yorkshire c1969	
D3626	C	C. F. Booth, Rotherham, South Yorkshire c1969	
D3627	C	C. F. Booth, Rotherham, South Yorkshire c1969	
D3628	C	C. F. Booth, Rotherham, South Yorkshire c1968	
D3629	C	G. Cohen, Kettering, Northamptonshire October 1969	
D3630	C	Cox & Danks, Park Royal c1969	
D3631	C	Cohen Ltd at Stratford depot October 1967	
D3632	C	C. F. Booth, Rotherham, South Yorkshire c1969	
D3633	C	G. Cohen, Kettering, Northamptonshire June 1969	
D3634	C	C. F. Booth, Rotherham, South Yorkshire June 1972	
D3635	C	G. Cohen, Kettering, Northamptonshire May 1969	
D3636	C	G. Cohen Ltd at Canning Town June 1969	
D3637	C	G. Cohen, Kettering, Northamptonshire August 1969	
D3638	C	NCB Ashington September 1975	Withdrawn July 1969, reinstated March 1970

BR 1957 No	*BR 1948 No*	*TOPS No*	*Built by*	*Works No*	*Date introduced*	*Date withdrawn*
D3639	—	—	BR Darlington	—	November 1958	July 1969
D3640	—	—	BR Darlington	—	November 1958	December 1968
D3641	—	—	BR Darlington	—	December 1958	December 1971
D3642	—	—	BR Darlington	—	December 1958	June 1969
D3643	—	—	BR Darlington	—	December 1958	October 1968
D3644	—	—	BR Darlington	—	December 1958	June 1970
D3645	—	—	BR Darlington	—	December 1958	March 1969
D3646	—	—	BR Darlington	—	December 1958	May 1971
D3647	—	—	BR Darlington	—	December 1958	March 1970
D3648	—	—	BR Darlington	—	January 1959	January 1971
D3649	—	—	BR Darlington	—	January 1959	July 1969
D3650	—	—	BR Darlington	—	January 1959	December 1971
D3651	—	—	BR Darlington	—	February 1959	December 1971
D3652	—	08 497	BR Doncaster	—	March 1958	
D3653	—	08 498	BR Doncaster	—	March 1958	
D3654	—	08 499	BR Doncaster	—	March 1958	
D3655	—	08 500	BR Doncaster	—	April 1958	
D3656	—	08 501	BR Doncaster	—	April 1958	
D3657	—	08 502	BR Doncaster	—	May 1958	
D3658	—	08 503	BR Doncaster	—	May 1958	
D3659	—	08 504	BR Doncaster	—	May 1958	
D3660	—	08 505	BR Doncaster	—	May 1958	February 1981
D3661	—	08 506	BR Doncaster	—	June 1958	
D3662	—	08 507	BR Doncaster	—	June 1958	
D3663	—	08 508	BR Doncaster	—	June 1958	
D3664	—	08 509	BR Doncaster	—	July 1958	
D3665	—	09 001	BR Darlington	—	February 1959	
D3666	—	09 002	BR Darlington	—	February 1959	
D3667	—	09 003	BR Darlington	—	February 1959	
D3668	—	09 004	BR Darlington	—	February 1959	
D3669	—	09 005	BR Darlington	—	February 1959	
D3670	—	09 006	BR Darlington	—	March 1959	
D3671	—	09 007	BR Darlington	—	March 1959	
D3672	—	08 510	BR Darlington	—	May 1958	
D3673	—	08 511	BR Darlington	—	May 1958	
D3674	—	08 512	BR Darlington	—	May 1958	
D3675	—	08 513	BR Darlington	—	June 1958	March 1978
D3676	—	08 514	BR Darlington	—	June 1958	
D3677	—	08 515	BR Darlington	—	June 1958	
D3678	—	08 516	BR Darlington	—	August 1958	
D3679	—	08 517	BR Darlington	—	August 1958	
D3680	—	08 518	BR Doncaster	—	July 1958	
D3681	—	08 519	BR Doncaster	—	July 1958	
D3682	—	08 520	BR Doncaster	—	August 1958	
D3683	—	08 521	BR Doncaster	—	August 1958	
D3684	—	08 522	BR Doncaster	—	September 1958	
D3685	—	08 523	BR Doncaster	—	September 1958	
D3686	—	08 524	BR Doncaster	—	September 1958	
D3687	—	08 525	BR Darlington	—	February 1959	

BR 1957 No	*Disposal code*	*Disposal details*	*Notes*
D3639	E	Guinea, West Africa March 1971	After withdrawal to Booth, Doncaster
D3640	C	G. Cohen, Kettering, Northamptonshire c1969	
D3641	C	C. F. Booth, Rotherham, South Yorkshire March 1973	
D3642	C	BSC Appleby-Frodingham October 1978	Formerly used at BSC Redbourne
D3643	C	G. Cohen, Kettering, Northamptonshire July 1969	
D3644	C	C. F. Booth, Rotherham, South Yorkshire c1971	
D3645	C	C. F. Booth, Rotherham, South Yorkshire c1970	
D3646	C	C. F. Booth, Rotherham, South Yorkshire c1972	
D3647	C	C. F. Booth, Rotherham, South Yorkshire c1971	Withdrawn July 1969, reinstated August 1969
D3648	C	L. Marley, Stanley, Durham February 1977	Previously used by NCB, Northumberland Area
D3649	E	Guinea, West Africa March 1971	After withdrawal to Booth, Doncaster
D3650	C	C. F. Booth, Rotherham, South Yorkshire June 1972	
D3651	C	C. F. Booth, Rotherham, South Yorkshire June 1972	
D3652			
D3653			Stored November 1981, reinstated August 1982
D3654			
D3655			Stored March 1983, reinstated May 1983
D3656			Stored September 1983, reinstated October 1983
D3657			
D3658			
D3659			
D3660	C	BREL Swindon March 1983	
D3661			
D3662			
D3663			
D3664			
D3665			
D3666			
D3667			
D3668			
D3669			
D3670			
D3671			
D3672			
D3673			
D3674			
D3675	C	BREL Doncaster October 1978	
D3676			
D3677			
D3678			
D3679			
D3680			
D3681			
D3682			
D3683			
D3684			
D3685			
D3686			
D3687			Stored January 1984, reinstated February 1984

BR 1957 No	*BR 1948 No*	*TOPS No*	*Built by*	*Works No*	*Date introduced*	*Date withdrawn*
D3688	—	08 526	BR Darlington	—	February 1959	
D3689	—	08 527	BR Darlington	—	March 1959	
D3690	—	08 528	BR Darlington	—	March 1959	
D3691	—	08 529	BR Darlington	—	March 1959	
D3692	—	08 530	BR Darlington	—	March 1959	
D3693	—	08 531	BR Darlington	—	April 1959	
D3694	—	08 532	BR Darlington	—	April 1959	
D3695	—	08 533	BR Darlington	—	April 1959	
D3696	—	08 534	BR Darlington	—	April 1959	
D3697	—	—	BR Darlington	—	May 1959	February 1965
D3698	—	—	BR Darlington	—	May 1959	February 1965
D3699	—	08 535	BR Darlington	—	May 1959	
D3700	—	08 536	BR Darlington	—	May 1959	
D3701	—	08 537	BR Darlington	—	May 1959	
D3702	—	08 538	BR Darlington	—	May 1959	
D3703	—	08 539	BR Darlington	—	June 1959	
D3704	—	08 540	BR Darlington	—	June 1959	
D3705	—	08 541	BR Darlington	—	June 1959	
D3706	—	08 542	BR Darlington	—	June 1959	
D3707	—	08 543	BR Darlington	—	June 1959	
D3708	—	08 544	BR Darlington	—	June 1959	
D3709	—	08 545	BR Darlington	—	July 1959	September 1980
D3710	—	08 546	BR Darlington	—	August 1959	
D3711	—	08 547	BR Darlington	—	August 1959	December 1981
D3712	—	08 548	BR Darlington	—	August 1959	December 1982
D3713	—	08 549	BR Darlington	—	September 1959	
D3714	—	08 550	BR Darlington	—	September 1959	March 1983
D3715	—	08 551	BR Darlington	—	September 1959	October 1982
D3716	—	08 552	BR Darlington	—	September 1959	August 1982
D3717	—	08 553	BR Darlington	—	October 1959	May 1981
D3718	—	08 554	BR Darlington	—	October 1959	August 1982
D3719	—	09 008	BR Darlington	—	October 1959	
D3720	—	09 009	BR Darlington	—	October 1959	
D3721	—	09 010	BR Darlington	—	October 1959	
D3722	—	08 555	BR Darlington	—	October 1959	August 1982
D3723	—	08 556	BR Darlington	—	October 1959	
D3724	—	08 557	BR Darlington	—	November 1959	December 1982
D3725	—	08 558	BR Darlington	—	November 1959	
D3726	—	08 559	BR Darlington	—	December 1959	December 1981
D3727	—	08 560	BR Darlington	—	December 1959	May 1981
D3728	—	08 561	BR Crewe	—	January 1959	
D3729	—	08 562	BR Crewe	—	January 1959	
D3730	—	08 563	BR Crewe	—	January 1959	
D3731	—	08 564	BR Crewe	—	February 1959	
D3732	—	08 565	BR Crewe	—	February 1959	
D3733	—	08 566	BR Crewe	—	April 1959	October 1975
D3734	—	08 567	BR Crewe	—	April 1959	
D3735	—	08 568	BR Crewe	—	April 1959	
D3736	—	08 569	BR Crewe	—	May 1959	
D3737	—	08 570	BR Crewe	—	May 1959	
D3738	—	08 571	BR Crewe	—	June 1959	
D3739	—	08 572	BR Crewe	—	May 1959	February 1981
D3740	—	08 573	BR Crewe	—	June 1959	
D3741	—	08 574	BR Crewe	—	June 1959	
D3742	—	08 575	BR Crewe	—	June 1959	

BR 1957 No	*Disposal code*	*Disposal details*	*Notes*
D3688			
D3689			
D3690			
D3691			
D3692			
D3693			
D3694			
D3695			
D3696			
D3697	R	Rebuilt into Class 13	
D3698	R	Rebuilt into Class 13	
D3699			
D3700			
D3701			
D3702			
D3703			
D3704			
D3705			
D3706			
D3707			
D3708			
D3709	C	BREL Swindon November 1983	
D3710			
D3711	C	BREL Swindon May 1981	Withdrawn August 1981, reinstated August 1981
D3712	C	BREL Doncaster December 1983	
D3713			
D3714	A	BREL Swindon	
D3715	C	BREL Doncaster November 1983	
D3716	C	BREL Doncaster January 1983	
D3717	C	BREL Swindon March 1983	
D3718	C	BREL Doncaster February 1983	
D3719			
D3720			
D3721			
D3722	C	BREL Doncaster November 1983	
D3723			
D3724	C	BREL Doncaster December 1983	
D3725			
D3726	C	BREL Swindon November 1983	Withdrawn April 1981, reinstated August 1981
D3727	C	BREL Swindon February 1982	
D3728			Stored July 1984
D3729			Withdrawn December 1981, reinstated (stored) January 1983
D3730			Stored April 1982
D3731			
D3732			Withdrawn July 1981, reinstated (stored) January 1983
D3733	C	BREL Glasgow November 1977	
D3734			
D3735			
D3736			
D3737			Stored March 1984, reinstated May 1984
D3738			Stored July 1984
D3739	C	BREL Swindon October 1983	
D3740			Stored January 1983, reinstated December 1983
D3741			Withdrawn March 1981, reinstated (stored) January 1983
D3742			

BR 1957 No	BR 1948 No	TOPS No	Built by	Works No	*Period Date introduced	Date withdrawn
D3743	—	08 576	BR Crewe	—	June 1959	
D3744	—	08 577	BR Crewe	—	June 1959	
D3745	—	08 578	BR Crewe	—	June 1959	
D3746	—	08 579	BR Crewe	—	July 1959	
D3747	—	08 580	BR Crewe	—	July 1959	
D3748	—	08 581	BR Crewe	—	July 1959	
D3749	—	08 582	BR Crewe	—	August 1959	
D3750	—	08 583	BR Crewe	—	August 1959	
D3751	—	08 584	BR Crewe	—	August 1959	
D3752	—	08 585	BR Crewe	—	August 1959	
D3753	—	08 586	BR Crewe	—	November 1959	
D3754	—	08 587	BR Crewe	—	November 1959	
D3755	—	08 588	BR Crewe	—	November 1959	
D3756	—	08 589	BR Crewe	—	October 1959	
D3757	—	08 590	BR Crewe	—	October 1959	
D3758	—	08 591	BR Crewe	—	October 1959	
D3759	—	08 592	BR Crewe	—	October 1959	
D3760	—	08 593	BR Crewe	—	December 1959	
D3761	—	08 594	BR Crewe	—	December 1959	
D3762	—	08 595	BR Crewe	—	December 1959	
D3763	—	08 596	BR Derby	—	4/59*	March 1977
D3764	—	08 597	BR Derby	—	5/59*	
D3765	—	08 598	BR Derby	—	5/59*	
D3766	—	08 599	BR Derby	—	5/59*	
D3767	—	08 600	BR Derby	—	5/59*	January 1979
D3768	—	08 601	BR Derby	—	5/59*	
D3769	—	08 602	BR Derby	—	6/59*	
D3770	—	08 603	BR Derby	—	6/59*	
D3771	—	08 604	BR Derby	—	6/59*	
D3772	—	08 605	BR Derby	—	6/59*	
D3773	—	08 606	BR Derby	—	7/59*	
D3774	—	08 607	BR Derby	—	7/59*	
D3775	—	08 608	BR Derby	—	7/59*	
D3776	—	08 609	BR Derby	—	7/59*	
D3777	—	08 610	BR Derby	—	8/59*	
D3778	—	08 611	BR Derby	—	8/59*	
D3779	—	08 612	BR Derby	—	9/59*	
D3780	—	08 613	BR Derby	—	9/59*	
D3781	—	08 614	BR Derby	—	9/59*	
D3782	—	08 615	BR Derby	—	9/59*	
D3783	—	08 616	BR Derby	—	9/59*	

BR 1957 No	*Disposal code*	*Disposal details*	*Notes*
D3743			
D3744			Stored February 1983, reinstated January 1984
D3745			Withdrawn December 1981, reinstated (stored) January 1983, reinstated (service) January 1984
D3746			
D3747			
D3748			
D3749			Withdrawn January 1982, reinstated April 1982
D3750			Stored December 1980, withdrawn October 1981, reinstated (stored) January 1983, reinstated (service) January 1984
D3751			
D3752			Withdrawn October 1981, reinstated (stored) January 1983, reinstated (service) January 1984
D3753			
D3754			Withdrawn December 1981, reinstated (stored) January 1983, reinstated (service) February 1984
D3755			
D3756			
D3757			
D3758			Stored February 1983, reinstated January 1984
D3759			
D3760			Withdrawn December 1981, reinstated (stored) January 1983, reinstated (service) January 1984
D3761			
D3762			
D3763	S	Bowaters, Sittingbourne, Kent	
D3764			Stored March 1983, reinstated December 1983
D3765			
D3766			
D3767	D	To Departmental fleet — 97800	
D3768			
D3769			
D3770			Withdrawn December 1981, reinstated (stored) January 1983, reinstated (service) February 1984
D3771			Withdrawn December 1981, reinstated (stored) January 1981, reinstated (service) February 1984
D3772			Stored January 1984
D3773			
D3774			
D3775			
D3776			Stored April 1982, reinstated March 1984
D3777			
D3778			
D3779			Stored April 1982, reinstated March 1984
D3780			
D3781			
D3782			Stored June 1982, reinstated March 1984
D3783			

BR 1957 No	BR 1948 No	TOPS No	Built by	Works No	*Period Date introduced	Date withdrawn
D3784	—	08 617	BR Derby	—	10/59*	
D3785	—	08 618	BR Derby	—	10/59*	
D3786	—	08 619	BR Derby	—	10/59*	
D3787	—	08 620	BR Derby	—	10/59*	
D3788	—	08 621	BR Derby	—	October 1959	
D3789	—	08 622	BR Derby	—	October 1959	
D3790	—	08 623	BR Derby	—	October 1959	
D3791	—	08 624	BR Derby	—	October 1959	
D3792	—	08 625	BR Derby	—	October 1959	
D3793	—	08 626	BR Derby	—	October 1959	
D3794	—	08 627	BR Derby	—	November 1959	
D3795	—	08 628	BR Derby	—	November 1959	
D3796	—	08 629	BR Derby	—	November 1959	
D3797	—	08 630	BR Derby	—	November 1959	
D3798	—	08 631	BR Derby	—	November 1959	
D3799	—	08 632	BR Derby	—	November 1959	
D3800	—	08 633	BR Derby	—	December 1959	
D3801	—	08 634	BR Derby	—	December 1959	
D3802	—	08 635	BR Derby	—	December 1959	
D3803	—	08 636	BR Horwich	—	December 1958	July 1980
D3804	—	08 637	BR Horwich	—	December 1958	
D3805	—	08 638	BR Horwich	—	December 1958	
D3806	—	08 639	BR Horwich	—	December 1958	
D3807	—	08 640	BR Horwich	—	December 1958	
D3808	—	08 641	BR Horwich	—	January 1959	
D3809	—	08 642	BR Horwich	—	January 1959	
D3810	—	08 643	BR Horwich	—	January 1959	
D3811	—	08 644	BR Horwich	—	February 1959	
D3812	—	08 645	BR Horwich	—	February 1959	
D3813	—	08 646	BR Horwich	—	February 1959	
D3814	—	08 647	BR Horwich	—	February 1959	
D3815	—	08 648	BR Horwich	—	March 1959	
D3816	—	08 649	BR Horwich	—	March 1959	
D3817	—	08 650	BR Horwich	—	March 1959	
D3818	—	08 651	BR Horwich	—	March 1959	
D3819	—	08 652	BR Horwich	—	March 1959	
D3820	—	08 653	BR Horwich	—	April 1959	
D3821	—	08 654	BR Horwich	—	April 1959	
D3822	—	08 655	BR Horwich	—	April 1959	
D3823	—	08 656	BR Horwich	—	April 1959	
D3824	—	08 657	BR Horwich	—	April 1959	
D3825	—	08 658	BR Horwich	—	May 1959	
D3826	—	08 659	BR Horwich	—	May 1959	
D3827	—	08 660	BR Horwich	—	May 1959	
D3828	—	08 661	BR Horwich	—	May 1959	
D3829	—	08 662	BR Horwich	—	May 1959	
D3830	—	08 663	BR Horwich	—	June 1959	
D3831	—	08 664	BR Horwich	—	June 1959	

BR 1957 No	*Disposal code*	*Disposal details*	*Notes*
D3784			Withdrawn October 1981, reinstated (stored) January 1983, reinstated (service) April 1984
D3785			Strored May 1984, reinstated June 1984
D3786			Withdrawn September 1981, reinstated (stored) January 1983, reinstated (service) March 1984
D3787			
D3788			
D3789			Withdrawn December 1981, reinstated (stored) January 1983, reinstated (service) April 1984
D3790			
D3791			
D3792			
D3793			
D3794			
D3795			Withdrawn October 1981, reinstated (stored) January 1983, reinstated (service) April 1984
D3796			Withdrawn November 1981, reinstated January 1983
D3797			
D3798			
D3799			
D3800			
D3801			
D3802			Withdrawn December 1981, reinstated (stored) January 1984, reinstated (service) May 1984
D3803	C	BREL Swindon June 1983	
D3804			
D3805			Withdrawn December 1981, reinstated (stored) January 1983, reinstated (service) May 1984
D3806			
D3807			
D3808			
D3809			
D3810			
D3811			
D3812			
D3813			
D3814			
D3815			
D3816			
D3817			
D3818			
D3819			
D3820			
D3821			
D3822			
D3823			
D3824			
D3825			
D3826			
D3827			
D3828			
D3829			
D3830			
D3831			

BR 1957 No	BR 1948 No	TOPS No	Built by	Works No	Date introduced	Date withdrawn
D3832	—	08 665	BR Crewe	—	January 1960	
D3833	—	08 666	BR Crewe	—	January 1960	
D3834	—	08 667	BR Crewe	—	January 1960	
D3835	—	08 668	BR Crewe	—	January 1960	
D3836	—	08 669	BR Crewe	—	January 1960	
D3837	—	08 670	BR Crewe	—	January 1960	
D3838	—	08 671	BR Crewe	—	January 1960	
D3839	—	08 672	BR Crewe	—	January 1960	
D3840	—	08 673	BR Crewe	—	January 1960	
D3841	—	08 674	BR Crewe	—	February 1960	January 1983
D3842	—	08 675	BR Horwich	—	July 1959	
D3843	—	08 676	BR Horwich	—	July 1959	
D3844	—	08 677	BR Horwich	—	July 1959	
D3845	—	08 678	BR Horwich	—	August 1959	
D3846	—	08 679	BR Horwich	—	August 1959	
D3847	—	08 680	BR Horwich	—	September 1959	
D3848	—	08 681	BR Horwich	—	September 1959	
D3849	—	08 682	BR Horwich	—	September 1959	
D3850	—	08 683	BR Horwich	—	September 1959	
D3851	—	08 684	BR Horwich	—	October 1959	
D3852	—	08 685	BR Horwich	—	October 1959	
D3853	—	08 686	BR Horwich	—	October 1959	
D3854	—	08 687	BR Horwich	—	October 1959	
D3855	—	08 688	BR Horwich	—	October 1959	
D3856	—	08 689	BR Horwich	—	October 1959	
D3857	—	08 690	BR Horwich	—	October 1959	
D3858	—	08 691	BR Horwich	—	October 1959	
D3859	—	08 692	BR Horwich	—	November 1959	
D3860	—	08 693	BR Horwich	—	November 1959	
D3861	—	08 694	BR Horwich	—	November 1959	
D3862	—	08 695	BR Horwich	—	November 1959	
D3863	—	08 696	BR Horwich	—	November 1959	
D3864	—	08 697	BR Horwich	—	December 1959	
D3865	—	08 698	BR Horwich	—	December 1959	
D3866	—	08 699	BR Horwich	—	January 1960	
D3867	—	08 700	BR Horwich	—	January 1960	
D3868	—	08 701	BR Horwich	—	February 1960	
D3869	—	08 702	BR Horwich	—	February 1960	
D3870	—	08 703	BR Horwich	—	February 1960	
D3871	—	08 704	BR Horwich	—	February 1960	
D3872	—	08 705	BR Crewe	—	March 1960	
D3873	—	08 706	BR Crewe	—	March 1960	
D3874	—	08 707	BR Crewe	—	March 1960	
D3875	—	08 708	BR Crewe	—	March 1960	
D3876	—	08 709	BR Crewe	—	April 1960	
D3877	—	08 710	BR Crewe	—	April 1960	
D3878	—	08 711	BR Crewe	—	May 1960	
D3879	—	08 712	BR Crewe	—	May 1960	
D3880	—	08 713	BR Crewe	—	May 1960	
D3881	—	08 714	BR Crewe	—	May 1960	
D3882	—	08 715	BR Crewe	—	May 1960	
D3883	—	08 716	BR Crewe	—	May 1960	
D3884	—	08 717	BR Crewe	—	May 1960	

BR 1957 No	*Disposal code*	*Disposal details*	*Notes*
D3832			
D3833			
D3834			Stored January 1984
D3835			
D3836			
D3837			Stored October 1981, reinstated March 1982
D3838			
D3839			
D3840			Stored 1982, reinstated June 1984
D3841	C	BREL Swindon July 1983	
D3842			
D3843			Stored 1983, reinstated June 1984
D3844			
D3845			
D3846			
D3847			Stored October 1981, reinstated July 1982
D3848			Stored April 1984, reinstated May 1984
D3849			
D3850			
D3851			
D3852			Stored April 1984, reinstated April 1984
D3853			
D3854			
D3855			
D3856			
D3857			Withdrawn October 1981, reinstated July 1984
D3858			
D3859			Stored April 1984
D3860			Stored December 1983, reinstated February 1984
D3861			
D3862			
D3863			
D3864			Stored January 1984, reinstated May 1984
D3865			Stored October 1981, reinstated March 1982
D3866			Stored April 1984
D3867			
D3868			
D3869			
D3870			
D3871			Withdrawn November 1981, reinstated January 1983
D3872			
D3873			
D3874			
D3875			
D3876			
D3877			
D3878			
D3879			Stored December 1983, reinstated February 1984
D3880			
D3881			
D3882			
D3883			
D3884			Withdrawn October 1981, reinstated (stored) January 1983

BR 1957 No	BR 1948 No	TOPS No	Built by	Works No	Date introduced	Date withdrawn
D3885	—	—	BR Crewe	—	May 1960	February 1972
D3886	—	08 718	BR Crewe	—	June 1960	
D3887	—	08 719	BR Crewe	—	June 1960	
D3888	—	08 720	BR Crewe	—	June 1960	
D3889	—	08 721	BR Crewe	—	June 1960	
D3890	—	08 722	BR Crewe	—	July 1960	
D3891	—	08 723	BR Crewe	—	July 1960	
D3892	—	08 724	BR Crewe	—	July 1960	
D3893	—	08 725	BR Crewe	—	July 1960	
D3894	—	08 726	BR Crewe	—	July 1960	
D3895	—	08 727	BR Crewe	—	August 1960	
D3896	—	08 728	BR Crewe	—	August 1960	
D3897	—	08 729	BR Crewe	—	August 1960	
D3898	—	08 730	BR Crewe	—	August 1960	
D3899	—	08 731	BR Crewe	—	September 1960	
D3900	—	08 732	BR Crewe	—	September 1960	
D3901	—	08 733	BR Crewe	—	September 1960	
D3902	—	08 734	BR Crewe	—	September 1960	
D3903	—	08 735	BR Crewe	—	October 1960	
D3904	—	08 736	BR Crewe	—	October 1960	
D3905	—	08 737	BR Crewe	—	October 1960	
D3906	—	08 738	BR Crewe	—	November 1960	
D3907	—	08 739	BR Crewe	—	November 1960	
D3908	—	08 740	BR Crewe	—	November 1960	
D3909	—	08 741	BR Crewe	—	November 1960	
D3910	—	08 742	BR Crewe	—	November 1960	
D3911	—	08 743	BR Crewe	—	November 1960	
D3912	—	08 744	BR Crewe	—	November 1960	
D3913	—	08 745	BR Crewe	—	November 1960	
D3914	—	08 746	BR Crewe	—	December 1960	
D3915	—	08 747	BR Crewe	—	December 1960	
D3916	—	08 748	BR Crewe	—	December 1960	
D3917	—	08 749	BR Crewe	—	December 1960	
D3918	—	08 750	BR Crewe	—	December 1960	
D3919	—	08 751	BR Crewe	—	December 1960	
D3920	—	08 752	BR Crewe	—	December 1960	
D3921	—	08 753	BR Crewe	—	December 1960	
D3922	—	08 754	BR Horwich	—	January 1961	
D3923	—	08 755	BR Horwich	—	January 1961	
D3924	—	08 756	BR Horwich	—	January 1961	
D3925	—	08 757	BR Horwich	—	February 1961	
D3926	—	08 758	BR Horwich	—	February 1961	
D3927	—	08 759	BR Horwich	—	February 1961	
D3928	—	08 760	BR Horwich	—	February 1961	
D3929	—	08 761	BR Horwich	—	March 1961	
D3930	—	08 762	BR Horwich	—	March 1961	
D3931	—	08 763	BR Horwich	—	March 1961	
D3932	—	08 764	BR Horwich	—	March 1961	
D3933	—	08 765	BR Horwich	—	March 1961	
D3934	—	08 766	BR Horwich	—	April 1961	
D3935	—	08 767	BR Horwich	—	April 1961	
D3936	—	08 768	BR Horwich	—	April 1961	
D3937	—	08 769	BR Derby	—	March 1960	
D3938	—	08 770	BR Derby	—	March 1960	
D3939	—	08 771	BR Derby	—	March 1960	
D3940	—	08 772	BR Derby	—	March 1960	
D3941	—	08 773	BR Derby	—	March 1960	

BR 1957 No	*Disposal code*	*Disposal details*	*Notes*
D3885	C	BREL Glasgow	
D3886			Stored January 1983, reinstated May 1983
D3887			
D3888			
D3889			
D3890			
D3891			Stored May 1984
D3892			
D3893			Withdrawn December 1981, reinstated May 1983
D3894			
D3895			Stored May 1984
D3896			
D3897			
D3898			Stored May 1984, reinstated August 1984
D3899			
D3900			
D3901			Stored July 1983, reinstated December 1983
D3902			
D3903			Stored May 1983, reinstated February 1984
D3904			
D3905			
D3906			
D3907			
D3908			
D3909			
D3910			
D3911			
D3912			
D3913			
D3914			
D3915			
D3916			
D3917			
D3918			
D3919			
D3920			
D3921			
D3922			
D3923			
D3924			
D3925			
D3926			
D3927			
D3928			
D3929			
D3930			
D3931			
D3932			
D3933			
D3934			
D3935			
D3936			
D3937			
D3938			
D3939			
D3940			
D3941			Withdrawn August 1982, reinstated October 1982

BR 1957 No	*BR 1948 No*	*TOPS No*	*Built by*	*Works No*	*Date introduced*	*Date withdrawn*
D3942	—	08 774	BR Derby	—	April 1960	
D3943	—	08 775	BR Derby	—	April 1960	
D3944	—	08 776	BR Derby	—	April 1960	
D3945	—	08 777	BR Derby	—	April 1960	
D3946	—	08 778	BR Derby	—	April 1960	
D3947	—	08 779	BR Derby	—	April 1960	
D3948	—	08 780	BR Derby	—	April 1960	
D3949	—	08 781	BR Derby	—	April 1960	
D3950	—	08 782	BR Derby	—	April 1960	
D3951	—	08 783	BR Derby	—	April 1960	
D3952	—	08 784	BR Derby	—	April 1960	
D3953	—	08 785	BR Derby	—	April 1960	
D3954	—	08 786	BR Derby	—	April 1960	
D3955	—	08 787	BR Derby	—	April 1960	
D3956	—	08 788	BR Derby	—	April 1960	
D3957	—	08 789	BR Derby	—	May 1960	
D3958	—	08 790	BR Derby	—	May 1960	
D3959	—	08 791	BR Derby	—	May 1960	
D3960	—	08 792	BR Derby	—	May 1960	
D3961	—	08 793	BR Derby	—	May 1960	
D3962	—	08 794	BR Derby	—	May 1960	
D3963	—	08 795	BR Derby	—	May 1960	
D3964	—	08 796	BR Derby	—	May 1960	
D3965	—	08 797	BR Derby	—	May 1960	
D3966	—	08 798	BR Derby	—	May 1960	
D3967	—	08 799	BR Derby	—	June 1960	
D3968	—	08 800	BR Derby	—	June 1960	
D3969	—	08 801	BR Derby	—	June 1960	
D3970	—	08 802	BR Derby	—	June 1960	
D3971	—	08 803	BR Derby	—	June 1960	
D3972	—	08 804	BR Derby	—	June 1960	
D3973	—	08 805	BR Derby	—	June 1960	
D3974	—	08 806	BR Derby	—	June 1960	
D3975	—	08 807	BR Derby	—	July 1960	
D3976	—	08 808	BR Derby	—	July 1960	
D3977	—	08 809	BR Derby	—	July 1960	
D3978	—	08 810	BR Derby	—	July 1960	
D3979	—	08 811	BR Derby	—	July 1960	
D3980	—	08 812	BR Derby	—	July 1960	February 1978
D3981	—	08 813	BR Derby	—	August 1960	
D3982	—	08 814	BR Derby	—	August 1960	
D3983	—	08 815	BR Derby	—	August 1960	
D3984	—	08 816	BR Derby	—	August 1960	
D3985	—	08 817	BR Derby	—	August 1960	
D3986	—	08 818	BR Derby	—	August 1960	
D3987	—	08 819	BR Derby	—	August 1960	
D3988	—	08 820	BR Derby	—	August 1960	
D3989	—	08 821	BR Derby	—	September 1960	
D3990	—	08 822	BR Derby	—	September 1960	
D3991	—	08 823	BR Derby	—	September 1960	
D3992	—	08 824	BR Derby	—	September 1960	
D3993	—	08 825	BR Derby	—	September 1960	
D3994	—	08 826	BR Derby	—	September 1960	

BR 1957 No	Disposal code	Disposal details	Notes
D3942			
D3943			Withdrawn August 1982, reinstated October 1982
D3944			
D3945			
D3946			
D3947			
D3948			
D3949			
D3950			
D3951			Stored April 1984, reinstated April 1984
D3952			
D3953			
D3954			Withdrawn December 1981, reinstated (stored) January 1982, reinstated (service) May 1982
D3955			
D3956			
D3957			Stored November 1980, reinstated March 1981
D3958			
D3959			
D3960			
D3961			
D3962			
D3963			
D3964			
D3965			
D3966			
D3967			
D3968			
D3969			
D3970			
D3971			
D3972			
D3973			
D3974			
D3975			
D3976			Stored January 1984, reinstated March 1984
D3977			
D3978			
D3979			
D3980	C	BREL Swindon March 1978	
D3981			Stored September 1982, reinstated March 1982
D3982			
D3983			
D3984			
D3985			Stored February 1984, reinstated July 1984
D3986			
D3987			
D3988			
D3989			
D3990			
D3991			
D3992			
D3993			
D3994			

BR 1957 No	*BR 1948 No*	*TOPS No*	*Built by*	*Works No*	*Date introduced*	*Date withdrawn*
D3995	—	08 827	BR Derby	—	September 1960	
D3996	—	08 828	BR Derby	—	October 1960	
D3997	—	08 829	BR Derby	—	October 1960	
D3998	—	08 830	BR Derby	—	November 1960	
D3999	—	08 831	BR Derby	—	November 1960	
D4000	—	08 832	BR Derby	—	November 1960	
D4001	—	08 833	BR Derby	—	November 1960	
D4002	—	08 834	BR Derby	—	November 1960	
D4003	—	08 835	BR Derby	—	November 1960	
D4004	—	08 836	BR Derby	—	December 1960	
D4005	—	08 837	BR Derby	—	December 1960	
D4006	—	08 838	BR Derby	—	December 1960	
D4007	—	08 839	BR Derby	—	December 1960	
D4008	—	08 840	BR Derby	—	December 1960	
D4009	—	08 841	BR Derby	—	December 1960	
D4010	—	08 842	BR Derby	—	December 1960	
D4011	—	08 843	BR Horwich	—	April 1961	
D4012	—	08 844	BR Horwich	—	April 1961	
D4013	—	08 845	BR Horwich	—	May 1961	
D4014	—	08 846	BR Horwich	—	May 1961	
D4015	—	08 847	BR Horwich	—	May 1961	
D4016	—	08 848	BR Horwich	—	May 1961	
D4017	—	08 849	BR Horwich	—	May 1961	
D4018	—	08 850	BR Horwich	—	June 1961	
D4019	—	08 851	BR Horwich	—	June 1961	
D4020	—	08 852	BR Horwich	—	June 1961	
D4021	—	08 853	BR Horwich	—	June 1961	
D4022	—	08 854	BR Horwich	—	June 1961	
D4023	—	08 855	BR Horwich	—	June 1961	
D4024	—	08 856	BR Horwich	—	July 1961	
D4025	—	08 857	BR Horwich	—	July 1961	
D4026	—	08 858	BR Horwich	—	August 1961	
D4027	—	08 859	BR Horwich	—	August 1961	
D4028	—	08 860	BR Darlington	—	May 1960	March 1981
D4029	—	08 861	BR Darlington	—	May 1960	October 1981
D4030	—	08 862	BR Darlington	—	June 1960	December 1980
D4031	—	08 863	BR Darlington	—	July 1960	December 1980
D4032	—	08 864	BR Darlington	—	August 1960	August 1981
D4033	—	08 865	BR Darlington	—	September 1960	
D4034	—	08 866	BR Darlington	—	October 1960	
D4035	—	08 867	BR Darlington	—	November 1960	
D4036	—	08 868	BR Darlington	—	November 1960	
D4037	—	08 869	BR Darlington	—	November 1960	
D4038	—	08 870	BR Darlington	—	November 1960	
D4039	—	08 871	BR Darlington	—	December 1960	
D4040	—	08 872	BR Darlington	—	December 1960	
D4041	—	08 873	BR Darlington	—	December 1960	
D4042	—	08 874	BR Darlington	—	December 1960	
D4043	—	08 875	BR Darlington	—	December 1960	
D4044	—	08 876	BR Darlington	—	December 1960	
D4045	—	08 877	BR Darlington	—	January 1961	
D4046	—	08 878	BR Darlington	—	January 1961	
D4047	—	08 879	BR Darlington	—	January 1961	
D4048	—	08 880	BR Darlington	—	January 1961	
D4049	—	—	BR Darlington	—	January 1961	January 1972

BR 1957 No	*Disposal Code*	*Disposal details*	*Notes*
D3995			
D3996			
D3997			
D3998			
D3999			
D4000			
D4001			
D4002			
D4003			
D4004			
D4005			
D4006			
D4007			
D4008			
D4009			
D4010			
D4011			
D4012			
D4013			
D4014			
D4015			
D4016			
D4017			
D4018			
D4019			
D4020			
D4021			
D4022			
D4023			
D4024			
D4025			
D4026			
D4027			
D4028	C	BREL Swindon June 1981	
D4029	C	BREL Swindon March 1982	
D4030	C	BREL Swindon October 1981	Stored from September 1980
D4031	C	BREL Swindon October 1981	Stored from September 1980
D4032	C	BREL Swindon March 1982	
D4033			
D4034			Stored March 1983, reinstated March 1984
D4035			
D4036			
D4037			Withdrawn November 1981, reinstated (stored) May 1983, reinstated (service) January 1984
D4038			
D4039			
D4040			
D4041			
D4042			
D4043			
D4044			
D4045			
D4046			
D4047			
D4048			
D4049	C	G. Cohen, Kettering, Northamptonshire August 1972	

BR 1957 No	*BR 1948 No*	*TOPS No*	*Built by*	*Works No*	*Date introduced*	*Date withdrawn*
D4050	—	—	BR Darlington	—	January 1961	December 1971
D4051	—	—	BR Darlington	—	January 1961	July 1971
D4052	—	—	BR Darlington	—	January 1961	October 1970
D4053	—	—	BR Darlington	—	January 1961	December 1971
D4054	—	—	BR Darlington	—	February 1961	June 1972
D4055	—	—	BR Darlington	—	February 1961	December 1971
D4056	—	—	BR Darlington	—	February 1961	June 1972
D4057	—	—	BR Darlington	—	February 1961	January 1972
D4058	—	—	BR Darlington	—	February 1961	January 1972
D4059	—	—	BR Darlington	—	March 1961	December 1971
D4060	—	—	BR Darlington	—	March 1961	December 1971
D4061	—	—	BR Darlington	—	March 1961	January 1972
D4062	—	—	BR Darlington	—	March 1961	February 1972
D4063	—	—	BR Darlington	—	April 1961	June 1972
D4064	—	—	BR Darlington	—	April 1961	August 1968
D4065	—	—	BR Darlington	—	April 1961	November 1971
D4066	—	—	BR Darlington	—	April 1961	June 1972
D4067	—	—	BR Darlington	—	May 1961	December 1970
D4068	—	—	BR Darlington	—	May 1961	June 1972
D4069	—	—	BR Darlington	—	May 1961	April 1972
D4070	—	—	BR Darlington	—	June 1961	April 1972
D4071	—	—	BR Darlington	—	June 1961	July 1968
D4072	—	—	BR Darlington	—	July 1961	April 1972
D4073	—	—	BR Darlington	—	August 1961	June 1972
D4074	—	—	BR Darlington	—	August 1961	April 1972
D4075	—	—	BR Darlington	—	September 1961	June 1972
D4076	—	—	BR Darlington	—	October 1961	July 1968
D4077	—	—	BR Darlington	—	October 1961	November 1970
D4078	—	—	BR Darlington	—	November 1961	June 1972
D4079	—	—	BR Darlington	—	November 1961	June 1972
D4080	—	—	BR Darlington	—	December 1961	February 1968
D4081	—	—	BR Darlington	—	January 1962	June 1968
D4082	—	—	BR Darlington	—	January 1962	June 1968

BR 1957 No	*Disposal code*	*Disposal details*	*Notes*
D4050	C	C. F. Booth, Rotherham, South Yorkshire c1972	
D4051	C	C. F. Booth, Rotherham, South Yorkshire July 1972	
D4052	C	C. F. Booth, Rotherham, South Yorkshire February 1971	
D4053	C	C. F. Booth, Rotherham, South Yorkshire c1972	
D4054	C	G. Cohen, Kettering, Northamptonshire May 1973	
D4055	C	C. F. Booth, Rotherham, South Yorkshire May 1973	
D4056	C	NCB Shilbottle Colliery c1980	
D4057	C	C. F. Booth, Rotherham, South Yorkshire April 1973	
D4058	C	G. Cohen, Kettering, Northamptonshire August 1972	
D4059	C	G. Cohen, Kettering, Northamptonshire August 1972	
D4060	C	C. F. Booth, Rotherham, South Yorkshire June 1972	
D4061	C	C. F. Booth, Rotherham, South Yorkshire November 1972	
D4062	C	C. F. Booth, Rotherham, South Yorkshire November 1972	
D4063	C	G. Cohen, Kettering, Northamptonshire May 1973	
D4064	C	C. F. Booth, Rotherham, South Yorkshire c1969	
D4065	C	C. F. Booth, Rotherham, South Yorkshire June 1972	
D4066	C	G. Cohen, Kettering, Northamptonshire c1973	
D4067	P	Great Central Railway, Loughborough	Formerly used by NCB Kent coalfields
D4068	S	NCB Whittle Colliery as No 56	
D4069	S	NCB Whittle Colliery as No 9300/111	
D4070	S	NCB Whittle Colliery as No 52	
D4071	C	G. Cohen, Kettering, Northamptonshire March 1969	
D4072	S	NCB Philadelphia Colliery as No 9300/114	
D4073	C	G. Cohen, Kettering, Northamptonshire April 1973	
D4074	C	NCB Whittle Colliery August 1978	
D4075	C	G. Cohen, Kettering, Northamptonshire April 1973	
D4076	C	C. F. Booth, Rotherham, South Yorkshire c1969	
D4077	C	C. F. Booth, Rotherham, South Yorkshire August 1971	
D4078	C	G. Cohen, Kettering, Northamptonshire May 1973	
D4079	C	G. Cohen, Kettering, Northamptonshire May 1973	
D4080	C	C. F. Booth, Rotherham, South Yorkshire c1969	
D4081	C	C. F. Booth, Rotherham, South Yorkshire April 1969	
D4082	C	C. F. Booth, Rotherham, South Yorkshire April 1969	

BR 1957 No	*BR 1948 No*	*TOPS No*	*Built by*	*Works No*	*Date introduced*	*Date withdrawn*
D4083	—	—	BR Darlington	—	January 1962	July 1968
D4084	—	—	BR Darlington	—	February 1962	July 1968
D4085	—	—	BR Darlington	—	February 1962	June 1968
D4086	—	—	BR Darlington	—	February 1962	August 1968
D4087	—	—	BR Darlington	—	February 1962	September 1968
D4088	—	—	BR Darlington	—	March 1962	August 1968
D4089	—	—	BR Darlington	—	March 1962	August 1968
D4090	—	—	BR Darlington	—	March 1962	August 1968
D4091	—	—	BR Darlington	—	April 1962	August 1968
D4092	—	—	BR Darlington	—	May 1962	September 1968
D4093	—	—	BR Darlington	—	May 1962	August 1968
D4094	—	—	BR Darlington	—	June 1962	August 1968
D4095	—	08 881	BR Horwich	—	August 1961	
D4096	—	08 882	BR Horwich	—	September 1961	
D4097	—	08 883	BR Horwich	—	September 1961	
D4098	—	08 884	BR Horwich	—	September 1961	
D4099	—	09 011	BR Horwich	—	October 1961	
D4100	—	09 012	BR Horwich	—	October 1961	
D4101	—	09 013	BR Horwich	—	October 1961	
D4102	—	09 014	BR Horwich	—	November 1961	
D4103	—	09 015	BR Horwich	—	November 1961	
D4104	—	09 016	BR Horwich	—	November 1961	
D4105	—	09 017	BR Horwich	—	December 1961	
D4106	—	09 018	BR Horwich	—	December 1961	
D4107	—	09 019	BR Horwich	—	December 1961	
D4108	—	09 020	BR Horwich	—	December 1961	
D4109	—	09 021	BR Horwich	—	December 1961	
D4110	—	09 022	BR Horwich	—	December 1961	
D4111	—	09 023	BR Horwich	—	December 1961	
D4112	—	09 024	BR Horwich	—	December 1961	
D4113	—	09 025	BR Horwich	—	January 1962	
D4114	—	09 026	BR Horwich	—	January 1962	
D4115	—	08 885	BR Horwich	—	January 1962	
D4116	—	08 886	BR Horwich	—	January 1962	
D4117	—	08 887	BR Horwich	—	February 1962	
D4118	—	08 888	BR Horwich	—	February 1962	
D4119	—	08 889	BR Horwich	—	February 1962	
D4120	—	08 890	BR Horwich	—	February 1962	
D4121	—	08 891	BR Horwich	—	March 1962	
D4122	—	08 892	BR Horwich	—	March 1962	
D4123	—	08 893	BR Horwich	—	March 1962	
D4124	—	08 894	BR Horwich	—	April 1962	
D4125	—	08 895	BR Horwich	—	April 1962	
D4126	—	08 896	BR Horwich	—	April 1962	
D4127	—	08 897	BR Horwich	—	April 1962	
D4128	—	08 898	BR Horwich	—	May 1962	
D4129	—	08 899	BR Horwich	—	May 1962	
D4130	—	08 900	BR Horwich	—	May 1962	
D4131	—	08 901	BR Horwich	—	May 1962	
D4132	—	08 902	BR Horwich	—	June 1962	

BR 1957 No	*Disposal code*	*Disposal details*	*Notes*
D4083	C	C. F. Booth, Rotherham, South Yorkshire c1969	
D4084	C	C. F. Booth, Rotherham, South Yorkshire c1969	
D4085	C	C. F. Booth, Rotherham, South Yorkshire c1969	
D4086	C	G. Cohen, Kettering, Northamptonshire January 1969	
D4087	C	G. Cohen, Kettering, Northamptonshire April 1969	
D4088	C	C. F. Booth, Rotherham, South Yorkshire c1969	
D4089	C	C. F. Booth, Rotherham, South Yorkshire c1969	
D4090	C	G. Cohen, Kettering, Northamptonshire April 1969	
D4091	C	Slag Reduction, Ickles, Rotherham c1970	
D4092	S	NCB Gwaun-cae-Gurwen Disposal Point	as *Christine*
D4093	C	G. Cohen, Kettering, Northamptonshire April 1969	
D4094	C	G. Cohen, Kettering, Northamptonshire April 1969	
D4095			
D4096			
D4097			
D4098			
D4099			
D4100			
D4101			
D4102			
D4103			
D4104			
D4105			
D4106			
D4107			
D4108			
D4109			
D4110			
D4111			
D4112			
D4113			
D4114			
D4115			
D4116			
D4117			
D4118			
D4119			
D4120			
D4121			
D4122			
D4123			
D4124			
D4125			
D4126			
D4127			
D4128			
D4129			
D4130			
D4131			
D4132			

BR 1957 No	BR 1948 No	TOPS No	Built by	Works No	Date introduced	Date withdrawn
D4133	—	08 903	BR Horwich	—	June 1962	
D4134	—	08 904	BR Horwich	—	June 1962	
D4135	—	08 905	BR Horwich	—	July 1962	
D4136	—	08 906	BR Horwich	—	July 1962	
D4137	—	08 907	BR Horwich	—	July 1962	
D4138	—	08 908	BR Horwich	—	July 1962	
D4139	—	08 909	BR Horwich	—	July 1962	
D4140	—	08 910	BR Horwich	—	September 1962	
D4141	—	08 911	BR Horwich	—	September 1962	
D4142	—	08 912	BR Horwich	—	September 1962	
D4143	—	08 913	BR Horwich	—	September 1962	
D4144	—	08 914	BR Horwich	—	September 1962	
D4145	—	08 915	BR Horwich	—	October 1962	
D4146	—	08 916	BR Horwich	—	October 1962	
D4147	—	08 917	BR Horwich	—	October 1962	
D4148	—	08 918	BR Horwich	—	November 1962	
D4149	—	08 919	BR Horwich	—	November 1962	
D4150	—	08 920	BR Horwich	—	November 1962	
D4151	—	08 921	BR Horwich	—	November 1962	
D4152	—	08 922	BR Horwich	—	November 1962	
D4153	—	08 923	BR Horwich	—	December 1962	
D4154	—	08 924	BR Horwich	—	December 1962	
D4155	—	08 925	BR Horwich	—	December 1962	
D4156	—	08 926	BR Horwich	—	December 1962	
D4157	—	08 927	BR Horwich	—	December 1962	
D4158	—	08 928	BR Darlington	—	May 1962	
D4159	—	08 929	BR Darlington	—	May 1962	
D4160	—	08 930	BR Darlington	—	May 1962	
D4161	—	08 931	BR Darlington	—	May 1962	
D4162	—	08 932	BR Darlington	—	May 1962	
D4163	—	08 933	BR Darlington	—	May 1962	
D4164	—	08 934	BR Darlington	—	May 1962	
D4165	—	08 935	BR Darlington	—	May 1962	
D4166	—	08 936	BR Darlington	—	May 1962	
D4167	—	08 937	BR Darlington	—	June 1962	
D4168	—	08 938	BR Darlington	—	June 1962	
D4169	—	08 939	BR Darlington	—	June 1962	
D4170	—	08 940	BR Darlington	—	June 1962	
D4171	—	08 941	BR Darlington	—	June 1962	
D4172	—	08 942	BR Darlington	—	July 1962	
D4173	—	08 943	BR Darlington	—	July 1962	
D4174	—	08 944	BR Darlington	—	August 1962	
D4175	—	08 945	BR Darlington	—	August 1962	
D4176	—	08 946	BR Darlington	—	September 1962	
D4177	—	08 947	BR Darlington	—	September 1962	
D4178	—	08 948	BR Darlington	—	September 1962	
D4179	—	08 949	BR Darlington	—	September 1962	
D4180	—	08 950	BR Darlington	—	October 1962	
D4181	—	08 951	BR Darlington	—	October 1962	
D4182	—	08 952	BR Darlington	—	October 1962	
D4183	—	08 953	BR Darlington	—	January 1963	
D4184	—	08 954	BR Darlington	—	January 1963	
D4185	—	08 955	BR Darlington	—	January 1963	
D4186	—	08 956	BR Darlington	—	July 1962	
D4187	—	—	BR Darlington	—	July 1962	February 1965
D4188	—	—	BR Darlington	—	July 1962	February 1965
D4189	—	—	BR Darlington	—	July 1962	February 1965
D4190	—	—	BR Darlington	—	August 1962	February 1965
D4191	—	08 957	BR Darlington	—	September 1962	
D4192	—	08 958	BR Darlington	—	September 1962	

BR 1957 No	*Disposal code*	*Disposal details*	*Notes*
D4133			
D4134			
D4135			
D4136			
D4137			
D4138			
D4139			
D4140			
D4141			
D4142			
D4143			
D4144			
D4145			
D4146			
D4147			
D4148			
D4149			
D4150			
D4151			
D4152			
D4153			
D4154			
D4155			
D4156			
D4157			
D4158			
D4159			
D4160			
D4161			
D4162			
D4163			
D4164			
D4165			
D4166			
D4167			
D4168			
D4169			
D4170			
D4171			
D4172			
D4173			
D4174			
D4175			
D4176			
D4177			
D4178			
D4179			
D4180			
D4181			
D4182			
D4183			
D4184			
D4185			
D4186			
D4187	R	Rebuilt into Class 13	
D4188	R	Rebuilt into Class 13	
D4189	R	Rebuilt into Class 13	
D4190	R	Rebuilt into Class 13	
D4191			
D4192			

Class 13

Three special locomotives formed by permanently coupling two Class 08s together, one with its cab removed. Built for use on shunting humps at Tinsley (Sheffield). The loco retaining its cab is the master, and the other the slave.

BR 1957 No	*TOPS No*	*Former Nos*	*Built by*	*Works No*	*Date introduced*
D4500	13 003	(M) D4188 (S) D3698	BR Darlington	—	May 1965
D4501	13 001	(M) D4190 (S) D4189	BR Darlington	—	June 1965
D4502	13 002	(M) D4187 (S) D3697	BR Darlington	—	July 1965

Class 24

The first orders, for 20 locomotives of this design were placed under the 1955 Modernisation Scheme, as the first step to provide a replacement for many steam locomotives of the medium power group, then up for replacement. Several subsequent orders were placed.

BR 1957 No	*TOPS No*	*Built by*	*Works No*	*Period* Date introduced*	*Date withdrawn*	*Disposal code*
D5000	24 005	BR Derby	—	9/58*	January 1976	C
D5001	24 001	BR Derby	—	11/58*	October 1975	C
D5002	24 002	BR Derby	—	13/58*	October 1975	C
D5003	24 003	BR Derby	—	13/58*	August 1975	C
D5004	24 004	BR Derby	—	13/58*	October 1975	C
D5005	—	BR Derby	—	1/59*	January 1969	C
D5006	24 006	BR Derby	—	1/59*	August 1975	C
D5007	24 007	BR Derby	—	2/59*	October 1975	C
D5008	24 008	BR Derby	—	3/59*	August 1975	C
D5009	24 009	BR Derby	—	3/59*	July 1976	C
D5010	24 010	BR Derby	—	3/59*	October 1975	C
D5011	24 011	BR Derby	—	4/59*	October 1975	C
D5012	24 012	BR Derby	—	4/59*	August 1975	C
D5013	24 013	BR Derby	—	4/59*	October 1975	C
D5014	24 014	BR Derby	—	5/59*	October 1975	C
D5015	24 015	BR Derby	—	6/59*	August 1975	C
D5016	24 016	BR Derby	—	6/59*	August 1975	C
D5017	24 017	BR Derby	—	6/59*	October 1975	C
D5018	24 018	BR Derby	—	7/59*	August 1975	C
D5019	24 019	BR Derby	—	7/59*	October 1975	C
D5020	24 020	BR Derby	—	August 1959	August 1975	C
D5021	24 021	BR Derby	—	August 1959	August 1975	C
D5022	24 022	BR Derby	—	September 1959	January 1976	C
D5023	24 023	BR Derby	—	September 1959	September 1978	C
D5024	24 024	BR Derby	—	October 1959	August 1975	C
D5025	24 025	BR Derby	—	October 1959	January 1976	C
D5026	24 026	BR Derby	—	October 1959	August 1975	C
D5027	24 027	BR Derby	—	October 1959	July 1976	C
D5028	—	BR Derby	—	November 1959	June 1972	C
D5029	24 029	BR Derby	—	November 1959	August 1975	C
D5030	24 030	BR Crewe	—	June 1959	July 1976	C
D5031	24 031	BR Crewe	—	June 1959	October 1975	C
D5032	24 032	BR Crewe	—	July 1959	July 1976	P

Engine: (2) EE6K of 350hp giving 700hp
Weight: 120 ton
Wheel dia: 54in
Max speed: 20mph
Class code: 7/1 later BR Class 13

Tractive effort: 70,000lb
Length: 60ft 1in
Height: 12ft 8⅝in
Width: 8ft 6in

BR 1957 No	*Date withdrawn*	*Disposal code*	*Disposal details*	*Notes*
D4500				
D4501				
D4502	June 1981	C	BREL Swindon October 1982	

Engine: Sulzer 6LDA28A of 1,160hp
Weight: 71 ton
Bogie type: Bo-Bo
Max speed: 75mph
Class code: D11/3, later 11/1 and 11/1A, and BR Class 24

Tractive effort: 39,000lb
Length: 50ft 6in
Height: 12ft 8in
Width: 9ft 1in

BR 1957 No	*Disposal details*	*Notes*
D5000	BREL Swindon April 1977	Withdrawn January 1969, reinstated October 1969
D5001	BREL Doncaster November 1977	Withdrawn January 1969, reinstated October 1969
D5002	BREL Glasgow July 1977	
D5003	BREL Doncaster July 1976	
D5004	BREL Glasgow April 1977	
D5005	BREL Derby September 1969	
D5006	BREL Glasgow December 1980	
D5007	BREL Doncaster January 1978	
D5008	BREL Doncaster May 1976	
D5009	BREL Doncaster November 1977	
D5010	BREL Doncaster February 1977	Withdrawn January 1969, reinstated July 1969
D5011	BREL Glasgow April 1977	
D5012	BREL Doncaster February 1976	
D5013	BREL Doncaster February 1978	
D5014	BREL Doncaster March 1978	
D5015	BREL Doncaster January 1977	
D5016	BREL Doncaster March 1977	
D5017	BREL Doncaster March 1977	
D5018	BREL Doncaster June 1976	
D5019	BREL Doncaster May 1978	Withdrawn January 1969, reinstated October 1969
D5020	BREL Swindon April 1977	
D5021	BREL Swindon April 1977	
D5022	BREL Doncaster August 1978	
D5023	BREL Doncaster November 1978	
D5024	BREL Swindon April 1977	
D5025	BREL Swindon July 1977	
D5026	BREL Swindon January 1977	
D5027	BREL Swindon May 1977	
D5028	BREL Crewe September 1972	
D5029	BREL Swindon March 1977	
D5030	BREL Swindon May 1977	
D5031	BREL Swindon December 1976	
D5032	North Yorkshire Moors Railway, Grosmont	After withdrawal to T. J. Thomson scrap dealer

BR 1957 No	*TOPS No*	*Built by*	*Works No*	*Date introduced*	*Date withdrawn*	*Disposal code*
D5033	24 033	BR Crewe	—	August 1959	October 1975	C
D5034	24 034	BR Crewe	—	September 1959	January 1976	C
D5035	24 035	BR Crewe	—	August 1959	October 1978	C
D5036	24 036	BR Crewe	—	September 1959	November 1977	C
D5037	24 037	BR Crewe	—	September 1959	July 1976	C
D5038	24 038	BR Crewe	—	September 1959	July 1976	C
D5039	24 039	BR Crewe	—	September 1959	July 1976	C
D5040	24 040	BR Crewe	—	October 1959	January 1976	C
D5041	24 041	BR Crewe	—	September 1959	July 1976	C
D5042	24 042	BR Crewe	—	October 1959	August 1975	C
D5043	—	BR Crewe	—	October 1959	August 1969	C
D5044	24 044	BR Crewe	—	October 1959	January 1976	C
D5045	24 045	BR Crewe	—	November 1959	August 1975	C
D5046	24 046	BR Crewe	—	October 1959	July 1976	C
D5047	24 047	BR Crewe	—	November 1959	November 1978	C
D5048	24 048	BR Crewe	—	November 1959	August 1975	C
D5049	24 049	BR Crewe	—	April 1960	January 1976	C
D5050	24 050	BR Crewe	—	November 1959	October 1975	C
D5051	—	BR Crewe	—	December 1959	November 1967	C
D5052	24 052	BR Crewe	—	December 1959	December 1976	C
D5053	24 053	BR Crewe	—	December 1959	January 1976	C
D5054	24 054	BR Crewe	—	December 1959	July 1976	D
D5055	24 055	BR Crewe	—	December 1959	October 1975	C
D5056	24 056	BR Crewe	—	December 1959	October 1975	C
D5057	24 057	BR Crewe	—	December 1959	January 1978	C
D5058	24 058	BR Crewe	—	January 1960	October 1975	C
D5059	24 059	BR Crewe	—	December 1959	October 1975	C
D5060	24 060	BR Crewe	—	January 1960	October 1975	C
D5061	24 061	BR Crewe	—	January 1960	August 1975	D
D5062	24 062	BR Crewe	—	January 1960	October 1975	C
D5063	24 063	BR Crewe	—	January 1960	April 1979	C
D5064	24 064	BR Crewe	—	January 1960	January 1976	C
D5065	24 065	BR Crewe	—	February 1960	December 1976	C
D5066	24 066	BR Derby	—	December 1959	February 1976	C
D5067	—	BR Derby	—	December 1959	October 1972	C
D5068	—	BR Derby	—	December 1959	October 1972	C
D5069	24 069	BR Derby	—	January 1960	December 1976	C
D5070	24 070	BR Derby	—	January 1960	February 1976	C
D5071	24 071	BR Derby	—	February 1960	August 1975	C
D5072	24 072	BR Derby	—	February 1960	October 1975	C
D5073	24 073	BR Derby	—	March 1960	December 1978	C
D5074	24 074	BR Derby	—	March 1960	October 1975	C
D5075	24 075	BR Derby	—	March 1960	January 1976	C
D5076	24 076	BR Crewe	—	February 1960	October 1975	C
D5077	24 077	BR Crewe	—	February 1960	July 1976	C
D5078	24 078	BR Crewe	—	February 1960	April 1976	C
D5079	24 079	BR Crewe	—	February 1960	July 1976	C
D5080	24 080	BR Crewe	—	March 1960	September 1976	C
D5081	24 081	BR Crewe	—	March 1960	October 1980	P
D5082	24 082	BR Crewe	—	March 1960	March 1979	C
D5083	24 083	BR Crewe	—	April 1960	March 1976	C
D5084	24 084	BR Crewe	—	April 1960	July 1976	C
D5085	24 085	BR Crewe	—	May 1960	July 1976	C
D5086	24 086	BR Crewe	—	May 1960	January 1976	C
D5087	24 087	BR Crewe	—	June 1960	February 1978	C
D5088	—	BR Crewe	—	June 1960	July 1970	C
D5089	24 089	BR Crewe	—	June 1960	January 1976	C
D5090	24 090	BR Crewe	—	June 1960	February 1976	C

BR 1957 No	*Disposal details*	*Notes*
D5033	BREL Swindon March 1977	
D5034	BREL Swindon May 1977	
D5035	BREL Doncaster January 1979	
D5036	BREL Doncaster June 1978	
D5037	BREL Swindon June 1977	
D5038	BREL Swindon June 1977	
D5039	BREL Swindon July 1978	
D5040	BREL Swindon February 1977	
D5041	BREL Swindon June 1978	
D5042	BREL Swindon February 1976	
D5043	J. Cashmore, Great Bridge, Tipton June 1970	
D5044	BREL Swindon January 1977	
D5045	BREL Swindon December 1976	
D5046	BREL Swindon July 1977	
D5047	BREL Doncaster February 1979	
D5048	BREL Doncaster March 1976	
D5049	BREL Doncaster November 1976	Completed November 1959
D5050	BREL Doncaster December 1976	
D5051	BR Workshops, Inverurie August 1968	
D5052	BREL Swindon May 1978	
D5053	BREL Swindon May 1976	
D5054	Departmental Stock — 968008	
D5055	BREL Swindon December 1976	
D5056	BREL Swindon November 1976	
D5057	BREL Doncaster May 1978	
D5058	BREL Swindon October 1976	
D5059	BREL Swindon March 1977	
D5060	BREL Swindon January 1977	
D5061	Departmental Stock — 97201	
D5062	BREL Swindon October 1976	
D5063	BREL Doncaster July 1979	
D5064	BREL Swindon December 1976	
D5065	BREL Swindon June 1977	
D5066	BREL Doncaster August 1978	
D5067	BREL Glasgow October 1973	
D5068	BREL Glasgow April 1973	
D5069	BREL Doncaster September 1977	
D5070	BREL Doncaster June 1976	
D5071	BREL Doncaster January 1977	
D5072	BREL Doncaster December 1977	
D5073	BREL Doncaster December 1978	Withdrawn December 1976, reinstated February 1977
D5074	J. Cashmore, Great Bridge, Tipton c1976	
D5075	BREL Swindon July 1976	
D5076	BREL Swindon January 1977	
D5077	BREL Swindon June 1978	
D5078	BREL Swindon June 1978	
D5079	BREL Swindon September 1978	
D5080	BREL Doncaster June 1978	
D5081	Steamport, Southport	
D5082	BREL Doncaster April 1979	
D5083	BREL Swindon May 1977	
D5084	BREL Swindon May 1978	
D5085	BREL Swindon October 1978	
D5086	BREL Doncaster January 1977	
D5087	BREL Doncaster August 1978	
D5088	G. Cohen, Kettering, Northamptonshire January 1972	
D5089	BREL Swindon July 1977	
D5090	BREL Doncaster January 1978	

BR 1957 No	TOPS No	Built by	Works No	Period* Date introduced	Date withdrawn	Disposal code
D5091	24 091	BR Crewe	—	June 1960	November 1977	C
D5092	24 092	BR Crewe	—	July 1960	October 1975	C
D5093	—	BR Crewe	—	July 1960	August 1969	C
D5094	24 094	BR Darlington	—	February 1960	December 1976	C
D5095	24 095	BR Darlington	—	March 1960	August 1975	C
D5096	24 096	BR Darlington	—	April 1960	August 1975	C
D5097	24 097	BR Darlington	—	May 1960	February 1976	C
D5098	24 098	BR Darlington	—	May 1960	August 1975	C
D5099	24 099	BR Darlington	—	June 1960	February 1976	C
D5100	24 100	BR Darlington	—	June 1960	February 1976	C
D5101	24 101	BR Darlington	—	July 1960	February 1976	C
D5102	24 102	BR Darlington	—	July 1960	February 1976	C
D5103	24 103	BR Darlington	—	August 1960	December 1976	C
D5104	24 104	BR Darlington	—	August 1960	December 1976	C
D5105	24 105	BR Darlington	—	September 1960	October 1975	C
D5106	24 106	BR Darlington	—	September 1960	December 1976	C
D5107	24 107	BR Darlington	—	October 1960	December 1976	C
D5108	24 108	BR Darlington	—	October 1960	July 1976	C
D5109	24 109	BR Darlington	—	November 1960	February 1976	C
D5110	24 110	BR Darlington	—	November 1960	December 1976	C
D5111	24 111	BR Darlington	—	November 1960	February 1976	C
D5112	24 112	BR Darlington	—	December 1960	December 1976	C
D5113	24 113	BR Darlington	—	January 1961	December 1976	C
D5114	—	BR Derby	—	4/60*	October 1972	C
D5115	24 115	BR Derby	—	5/60*	December 1976	C
D5116	24 116	BR Derby	—	5/60*	September 1976	C
D5117	24 117	BR Derby	—	5/60*	February 1976	C
D5118	24 118	BR Derby	—	5/60*	December 1976	C
D5119	24 119	BR Derby	—	6/60*	July 1976	C
D5120	24 120	BR Derby	—	6/60*	December 1976	C
D5121	24 121	BR Derby	—	6/60*	December 1976	C
D5122	—	BR Derby	—	6/60*	September 1968	C
D5123	24 123	BR Derby	—	7/60*	July 1976	C
D5124	24 124	BR Derby	—	7/60*	December 1976	C
D5125	24 125	BR Derby	—	7/60*	March 1976	C
D5126	24 126	BR Derby	—	8/60*	February 1976	C
D5127	24 127	BR Derby	—	8/60*	February 1976	C
D5128	24 128	BR Derby	—	8/60*	July 1976	C
D5129	24 129	BR Derby	—	9/60*	December 1976	C
D5130	24 130	BR Derby	—	9/60*	December 1976	C
D5131	—	BR Derby	—	10/60*	September 1971	C
D5132	24 132	BR Derby	—	10/60*	February 1976	C
D5133	24 133	BR Derby	—	10/60*	March 1978	C
D5134	24 134	BR Derby	—	10/60*	December 1976	C
D5135	24 135	BR Derby	—	10/60*	January 1976	C
D5136	24 136	BR Derby	—	11/60*	October 1975	C
D5137	24 137	BR Derby	—	11/60*	July 1976	C
D5138	—	BR Derby	—	11/60*	August 1969	C
D5139	—	BR Derby	—	11/60*	August 1969	C
D5140	24 140	BR Derby	—	11/60*	January 1976	C
D5141	24 141	BR Derby	—	12/60*	July 1976	C
D5142	24 142	BR Derby	—	12/60*	July 1976	D
D5143	24 143	BR Derby	—	12/60*	January 1976	C
D5144	24 144	BR Derby	—	12/60*	January 1976	C
D5145	24 145	BR Derby	—	13/60*	January 1976	C
D5146	24 146	BR Derby	—	13/60*	January 1976	C
D5147	24 147	BR Derby	—	December 1960	July 1976	C
D5148	24 148	BR Derby	—	December 1960	October 1975	C
D5149	—	BR Derby	—	January 1961	October 1972	C
D5150	24 150	BR Derby	—	January 1961	December 1976	C

BR 1957 No	*Disposal details*	*Notes*
D5091	BREL Doncaster June 1978	
D5092	BREL Swindon December 1976	
D5093	J. Cashmore, Great Bridge, Tipton June 1970	
D5094	BREL Doncaster September 1977	
D5095	BREL Doncaster June 1976	
D5096	BREL Doncaster August 1976	
D5097	BREL Doncaster February 1977	
D5098	BREL Doncaster May 1976	
D5099	BREL Doncaster August 1977	
D5100	BREL Doncaster April 1976	
D5101	BREL Doncaster March 1976	
D5102	BREL Doncaster April 1978	
D5103	BREL Doncaster July 1977	
D5104	BREL Doncaster September 1977	
D5105	BREL Doncaster March 1978	
D5106	BREL Doncaster October 1977	
D5107	BREL Swindon June 1977	
D5108	BREL Doncaster February 1978	
D5109	BREL Doncaster March 1978	
D5110	BREL Doncaster April 1977	
D5111	BREL Doncaster February 1978	
D5112	BREL Doncaster October 1977	
D5113	BREL Doncaster October 1977	
D5114	BREL Glasgow October 1973	
D5115	BREL Swindon June 1977	
D5116	BREL Doncaster July 1977	
D5117	BREL Doncaster January 1977	
D5118	BREL Doncaster June 1977	
D5119	BREL Doncaster May 1977	
D5120	BREL Doncaster August 1977	
D5121	BREL Doncaster May 1978	
D5122	BREL Glasgow March 1971	
D5123	BREL Doncaster July 1977	
D5124	BREL Swindon May 1977	
D5125	BREL Doncaster July 1977	
D5126	BREL Doncaster July 1977	
D5127	BREL Doncaster March 1977	
D5128	BREL Doncaster October 1977	
D5129	BREL Doncaster April 1977	
D5130	BREL Doncaster August 1977	
D5131	BREL Glasgow November 1971	
D5132	BREL Doncaster March 1976	
D5133	BREL Doncaster September 1978	
D5134	BREL Swindon September 1978	
D5135	BREL Swindon July 1977	
D5136	BREL Swindon January 1977	
D5137	BREL Doncaster October 1978	
D5138	J. Cashmore, Great Bridge, Tipton June 1970	
D5139	J. Cashmore, Great Bridge, Tipton June 1970	
D5140	BREL Swindon September 1976	
D5141	BREL Swindon June 1978	
D5142	Departmental Stock — 968009	
D5143	BREL Swindon May 1976	
D5144	BREL Swindon September 1976	
D5145	BREL Swindon June 1976	
D5146	BREL Swindon October 1976	
D5147	BREL Doncaster November 1977	
D5148	BREL Doncaster December 1977	
D5149	BREL Glasgow April 1973	
D5150	BREL Doncaster August 1977	

BR/Sulzer Type 2 No D5082, classified as Class 24, No 24 082 under TOPS numbering. This locomotive was built at Crewe in March 1960. *GEC Traction Ltd*

Under BR TOPS classification the Brush Type 2 locomotives became Class 31. No 31 268, formerly D5698 (BEM works number 300), stands at Duxford in 1981. *Colin J. Marsden*

An unusual fleet of 20 locomotives were built by Metropolitan Vickers in 1958, having a three-axle bogie at one end and a two-axle bogie at the other. No D5700, the first of the class, is shown here. *BR*

English Electric built 'Baby Deltic' Class 23 locomotives were introduced from 1959 for ER suburban duties. However the class was wholly unsuccessful and all were withdrawn by the end of 1973. D5903 is seen in original condition painted in green livery with white base band.
GEC Traction Ltd

Class 25

The fleets of Type 2 1,160hp locomotives proved themselves, and in 1960 orders were placed for a subsequent build with detail modifications and different internal equipment. Two different body designs were built.

BR 1957 No	*TOPS No*	*Built by*	*Works No*	*Period* Date introduced*	*Date withdrawn*	*Disposal code*
D5151	25 001	BR Darlington	—	April 1961	September 1980	C
D5152	25 002	BR Darlington	—	May 1961	December 1980	C
D5153	25 003	BR Darlington	—	May 1961	August 1976	C
D5154	25 004	BR Darlington	—	May 1961	September 1976	C
D5155	25 005	BR Darlington	—	June 1961	December 1980	C
D5156	25 006	BR Darlington	—	June 1961	December 1980	C
D5157	25 007	BR Darlington	—	July 1961	December 1980	C
D5158	25 008	BR Darlington	—	July 1961	June 1980	C
D5159	25 009	BR Darlington	—	July 1961	July 1980	C
D5160	25 010	BR Darlington	—	August 1961	February 1980	C
D5161	25 011	BR Darlington	—	September 1961	December 1980	C
D5162	25 012	BR Darlington	—	September 1961	February 1977	C
D5163	25 013	BR Darlington	—	September 1961	September 1980	C
D5164	25 014	BR Darlington	—	October 1961	July 1977	C
D5165	25 015	BR Darlington	—	October 1961	December 1975	C
D5166	25 016	BR Darlington	—	November 1961	January 1976	C
D5167	25 017	BR Darlington	—	November 1961	January 1976	C
D5168	25 018	BR Darlington	—	December 1961	November 1976	C
D5169	25 019	BR Darlington	—	December 1961	September 1980	C
D5170	25 020	BR Darlington	—	December 1961	January 1976	C
D5171	25 021	BR Darlington	—	February 1962	September 1980	C
D5172	25 022	BR Darlington	—	February 1962	January 1976	C
D5173	25 023	BR Darlington	—	March 1962	September 1980	C
D5174	25 024	BR Darlington	—	March 1962	January 1976	C
D5175	25 025	BR Darlington	—	April 1962	April 1977	C
D5176	25 026	BR Darlington	—	January 1963	November 1980	C
D5177	25 027	BR Darlington	—	February 1963	May 1983	A
D5178	25 028	BR Darlington	—	February 1963	December 1980	A
D5179	25 029	BR Darlington	—	February 1963	August 1977	C
D5180	25 030	BR Darlington	—	February 1963	August 1976	C
D5181	25 031	BR Darlington	—	March 1963	December 1977	C
D5182	25 032	BR Darlington	—	March 1963		
D5183	25 033	BR Darlington	—	4/63*	April 1983	A
D5184	25 034	BR Darlington	—	5/63*		
D5185	25 035	BR Darlington	—	6/63*		
D5186	25 036	BR Derby	—	3/63*	December 1982	A
D5187	25 037	BR Derby	—	3/63*		
D5188	25 038	BR Derby	—	3/63*	May 1981	C
D5189	25 039	BR Derby	—	4/63*	May 1981	C
D5190	25 040	BR Derby	—	4/63*	November 1980	C
D5191	25 041	BR Derby	—	5/63*	May 1981	C
D5192	25 042	BR Derby	—	5/63*		
D5193	25 043	BR Derby	—	5/63*	February 1981	C
D5194	25 044	BR Derby	—	5/63*		
D5195	25 045	BR Derby	—	5/63*	October 1975	C
D5196	25 046	BR Derby	—	5/63*	February 1981	A
D5197	25 047	BR Derby	—	5/63*	September 1980	C
D5198	25 048	BR Derby	—	5/63*		
D5199	25 049	BR Derby	—	5/63*	January 1984	A
D5200	25 050	BR Derby	—	6/63*	April 1983	A
D5201	25 051	BR Derby	—	6/63*		
D5202	25 052	BR Derby	—	6/63*	October 1980	C
D5203	25 053	BR Derby	—	6/63*	December 1980	C

Engine: Sulzer 6LDA28B of 1,250hp
Weight: 73 ton
Bogie type: Bo-Bo
Max speed: 90mph
Class code: D12/4, later 12/1 and 12/1A.
BR Class 25

Tractive effort: 45,000lb
Length: 50ft 6in
Height: 12ft 8in
Width: 9ft 1in

BR 1957 No	*Disposal details*	*Notes*
D5151	BREL Swindon November 1980	
D5152	BREL Swindon April 1981	
D5153	BREL Glasgow January 1979	
D5154	BREL Glasgow September 1977	
D5155	BREL Swindon August 1981	
D5156	BREL Swindon May 1983	Stored from September 1980
D5157	BREL Swindon September 1982	Stored from September 1980
D5158	BREL Glasgow September 1980	
D5159	BREL Glasgow October 1980	
D5160	BREL Swindon May 1981	
D5161	BREL Swindon March 1981	
D5162	BREL Glasgow September 1977	
D5163	BREL Swindon January 1981	
D5164	BREL Swindon September 1977	
D5165	BREL Doncaster February 1977	
D5166	BREL Swindon December 1976	
D5167	BREL Swindon July 1976	
D5168	BREL Glasgow September 1978	
D5169	BREL Swindon January 1981	
D5170	BREL Swindon August 1976	
D5171	BREL Swindon December 1980	
D5172	BREL Glasgow January 1979	
D5173	BREL Swindon March 1983	
D5174	BREL Glasgow January 1977	
D5175	BREL Glasgow June 1978	
D5176	BREL Swindon March 1981	
D5177	BR Saltley depot	
D5178	BREL Glasgow	Stored from October 1980
D5179	BREL Glasgow January 1978	
D5180	BREL Derby May 1980	
D5181	BREL Glasgow May 1978	
D5182		
D5183	BREL Derby	
D5184		
D5185		
D5186	BREL Derby	
D5187		
D5188	BREL Derby November 1982	
D5189	BREL Swindon December 1981	
D5190	BREL Swindon February 1982	
D5191	BREL Swindon May 1983	
D5192		
D5193	BREL Derby August 1981	
D5194		
D5195	BREL Derby August 1979	
D5196	BR Polmadie depot	
D5197	BREL Swindon January 1981	
D5198		
D5199	BREL Derby	
D5200	BREL Derby	
D5201		
D5202	BREL Swindon November 1980	
D5203	BREL Swindon November 1981	Stored from November 1980

BR 1957 No	*TOPS No*	*Built by*	*Works No*	*Period* Date introduced*	*Date withdrawn*	*Disposal code*
D5204	25 054	BR Derby	—	6/63*		
D5205	25 055	BR Derby	—	6/63*	November 1980	C
D5206	25 056	BR Derby	—	7/63*	August 1982	A
D5207	25 057	BR Derby	—	7/63*		
D5208	25 058	BR Derby	—	7/63*		
D5209	25 059	BR Derby	—	7/63*		
D5210	25 060	BR Derby	—	7/63*		
D5211	25 061	BR Derby	—	7/63*	November 1980	C
D5212	25 062	BR Derby	—	7/63*	December 1982	A
D5213	25 063	BR Derby	—	7/63*	November 1980	C
D5214	25 064	BR Derby	—	7/63*		
D5215	25 065	BR Derby	—	8/63*	February 1981	C
D5216	25 066	BR Derby	—	7/63*	June 1981	C
D5217	25 067	BR Derby	—	8/63*	December 1982	A
D5218	25 068	BR Derby	—	8/63*	July 1980	C
D5219	25 069	BR Derby	—	8/63*	December 1983	A
D5220	25 070	BR Derby	—	10/63*	November 1980	C
D5221	25 071	BR Derby	—	9/63*	June 1981	C
D5222	25 072	BR Derby	—	10/63*		
D5223	25 073	BR Darlington	—	7/63*	September 1981	C
D5224	25 074	BR Darlington	—	8/63*	September 1980	C
D5225	25 075	BR Darlington	—	8/63*	March 1983	A
D5226	25 076	BR Darlington	—	9/63*		
D5227	25 077	BR Darlington	—	9/63*	May 1978	C
D5228	25 078	BR Darlington	—	10/63*		
D5229	25 079	BR Darlington	—	10/63*	August 1983	C
D5230	25 080	BR Darlington	—	11/63*		
D5231	25 081	BR Darlington	—	13/63*	February 1982	C
D5232	25 082	BR Darlington	—	12/63*	May 1981	C
D5233	25 083	BR Derby	—	13/63*	July 1984	
D5234	25 084	BR Derby	—	13/63*	December 1983	A
D5235	25 085	BR Derby	—	13/63*	March 1982	C
D5236	25 086	BR Derby	—	13/63*	October 1983	A
D5237	25 087	BR Derby	—	13/63*	September 1980	C
D5238	25 088	BR Derby	—	13/63*	August 1981	A
D5239	25 089	BR Derby	—	13/63*		
D5240	25 090	BR Derby	—	1/64*	May 1983	A
D5241	25 091	BR Derby	—	1/64*	October 1978	C
D5242	25 092	BR Derby	—	1/64*	May 1980	C
D5243	25 093	BR Derby	—	1/64*	November 1982	A
D5244	25 094	BR Derby	—	1/64*	February 1981	C
D5245	25 095	BR Derby	—	1/64*		
D5246	25 096	BR Derby	—	1/64*	December 1977	C
D5247	25 097	BR Derby	—	2/64*	November 1983	A
D5248	25 098	BR Derby	—	2/64*	October 1978	C
D5249	25 099	BR Derby	—	2/64*	December 1980	C
D5250	25 100	BR Derby	—	2/64*	February 1981	C
D5251	25 101	BR Derby	—	2/64*	January 1983	A
D5252	25 102	BR Derby	—	2/64*	May 1980	C
D5253	25 103	BR Derby	—	3/64*	September 1980	C
D5254	25 104	BR Derby	—	3/64*	September 1982	A
D5255	25 105	BR Derby	—	3/64*	April 1982	A
D5256	25 106	BR Derby	—	3/64*	November 1983	C
D5257	25 107	BR Derby	—	3/64*	May 1981	C
D5258	25 108	BR Derby	—	3/64*	July 1980	C
D5259	25 109	BR Derby	—	4/64*		
D5260	25 110	BR Derby	—	4/64*	November 1980	C
D5261	25 111	BR Derby	—	4/64*	March 1980	C
D5262	25 112	BR Derby	—	4/64*	November 1980	C
D5263	25 113	BR Derby	—	4/64*	June 1983	C
D5264	25 114	BR Derby	—	4/64*	February 1981	C

BR 1957 No	*Disposal details*	*Notes*
D5204		
D5205	BREL Swindon January 1982	
D5206	BREL Swindon	
D5207		
D5208		
D5209		
D5210		
D5211	BREL Swindon March 1983	
D5212	BREL Derby	
D5213	BREL Swindon February 1983	
D5214		
D5215	BREL Swindon February 1982	
D5216	BREL Derby January 1983	
D5217	BREL Swindon	
D5218	BREL Glasgow August 1981	
D5219	BR Springs Branch depot	
D5220	BREL Swindon May 1983	
D5221	BREL Swindon January 1983	
D5222		
D5223	BREL Swindon August 1982	
D5224	BREL Swindon May 1982	
D5225	BR Cricklewood depot	
D5226		
D5227	BREL Glasgow September 1978	
D5228		
D5229	BREL Swindon January 1984	
D5230		
D5231	BREL Swindon June 1982	
D5232	BREL Swindon January 1983	
D5233		
D5234	BR Newton Heath depot	
D5235	BREL Derby June 1983	
D5236	BR Newton Heath depot	
D5237	BREL Swindon April 1981	
D5238	BREL Derby	
D5239		
D5240	BREL Swindon	
D5241	BREL Glasgow November 1979	
D5242	BREL Derby June 1982	
D5243	BREL Derby	
D5244	BREL Derby April 1982	
D5245		
D5246	BREL Glasgow May 1978	
D5247	BREL Swindon	
D5248	BREL Glasgow July 1979	
D5249	BREL Swindon February 1981	Stored from November 1980
D5250	BREL Swindon February 1983	
D5251	BREL Swindon	
D5252	BREL Swindon October 1980	
D5253	BREL Swindon March 1983	
D5254	BREL Swindon	
D5255	BREL Derby	
D5256	BREL Swindon February 1984	
D5257	BREL Swindon September 1981	
D5258	BREL Glasgow February 1981	
D5259		
D5260	BREL Swindon March 1982	
D5261	BREL Swindon October 1980	
D5262	BREL Swindon March 1982	
D5263	BREL Swindon October 1983	
D5264	BREL Swindon July 1981	

BR 1957 No	TOPS No	Built by	Works No	Period* Date introduced	Date withdrawn	Disposal code
D5265	25 115	BR Derby	—	5/64*	October 1983	C
D5266	25 116	BR Derby	—	5/64*	November 1980	C
D5267	25 117	BR Derby	—	5/64*	January 1984	C
D5268	25 118	BR Derby	—	5/64*	January 1981	C
D5269	25 119	BR Derby	—	5/64*		
D5270	25 120	BR Derby	—	5/64*	November 1983	C
D5271	25 121	BR Derby	—	6/64*	November 1980	C
D5272	25 122	BR Derby	—	6/64*	November 1980	C
D5273	25 123	BR Derby	—	6/64*	May 1983	A
D5274	25 124	BR Derby	—	6/64*	November 1983	A
D5275	25 125	BR Derby	—	6/64*	December 1981	C
D5276	25 126	BR Derby	—	6/64*	November 1982	A
D5277	25 127	BR Derby	—	7/64*	November 1980	C
D5278	—	BR Derby	—	6/64*	May 1971	C
D5279	25 129	BR Derby	—	7/64*	February 1982	A
D5280	25 130	BR Derby	—	7/64*	December 1982	A
D5281	25 131	BR Derby	—	7/64*	December 1982	D
D5282	25 132	BR Derby	—	7/64*	December 1982	A
D5283	25 133	BR Derby	—	7/64*	August 1983	A
D5284	25 134	BR Derby	—	7/64*	December 1982	A
D5285	25 135	BR Derby	—	7/64*	January 1983	A
D5286	25 136	BR Derby	—	9/64*	March 1983	A
D5287	25 137	BR Derby	—	9/64*	October 1980	C
D5288	25 138	BR Derby	—	9/64*	December 1983	A
D5289	25 139	BR Derby	—	9/64*	November 1982	A
D5290	25 140	BR Derby	—	9/64*	December 1983	A
D5291	25 141	BR Derby	—	9/64*	September 1982	A
D5292	25 142	BR Derby	—	9/64*	October 1981	C
D5293	25 143	BR Derby	—	9/64*	November 1982	A
D5294	25 144	BR Derby	—	10/64*	April 1983	A
D5295	25 145	BR Derby	—	10/64*		
D5296	25 146	BR Derby	—	10/64*	August 1983	A
D5297	25 147	BR Derby	—	10/64*	March 1980	C
D5298	25 148	BR Derby	—	10/64*	September 1981	C
D5299	25 149	BR Derby	—	11/65*	January 1982	C

Class continued with D7500

Class 26

Ordered by the BTC under the modernisation scheme, these BRCW Type 2s for use on ER and ScR incorporated the Sulzer 6LDA28A power unit, as in the BR Type 2s. The first order for 20 locomotives was soon increased to 47 examples.

BR 1957 No	TOPS No	Built by	Works No	Date introduced	Date withdrawn	Disposal code
D5300	26 007	BRCW	DEL 45	July 1958		
D5301	26 001	BRCW	DEL 46	September 1958		
D5302	26 002	BRCW	DEL 47	October 1958		
D5303	26 003	BRCW	DEL 48	October 1958		
D5304	26 004	BRCW	DEL 49	October 1958		
D5305	26 005	BRCW	DEL 50	November 1958		
D5306	26 006	BRCW	DEL 51	November 1958		
D5307	26 020	BRCW	DEL 52	December 1958	February 1977	C
D5308	26 008	BRCW	DEL 53	December 1958		
D5309	26 009	BRCW	DEL 54	December 1958	January 1977	C
D5310	26 010	BRCW	DEL 55	January 1959		

BR 1957 No	*Disposal details*	*Notes*
D5265	BREL Swindon November 1983	
D5266	BREL Swindon July 1982	
D5267	BREL Swindon May 1984	
D5268	BREL Swindon August 1983	
D5269		
D5270	BREL Swindon May 1984	
D5271	BREL Swindon August 1982	
D5272	BREL Swindon May 1983	
D5273	BR Bristol Bath Road depot	
D5274	BREL Swindon	
D5275	BREL Swindon March 1983	
D5276	BREL Swindon	
D5277	BREL Swindon April 1983	
D5278	Peak Forest by G. Cohen October 1971	
D5279	BREL Derby	
D5280	BREL Swindon	
D5281	BREL Swindon	Transferred to departmental stock in early 1984 as 97202
D5282	BREL Swindon	
D5283	BREL Derby	
D5284	BREL Swindon	
D5285	BREL Swindon	
D5286	BREL Swindon	
D5287	BREL Swindon April 1983	
D5288	BR Crewe depot	
D5289	BREL Swindon	
D5290	BR Crewe depot	
D5291	BREL Swindon	
D5292	BREL Swindon November 1982	
D5293	BREL Swindon	
D5294	BREL Swindon	Stored April 1983
D5295		
D5296	BREL Derby	
D5297	BREL Swindon September 1980	
D5298	BREL Swindon May 1982	
D5299	BREL Swindon May 1983	Completed October 1964 under test until November 1965

Engine: Sulzer 6LDA28A of 1,160hp
Weight: 77 ton
Bogie type: Bo-Bo
Max speed: 75mph
Class code: D11/4, later 11/6 and 11/6A, and BR Class 26

Tractive effort: 42,000lb
Length: 50ft 9in
Height: 12ft 8in
Width: 8ft 10in

BR 1957 No	*Disposal details*	*Notes*
D5300		
D5301		
D5302		
D5303		
D5304		
D5305		
D5306		
D5307	BREL Glasgow March 1978	
D5308		
D5309	BREL Glasgow April 1978	
D5310		

BR 1957 No	*TOPS No*	*Built by*	*Works No*	*Period* Date introduced*	*Date withdrawn*	*Disposal code*
D5311	26 011	BRCW	DEL 56	January 1959		
D5312	26 012	BRCW	DEL 57	January 1959	January 1982	C
D5313	26 013	BRCW	DEL 58	January 1959		
D5314	26 014	BRCW	DEL 59	January 1959		
D5315	26 015	BRCW	DEL 60	February 1959		
D5316	26 016	BRCW	DEL 61	February 1959	October 1975	C
D5317	26 017	BRCW	DEL 62	February 1959	August 1977	C
D5318	26 018	BRCW	DEL 63	March 1959	January 1982	C
D5319	26 019	BRCW	DEL 64	March 1959		
D5320	26 028	BRCW	DEL 65	4/59*		
D5321	26 021	BRCW	DEL 66	4/59*		
D5322	26 022	BRCW	DEL 67	5/59*	February 1981	C
D5323	26 023	BRCW	DEL 68	5/59*		
D5324	26 024	BRCW	DEL 69	5/59*		
D5325	26 025	BRCW	DEL 70	5/59*		
D5326	26 026	BRCW	DEL 71	6/59*		
D5327	26 027	BRCW	DEL 72	6/59*		
D5328	—	BRCW	DEL 73	6/59*	July 1972	C
D5329	26 029	BRCW	DEL 74	6/59*		
D5330	26 030	BRCW	DEL 75	7/59*		
D5331	26 031	BRCW	DEL 76	7/59*		
D5332	26 032	BRCW	DEL 77	7/59*		
D5333	26 033	BRCW	DEL 78	7/59*		
D5334	26 034	BRCW	DEL 79	8/59*		
D5335	26 035	BRCW	DEL 80	8/59*		
D5336	26 036	BRCW	DEL 81	9/59*		
D5337	26 037	BRCW	DEL 82	9/59*		
D5338	26 038	BRCW	DEL 83	9/59*		
D5339	26 039	BRCW	DEL 84	9/59*		
D5340	26 040	BRCW	DEL 85	10/59*		
D5341	26 041	BRCW	DEL 86	10/59*		
D5342	26 042	BRCW	DEL 87	10/59*		
D5343	26 043	BRCW	DEL 88	10/59*		
D5344	26 044	BRCW	DEL 89	11/59*	January 1984	A
D5345	26 045	BRCW	DEL 90	11/59*	July 1983	A
D5346	26 046	BRCW	DEL 91	11/59*		

Class 27

Subsequent BRCW Type 2 locomotives were built with the Sulzer 6LDA28B power unit of 1,250hp and now classified as 27. When built, locomotives were allocated to LMR/ER/ScR, but in common with the Class 26s all now operate in Scotland.

BR 1957 No	*TOPS No*	*TOPS re-No: 1*	*TOPS re-No: 2*	*Built by*	*Works No*	*Period* Date introduced*	*Date withdrawn*
D5347	27 001	—	—	BRCW	DEL 190	7/61*	
D5348	27 002	—	—	BRCW	DEL 191	8/61*	
D5349	27 003	—	—	BRCW	DEL 192	8/61*	
D5350	27 004	—	—	BRCW	DEL 193	9/61*	
D5351	27 005	—	—	BRCW	DEL 194	9/61*	
D5352	27 006	—	—	BRCW	DEL 195	9/61*	January 1976
D5353	27 007	—	—	BRCW	DEL 196	10/61*	
D5354	27 008	—	—	BRCW	DEL 197	10/61*	
D5355	27 009	—	—	BRCW	DEL 198	10/61*	July 1980
D5356	27 010	—	—	BRCW	DEL 199	11/61*	
D5357	27 011	—	—	BRCW	DEL 200	11/61*	March 1981

BR 1957 No	*Disposal details*	*Notes*
D5311		
D5312	BREL Glasgow August 1982	
D5313		Stored September 1982
D5314		Stored September 1982, reinstated May 1984
D5315		
D5316	BREL Glasgow September 1976	
D5317	BREL Glasgow February 1978	
D5318	BREL Glasgow May 1982	
D5319		Stored February 1983
D5320		Stored 1983, reinstated June 1983
D5321		
D5322	BREL Glasgow March 1981	
D5323		
D5324		
D5325		
D5326		
D5327		Stored November 1982, reinstated May 1983, stored April 1984
D5328	BREL Glasgow December 1972	
D5329		
D5330		Stored October 1983
D5331		
D5332		
D5333		Stored October 1982
D5334		
D5335		
D5336		
D5337		
D5338		
D5339		Stored April 1984
D5340		
D5341		
D5342		
D5343		
D5344	BR Inverness depot	
D5345	BR Polmadie depot	Stored January 1983
D5346		

Engine: Sulzer 6LDA28B of 1,250hp
Weight: 71-76 tons†
Bogie type: Bo-Bo
Max speed: 90mph
Class code: D12/3, later 12/6, BR Class 27
†Dependent on fittings

Tractive effort: 40,000lb
Length: 50ft 9in
Height: 12ft 8in
Width: 8ft 10in

BR 1957 No	*Disposal code*	*Disposal details*	*Notes*
D5347			Stored September 1982, reinstated June 1983
D5348			Stored March 1984, reinstated May 1984
D5349			
D5350			
D5351			
D5352	C	BREL Glasgow January 1977	
D5353			
D5354			
D5355	C	BREL Glasgow January 1982	
D5356			
D5357	C	BREL Derby August 1982	

BR 1957 No	TOPS No	TOPS re-No: 1	TOPS re-No: 2	Built by	Works No	Period* Date introduced	Date withdrawn
D5358	27 012	—	—	BRCW	DEL 201	11/61*	
D5359	27 013	—	—	BRCW	DEL 202	11/61*	July 1976
D5360	27 014	—	—	BRCW	DEL 203	12/61*	
D5361	27 015	—	—	BRCW	DEL 204	12/61*	January 1977
D5362	27 016	—	—	BRCW	DEL 205	12/61*	April 1984
D5363	27 017	—	—	BRCW	DEL 206	13/61*	
D5364	27 018	—	—	BRCW	DEL 207	13/61*	
D5365	27 019	—	—	BRCW	DEL 208	13/61*	April 1984
D5366	27 020	—	—	BRCW	DEL 209	1/62*	
D5367	27 021	—	—	BRCW	DEL 210	1/62*	
D5368	27 022	—	—	BRCW	DEL 211	1/62*	
D5369	27 023	—	—	BRCW	DEL 212	1/62*	
D5370	27 024	—	—	BRCW	DEL 213	January 1962	
D5371	27 025	—	—	BRCW	DEL 214	January 1962	
D5372	27 026	—	—	BRCW	DEL 215	January 1962	
D5373	27 027	—	—	BRCW	DEL 216	January 1962	June 1983
D5374	27 101	—	27 045	BRCW	DEL 217	February 1962	
D5375	27 028	—	—	BRCW	DEL 218	February 1962	
D5376	27 029	—	—	BRCW	DEL 219	February 1962	
D5377	27 030	—	—	BRCW	DEL 220	February 1962	
D5378	27 031	—	—	BRCW	DEL 221	March 1962	May 1978
D5379	27 032	—	—	BRCW	DEL 222	4/62*	
D5380	27 102	—	27 046	BRCW	DEL 223	4/62*	
D5381	27 033	—	—	BRCW	DEL 224	4/62*	
D5382	27 034	—	—	BRCW	DEL 225	4/62*	July 1984
D5383	—	—	—	BRCW	DEL 226	5/62*	January 1966
D5384	27 035	—	—	BRCW	DEL 227	5/62*	September 1976
D5385	27 036	—	—	BRCW	DEL 228	5/62*	
D5386	27 103	27 212	27 066	BRCW	DEL 229	5/62*	
D5387	27 104	—	27 048	BRCW	DEL 230	6/62*	
D5388	27 105	—	27 049	BRCW	DEL 231	6/62*	
D5389	27 037	—	—	BRCW	DEL 232	6/62*	
D5390	27 038	—	—	BRCW	DEL 233	6/62*	
D5391	27 119	27 201	—	BRCW	DEL 234	6/62*	January 1979
D5392	27 120	27 202	—	BRCW	DEL 235	6/62*	August 1980
D5393	27 121	27 203	27 057	BRCW	DEL 236	7/62*	May 1983
D5394	27 106	—	27 050	BRCW	DEL 237	7/62*	
D5395	27 107	—	27 051	BRCW	DEL 238	7/62*	
D5396	27 108	—	27 052	BRCW	DEL 239	7/62*	
D5397	27 109	—	27 053	BRCW	DEL 240	8/62*	
D5398	27 039	—	—	BRCW	DEL 241	7/62*	October 1975
D5399	27 110	—	27 054	BRCW	DEL 242	7/62*	
D5400	27 111	—	27 055	BRCW	DEL 243	7/62*	
D5401	27 112	—	27 056	BRCW	DEL 244	7/62*	
D5402	27 040	—	—	BRCW	DEL 245	7/62*	
D5403	27 122	27 204	27 058	BRCW	DEL 246	8/62*	
D5404	27 113	27 207	27 061	BRCW	DEL 247	8/62*	
D5405	27 041	—	—	BRCW	DEL 248	8/62*	
D5406	27 042	—	—	BRCW	DEL 249	8/62*	
D5407	27 114	27 208	27 062	BRCW	DEL 250	8/62*	
D5408	27 115	27 209	27 063	BRCW	DEL 251	9/62*	
D5409	27 116	27 210	27 064	BRCW	DEL 252	8/62*	
D5410	27 123	27 205	27 059	BRCW	DEL 253	9/62*	
D5411	27 117	27 211	27 065	BRCW	DEL 254	9/62*	
D5412	27 124	27 206	27 060	BRCW	DEL 255	9/62*	
D5413	27 118	27 103	27 047	BRCW	DEL 256	10/62*	
D5414	27 043	—	—	BRCW	DEL 257	10/62*	April 1980
D5415	27 044	—	—	BRCW	DEL 258	10/62*	July 1980

BR 1957 No	*Disposal code*	*Disposal details*	*Notes*
D5358			
D5359	C	BREL Glasgow July 1977	
D5360			
D5361	C	BREL Glasgow April 1977	
D5362	A	BREL Glasgow	Stored April 1983
D5363			
D5364			
D5365	A	BREL Swindon	Stored July 1983, reinstated December 1983, stored March 1984
D5366			
D5367			
D5368			
D5369			
D5370			
D5371			
D5372			
D5373	A	BREL Glasgow	Stored September 1982
D5374			
D5375			Stored March 1983, reinstated August 1984
D5376			
D5377			
D5378	C	BREL Glasgow September 1978	
D5379			
D5380			
D5381			
D5382			
D5383	C	J. Cashmore, Great Bridge, Tipton	
D5384	C	BREL Glasgow March 1977	
D5385			Stored December 1983, reinstated June 1984
D5386			
D5387			
D5388			
D5389			
D5390			
D5391	C	BREL Glasgow September 1979	
D5392	C	BREL Glasgow January 1982	
D5393	A	BREL Derby	Stored December 1982
D5394			
D5395			
D5396			
D5397			
D5398	C	BREL Glasgow April 1977	
D5399			
D5400			
D5401			
D5402			
D5403			
D5404			
D5405			Stored January 1983, reinstated April 1983
D5406			
D5407			
D5408			
D5409			Number 27116 never carried
D5410			
D5411			
D5412			
D5413			
D5414	A	BR Eastfield depot	
D5415	C	BREL Glasgow February 1982	

Class 31

Several different builders were awarded contracts for Type 2 locomotives under the BTC Modernisation Scheme. Brush was given 20 locomotives to build to a design which led to subsequent orders being placed for over 200 locomotives. When built all had a Mirrlees 12JVS12T power unit later changed to EE12SVT unit.

BR 1957 No	*TOPS No*	*TOPS re-No*	*Built by*	*Works No*	*Date introduced*	*Date withdrawn*
D5500	31 018	—	Brush	71	October 1957	July 1976
D5501	31 001	—	Brush	72	November 1957	July 1976
D5502	31 002	—	Brush	73	December 1957	January 1980
D5503	31 003	—	Brush	74	January 1958	February 1980
D5504	31 004	—	Brush	75	January 1958	October 1980
D5505	31 005	—	Brush	76	February 1958	February 1980
D5506	31 006	—	Brush	77	March 1958	January 1980
D5507	31 007	—	Brush	78	April 1958	November 1976
D5508	31 008	—	Brush	79	April 1958	October 1980
D5509	31 009	—	Brush	80	May 1958	July 1976
D5510	31 010	—	Brush	81	May 1958	July 1976
D5511	31 011	—	Brush	82	June 1958	July 1976
D5512	31 012	—	Brush	83	June 1958	November 1976
D5513	31 013	—	Brush	84	July 1958	March 1979
D5514	31 014	—	Brush	85	July 1958	November 1976
D5515	31 015	—	Brush	86	July 1958	May 1980
D5516	31 016	—	Brush	87	September 1958	July 1976
D5517	31 017	—	Brush	88	September 1958	May 1980
D5518	31 101	—	Brush	89	October 1958	
D5519	31 019	—	Brush	90	December 1958	October 1980
D5520	31 102	—	Brush	119	February 1959	
D5521	31 103	—	Brush	120	March 1959	October 1980
D5522	31 104*	31 418	Brush	121	March 1959	
D5523	31 105	—	Brush	122	March 1959	
D5524	31 106	—	Brush	123	March 1959	
D5525	31 107	—	Brush	124	March 1959	
D5526	31 108	—	Brush	125	April 1959	
D5527	31 109	—	Brush	126	April 1959	
D5528	31 110	—	Brush	127	April 1959	
D5529	31 111	—	Brush	128	May 1959	June 1983
D5530	31 112	—	Brush	129	May 1959	
D5531	31 113	—	Brush	130	May 1959	
D5532	31 114	—	Brush	131	June 1959	
D5533	31 115	—	Brush	132	June 1959	
D5534	31 116	—	Brush	133	June 1959	
D5535	31 117	—	Brush	134	June 1959	
D5536	31 118	—	Brush	135	June 1959	
D5537	31 119	—	Brush	136	June 1959	
D5538	31 120	—	Brush	137	July 1959	
D5539	31 121	—	Brush	138	July 1959	
D5540	31 122	—	Brush	139	July 1959	
D5541	31 123	—	Brush	140	July 1959	
D5542	31 124	—	Brush	141	July 1959	
D5543	31 125	—	Brush	142	July 1959	
D5544	31 126	—	Brush	143	August 1959	
D5545	31 127	—	Brush	144	October 1959	
D5546	31 128	—	Brush	145	August 1959	

Engine: EE12SVT of 1,470hp†
Weight: 107-113 ton (various)
Bogie type: A1A-A1A
Max speed: 80-90mph‡
Class code: D12/2 later 12/2 Class 30 (Mirrlees)
D13/1, 13/2 Class 31 (EE)
†Mirrlees JVS12T of 1,250hp when built
‡Dependent on build
*Number allocated, but not carried

Tractive effort: 35,900-42,800lb‡
Length: 56ft 9in
Height: 12ft 7in
Width: 8ft 9in

BR 1957 No	*Disposal code*	*Disposal details*	*Notes*
D5500	P	National Railway Museum, York	
D5501	C	BREL Doncaster January 1977	
D5502	D	Departmental Stock — 968014	
D5503	C	BREL Doncaster April 1980	
D5504	C	BREL Swindon August 1981	
D5505	C	BREL Doncaster March 1980	
D5506	C	BREL Doncaster December 1980	
D5507	C	BREL Doncaster June 1978	
D5508	D	Departmental Stock — 968016	
D5509	C	BREL Doncaster November 1977	
D5510	C	BREL Doncaster December 1976	
D5511	C	BREL Doncaster January 1977	
D5512	C	BREL Doncaster October 1978	
D5513	D	Departmental Stock — 968013	
D5514	D	Departmental Stock — 968015	
D5515	C	BREL Doncaster October 1980	
D5516	C	BREL Doncaster December 1976	
D5517	C	BREL Swindon January 1983	
D5518			Stored May 1981, reinstated September 1982
D5519	C	BREL Swindon August 1981	
D5520			
D5521	C	BREL Swindon February 1983	
D5522			
D5523			
D5524			
D5525			
D5526			
D5527			
D5528			
D5529	A	BREL Swindon	
D5530			
D5531			
D5532			
D5533			
D5534			
D5535			
D5536			
D5537			
D5538			
D5539			
D5540			Stored May 1981, reinstated January 1982
D5541			
D5542			
D5543			
D5544			
D5545			
D5546			

BR 1957 No	TOPS No	TOPS re-No	Built by	Works No	Date introduced	Date withdrawn
D5547	31 129	—	Brush	146	August 1959	
D5548	31 130	—	Brush	147	September 1959	
D5549	31 131	—	Brush	148	September 1959	
D5550	31 132	—	Brush	149	September 1959	
D5551	31 133	31 450	Brush	150	September 1959	
D5552	31 134	—	Brush	151	September 1959	
D5553	31 135	—	Brush	152	September 1959	
D5554	31 136	—	Brush	153	October 1959	August 1980
D5555	31 137	31 444	Brush	154	October 1959	
D5556	31 138	—	Brush	155	October 1959	
D5557	31 139	31 438	Brush	156	October 1959	
D5558	31 140	31 421	Brush	157	October 1959	
D5559	31 141	—	Brush	158	October 1959	
D5560	31 142	—	Brush	159	October 1959	
D5561	31 143	—	Brush	160	October 1959	
D5562	31 144	—	Brush	161	November 1959	
D5563	31 145	—	Brush	162	November 1959	
D5564	31 146	—	Brush	163	November 1959	
D5565	31 147	—	Brush	164	November 1959	
D5566	31 148	31 448	Brush	165	November 1959	
D5567	31 149	—	Brush	166	November 1959	
D5568	31 150	—	Brush	167	December 1959	October 1975
D5569	31 151	31 436	Brush	168	December 1959	
D5570	31 152	—	Brush	169	December 1959	
D5571	31 153	31 432	Brush	170	December 1959	
D5572	31 154	—	Brush	171	December 1959	
D5573	31 155	—	Brush	172	December 1959	
D5574	31 156	—	Brush	173	December 1959	
D5575	31 157	31 424	Brush	174	December 1959	
D5576	31 158	—	Brush	175	December 1959	
D5577	31 159	—	Brush	176	December 1959	
D5578	31 160	—	Brush	177	January 1960	
D5579	31 161	—	Brush	178	January 1960	
D5580	31 162	—	Brush	180	January 1960	
D5581	31 163	—	Brush	181	January 1960	
D5582	31 164	—	Brush	182	January 1960	
D5583	31 165	—	Brush	183	January 1960	
D5584	31 166	—	Brush	184	January 1960	
D5585	31 167	—	Brush	185	January 1960	
D5586	31 168	—	Brush	186	February 1960	
D5587	31 169	—	Brush	187	February 1960	
D5588	31 170	—	Brush	188	February 1960	
D5589	31 401	—	Brush	189	February 1960	
D5590	31 171	—	Brush	190	February 1960	
D5591	31 172	31 420	Brush	191	February 1960	
D5592	31 402	—	Brush	192	February 1960	
D5593	31 173	—	Brush	193	March 1960	
D5594	31 174	—	Brush	194	March 1960	
D5595	31 175	—	Brush	195	March 1960	
D5596	31 403	—	Brush	196	March 1960	
D5597	31 176	—	Brush	197	March 1960	
D5598	31 177	31 443	Brush	198	March 1960	
D5599	31 178	—	Brush	199	March 1960	
D5600	31 179	31 435	Brush	200	March 1960	
D5601	31 180	—	Brush	201	March 1960	
D5602	31 181	—	Brush	202	March 1960	
D5603	31 182	31 437	Brush	203	March 1960	
D5604	31 183	—	Brush	204	April 1960	
D5605	31 404	—	Brush	205	April 1960	

BR 1957 No	*Disposal code*	*Disposal details*	*Notes*
D5547			
D5548			
D5549			
D5550			
D5551			
D5552			
D5553			
D5554	C	BREL Swindon November 1980	Stored from July 1980
D5555			
D5556			
D5557			Stored May 1981, reinstated February 1982
D5558			
D5559			
D5560			
D5561			
D5562			
D5563			
D5564			
D5565			
D5566			
D5567			
D5568	C	BREL Doncaster December 1975	
D5569			
D5570			
D5571			
D5572			
D5573			
D5574			
D5575			
D5576			
D5577			
D5578			
D5579			
D5580			
D5581			
D5582			
D5583			
D5584			
D5585			Stored May 1981, reinstated March 1982
D5586			
D5587			
D5588			
D5589			
D5590			
D5591			
D5592			
D5593			
D5594			
D5595			
D5596			
D5597			
D5598			
D5599			
D5600			
D5601			
D5602			
D5603			
D5604			
D5605			

BR 1957 No	*TOPS No*	*TOPS re-No*	*Built by*	*Works No*	*Date introduced*	*Date withdrawn*
D5606	31 405	—	Brush	206	April 1960	
D5607	31 184	—	Brush	207	April 1960	
D5608	31 185	—	Brush	208	April 1960	
D5609	31 186	—	Brush	209	April 1960	
D5610	31 187	—	Brush	210	April 1960	
D5611	31 188	—	Brush	211	April 1960	
D5612	31 189	—	Brush	212	May 1960	
D5613	31 190	—	Brush	213	May 1960	
D5614	31 191	—	Brush	214	May 1960	
D5615	31 192	—	Brush	215	May 1960	October 1982
D5616	31 406	—	Brush	216	May 1960	
D5617	31 193	31 426	Brush	217	May 1960	
D5618	31 194	31 427	Brush	218	May 1960	
D5619	31 195	—	Brush	219	May 1960	
D5620	31 196	—	Brush	220	June 1960	
D5621	31 197	31 423	Brush	221	June 1960	
D5622	31 198	—	Brush	222	June 1960	
D5623	31 199	—	Brush	223	June 1960	
D5624	31 200	—	Brush	224	June 1960	
D5625	31 201	—	Brush	225	June 1960	
D5626	31 202	—	Brush	226	June 1960	
D5627	31 203	—	Brush	227	June 1960	
D5628	31 204	31 440	Brush	228	June 1960	
D5629	31 205	—	Brush	229	June 1960	
D5630	31 206	—	Brush	230	July 1960	
D5631	31 207	—	Brush	231	July 1960	
D5632	31 208	—	Brush	232	July 1960	
D5633	31 209	—	Brush	233	July 1960	
D5634	31 210	—	Brush	234	July 1960	
D5635	31 211	31 428	Brush	235	July 1960	
D5636	31 212	—	Brush	236	July 1960	
D5637	31 213	—	Brush	237	July 1960	
D5638	31 214	—	Brush	238	August 1960	May 1983
D5639	31 215	—	Brush	239	August 1960	
D5640	31 407	—	Brush	240	August 1960	
D5641	31 216	—	Brush	241	August 1960	
D5642	31 217	—	Brush	242	August 1960	
D5643	31 218	—	Brush	243	August 1960	
D5644	31 219	—	Brush	244	August 1960	
D5645	31 220	31 441	Brush	245	September 1960	
D5646	31 408	—	Brush	246	September 1960	
D5647	31 221	—	Brush	247	September 1960	
D5648	31 222	—	Brush	248	September 1960	
D5649	31 223	—	Brush	249	September 1960	
D5650	31 224	—	Brush	250	September 1960	
D5651	31 225	—	Brush	251	September 1960	
D5652	31 226	—	Brush	252	September 1960	
D5653	31 227	—	Brush	253	September 1960	
D5654	31 228	—	Brush	254	September 1960	
D5655	31 229	—	Brush	255	September 1960	
D5656	31 409	—	Brush	256	October 1960	
D5657	31 230	—	Brush	257	October 1960	
D5658	31 231	—	Brush	258	October 1960	
D5659	31 232	—	Brush	259	October 1960	
D5660	31 233	—	Brush	260	October 1960	
D5661	31 234	—	Brush	261	October 1960	
D5662	31 235	—	Brush	262	October 1960	

BR 1957 No	*Disposal code*	*Disposal details*	*Notes*
D5606			
D5607			
D5608			
D5609			
D5610			
D5611			
D5612			
D5613			
D5614			
D5615	C	BREL Doncaster January 1983	
D5616			
D5617			Stored May 1981, reinstated September 1982
D5618			Stored May 1981, reinstated September 1982
D5619			
D5620			
D5621			
D5622			
D5623			
D5624			
D5625			
D5626			
D5627			
D5628			
D5629			
D5630			
D5631			
D5632			
D5633			
D5634			
D5635			Stored May 1981, reinstated September 1982
D5636			
D5637			
D5638	C	BREL Doncaster October 1983	
D5639			
D5640			
D5641			
D5642			
D5643			
D5644			
D5645			
D5646			
D5647			
D5648			
D5649			
D5650			
D5651			
D5652			
D5653			
D5654			Stored May 1981, reinstated February 1982
D5655			
D5656			
D5657			
D5658			
D5659			
D5660			
D5661			
D5662			

BR 1957 No	TOPS No	TOPS re-No	Built by	Works No	Date introduced	Date withdrawn
D5663	31 236	31 433	Brush	263	November 1960	
D5664	31 237	—	Brush	264	November 1960	
D5665	31 238	—	Brush	265	November 1960	
D5666	31 239	31 439	Brush	266	November 1960	
D5667	31 240	—	Brush	267	November 1960	
D5668	31 241	—	Brush	268	November 1960	March 1982
D5669	31 410	—	Brush	269	November 1960	
D5670	31 242	—	Brush	270	January 1961	
D5671	31 243	—	Brush	271	October 1960	
D5672	31 244	—	Brush	272	November 1960	May 1983
D5673	31 245	—	Brush	273	December 1960	
D5674	31 246	—	Brush	274	December 1960	
D5675	31 247	—	Brush	275	December 1960	
D5676	31 248	—	Brush	276	December 1960	
D5677	31 249	—	Brush	277	December 1960	
D5678	31 250	—	Brush	278	December 1960	
D5679	31 251	31 442	Brush	279	December 1960	
D5680	31 252	—	Brush	281	December 1960	
D5681	31 253	31 431	Brush	282	January 1961	
D5682	31 254	—	Brush	283	January 1961	December 1979
D5683	31 255	—	Brush	284	January 1961	
D5684	31 256	—	Brush	285	January 1961	
D5685	31 257	—	Brush	286	February 1961	
D5686	31 258	31 434	Brush	287	February 1961	
D5687	31 259	—	Brush	288	February 1961	
D5688	31 260	—	Brush	289	February 1961	
D5689	31 261	—	Brush	290	March 1961	
D5690	31 262	—	Brush	291	March 1961	May 1983
D5691	31 411	—	Brush	292	March 1961	
D5692	31 412	—	Brush	293	March 1961	
D5693	31 263	—	Brush	294	March 1961	
D5694	31 264	—	Brush	295	April 1961	
D5695	31 265	31 430	Brush	296	April 1961	
D5696	31 266	—	Brush	297	May 1961	
D5697	31 267*	31 419	Brush	299	May 1961	
D5698	31 268	—	Brush	300	May 1961	
D5699	31 269	31 429	Brush	298	April 1961	

Class continued with D5800

Class 28

These 20 Metropolitan-Vickers built Type 2s were delivered in 1958-59 to the LMR, and were of a most unusual bogie layout — Co-Bo (four wheels at one end, and six at the other). The power unit was of the two-stroke type. The design was not successful and the locomotives scrapped.

BR 1957 No	Built by	Works No	Date introduced	Date withdrawn	Disposal code
D5700	M/Vickers	—	July 1958	December 1967	C
D5701	M/Vickers	—	August 1958	September 1968	C
D5702	M/Vickers	—	September 1958	September 1968	C

BR 1957 No	*Disposal code*	*Disposal details*	*Notes*
D5663			
D5664			
D5665			
D5666			
D5667			
D5668	C	BREL Swindon May 1982	Stored from March 1982
D5669			
D5670			Built November 1960
D5671			
D5672	C	BREL Doncaster September 1983	
D5673			
D5674			
D5675			
D5676			
D5677			
D5678			
D5679			
D5680			
D5681			
D5682	C	BR at Old Oak Common depot July 1980	
D5683			
D5684			
D5685			
D5686			Stored September 1983, reinstated October 1983
D5687			
D5688			
D5689			
D5690	C	BREL Doncaster August 1983	
D5691			
D5692			
D5693			
D5694			Stored October 1980, withdrawn December 1980, reinstated September 1982
D5695			Stored October 1980, withdrawn December 1980, reinstated September 1982
D5696			
D5697			
D5698			
D5699			Stored May 1981, reinstated September 1982

Engine: Crossley HSTV8 of 1,200hp
Weight: 97 ton
Bogie type: Co-Bo
Max speed: 75mph
Class code: D12/1 later 12/5, and BR Class 28

Tractive effort: 50,000lb
Length: 56ft 7½in
Height: 12ft 8in
Width: 9ft 1in

BR 1957 No	*Disposal details*	*Notes*
D5700	J. McWilliam, Shettleston, Glasgow September 1968	
D5701	J. Cashmore, Great Bridge, Tipton October 1969	
D5702	J. Cashmore, Great Bridge, Tipton, November 1969	

BR 1957 No	Built by	Works No	Date introduced	Date withdrawn	Disposal code
D5703	M/Vickers	—	October 1958	December 1967	C
D5704	M/Vickers	—	November 1958	December 1967	C
D5705	M/Vickers	—	December 1958	September 1968	D
D5706	M/Vickers	—	December 1958	September 1968	C
D5707	M/Vickers	—	December 1958	September 1968	C
D5708	M/Vickers	—	January 1959	September 1968	C
D5709	M/Vickers	—	January 1959	December 1967	C
D5710	M/Vickers	—	February 1959	December 1967	C
D5711	M/Vickers	—	February 1959	September 1968	C
D5712	M/Vickers	—	February 1959	September 1968	C
D5713	M/Vickers	—	March 1959	December 1967	C
D5714	M/Vickers	—	March 1959	December 1968	C
D5715	M/Vickers	—	April 1959	April 1968	C
D5716	M/Vickers	—	May 1959	September 1968	C
D5717	M/Vickers	—	June 1959	September 1968	C
D5718	M/Vickers	—	July 1959	April 1968	C
D5719	M/Vickers	—	October 1959	September 1968	C

Class 31 — Continued from D5699

BR 1957 No	TOPS No	TOPS re-No	Built by	Works No	Date introduced	Date withdrawn
D5800	31 270	—	Brush	301	June 1961	
D5801	31 271	—	Brush	302	June 1961	
D5802	31 272	—	Brush	303	June 1961	
D5803	31 273	—	Brush	304	June 1961	
D5804	31 274	31 425	Brush	305	June 1961	
D5805	31 275	—	Brush	306	July 1961	
D5806	31 276	—	Brush	307	July 1961	
D5807	31 277	—	Brush	308	July 1961	
D5808	31 278	—	Brush	309	July 1961	

BR 1957 No	*Disposal details*	*Notes*
D5703	J. McWilliam, Shettleston, Glasgow, July 1968	
D5704	J. McWilliam, Shettleston, Glasgow September 1968	
D5705	Departmental Stock — 15705	
D5706	J. Cashmore, Great Bridge, Tipton November 1969	
D5707	J. Cashmore, Great Bridge, Tipton October 1969	
D5708	J. Cashmore, Great Bridge, Tipton November 1969	
D5709	J. McWilliam, Shettleston, Glasgow October 1968	
D5710	J. McWilliam, Shettleston, Glasgow October 1968	
D5711	J. Cashmore, Great Bridge, Tipton November 1969	
D5712	J. Cashmore, Great Bridge, Tipton December 1969	
D5713	J. McWilliam, Shettleston, Glasgow October 1968	
D5714	J. Cashmore, Great Bridge, Tipton October 1969	
D5715	J. McWilliam, Shettleston, Glasgow c1969	
D5716	J. Cashmore, Great Bridge, Tipton December 1969	
D5717	J. Cashmore, Great Bridge, Tipton November 1969	
D5718	J. McWilliam, Shettleston, Glasgow October 1968	
D5719	J. Cashmore, Great Bridge, Tipton October 1969	

BR 1957 No	*Disposal code*	*Disposal details*	*Notes*
D5800			
D5801			
D5802			
D5803			
D5804			Stored October 1980, withdrawn December 1980, reinstated September 1982
D5805			
D5806			
D5807			
D5808			

BR 1957 No	*TOPS No*	*TOPS re-No*	*Built by*	*Works No*	*Date introduced*	*Date withdrawn*
D5809	31 279	31 452	Brush	310	July 1961	
D5810	31 280	—	Brush	311	August 1961	
D5811	31 281	—	Brush	312	August 1961	
D5812	31 413	—	Brush	313	August 1961	
D5813	31 282	—	Brush	314	September 1961	
D5814	31 414	—	Brush	315	September 1961	
D5815	31 283	—	Brush	316	September 1961	
D5816	31 284	—	Brush	317	September 1961	
D5817	31 285	—	Brush	318	October 1961	
D5818	31 286	—	Brush	319	October 1961	
D5819	31 287	—	Brush	320	October 1961	
D5820	31 288	—	Brush	321	October 1961	
D5821	31 289	—	Brush	322	November 1961	
D5822	31 290	—	Brush	323	November 1961	
D5823	31 291	—	Brush	324	November 1961	
D5824	31 415	—	Brush	325	November 1961	
D5825	31 292	—	Brush	326	November 1961	
D5826	31 293	—	Brush	362	December 1961	
D5827	31 294	—	Brush	363	December 1961	
D5828	31 295	31 447	Brush	364	December 1961	
D5829	31 296	—	Brush	365	January 1962	
D5830	31 297	—	Brush	366	January 1962	
D5831	31 298	—	Brush	367	January 1962	
D5832	31 299	—	Brush	368	February 1962	
D5833	31 300	31 445	Brush	369	February 1962	
D5834	31 301	—	Brush	371	March 1962	
D5835	31 302	—	Brush	370	April 1962	
D5836	31 303	—	Brush	372	April 1962	
D5837	31 304	—	Brush	373	April 1962	
D5838	31 305	—	Brush	374	April 1962	
D5839	31 306	—	Brush	375	May 1962	
D5840	31 307	31 449	Brush	376	May 1962	
D5841	31 308	—	Brush	377	May 1962	
D5842	31 416	—	Brush	378	May 1962	
D5843	31 309	—	Brush	379	May 1962	
D5844	31 310	31 422	Brush	380	June 1962	
D5845	31 311	—	Brush	381	June 1962	
D5846	31 312	—	Brush	382	June 1962	
D5847	31 313	—	Brush	383	June 1962	May 1983
D5848	31 314	—	Brush	384	July 1962	September 1982
D5849	31 315	—	Brush	385	July 1962	
D5850	31 316	31 446	Brush	386	July 1962	
D5851	31 317	—	Brush	387	July 1962	
D5852	31 318	31 451	Brush	388	August 1962	
D5853	31 319	—	Brush	389	August 1962	
D5854	31 320	—	Brush	390	August 1962	
D5855	31 321	—	Brush	391	August 1962	
D5856	31 417	—	Brush	392	August 1962	
D5857	31 322	—	Brush	393	September 1962	
D5858	31 323	—	Brush	394	September 1962	
D5859	31 324	—	Brush	395	October 1962	
D5860	31 325	—	Brush	396	October 1962	
D5861	31 326	—	Brush	397	October 1962	
D5862	31 327	—	Brush	398	October 1962	

BR 1957 No	*Disposal code*	*Disposal details*	*Notes*
D5809			
D5810			Stored May 1981, reinstated January 1982
D5811			
D5812			
D5813			
D5814			
D5815			
D5816			
D5817			
D5818			
D5819			
D5820			
D5821			
D5822			
D5823			
D5824			
D5825			
D5826			
D5827			
D5828			
D5829			
D5830			
D5831			Stored May 1981, reinstated February 1982
D5832			
D5833			
D5834			
D5835			
D5836			
D5837			
D5838			Stored May 1981, reinstated March 1982
D5839			
D5840			
D5841			
D5842			
D5843			Stored May 1981, reinstated February 1982
D5844			
D5845			
D5846			
D5847	C	BREL Doncaster May 1983	
D5848	C	BREL Doncaster January 1983	
D5849			
D5850			
D5851			
D5852			
D5853			
D5854			
D5855			
D5856			
D5857			
D5858			
D5859			
D5860			
D5861			Stored May 1981, reinstated January 1982
D5862			

Class 23

Another of the small Type 2 designs were these 10 English Electric built locomotives powered by a Napier Deltic T9-29 ('Baby Deltic') engine. The locomotives were always problematical with BR and in 1963 all were removed from service and rebuilt, and then gave a further four-five years' service.

BR 1957 No	*Built by*	*Works No*	*Date introduced*	*Date withdrawn*	*Disposal code*
D5900	EE(VF)	E2377/D417	May 1959	November 1968	C
D5901	EE(VF)	E2378/D418	May 1959	December 1969	D
D5902	EE(VF)	E2379/D419	May 1959	November 1969	C
D5903	EE(VF)	E2380/D420	April 1959	November 1968	C
D5904	EE(VF)	E2381/D421	April 1959	January 1969	C
D5905	EE(VF)	E2382/D422	May 1959	February 1971	C
D5906	EE(VF)	E2383/D423	May 1959	September 1968	C
D5907	EE(VF)	E2384/D424	May 1959	October 1968	C
D5908	EE(VF)	E2385/D425	May 1959	March 1969	C
D5909	EE(VF)	E2386/D426	June 1959	March 1971	C

Class 21/29

Again ordered under the Modernisation Scheme were 10 Type 2 Bo-Bos from NBL for ER operation, prior to the first loco being delivered a total of 58 were ordered. After ER operation all were re-allocated to ScR. Twenty locomotives rebuilt in 1965 with new power unit, and revised equipment, and reclassified Class 29*.

BR 1957 No	*Built by*	*Works No*	*Date introduced*	*Date withdrawn*	*Disposal code*
D6100*	NBL	27681	December 1958	October 1971	C
D6101*	NBL	27682	December 1958	August 1971	C
D6102*	NBL	27683	December 1958	October 1971	C
D6103*	NBL	27684	May 1959	October 1971	C
D6104	NBL	27685	February 1959	December 1967	C
D6105	NBL	27686	March 1959	June 1968	C
D6106*	NBL	27687	March 1959	July 1971	C
D6107*	NBL	27688	March 1959	October 1971	C
D6108*	NBL	27689	April 1959	May 1969	C
D6109	NBL	27690	April 1959	April 1968	C
D6110	NBL	27840	May 1959	April 1968	C
D6111	NBL	27841	May 1959	August 1968	C
D6112*	NBL	27842	May 1959	December 1971	C
D6113*	NBL	27843	May 1959	October 1971	C
D6114*	NBL	27844	May 1959	October 1971	C
D6115	NBL	27845	June 1959	June 1968	C
D6116*	NBL	27846	June 1959	December 1968	C
D6117	NBL	27847	June 1959	August 1968	C
D6118	NBL	27848	June 1959	December 1967	C
D6119*	NBL	27849	June 1959	December 1971	C
D6120	NBL	27850	July 1959	December 1967	C
D6121*	NBL	27851	August 1959	October 1971	C
D6122	NBL	27852	August 1959	December 1971	C
D6123*	NBL	27853	September 1959	September 1971	C
D6124*	NBL	27854	September 1959	October 1971	C
D6125	NBL	27855	September 1959	December 1967	C

Engine: Napier T9-29 of 1,100hp
Weight: 74 ton
Bogie type: Bo-Bo
Max speed: 75mph
Class code: D11/1 then 11/3 and BR Class 23

Tractive effort: 47,000lb
Length: 52ft 6in
Height: 12ft 8in
Width: 8ft 10½in

BR 1957 No	*Disposal details*	*Notes*
D5900	G. Cohen, Kettering, Northamptonshire August 1969	
D5901	Departmental Stock — D5901	
D5902	G. Cohen, Kettering, Northamptonshire September 1970	
D5903	G. Cohen, Kettering, Northamptonshire October 1969	
D5904	G. Cohen, Kettering, Northamptonshire August 1969	
D5905	G. Cohen, Kettering, Northamptonshire October 1973	
D5906	G. Cohen, Kettering, Northamptonshire July 1969	
D5907	G. Cohen, Kettering, Northamptonshire July 1969	
D5908	J. Cashmore, Great Bridge, Tipton, February 1970	
D5909	G. Cohen, Kettering, Northamptonshire October 1973	

Engine (New): NBL/MAN L12V18/21 of 1,100hp (derated to 1,000hp)
Engine (Rebuilt): Paxman 12YJXL of 1,350hp
Weight: 73 ton
Bogie type: Bo-Bo
Max speed: 75mph (80mph Class 29)
Class code: D10/1 later 10/4 (1,000hp), D11/2 later 11/4 (1,100hp), then BR Class 21. Rebuilds D13/1, later 13/4 then BR Class 29

Tractive effort: 45,000lb
Length: 51ft 6in
Height: 12ft 6⅞in
Width: 8ft 8in

BR 1957 No	*Disposal details*	*Notes*
D6100	BREL Glasgow November 1972	
D6101	BREL Glasgow October 1972	
D6102	BREL Glasgow August 1972	
D6103	BREL Glasgow November 1972	Built January 1959
D6104	Barnes & Bell, Coatbridge, Lanarkshire c1968	
D6105	J. McWilliam, Shettleston, Glasgow c1968	
D6106	BREL Glasgow July 1972	
D6107	BREL Glasgow October 1972	
D6108	J. McWilliam, Shettleston, Glasgow July 1971	
D6109	J. McWilliam, Shettleston, Glasgow January 1969	
D6110	J. McWilliam, Shettleston, Glasgow February 1969	
D6111	J. McWilliam, Shettleston, Glasgow c1969	
D6112	BREL Glasgow June 1972	
D6113	BREL Glasgow November 1972	
D6114	BREL Glasgow September 1972	
D6115	J. McWilliam, Shettleston, Glasgow August 1968	
D6116	BREL Glasgow May 1972	
D6117	J. McWilliam, Shettleston, Glasgow c1969	
D6118	J. McWilliam, Shettleston, Glasgow c1968	
D6119	BREL Glasgow August 1972	
D6120	J. McWilliam, Shettleston, Glasgow October 1968	
D6121	BREL Glasgow September 1972	
D6122	D. Woodham, Barry June 1980	
D6123	BREL Glasgow October 1972	
D6124	BREL Glasgow September 1972	
D6125	Barnes & Bell, Coatbridge, Lanarkshire c1968	

BR 1957 No	*Built by*	*Works No*	*Date introduced*	*Date withdrawn*	*Disposal code*
D6126	NBL	27856	October 1959	April 1968	C
D6127	NBL	27857	October 1959	December 1967	C
D6128	NBL	27858	October 1959	December 1967	C
D6129*	NBL	27859	October 1959	October 1971	C
D6130*	NBL	27860	October 1959	October 1971	C
D6131	NBL	27861	November 1959	December 1967	C
D6132*	NBL	27862	November 1959	October 1971	C
D6133*	NBL	27863	November 1959	December 1971	C
D6134	NBL	27864	November 1959	December 1967	C
D6135	NBL	27865	December 1959	December 1967	C
D6136	NBL	27866	December 1959	December 1967	C
D6137*	NBL	27867	December 1959	April 1971	C
D6138	NBL	27942	February 1960	December 1967	C
D6139	NBL	27943	February 1960	December 1967	C
D6140	NBL	27944	February 1960	December 1967	C
D6141	NBL	27945	March 1960	December 1967	C
D6142	NBL	27946	March 1960	December 1967	C
D6143	NBL	27947	March 1960	December 1967	C
D6144	NBL	27948	March 1960	December 1967	C
D6145	NBL	27949	April 1960	December 1967	C
D6146	NBL	27950	April 1960	December 1967	C
D6147	NBL	27951	April 1960	December 1967	C
D6148	NBL	27952	May 1960	December 1967	C
D6149	NBL	27953	May 1960	December 1967	C
D6150	NBL	27954	July 1960	December 1967	C
D6151	NBL	27955	July 1960	December 1967	C
D6152	NBL	27956	July 1960	August 1968	C
D6153	NBL	27957	July 1960	December 1967	C
D6154	NBL	27958	July 1960	December 1967	C
D6155	NBL	27959	October 1960	December 1967	C
D6156	NBL	27960	October 1960	December 1967	C
D6157	NBL	27961	November 1960	December 1967	C

Class 22

Ordered under the modernisation plan for use on the WR, was this fleet of Type 2 diesel-hydraulic locomotives, introduced to replace steam on secondary passenger and freight duties, early withdrawal due to locos being non standard.

BR 1957 No	*Built by*	*Works No*	*Date introduced*	*Date withdrawn*	*Disposal code*
D6300	NBL	27665	January 1959	May 1968	C
D6301	NBL	27666	February 1959	December 1967	C
D6302	NBL	27667	February 1959	May 1968	C
D6303	NBL	27668	May 1959	May 1968	C
D6304	NBL	27669	June 1959	May 1968	C
D6305	NBL	27670	January 1960	May 1968	C
D6306	NBL	27879	October 1959	December 1968	C
D6307	NBL	27880	October 1959	March 1971	C
D6308	NBL	27881	January 1960	September 1971	C
D6309	NBL	27882	January 1960	May 1971	C
D6310	NBL	27883	January 1960	March 1971	C
D6311	NBL	27884	January 1960	September 1968	C
D6312	NBL	27885	January 1960	May 1971	C
D6313	NBL	27886	January 1960	August 1968	C
D6314	NBL	27887	January 1960	April 1969	C
D6315	NBL	27888	January 1960	May 1971	C

BR 1957 No	*Disposal details*	*Notes*
D6126	J. McWilliam, Shettleston, Glasgow February 1969	
D6127	Barnes & Bell, Coatbridge, Larnarkshire c1968	
D6128	J. McWilliam, Shettleston, Glasgow c1968	
D6129	BREL Glasgow June 1972	
D6130	BREL Glasgow October 1972	
D6131	J. McWilliam, Shettleston, Glasgow c1968	
D6132	BREL Glasgow September 1972	
D6133	BREL Glasgow July 1972	
D6134	Barnes & Bell, Coatbridge, Lanarkshire c1968	
D6135	J. McWilliam, Shettleston, Glasgow c1968	
D6136	Barnes & Bell, Coatbridge, Lanarkshire c1968	
D6137	BREL Glasgow August 1972	
D6138	J. McWilliam, Shettleston, Glasgow June 1968	
D6139	J. McWilliam, Shettleston, Glasgow June 1968	
D6140	J. McWilliam, Shettleston, Glasgow May 1968	
D6141	J. McWilliam, Shettleston, Glasgow August 1968	
D6142	J. McWilliam, Shettleston, Glasgow October 1968	
D6143	J. McWilliam, Shettleston, Glasgow c1968	
D6144	J. McWilliam, Shettleston, Glasgow August 1968	
D6145	J. McWilliam, Shettleston, Glasgow August 1968	
D6146	BR Workshops Inverurie August 1968	
D6147	J. McWilliam, Shettleston, Glasgow July 1968	
D6148	J. McWilliam, Shettleston, Glasgow July 1968	
D6149	J. McWilliam, Shettleston, Glasgow June 1968	
D6150	J. McWilliam, Shettleston, Glasgow August 1968	
D6151	J. McWilliam, Shettleston, Glasgow August 1968	
D6152	J. McWilliam, Shettleston, Glasgow c1969	
D6153	J. McWilliam, Shettleston, Glasgow May 1968	
D6154	J. McWilliam, Shettleston, Glasgow August 1968	
D6155	J. McWilliam, Shettleston, Glasgow August 1968	
D6156	J. McWilliam, Shettleston, Glasgow May 1968	
D6157	J. McWilliam, Shettleston, Glasgow August 1968	

Engine: MAN L12V18/21BS of 1,000-1,100hp
Weight: 65-68 ton
Bogie type: B-B
Max speed: 75mph
Class code: D10/2 later 10/4A (D6300-5), others D11/5, later 11/4A BR Class 22

Tractive effort: 40,000lb
Length: 46ft 8in
Height: 12ft 10in
Width: 8ft 8in

BR 1957 No	*Disposal details*	*Notes*
D6300	J. Cashmore, Newport, Gwent c1969	
D6301	G. Cohen, Morriston, Swansea c1968	
D6302	J. Cashmore, Newport, Gwent, c1969	
D6303	J. Cashmore, Newport, Gwent c1969	
D6304	J. Cashmore, Newport, Gwent c1969	
D6305	J. Cashmore, Newport, Gwent c1969	Built July 1959
D6306	J. Cashmore, Newport, Gwent c1969	
D6307	BREL Swindon December 1971	
D6308	BREL Swindon May 1972	
D6309	BREL Swindon December 1971	
D6310	BREL Swindon May 1972	
D6311	J. Cashmore, Newport, Gwent c1969	
D6312	BREL Swindon January 1972	
D6313	J. Cashmore, Newport, Gwent c1969	
D6314	J. Cashmore, Newport, Gwent c1969	
D6315	BREL Swindon January 1972	

BR 1957 No	Built by	Works No	Date introduced	Date withdrawn	Disposal code
D6316	NBL	27889	March 1960	March 1968	C
D6317	NBL	27890	March 1960	September 1968	C
D6318	NBL	27891	March 1960	May 1971	C
D6319	NBL	27892	April 1960	September 1971	C
D6320	NBL	27893	March 1960	May 1971	C
D6321	NBL	27894	April 1960	August 1968	C
D6322	NBL	27895	April 1960	October 1971	C
D6323	NBL	27896	April 1960	May 1971	C
D6324	NBL	27897	June 1960	September 1968	C
D6325	NBL	27898	June 1960	October 1968	C
D6326	NBL	27899	May 1960	October 1971	C
D6327	NBL	27900	August 1960	May 1971	C
D6328	NBL	27901	June 1960	July 1971	C
D6329	NBL	27902	June 1960	November 1968	C
D6330	NBL	27903	June 1960	October 1971	C
D6331	NBL	27904	July 1960	March 1971	C
D6332	NBL	27905	July 1960	May 1971	C
D6333	NBL	27906	August 1960	January 1972	C
D6334	NBL	27907	December 1960	October 1971	C
D6335	NBL	27908	February 1961	September 1968	C
D6336	NBL	27909	July 1961	January 1972	C
D6337	NBL	27910	March 1962	October 1971	C
D6338	NBL	27911	March 1962	January 1972	C
D6339	NBL	27912	April 1962	January 1972	C
D6340	NBL	27913	April 1962	May 1971	C
D6341	NBL	27914	May 1962	November 1968	C
D6342	NBL	27915	May 1962	December 1968	C
D6343	NBL	27916	May 1962	October 1971	C
D6344	NBL	27917	May 1962	September 1968	C
D6345	NBL	27918	May 1962	September 1968	C
D6346	NBL	27919	June 1962	April 1969	C
D6347	NBL	27920	June 1962	March 1968	C
D6348	NBL	27921	June 1962	July 1971	C
D6349	NBL	27922	June 1962	September 1968	C
D6350	NBL	27923	June 1962	September 1968	C
D6351	NBL	27924	June 1962	November 1968	C
D6352	NBL	27925	July 1962	May 1971	C
D6353	NBL	27926	July 1962	September 1968	C
D6354	NBL	27927	August 1962	May 1971	C
D6355	NBL	27928	August 1962	September 1968	C
D6356	NBL	27929	September 1962	October 1971	C
D6357	NBL	27930	November 1962	December 1968	C

Class 33

Designed and built expressly for the SR were these 98 Type 3 BRCW locomotives, derived from the builder's previous Type 2 Class 26/27 locomotives. This fleet were the first locos built with ETH from new. The final 12 examples built to the narrow 'Hastings' gauge.

BR 1957 No	TOPS No	Name	Built by	Works No	Date introduced	Date withdrawn
D6500	33 001	—	BRCW	DEL 92	January 1960	
D6501	33 002	—	BRCW	DEL 93	February 1960	
D6502	—	—	BRCW	DEL 94	March 1960	May 1964
D6503	33 003	—	BRCW	DEL 95	March 1960	

BR 1957 No	*Disposal details*	*Notes*
D6316	J. Cashmore, Newport, Gwent c1969	
D6317	J. Cashmore, Newport, Gwent c1969	
D6318	BREL Swindon March 1972	
D6319	BREL Swindon November 1972	Withdrawn March 1971, reinstated September 1971
D6320	BREL Swindon June 1972	
D6321	J. Cashmore, Newport, Gwent c1969	
D6322	BREL Swindon May 1972	
D6323	BREL Swindon August 1972	
D6324	J. Cashmore, Newport, Gwent c1969	
D6325	J. Cashmore, Newport, Gwent c1969	
D6326	BREL Swindon March 1972	
D6327	BREL Swindon July 1972	Completed May 1960
D6328	BREL Swindon May 1972	
D6329	J. Cashmore, Newport, Gwent	
D6330	BREL Swindon June 1972	Withdrawn September 1968, reinstated September 1969
D6331	BREL Swindon March 1972	
D6332	BREL Swindon December 1971	
D6333	BREL Swindon August 1972	
D6334	BREL Swindon April 1972	
D6335	J. Cashmore, Newport, Gwent	
D6336	BREL Swindon June 1972	Withdrawn October 1971, reinstated October 1971
D6337	BREL Swindon May 1972	
D6338	BREL Swindon February 1972	
D6339	BREL Swindon June 1972	Withdrawn October 1971, reinstated October 1971
D6340	BREL Swindon April 1972	
D6341	J. Cashmore, Newport, Gwent c1969	
D6342	J. Cashmore, Newport, Gwent c1969	
D6343	BREL Swindon January 1972	
D6344	J. Cashmore, Newport, Gwent c1969	
D6345	J. Cashmore, Newport, Gwent c1969	
D6346	J. Cashmore, Newport, Gwent c1969	
D6347	J. Cashmore, Newport, Gwent c1969	
D6348	BREL Swindon May 1972	
D6349	BREL Swindon October 1971	
D6350	J. Cashmore, Newport, Gwent c1969	
D6351	J. Cashmore, Newport, Gwent c1969	
D6352	BREL Swindon November 1971	
D6353	J. Cashmore, Newport, Gwent c1969	
D6354	BREL Swindon February 1972	
D6355	J. Cashmore, Newport, Gwent c1969	
D6356	BREL Swindon January 1972	
D6357	J. Cashmore, Newport, Gwent c1969	

Engine: Sulzer 8LDA28B of 1,550hp
Weight: 74-78 ton (various)
Bogie type: Bo-Bo
Max speed: 85mph
Class code: D15/1 later 15/6 (STD loco) D15/2, later 15/6A (slim loco) BR Class 33

Tractive effort: 45,000lb
Length: 50ft 9in
Height: 12ft 8in
Width: 9ft 3in (33/2 — 8ft 8in)

BR 1957 No	*Disposal code*	*Disposal details*	*Notes*
D6500			
D6501			
D6502	C	BR Workshops Eastleigh July 1964	
D6503			

BR 1957 No	*TOPS No*	*Name*	*Built by*	*Works No*	*Date introduced*	*Date withdrawn*
D6504	33 004	—	BRCW	DEL 96	March 1960	
D6505	33 005	—	BRCW	DEL 97	April 1960	
D6506	33 006	—	BRCW	DEL 98	April 1960	
D6507	33 007	—	BRCW	DEL 99	May 1960	
D6508	33 008	*Eastleigh,* April 1980	BRCW	DEL 100	May 1960	
D6509	33 009	—	BRCW	DEL 101	May 1960	
D6510	33 010	—	BRCW	DEL 102	June 1960	
D6511	33 101	—	BRCW	DEL 103	June 1960	
D6512	33 011	—	BRCW	DEL 104	June 1960	
D6513	33 102	—	BRCW	DEL 105	June 1960	
D6514	33 103	—	BRCW	DEL 106	July 1960	
D6515	33 012	—	BRCW	DEL 107	July 1960	
D6516	33 104	—	BRCW	DEL 108	July 1960	
D6517	33 105	—	BRCW	DEL 109	July 1960	
D6518	33 013	—	BRCW	DEL 110	August 1960	
D6519	33 106	—	BRCW	DEL 111	August 1960	
D6520	33 107	—	BRCW	DEL 112	September 1960	
D6521	33 108	—	BRCW	DEL 113	September 1960	
D6522	33 014	—	BRCW	DEL 114	September 1960	
D6523	33 015	—	BRCW	DEL 115	September 1960	
D6524	33 016	—	BRCW	DEL 116	October 1960	
D6525	33 109	—	BRCW	DEL 117	October 1960	
D6526	33 017	—	BRCW	DEL 118	October 1960	
D6527	33 110	—	BRCW	DEL 119	October 1960	
D6528	33 111	—	BRCW	DEL 120	October 1960	
D6529	33 112	—	BRCW	DEL 121	November 1960	
D6530	33 018	—	BRCW	DEL 122	November 1960	
D6531	33 113	—	BRCW	DEL 123	November 1960	
D6532	33 114	—	BRCW	DEL 124	November 1960	
D6533	33 115	—	BRCW	DEL 125	December 1960	
D6534	33 019	—	BRCW	DEL 126	December 1960	
D6535	33 116	—	BRCW	DEL 127	December 1960	
D6536	33 117	—	BRCW	DEL 128	December 1960	
D6537	33 020	—	BRCW	DEL 129	December 1960	
D6538	33 118	—	BRCW	DEL 130	January 1961	
D6539	33 021	—	BRCW	DEL 131	January 1961	
D6540	33 022	—	BRCW	DEL 132	January 1961	
D6541	33 023	—	BRCW	DEL 133	January 1961	
D6542	33 024	—	BRCW	DEL 134	February 1961	
D6543	33 025	*Sultan,* August 1981	BRCW	DEL 135	February 1961	
D6544	33 026	—	BRCW	DEL 136	February 1961	
D6545	33 027	*Earl Mountbatten of Burma,* September 1980	BRCW	DEL 137	March 1961	
D6546	33 028	—	BRCW	DEL 138	March 1961	
D6547	33 029	—	BRCW	DEL 139	March 1961	
D6548	33 030	—	BRCW	DEL 140	April 1961	
D6549	33 031	—	BRCW	DEL 141	April 1961	
D6550	33 032	—	BRCW	DEL 142	April 1961	
D6551	33 033	—	BRCW	DEL 143	April 1961	
D6552	33 034	—	BRCW	DEL 144	April 1961	
D6553	33 035	—	BRCW	DEL 145	May 1961	
D6554	33 036	—	BRCW	DEL 146	May 1961	July 1979
D6555	33 037	—	BRCW	DEL 147	May 1961	
D6556	33 038	—	BRCW	DEL 148	June 1961	
D6557	33 039	—	BRCW	DEL 149	June 1961	
D6558	33 040	—	BRCW	DEL 150	June 1961	
D6559	33 041	—	BRCW	DEL 151	June 1961	
D6560	33 042	—	BRCW	DEL 152	July 1961	

BR 1957 No	*Disposal code*	*Disposal details*	*Notes*
D6504			
D6505			
D6506			
D6507			
D6508			
D6509			
D6510			
D6511			
D6512			
D6513			
D6514			
D6515			
D6516			
D6517			
D6518			
D6519			
D6520			
D6521			
D6522			
D6523			
D6524			
D6525			
D6526			
D6527			
D6528			
D6529			
D6530			
D6531			
D6532			
D6533			
D6534			
D6535			
D6536			
D6537			
D6538			
D6539			
D6540			
D6541			
D6542			
D6543			
D6544			
D6545			
D6546			
D6547			
D6548			
D6549			
D6550			
D6551			
D6552			
D6553			
D6554	C	BR Slade Green depot October 1979	
D6555			
D6556			
D6557			
D6558			
D6559			
D6560			

BR 1957 No	*TOPS No*	*Name*	*Built by*	*Works No*	*Date introduced*	*Date withdrawn*
D6561	33 043	—	BRCW	DEL 153	July 1961	
D6562	33 044	—	BRCW	DEL 154	July 1961	
D6563	33 045	—	BRCW	DEL 155	July 1961	
D6564	33 046	—	BRCW	DEL 156	July 1961	
D6565	33 047	—	BRCW	DEL 169	August 1961	
D6566	33 048	—	BRCW	DEL 170	August 1961	
D6567	33 049	—	BRCW	DEL 171	September 1961	
D6568	33 050	—	BRCW	DEL 172	September 1961	
D6569	33 051	—	BRCW	DEL 173	September 1961	
D6570	33 052	*Ashford,* May 1980	BRCW	DEL 174	September 1961	
D6571	33 053	—	BRCW	DEL 175	October 1961	
D6572	33 054	—	BRCW	DEL 176	October 1961	
D6573	33 055	—	BRCW	DEL 177	November 1961	
D6574	33 056	*The Burma Star,* September 1980	BRCW	DEL 178	October 1961	
D6575	33 057	—	BRCW	DEL 179	November 1961	
D6576	—	—	BRCW	DEL 180	November 1961	November 1968
D6577	33 058	—	BRCW	DEL 181	November 1961	
D6578	33 059	—	BRCW	DEL 182	November 1961	
D6579	33 060	—	BRCW	DEL 183	December 1961	
D6580	33 119	—	BRCW	DEL 184	December 1961	
D6581	33 061	—	BRCW	DEL 185	December 1961	
D6582	33 062	—	BRCW	DEL 186	December 1961	
D6583	33 063	—	BRCW	DEL 187	January 1962	
D6584	33 064	—	BRCW	DEL 188	January 1962	
D6585	33 065	—	BRCW	DEL 189	January 1962	
D6586	33 201	—	BRCW	DEL 157	February 1962	
D6587	33 202	—	BRCW	DEL 158	February 1962	
D6588	33 203	—	BRCW	DEL 159	February 1962	
D6589	33 204	—	BRCW	DEL 160	February 1962	
D6590	33 205	—	BRCW	DEL 161	February 1962	
D6591	33 206	—	BRCW	DEL 162	March 1962	
D6592	33 207	—	BRCW	DEL 163	March 1962	
D6593	33 208	—	BRCW	DEL 164	March 1962	
D6594	33 209	—	BRCW	DEL 165	March 1962	
D6595	33 210	—	BRCW	DEL 166	April 1962	
D6596	33 211	—	BRCW	DEL 167	April 1962	
D6597	33 212	—	BRCW	DEL 168	May 1962	

Class 37

To cater for the Type 3 power requirement the BTC ordered a fleet of locomotives from English Electric, based on the Type 4 later Class 40s then under construction. Eventually over 300 of the type were built forming a major backbone of the mixed traffic fleet.

BR 1957 No	*TOPS No*	*Name*	*Built by*	*Works No*	*Date introduced*
D6600	37 300	—	EE(VF)	E3560/D989	August 1965
D6601	37 301	—	EE(VF)	E3561/D990	September 1965
D6602	37 302	—	EE(VF)	E3562/D991	September 1965
D6603	37 303	—	EE(VF)	E3563/D992	September 1965
D6604	37 304	—	EE(VF)	E3564/D993	September 1965
D6605	37 305	—	EE(VF)	E3565/D994	October 1965
D6606	37 306	—	EE(VF)	E3566/D995	October 1965
D6607	37 307	—	EE(VF)	E3567/D996	October 1965
D6608	37 308	—	EE(VF)	E3568/D997	November 1965
D6700	37 119	—	EE(VF)	E2863/D579	December 1960
D6701	37 001	—	EE(VF)	E2864/D580	December 1960

BR 1957 No	*Disposal code*	*Disposal details*	*Notes*
D6561			
D6562			
D6563			
D6564			
D6565			
D6566			
D6567			
D6568			
D6569			
D6570			
D6571			
D6572			
D6573			
D6574			
D6575			
D6576	C	BR Workshops Eastleigh March 1969	
D6577			
D6578			
D6579			
D6580			
D6581			
D6582			
D6583			
D6584			
D6585			
D6586			
D6587			
D6588			
D6589			
D6590			
D6591			
D6592			
D6593			
D6594			
D6595			
D6596			
D6597			

Engine: EE 12CSVT of 1,750hp
Weight: 100-105 ton (various)
Bogie type: Co-Co
Max speed: 90mph
Class code: D17/1, later 17/3 and BR Class 37
*Allocated but not carried

Tractive effort: 55,000lb
Length: 61ft 6in
Height: 12ft 9$\frac{1}{16}$in
Width: 8ft 10$\frac{1}{2}$in

BR 1957 No	*Date withdrawn*	*Disposal code*	*Disposal details*	*Notes*
D6600				
D6601				
D6602				
D6603				
D6604				
D6605				
D6606				
D6607				
D6608				
D6700				
D6701				

BR 1957 No	*TOPS No*	*Name*	*Built by*	*Works No*	*Date introduced*
D6702	37 002	—	EE(VF)	E2865/D581	December 1960
D6703	37 003	*First East Anglian Regiment**	EE(VF)	E2866/D582	December 1960
D6704	37 004	*Second East Anglian Regiment**	EE(VF)	E2867/D583	January 1961
D6705	37 005	—	EE(VF)	E2868/D584	January 1961
D6706	37 006	—	EE(VF)	E2869/D585	January 1961
D6707	37 007	*Third East Anglian Regiment**	EE(VF)	E2870/D586	February 1961
D6708	37 008	—	EE(VF)	E2871/D587	February 1961
D6709	37 009	—	EE(VF)	E2872/D588	February 1961
D6710	37 010	—	EE(VF)	E2874/D590	February 1961
D6711	37 011	—	EE(VF)	E2875/D591	March 1961
D6712	37 012	*Loch Rannoch,* March 1982	EE(VF)	E2873/D589	March 1961
D6713	37 013	—	EE(VF)	E2876/D592	March 1961
D6714	37 014	—	EE(VF)	E2877/D593	March 1961
D6715	37 015	—	EE(VF)	E2878/D594	May 1961
D6716	37 016	—	EE(VF)	E2879/D595	June 1961
D6717	37 017	—	EE(VF)	E2880/D596	May 1961
D6718	37 018	—	EE(VF)	E2881/D597	June 1961
D6719	37 019	—	EE(VF)	E2882/D598	June 1961
D6720	37 020	—	EE(VF)	E2883/D599	June 1961
D6721	37 021	—	EE(VF)	E2884/D600	July 1961
D6722	37 022	—	EE(VF)	E2885/D601	July 1961
D6723	37 023	—	EE(VF)	E2886/D602	July 1961
D6724	37 024	—	EE(VF)	E2887/D603	August 1961
D6725	37 025	—	EE(VF)	E2888/D604	August 1961
D6726	37 026	*Loch Awe,* October 1981	EE(VF)	E2889/D605	September 1961
D6727	37 027	*Loch Eil,* October 1981	EE(VF)	E2890/D606	September 1961
D6728	37 028	—	EE(VF)	E2891/D607	September 1961
D6729	37 029	—	EE(VF)	E2892/D608	October 1961
D6730	37 030	—	EE(VF)	E2893/D609	October 1961
D6731	37 031	—	EE(VF)	E2894/D610	October 1961
D6732	37 032	—	EE(VF)	E2895/D611	March 1962
D6733	37 033	—	EE(VF)	E2896/D612	March 1962
D6734	37 034	—	EE(VF)	E2897/D613	March 1962
D6735	37 035	—	EE(VF)	E2898/D614	April 1962
D6736	37 036	—	EE(VF)	E2899/D615	April 1962
D6737	37 037	—	EE(VF)	E2900/D616	May 1962
D6738	37 038	—	EE(VF)	E2901/D617	May 1962
D6739	37 039	—	EE(VF)	E2902/D618	May 1962
D6740	37 040	—	EE(VF)	E2903/D619	June 1962
D6741	37 041	—	EE(VF)	E2904/D620	June 1962
D6742	37 042	—	EE(VF)	E3034/D696	June 1962
D6743	37 043	*Loch Lomond,* October 1981	EE(VF)	E3035/D697	June 1962
D6744	37 044	—	EE(VF)	E3036/D698	June 1962
D6745	37 045	—	EE(VF)	E3037/D699	July 1962
D6746	37 046	—	EE(VF)	E3038/D700	July 1962
D6747	37 047	—	EE(VF)	E3039/D701	July 1962
D6748	37 048	—	EE(VF)	E3040/D702	August 1962
D6749	37 049	—	EE(VF)	E3041/D703	August 1962
D6750	37 050	—	EE(VF)	E3042/D704	August 1962
D6751	37 051	—	EE(VF)	E3043/D705	August 1962
D6752	37 052	—	EE(VF)	E3044/D706	September 1962
D6753	37 053	—	EE(VF)	E3045/D707	September 1962
D6754	37 054	—	EE(VF)	E3046/D708	September 1962
D6755	37 055	—	EE(VF)	E3047/D709	September 1962
D6756	37 056	—	EE(VF)	E3048/D710	September 1962
D6757	37 057	—	EE(VF)	E3049/D711	October 1962
D6758	37 058	—	EE(VF)	E3050/D712	October 1962
D6759	37 059	—	EE(VF)	E3051/D713	October 1962
D6760	37 060	—	EE(VF)	E3052/D714	October 1962
D6761	37 061	—	EE(VF)	E3053/D715	October 1962

BR 1957 No	*Date withdrawn*	*Disposal code*	*Disposal details*	*Notes*
D6702				
D6703				
D6704				
D6705				
D6706				
D6707				
D6708				
D6709				
D6710				
D6711				
D6712				
D6713				
D6714				
D6715				
D6716				
D6717				
D6718				
D6719				
D6720				
D6721				
D6722				
D6723				
D6724				
D6725				
D6726				
D6727				
D6728				
D6729				
D6730				
D6731				
D6732				
D6733				
D6734				
D6735				
D6736				
D6737				
D6738				
D6739				
D6740				
D6741				
D6742				
D6743				
D6744				
D6745				
D6746				
D6747				
D6748				
D6749				
D6750				
D6751				
D6752				
D6753				
D6754				
D6755				
D6756				
D6757				
D6758				
D6759				
D6760				
D6761				

BR 1957 No	*TOPS No*	*Name*	*Built by*	*Works No*	*Date introduced*
D6762	37 062	—	EE(VF)	E3054/D716	October 1962
D6763	37 063	—	EE(VF)	E3055/D717	November 1962
D6764	37 064	—	EE(VF)	E3056/D718	November 1962
D6765	37 065	—	EE(VF)	E3057/D719	November 1962
D6766	37 066	—	EE(VF)	E3058/D720	November 1962
D6767	37 067	—	EE(VF)	E3059/D721	November 1962
D6768	37 068	—	EE(VF)	E3060/D722	November 1962
D6769	37 069	—	RSH	E3061/8315	July 1962
D6770	37 070	—	RSH	E3062/8316	August 1962
D6771	37 071	—	RSH	E3063/8317	August 1962
D6772	37 072	—	RSH	E3064/8318	September 1962
D6773	37 073	—	RSH	E3065/8319	September 1962
D6774	37 074	—	RSH	E3066/8320	September 1962
D6775	37 075	—	RSH	E3067/8321	September 1962
D6776	37 076	—	RSH	E3068/8322	October 1962
D6777	37 077	—	RSH	E3069/8323	October 1962
D6778	37 078	*Teesside Steelmaster,* June 1984	RSH	E3070/8324	October 1962
D6779	37 079	—	RSH	E3206/8325	November 1962
D6780	37 080	—	RSH	E3207/8326	November 1962
D6781	37 081	*Loch Long,* October 1981	RSH	E3208/8327	November 1962
D6782	37 082	—	RSH	E3209/8328	November 1962
D6783	37 083	—	RSH	E3210/8329	December 1962
D6784	37 084	—	RSH	E3211/8330	December 1962
D6785	37 085	—	RSH	E3212/8331	December 1962
D6786	37 086	—	RSH	E3213/8332	December 1962
D6787	37 087	—	RSH	E3214/8333	December 1962
D6788	37 088	—	RSH	E3215/8334	January 1963
D6789	37 089	—	RSH	E3216/8335	January 1963
D6790	37 090	—	RSH	E3217/8336	January 1963
D6791	37 091	—	RSH	E3218/8337	January 1963
D6792	37 092	—	RSH	E3219/8338	February 1963
D6793	37 093	—	RSH	E3220/8339	February 1963
D6794	37 094	—	RSH	E3221/8341	February 1963
D6795	37 095	—	RSH	E3222/8342	March 1963
D6796	37 096	—	EE(VF)	E3225/D750	November 1962
D6797	37 097	—	EE(VF)	E3226/D751	December 1962
D6798	37 098	—	EE(VF)	E3227/D752	December 1962
D6799	37 099	—	EE(VF)	E3228/D753	December 1962
D6800	37 100	—	EE(VF)	E3229/D754	December 1962
D6801	37 101	—	EE(VF)	E3230/D755	December 1962
D6802	37 102	—	EE(VF)	E3231/D756	January 1963
D6803	37 103	—	EE(VF)	E3232/D757	January 1963
D6804	37 104	—	EE(VF)	E3233/D758	January 1963
D6805	37 105	—	EE(VF)	E3234/D759	January 1963
D6806	37 106	—	EE(VF)	E3235/D760	January 1963
D6807	37 107	—	EE(VF)	E3236/D761	January 1963
D6808	37 108	—	EE(VF)	E3237/D762	January 1963
D6809	37 109	—	EE(VF)	E3238/D763	February 1963
D6810	37 110	—	EE(VF)	E3239/D764	February 1963
D6811	37 111	—	EE(VF)	E3240/D765	February 1963
D6812	37 112	—	EE(VF)	E3241/D766	February 1963
D6813	37 113	—	EE(VF)	E3242/D767	February 1963
D6814	37 114	—	EE(VF)	E3243/D768	February 1963
D6815	37 115	—	EE(VF)	E3244/D769	February 1963
D6816	37 116	—	EE(VF)	E3245/D770	March 1963
D6817	37 117	—	EE(VF)	E3246/D771	March 1963
D6818	37 118	—	EE(VF)	E3247/D772	March 1963
D6819	37 283	—	RSH	E3264/8379	March 1963
D6820	37 120	—	RSH	E3265/8380	March 1963
D6821	37 121	—	RSH	E3266/8381	April 1963

BR 1957 No	Date withdrawn	Disposal code	Disposal details	Notes
D6762				
D6763				
D6764				
D6765				
D6766				
D6767				
D6768				
D6769				
D6770				
D6771				
D6772				
D6773				
D6774				
D6775				
D6776				
D6777				
D6778				
D6779				
D6780				
D6781				
D6782				
D6783				
D6784				
D6785				
D6786				
D6787				
D6788				
D6789				
D6790				
D6791				
D6792				
D6793				
D6794				
D6795				
D6796				
D6797				
D6798				
D6799				
D6800				
D6801				
D6802				
D6803				
D6804				
D6805				
D6806				
D6807				
D6808				
D6809				
D6810				
D6811				
D6812				
D6813				
D6814				
D6815				
D6816				
D6817				
D6818				
D6819				
D6820				
D6821				

BR 1957 No	TOPS No	Name	Built by	Works No	Date introduced
D6822	37 122	—	RSH	E3267/8382	May 1963
D6823	37 123	—	RSH	E3268/8383	April 1963
D6824	37 124	—	RSH	E3269/8384	April 1963
D6825	37 125	—	RSH	E3270/8385	May 1963
D6826	37 126	—	RSH	E3271/8386	May 1963
D6827	37 127	—	RSH	E3272/8387	May 1963
D6828	37 128	—	RSH	E3273/8388	June 1963
D6829	37 129	—	EE(VF)	E3274/D803	March 1963
D6830	37 130	—	EE(VF)	E3275/D804	March 1963
D6831	37 131	—	EE(VF)	E3276/D805	March 1963
D6832	37 132	—	EE(VF)	E3277/D806	April 1963
D6833	37 133	—	EE(VF)	E3278/D807	April 1963
D6834	37 134	—	EE(VF)	E3279/D808	April 1963
D6835	37 135	—	EE(VF)	E3280/D809	April 1963
D6836	37 136	—	EE(VF)	E3281/D810	April 1963
D6837	37 137	—	EE(VF)	E3282/D811	April 1963
D6838	37 138	—	EE(VF)	E3283/D812	April 1963
D6839	37 139	—	EE(VF)	E3314/D813	May 1963
D6840	37 140	—	EE(VF)	E3315/D814	May 1963
D6841	37 141	—	EE(VF)	E3316/D815	May 1963
D6842	37 142	—	EE(VF)	E3317/D816	May 1963
D6843	37 143	—	EE(VF)	E3318/D817	May 1963
D6844	37 144	—	EE(VF)	E3319/D818	June 1963
D6845	37 145	—	EE(VF)	E3320/D819	June 1963
D6846	37 146	—	EE(VF)	E3321/D820	June 1963
D6847	37 147	—	EE(VF)	E3322/D821	June 1963
D6848	37 148	—	EE(VF)	E3323/D822	June 1963
D6849	37 149	—	EE(VF)	E3324/D823	June 1963
D6850	37 150	—	EE(VF)	E3325/D824	July 1963
D6851	37 151	—	EE(VF)	E3326/D825	July 1963
D6852	37 152	—	EE(VF)	E3327/D826	July 1963
D6853	37 153	—	EE(VF)	E3328/D827	July 1963
D6854	37 154	—	EE(VF)	E3329/D828	July 1963
D6855	37 155	—	EE(VF)	E3330/D829	July 1963
D6856	37 156	—	EE(VF)	E3331/D830	July 1963
D6857	37 157	—	EE(VF)	E3332/D831	July 1963
D6858	37 158	—	EE(VF)	E3333/D832	August 1963
D6859	37 159	—	RSH	E3337/8390	June 1963
D6860	37 160	—	RSH	E3338/8391	July 1963
D6861	37 161	—	RSH	E3339/8392	July 1963
D6862	37 162	—	RSH	E3340/8393	July 1963
D6863	37 163	—	RSH	E3341/8394	August 1963
D6864	37 164	—	RSH	E3342/8395	August 1963
D6865	37 165	—	RSH	E3343/8396	August 1963
D6866	37 166	—	RSH	E3344/8397	September 1963
D6867	37 167	—	RSH	E3345/8398	September 1963
D6868	37 168	—	RSH	E3346/8399	October 1963
D6869	37 169	—	EE(VF)	E3347/D833	August 1963
D6870	37 170	—	EE(VF)	E3348/D834	August 1963
D6871	37 171	—	EE(VF)	E3349/D835	September 1963
D6872	37 172	—	EE(VF)	E3350/D836	September 1963
D6873	37 173	—	EE(VF)	E3351/D837	September 1963
D6874	37 174	—	EE(VF)	E3352/D838	September 1963
D6875	37 175	—	EE(VF)	E3353/D839	September 1963
D6876	37 176	—	EE(VF)	E3354/D840	October 1963
D6877	37 177	—	EE(VF)	E3355/D841	October 1963
D6878	37 178	—	EE(VF)	E3356/D842	October 1963
D6879	37 179	—	RSH	E3357/8400	October 1963
D6880	37 180	*Sir Dyfed/County of Dyfed,* May 1981	RSH	E3358/8401	October 1963
D6881	37 181	—	RSH	E3359/8402	October 1963

BR 1957 No	*Date withdrawn*	*Disposal code*	*Disposal details*	*Notes*
D6822				
D6823				
D6824				
D6825				
D6826				
D6827				
D6828				
D6829				
D6830				
D6831				
D6832				
D6833				
D6834				
D6835				
D6836				
D6837				
D6838				
D6839				
D6840				
D6841				
D6842				
D6843				
D6844				
D6845				
D6846				
D6847				
D6848				
D6849				
D6850				
D6851				
D6852				
D6853				
D6854				
D6855				
D6856				
D6857				
D6858				
D6859				
D6860				
D6861				
D6862				
D6863				
D6864				
D6865				
D6866				
D6867				
D6868				
D6869				
D6870				
D6871				
D6872				
D6873				
D6874				
D6875				
D6876				
D6877				
D6878				
D6879				
D6880				
D6881				

BR 1957 No	*TOPS No*	*Name*	*Built by*	*Works No*	*Date introduced*
D6882	37 182	—	RSH	E3360/8403	October 1963
D6883	37 183	—	RSH	E3361/8404	November 1963
D6884	37 184	—	RSH	E3362/8405	November 1963
D6885	37 185	—	RSH	E3363/8406	December 1963
D6886	37 186	—	RSH	E3364/8407	November 1963
D6887	37 187	—	RSH	E3365/8408	January 1964
D6888	37 188	—	RSH	E3366/8409	January 1964
D6889	37 189	—	RSH	E3367/8410	January 1964
D6890	37 190	—	RSH	E3368/8411	January 1964
D6891	37 191	—	RSH	E3369/8412	February 1964
D6892	37 192	—	RSH	E3370/8413	February 1964
D6893	37 193	—	RSH	E3371/8414	February 1964
D6894	37 194	—	RSH	E3372/8415	March 1964
D6895	37 195	—	RSH	E3373/8416	March 1964
D6896	37 196	—	RSH	E3374/8417	April 1964
D6897	37 197	—	RSH	E3375/8418	April 1964
D6898	37 198	—	RSH	E3376/8419	May 1964
D6899	37 199	—	EE(VF)	E3377/D843	October 1963
D6900	37 200	—	EE(VF)	E3378/D844	October 1963
D6901	37 201	—	EE(VF)	E3379/D845	October 1963
D6902	37 202	—	EE(VF)	E3380/D846	October 1963
D6903	37 203	—	EE(VF)	E3381/D847	October 1963
D6904	37 204	—	EE(VF)	E3382/D848	November 1963
D6905	37 205	—	EE(VF)	E3383/D849	November 1963
D6906	37 206	—	EE(VF)	E3384/D850	November 1963
D6907	37 207	*William Cookworthy*, May 1982	EE(VF)	E3385/D851	November 1963
D6908	37 208	—	EE(VF)	E3386/D852	November 1963
D6909	37 209	—	EE(VF)	E3387/D853	December 1963
D6910	37 210	—	EE(VF)	E3388/D854	November 1963
D6911	37 211	—	EE(VF)	E3389/D855	December 1963
D6912	37 212	—	EE(VF)	E3390/D856	January 1964
D6913	37 213	—	EE(VF)	E3391/D857	January 1964
D6914	37 214	—	EE(VF)	E3392/D858	January 1964
D6915	37 215	—	EE(VF)	E3393/D859	January 1964
D6916	37 216	—	EE(VF)	E3394/D860	January 1964
D6917	37 217	—	EE(VF)	E3395/D861	January 1964
D6918	37 218	—	EE(VF)	E3396/D862	January 1964
D6919	37 219	—	EE(VF)	E3405/D863	January 1964
D6920	37 220	—	EE(VF)	E3406/D864	January 1964
D6921	37 221	—	EE(VF)	E3407/D865	January 1964
D6922	37 222	—	EE(VF)	E3408/D866	January 1964
D6923	37 223	—	EE(VF)	E3409/D867	February 1964
D6924	37 224	—	EE(VF)	E3410/D868	January 1964
D6925	37 225	—	EE(VF)	E3411/D869	February 1964
D6926	37 226	—	EE(VF)	E3412/D870	February 1964
D6927	37 227	—	EE(VF)	E3413/D871	February 1964
D6928	37 228	—	EE(VF)	E3414/D872	February 1964
D6929	37 229	—	EE(VF)	E3415/D873	February 1964
D6930	37 230	—	EE(VF)	E3416/D874	March 1964
D6931	37 231	—	EE(VF)	E3417/D875	March 1964
D6932	37 232	—	EE(VF)	E3418/D876	March 1964
D6933	37 233	—	EE(VF)	E3419/D877	April 1964
D6934	37 234	—	EE(VF)	E3420/D878	April 1964
D6935	37 235	—	EE(VF)	E3421/D879	April 1964
D6936	37 236	—	EE(VF)	E3422/D880	April 1964
D6937	37 237	—	EE(VF)	E3423/D881	May 1964
D6938	37 238	—	EE(VF)	E3424/D882	June 1964
D6939	37 239	—	EE(VF)	E3496/D927	August 1964
D6940	37 240	—	EE(VF)	E3497/D928	August 1964

BR 1957 No	Date withdrawn	Disposal code	Disposal details	Notes
D6882				
D6883				
D6884				
D6885				
D6886				
D6887				
D6888				
D6889				
D6890				
D6891				
D6892				
D6893				
D6894				
D6895				
D6896				
D6897				
D6898				
D6899				
D6900				
D6901				
D6902				
D6903				
D6904				
D6905				
D6906				
D6907				
D6908				
D6909				
D6910				
D6911				
D6912				
D6913				
D6914				
D6915				
D6916				
D6917				
D6918				
D6919				
D6920				
D6921				
D6922				
D6923				
D6924				
D6925				
D6926				
D6927				
D6928				
D6929				
D6930				
D6931				
D6932				
D6933				
D6934				
D6935				
D6936				
D6937				
D6938				
D6939				
D6940				

BR 1957 No	*TOPS No*	*Name*	*Built by*	*Works No*	*Date introduced*
D6941	37 241	—	EE(VF)	E3498/D929	September 1964
D6942	37 242	—	EE(VF)	E3499/D930	September 1964
D6943	37 243	—	EE(VF)	E3500/D931	September 1964
D6944	37 244	—	EE(VF)	E3501/D932	September 1964
D6945	37 245	—	EE(VF)	E3502/D933	October 1964
D6946	37 246	—	EE(VF)	E3503/D934	October 1964
D6947	37 247	—	EE(VF)	E3504/D935	October 1964
D6948	37 248	—	EE(VF)	E3505/D936	October 1964
D6949	37 249	—	EE(VF)	E3506/D937	December 1964
D6950	37 250	—	EE(VF)	E3507/D938	December 1964
D6951	37 251	—	EE(VF)	E3508/D939	December 1964
D6952	37 252	—	EE(VF)	E3509/D940	January 1965
D6953	37 253	—	EE(VF)	E3510/D941	January 1965
D6954	37 254	—	EE(VF)	E3511/D942	January 1965
D6955	37 255	—	EE(VF)	E3512/D943	January 1965
D6956	37 256	—	EE(VF)	E3513/D944	January 1965
D6957	37 257	—	EE(VF)	E3514/D945	January 1965
D6958	37 258	—	EE(VF)	E3515/D946	January 1965
D6959	37 259	—	EE(VF)	E3519/D948	January 1965
D6960	37 260	*Radio Highland,* July 1984	EE(VF)	E3520/D949	January 1965
D6961	37 261	—	EE(VF)	E3521/D950	January 1965
D6962	37 262	—	EE(VF)	E3522/D951	January 1965
D6963	37 263	—	EE(VF)	E3523/D952	January 1965
D6964	37 264	—	EE(VF)	E3524/D953	January 1965
D6965	37 265	—	EE(VF)	E3525/D954	February 1965
D6966	37 266	—	EE(VF)	E3526/D955	February 1965
D6967	37 267	—	EE(VF)	E3527/D956	February 1965
D6968	37 401	—	EE(VF)	E3528/D957	February 1965
D6969	37 269	—	EE(VF)	E3529/D958	February 1965
D6970	37 270	—	EE(VF)	E3530/D959	March 1965
D6971	37 271	—	EE(VF)	E3531/D960	March 1965
D6972	37 272	—	EE(VF)	E3532/D961	March 1965
D6973	37 273	—	EE(VF)	E3533/D962	April 1965
D6974	37 274	—	EE(VF)	E3534/D963	April 1965
D6975	37 275	—	EE(VF)	E3535/D964	April 1965
D6976	37 276	—	EE(VF)	E3536/D965	April 1965
D6977	37 277	—	EE(VF)	E3537/D966	April 1965
D6978	37 278	—	EE(VF)	E3538/D967	April 1965
D6979	37 279	—	EE(VF)	E3539/D968	May 1965
D6980	37 280	—	EE(VF)	E3540/D969	May 1965
D6981	37 281	—	EE(VF)	E3541/D970	May 1965
D6982	37 282	—	EE(VF)	E3542/D971	May 1965
D6983	—	—	EE(VF)	E3543/D972	May 1965
D6984	37 284	—	EE(VF)	E3544/D973	May 1965
D6985	37 285	—	EE(VF)	E3545/D974	May 1965
D6986	37 286	—	EE(VF)	E3546/D975	June 1965
D6987	37 287	—	EE(VF)	E3547/D976	June 1965
D6988	37 288	—	EE(VF)	E3548/D977	June 1965
D6989	37 289	—	EE(VF)	E3549/D978	June 1965
D6990	37 290	—	EE(VF)	E3550/D979	June 1965
D6991	37 291	—	EE(VF)	E3551/D980	June 1965
D6992	37 292	—	EE(VF)	E3552/D981	July 1965
D6993	37 293	—	EE(VF)	E3553/D982	July 1965
D6994	37 294	—	EE(VF)	E3554/D983	July 1965
D6995	37 295	—	EE(VF)	E3555/D984	July 1965
D6996	37 296	—	EE(VF)	E3556/D985	July 1965
D6997	37 297	—	EE(VF)	E3557/D986	July 1965
D6998	37 298	—	EE(VF)	E3558/D987	August 1965
D6999	37 299	—	EE(VF)	E3559/D988	August 1965

BR 1957 No	Date withdrawn	Disposal code	Disposal details	Notes
D6941				
D6942				
D6943				
D6944				
D6945				
D6946				
D6947				
D6948				
D6949				
D6950				
D6951				
D6952				
D6953				
D6954				
D6955				
D6956				
D6957				
D6958				
D6959				
D6960				
D6961				
D6962				
D6963				
D6964				
D6965				
D6966				
D6967				
D6968				Formerly No 37 268
D6969				
D6970				
D6971				
D6972				
D6973				
D6974				
D6975				
D6976				
D6977				
D6978				
D6979				
D6980				
D6981				
D6982				
D6983	October 1966	C	Bridgend by R. S. Hayes	
D6984				
D6985				
D6986				
D6987				
D6988				
D6989				
D6990				
D6991				
D6992				
D6993				
D6994				
D6995				
D6996				
D6997				
D6998				
D6999				

North British Locomotive (NBL) Co Type 2 diesel-hydraulic No D6300 in as built condition. *NBL*

For use on push-pull services 19 standard Class 33s were re-built in 1966/67 for remote/ push-pull operation and reclassified as 33/1. No 33 114 is illustrated. *Colin J. Marsden*

BTH built 44 Type 1 locomotives under the 1955 modernisation plan Nos D8200-D8243. The first of the build, No D8200 carrying works number 1031, is seen here when new. *BR*

Perhaps the least successful of the Type 1 builds were 10 examples built by North British as Nos D8400-D8409, classified by BR as Class 16. None survived for TOPS renumbering and the class was extinct by 1971. No D8402, NBL No 27673 is illustrated. *BR*

Class 35

The WR Type 3 locomotive for mixed traffic duties was this fleet of 'Hymek' B-B locos introduced from 1961. The fleet was eliminated from service by 1975 as non-standard, after only some 10 years' service.

BR 1957 No	*Built by*	*Works No*	*Date introduced*	*Date withdrawn*	*Disposal code*
D7000	B/Peacock	7894	May 1961	July 1973	C
D7001	B/Peacock	7895	July 1961	March 1974	C
D7002	B/Peacock	7896	July 1961	October 1971	C
D7003	B/Peacock	7897	August 1961	January 1972	C
D7004	B/Peacock	7898	August 1961	June 1972	C
D7005	B/Peacock	7899	September 1961	July 1972	C
D7006	B/Peacock	7900	October 1961	September 1971	C
D7007	B/Peacock	7901	October 1961	April 1972	C
D7008	B/Peacock	7902	October 1961	January 1972	C
D7009	B/Peacock	7903	November 1961	May 1973	C
D7010	B/Peacock	7904	November 1961	January 1972	C
D7011	B/Peacock	7905	December 1961	March 1975	C
D7012	B/Peacock	7906	December 1961	January 1972	C
D7013	B/Peacock	7907	December 1961	January 1972	C
D7014	B/Peacock	7908	December 1961	January 1971	C
D7015	B/Peacock	7909	December 1961	June 1972	C
D7016	B/Peacock	7910	January 1962	July 1974	C
D7017	B/Peacock	7911	January 1962	March 1975	P
D7018	B/Peacock	7912	January 1962	March 1975	P
D7019	B/Peacock	7913	February 1962	September 1972	C
D7020	B/Peacock	7914	February 1962	January 1972	C
D7021	B/Peacock	7915	February 1962	January 1972	C
D7022	B/Peacock	7916	February 1962	March 1975	C
D7023	B/Peacock	7917	February 1962	May 1973	C
D7024	B/Peacock	7918	March 1962	January 1972	C
D7025	B/Peacock	7919	March 1962	January 1972	C
D7026	B/Peacock	7920	March 1962	October 1974	C
D7027	B/Peacock	7921	April 1962	November 1971	C
D7028	B/Peacock	7922	April 1962	January 1975	C
D7029	B/Peacock	7923	April 1962	February 1975	P
D7030	B/Peacock	7924	April 1962	May 1973	C
D7031	B/Peacock	7925	April 1962	May 1973	C
D7032	B/Peacock	7926	May 1962	May 1973	C
D7033	B/Peacock	7927	May 1962	January 1972	C
D7034	B/Peacock	7928	May 1962	January 1972	C
D7035	B/Peacock	7929	June 1962	January 1972	C
D7036	B/Peacock	7930	June 1962	June 1972	C
D7037	B/Peacock	7931	June 1962	September 1972	C
D7038	B/Peacock	7932	June 1962	July 1972	C
D7039	B/Peacock	7933	June 1962	June 1972	C
D7040	B/Peacock	7934	July 1962	January 1972	C
D7041	B/Peacock	7935	July 1962	January 1972	C

Engine: Maybach MD870 of 1,700hp
Weight: 74 ton
Bogie type: B-B
Max speed: 90mph
Class code: D17/2 later 17/7 and BR Class 35

Tractive effort: 49,700lb
Length: 51ft 8in
Height: 12ft 10½in
Width: 8ft 10in

BR 1957 No	*Disposal details*	*Notes*
D7000	BREL Swindon October 1975	
D7001	G. Cohen, Kettering, Northamptonshire May 1975	
D7002	BREL Swindon July 1972	
D7003	BREL Swindon August 1972	
D7004	BREL Swindon August 1972	Withdrawn January 1972, reinstated January 1972
D7005	BREL Swindon October 1972	Withdrawn January 1972, reinstated January 1972
D7006	BREL Swindon September 1972	
D7007	BREL Swindon June 1972	Withdrawn January 1972, reinstated January 1972
D7008	BREL Swindon September 1972	
D7009	BREL Swindon October 1974	
D7010	BREL Swindon November 1972	
D7011	Marple & Gillot Ltd, Sheffield, March 1977	
D7012	BREL Swindon July 1972	
D7013	BREL Swindon October 1972	
D7014	BREL Swindon August 1972	
D7015	BREL Swindon September 1972	
D7016	BREL Swindon June 1975	
D7017	Diesel & Electric Group, West Somerset Railway, Minehead	Withdrawn May 1973, reinstated May 1973
D7018	Diesel & Electric Group, Didcot	
D7019	BREL Swindon October 1972	Withdrawn July 1972, reinstated September 1972
D7020	BREL Swindon September 1972	
D7021	BREL Swindon June 1972	
D7022	G. Cohen, Kettering, Northamptonshire January 1977	
D7023	BREL Swindon May 1975	
D7024	BREL Swindon November 1972	
D7025	BREL Swindon July 1972	
D7026	G. Cohen, Kettering, Northamptonshire January 1977	
D7027	BREL Swindon August 1972	
D7028	G. Cohen, Kettering, Northamptonshire February 1977	
D7029	Diesel Traction Group, North York Moors Railway	
D7030	Birds Ltd, Long Marston March 1974	
D7031	BREL Swindon September 1975	
D7032	BREL Swindon July 1975	
D7033	BREL Swindon November 1972	
D7034	BREL Swindon September 1972	
D7035	BREL Swindon August 1972	
D7036	BREL Swindon October 1972	Withdrawn January 1972, reinstated April 1972
D7037	BREL Swindon November 1972	
D7038	BREL Swindon June 1973	Withdrawn January 1972, reinstated January 1972
D7039	BREL Swindon August 1972	
D7040	BREL Swindon August 1972	
D7041	BREL Swindon September 1972	

BR 1957 No	Built by	Works No	Date introduced	Date withdrawn	Disposal code
D7042	B/Peacock	7936	July 1962	January 1972	C
D7043	B/Peacock	7937	July 1962	January 1972	C
D7044	B/Peacock	7938	August 1962	May 1973	C
D7045	B/Peacock	7949	August 1962	November 1972	C
D7046	B/Peacock	7950	August 1962	January 1972	C
D7047	B/Peacock	7951	August 1962	January 1972	C
D7048	B/Peacock	7952	September 1962	January 1972	C
D7049	B/Peacock	7953	October 1962	January 1972	C
D7050	B/Peacock	7954	October 1962	November 1972	C
D7051	B/Peacock	7955	October 1962	January 1972	C
D7052	B/Peacock	7956	October 1962	November 1972	C
D7053	B/Peacock	7957	October 1962	January 1972	C
D7054	B/Peacock	7958	November 1962	December 1972	C
D7055	B/Peacock	7959	November 1962	April 1973	D
D7056	B/Peacock	7960	November 1962	January 1972	C
D7057	B/Peacock	7961	November 1962	January 1972	C
D7058	B/Peacock	7962	November 1962	October 1971	C
D7059	B/Peacock	7963	November 1962	October 1971	C
D7060	B/Peacock	7964	December 1962	October 1971	C
D7061	B/Peacock	7965	December 1962	January 1972	C
D7062	B/Peacock	7966	January 1963	October 1971	C
D7063	B/Peacock	7967	December 1962	October 1971	C
D7064	B/Peacock	7968	January 1963	October 1971	C
D7065	B/Peacock	7969	January 1963	January 1972	C
D7066	B/Peacock	7970	January 1963	November 1971	C
D7067	B/Peacock	7971	February 1963	October 1971	C
D7068	B/Peacock	7972	February 1963	December 1972	C
D7069	B/Peacock	7973	February 1963	October 1971	C
D7070	B/Peacock	7974	March 1963	September 1972	C
D7071	B/Peacock	7975	March 1963	January 1972	C
D7072	B/Peacock	7976	March 1963	October 1971	C
D7073	B/Peacock	7977	March 1963	December 1971	C
D7074	B/Peacock	7978	March 1963	December 1972	C
D7075	B/Peacock	7979	March 1963	May 1973	C
D7076	B/Peacock	7980	May 1963	May 1973	P
D7077	B/Peacock	7981	December 1963	July 1972	C
D7078	B/Peacock	7982	May 1963	October 1971	C
D7079	B/Peacock	7983	December 1963	October 1971	C
D7080	B/Peacock	7984	December 1963	November 1972	C
D7081	B/Peacock	7985	December 1963	September 1971	C
D7082	B/Peacock	7986	June 1963	April 1972	C
D7083	B/Peacock	7987	June 1963	October 1971	C
D7084	B/Peacock	7988	June 1963	October 1972	C
D7085	B/Peacock	7989	June 1963	October 1972	C
D7086	B/Peacock	7990	July 1963	January 1972	C
D7087	B/Peacock	7991	July 1963	October 1972	C
D7088	B/Peacock	7992	October 1963	January 1972	C
D7089	B/Peacock	7993	July 1963	May 1973	D
D7090	B/Peacock	7994	September 1963	June 1972	C
D7091	B/Peacock	7995	September 1963	August 1972	C
D7092	B/Peacock	7996	December 1963	June 1972	C
D7093	B/Peacock	7997	December 1963	November 1974	C

BR 1957 No	*Disposal details*	*Notes*
D7042	BREL Swindon July 1972	
D7043	BREL Swindon August 1972	
D7044	Birds Ltd, Long Marston March 1974	
D7045	BREL Swindon August 1973	
D7046	BREL Swindon July 1982	
D7047	BREL Swindon August 1972	
D7048	BREL Swindon August 1972	
D7049	BREL Swindon July 1972	
D7050	BREL Swindon June 1973	
D7051	BREL Swindon July 1972	
D7052	BREL Swindon May 1973	Withdrawn January 1972, reinstated May 1972, withdrawn July 1972, reinstated September 1972
D7053	BREL Swindon August 1972	
D7054	BREL Swindon April 1975	Withdrawn January 1972, reinstated April 1972, withdrawn July 1972, reinstated September 1972
D7055	Departmental Stock — 968004	
D7056	BREL Swindon July 1972	
D7057	BREL Swindon October 1972	
D7058	BREL Swindon June 1972	
D7059	BREL Swindon July 1972	
D7060	BREL Swindon October 1972	
D7061	BREL Swindon August 1972	
D7062	BREL Swindon August 1972	
D7063	BREL Swindon November 1972	
D7064	BREL Swindon September 1972	
D7065	BREL Swindon September 1972	
D7066	BREL Swindon September 1972	
D7067	BREL Swindon August 1972	
D7068	BREL Swindon April 1975	
D7069	BREL Swindon August 1972	
D7070	BREL Swindon October 1972	Withdrawn January 1972, reinstated May 1972, withdrawn July 1972, reinstated August 1972
D7071	BREL Swindon September 1972	
D7072	BREL Swindon September 1972	
D7073	BREL Swindon October 1972	
D7074	BREL Swindon August 1975	
D7075	Birds Ltd, Long Marston February 1974	
D7076	Privately at Bury Transport Museum December 1982	After withdrawal used by RCD as dead load vehicle
D7077	BREL Swindon October 1972	Completed May 1963 under test
D7078	BREL Swindon May 1972	
D7079	BREL Swindon August 1972	Completed May 1963
D7080	BREL Swindon May 1973	Completed May 1963
D7081	BREL Swindon August 1972	Completed May 1963
D7082	BREL Swindon October 1972	
D7083	BREL Swindon September 1972	
D7084	BREL Swindon November 1972	
D7085	BREL Swindon March 1973	Withdrawn July 1972, reinstated September 1972
D7086	BREL Swindon September 1972	
D7087	BREL Swindon September 1973	
D7088	BREL Swindon October 1972	
D7089	Departmental Stock — 968005	
D7090	BREL Swindon September 1972	
D7091	BREL Swindon October 1972	
D7092	BREL Swindon September 1972	
D7093	G. Cohen, Kettering, Northamptonshire February 1977	Withdrawn May 1973, reinstated August 1973

BR 1957 No	Built by	Works No	Date introduced	Date withdrawn	Disposal code
D7094	B/Peacock	7998	December 1963	November 1972	C
D7095	B/Peacock	7999	December 1963	October 1972	C
D7096	B/Peacock	8000	December 1963	December 1972	D
D7097	B/Peacock	8001	December 1963	December 1972	C
D7098	B/Peacock	8002	January 1964	December 1972	C
D7099	B/Peacock	8003	January 1964	October 1972	C
D7100	B/Peacock	8004	February 1965	November 1972	C

Class 25 — Continued from D5299

BR 1957 No	TOPS No	Built by	Works No	Period* Date introduced	Date withdrawn	Disposal code
D7500	25 150	BR Derby	—	10/64*	June 1982	A
D7501	25 151	BR Derby	—	11/64*	September 1982	A
D7502	25 152	BR Derby	—	11/64*	January 1984	A
D7503	25 153	BR Derby	—	11/64*	April 1983	A
D7504	25 154	BR Derby	—	11/64*		
D7505	25 155	BR Derby	—	11/64*	December 1980	C
D7506	25 156	BR Derby	—	11/64*	December 1981	C
D7507	25 157	BR Derby	—	11/64*	October 1982	A
D7508	25 158	BR Derby	—	12/64*	May 1983	A
D7509	25 159	BR Derby	—	12/64*	November 1980	C
D7510	25 160	BR Derby	—	12/64*	October 1982	A
D7511	25 161	BR Derby	—	12/64*		
D7512	25 162	BR Derby	—	12/64*	May 1981	C
D7513	25 163	BR Derby	—	12/64*	November 1980	C
D7514	25 164	BR Derby	—	12/64*	August 1983	A
D7515	25 165	BR Derby	—	13/64*	November 1978	C
D7516	25 166	BR Derby	—	13/64*	November 1980	C
D7517	25 167	BR Derby	—	13/64*	May 1983	C
D7518	25 168	BR Derby	—	13/64*	May 1983	C
D7519	25 169	BR Derby	—	1/65*	September 1981	C
D7520	25 170	BR Derby	—	13/64*	August 1982	A
D7521	25 171	BR Derby	—	1/65*	October 1978	C
D7522	25 172	BR Derby	—	1/65*	February 1981	C
D7523	25 173	BR Derby	—	1/65*		
D7524	25 174	BR Derby	—	1/65*	September 1976	C
D7525	25 175	BR Derby	—	1/65*		
D7526	25 176	BR Derby	—	1/65*		
D7527	25 177	BR Derby	—	1/65*	November 1982	A
D7528	25 178	BR Derby	—	2/65*		
D7529	25 179	BR Derby	—	2/65*	November 1982	A
D7530	25 180	BR Derby	—	2/65*	November 1982	A
D7531	25 181	BR Derby	—	2/65*		
D7532	25 182	BR Derby	—	2/65*		
D7533	25 183	BR Derby	—	2/65*	December 1980	C
D7534	25 184	BR Derby	—	3/65*	August 1983	C
D7535	25 185	BR Derby	—	3/65*		
D7536	25 186	BR Derby	—	3/65*	November 1982	A
D7537	25 187	BR Derby	—	3/65*	November 1982	A
D7538	25 188	BR Derby	—	3/65*	August 1982	A
D7539	25 189	BR Derby	—	3/65*		
D7540	25 190	BR Derby	—	4/65*		
D7541	25 191	BR Derby	—	4/65*		
D7542	25 192	BR Derby	—	4/65*		
D7543	25 193	BR Derby	—	4/65*		
D7544	25 194	BR Derby	—	5/65*		
D7545	25 195	BR Derby	—	5/65*		
D7546	25 196	BR Derby	—	5/65*		

BR 1957 No	*Disposal details*	*Notes*
D7094	BREL Swindon July 1973	
D7095	BREL Swindon December 1972	
D7096	Departmental Stock — D7096	
D7097	BREL Swindon March 1975	
D7098	BREL Swindon March 1975	
D7099	BREL Swindon October 1972	
D7100	BREL Swindon December 1974	

BR 1957 No	*Disposal details*	*Notes*
D7500	BREL Derby	
D7501	BR Toton depot	
D7502	BREL Swindon	
D7503	BREL Swindon	
D7504		
D7505	BREL Swindon September 1981	Stored from November 1980
D7506	BREL Swindon May 1982	
D7507	BREL Swindon	
D7508	BREL Swindon	
D7509	BREL Swindon March 1981	
D7510	BR Polmadie depot	
D7511		
D7512	BREL Swindon June 1982	
D7513	BREL Swindon March 1983	
D7514	BREL Derby	
D7515	BREL Derby October 1979	
D7516	BREL Swindon July 1981	
D7517	BREL Swindon April 1984	
D7518	BREL Swindon April 1984	
D7519	BREL Swindon February 1982	
D7520	BREL Derby	Withdrawn April 1982, reinstated June 1982
D7521	BR at Arbroath January 1979	
D7522	BREL Swindon June 1983	
D7523		
D7524	BREL Derby July 1978	
D7525		
D7526		
D7527	BREL Swindon	
D7528		
D7529	BREL Swindon	
D7530	BR Tyseley	
D7531		
D7532		
D7533	BREL Swindon September 1981	Stored from November 1980
D7534	BREL Swindon February 1984	
D7535		
D7536	BREL Swindon	Stored August 1982
D7537	BREL Swindon	
D7538	BREL Swindon	
D7539		
D7540		
D7541		
D7542		
D7543		
D7544		
D7545		
D7546		

BR 1957 No	TOPS No	Built by	Works No	Period* Date introduced	Date withdrawn	Disposal code
D7547	25 197	BR Derby	—	5/65*	December 1980	C
D7548	25 198	BR Derby	—	5/65*		
D7549	25 199	BR Derby	—	6/65*		
D7550	25 200	BR Derby	—	6/65*		
D7551	25 201	BR Derby	—	6/65*		
D7552	25 202	BR Derby	—	7/65*		
D7553	25 203	BR Derby	—	7/65*	December 1980	C
D7554	25 204	BR Derby	—	7/65*	July 1980	C
D7555	25 205	BR Derby	—	7/65*		
D7556	25 206	BR Derby	—	7/65*		
D7557	25 207	BR Derby	—	8/65*		
D7558	25 208	BR Derby	—	8/65*	May 1984	A
D7559	25 209	BR Derby	—	9/65*		
D7560	25 210	BR Derby	—	10/65*		
D7561	25 211	BR Derby	—	11/65*		
D7562	25 212	BR Derby	—	12/65*		
D7563	25 213	BR Derby	—	12/65*		
D7564	25 214	BR Derby	—	13/65*	November 1982	A
D7565	25 215	BR Derby	—	12/65*	June 1983	C
D7566	25 216	BR Derby	—	1/66*	December 1980	C
D7567	25 217	BR Derby	—	1/66*	February 1981	C
D7568	25 218	BR Derby	—	10/63*		
D7569	25 219	BR Derby	—	11/63*	April 1983	A
D7570	25 220	BR Derby	—	10/63*	June 1982	A
D7571	25 221	BR Derby	—	11/63*	February 1984	A
D7572	25 222	BR Derby	—	11/63*	December 1980	C
D7573	25 223	BR Derby	—	11/63*	October 1980	C
D7574	25 224	BR Derby	—	11/63*		
D7575	25 225	BR Derby	—	12/63*	October 1980	C
D7576	25 226	BR Derby	—	12/63*		
D7577	25 227	BR Derby	—	12/63*	June 1983	C
D7578	25 228	BR Darlington	—	12/63*	March 1984	A
D7579	25 229	BR Darlington	—	13/63*		
D7580	25 230	BR Darlington	—	13/63*		
D7581	25 231	BR Darlington	—	13/63*		
D7582	25 232	BR Darlington	—	1/64*	December 1980	C
D7583	25 233	BR Darlington	—	1/64*	March 1983	A
D7584	25 234	BR Darlington	—	2/64*		
D7585	25 235	BR Darlington	—	2/64*		
D7586	25 236	BR Darlington	—	3/64*		
D7587	25 237	BR Darlington	—	3/64*		
D7588	25 238	BR Darlington	—	3/64*	October 1980	C
D7589	25 239	BR Darlington	—	4/64*		
D7590	25 240	BR Darlington	—	5/64*	August 1983	C
D7591	25 241	BR Darlington	—	5/64*	May 1981	C
D7592	25 242	BR Darlington	—	5/64*	May 1984	A
D7593	25 243	BR Darlington	—	6/64*	September 1983	C
D7594	25 244	BR Darlington	—	6/64*		
D7595	25 245	BR Darlington	—	7/64*		
D7596	25 246	BR Darlington	—	7/64*	October 1981	C
D7597	25 247	BR Darlington	—	9/64*	June 1983	C
D7598	25 248	BR Derby	—	February 1966	November 1982	A
D7599	25 249	BR Derby	—	February 1966		
D7600	25 250	BR Derby	—	February 1966	May 1984	A
D7601	25 251	BR Derby	—	February 1966		
D7602	25 252	BR Derby	—	February 1966	March 1980	C
D7603	25 253	BR Derby	—	February 1966	September 1983	A
D7604	25 254	BR Derby	—	March 1966		

BR 1957 No	*Disposal details*	*Notes*
D7547	BREL Swindon February 1983	Stored from November 1980
D7548		
D7549		
D7550		
D7551		
D7552		
D7553	BREL Swindon February 1982	Stored from November 1980
D7554	BREL Swindon October 1980	
D7555		
D7556		
D7557		
D7558	BREL Swindon	
D7559		
D7560		
D7561		
D7562		
D7563		
D7564	BR Healey Mills depot	
D7565	BREL Swindon December 1983	
D7566	BREL Derby March 1983	
D7567	BREL Derby January 1982	
D7568		
D7569	BR Cricklewood depot	
D7570	BREL Derby	
D7571	BR Springs Branch depot	
D7572	BREL Swindon December 1981	
D7573	BREL Swindon November 1980	
D7574		Withdrawn January 1983, reinstated March 1983
D7575	BREL Swindon November 1980	
D7576		
D7577	BREL Swindon December 1983	
D7578	BREL Derby	
D7579		
D7580		
D7581		
D7582	BREL Swindon April 1983	
D7583	BREL Derby	
D7584		
D7585		
D7586		
D7587		Stored January 1984, reinstated January 1984
D7588	BREL Swindon July 1983	
D7589		
D7590	BREL Swindon December 1983	
D7591	BREL Swindon October 1981	
D7592	BREL Swindon	
D7593	BREL Swindon January 1984	
D7594		
D7595		
D7596	BREL Swindon January 1983	Stored from April 1981
D7597	BREL Swindon December 1983	
D7598	BREL Derby	
D7599		
D7600	BREL Swindon	
D7601		
D7602	BREL Swindon September 1980	
D7603	BREL Derby	
D7604		

BR 1957 No	*TOPS No*	*Built by*	*Works No*	*Period* Date introduced*	*Date withdrawn*	*Disposal code*
D7605	—	BR Derby	—	March 1966	March 1972	C
D7606	25 256	BR Derby	—	March 1966		
D7607	25 257	BR Derby	—	March 1966	December 1983	A
D7608	25 258	BR Derby	—	April 1966		
D7609	25 259	BR Derby	—	April 1966		
D7610	25 260	BR Derby	—	April 1966	December 1982	A
D7611	25 261	BR Derby	—	4/66*	January 1981	C
D7612	25 262	BR Derby	—	4/66*		
D7613	25 263	BR Derby	—	5/66*	November 1980	C
D7614	25 264	BR Derby	—	5/66*	December 1980	C
D7615	25 265	BR Derby	—	5/66*		
D7616	25 266	BR Derby	—	5/66*		
D7617	25 267	BR Derby	—	8/66*	February 1981	C
D7618	25 268	BR Derby	—	9/66*		
D7619	25 269	BR Derby	—	9/66*		
D7620	25 270	BR Derby	—	9/66*	November 1982	A
D7621	25 271	BR Derby	—	9/66*	October 1981	C
D7622	25 272	BR Derby	—	9/66*	July 1981	C
D7623	25 273	BR Derby	—	9/66*	February 1981	C
D7624	25 274	B/Peacock	8034	July 1965	May 1982	A
D7625	25 275	B/Peacock	8035	July 1965	April 1982	A
D7626	25 276	B/Peacock	8036	September 1965		
D7627	25 277	B/Peacock	8037	September 1965	April 1984	A
D7628	25 278	B/Peacock	8038	September 1965		
D7629	25 279	B/Peacock	8039	September 1965		
D7630	25 280	B/Peacock	8040	September 1965	November 1981	C
D7631	25 281	B/Peacock	8041	September 1965	February 1981	C
D7632	25 282	B/Peacock	8042	October 1965		
D7633	25 283	B/Peacock	8043	October 1965		
D7634	25 284	B/Peacock	8044	October 1965		
D7635	25 285	B/Peacock	8045	November 1965		
D7636	25 286	B/Peacock	8046	November 1965		
D7637	25 287	B/Peacock	8047	November 1965		
D7638	25 288	B/Peacock	8048	November 1965		
D7639	25 289	B/Peacock	8049	November 1965	January 1984	A
D7640	25 290	B/Peacock	8050	November 1965	October 1981	A
D7641	25 291	B/Peacock	8051	January 1966	May 1981	C
D7642	25 292	B/Peacock	8052	January 1966	October 1981	C
D7643	25 293	B/Peacock	8053	February 1966	February 1981	C
D7644	25 294	B/Peacock	8054	February 1966	October 1982	A
D7645	25 295	B/Peacock	8055	March 1966	June 1978	C
D7646	25 296	B/Peacock	8056	March 1966		
D7647	25 297	B/Peacock	8057	April 1966		
D7648	25 298	B/Peacock	8058	April 1966		
D7649	25 299	B/Peacock	8059	April 1966	October 1981	C
D7650	25 300	B/Peacock	8060	5/66*		
D7651	25 301	B/Peacock	8061	5/66*	December 1983	A
D7652	25 302	B/Peacock	8062	5/66*		
D7653	25 303	B/Peacock	8063	7/66*		
D7654	25 304	B/Peacock	8064	7/66*	November 1982	A
D7655	25 305	B/Peacock	8065	7/66*	July 1983	D
D7656	25 306	B/Peacock	8066	7/66*		
D7657	25 307	B/Peacock	8067	7/66*		
D7658	25 308	B/Peacock	8068	8/66*	October 1983	A
D7659	25 309	B/Peacock	8069	8/66*		
D7660	25 310	BR Derby	—	13/66*	October 1982	A
D7661	25 311	BR Derby	—	12/66*		
D7662	25 312	BR Derby	—	12/66*	June 1982	A

BR 1957 No	*Disposal details*	*Notes*
D7605	BREL Derby June 1972	
D7606		
D7607	BREL Swindon	
D7608		
D7609		
D7610	BR Derby depot	
D7611	BREL Derby December 1983	
D7612		
D7613	BREL Swindon April 1983	
D7614	BREL Swindon June 1983	
D7615		
D7616		
D7617	BREL Derby February 1982	
D7618		
D7619		
D7620	BR Newton Heath depot	
D7621	BREL Derby October 1982	
D7622	BREL Derby August 1982	
D7623	BREL Swindon April 1982	
D7624	BREL Derby	
D7625	BR Tyseley depot	
D7626		
D7627	BREL Derby	
D7628		
D7629		
D7630	BREL Swindon July 1983	
D7631	BREL Swindon May 1981	
D7632		
D7633		
D7634		
D7635		
D7636		
D7637		Withdrawn July 1976, reinstated September 1976
D7638		
D7639	BREL Swindon	
D7640	BREL Derby	
D7641	BREL Swindon November 1982	
D7642	BREL Swindon February 1983	
D7643	BREL Swindon August 1981	
D7644	BREL Derby	
D7645	BREL Derby November 1981	
D7646		
D7647		
D7648		
D7649	BREL Derby May 1982	
D7650		
D7651	BREL Swindon	
D7652		
D7653		
D7654	BREL Derby	
D7655	Departmental Stock — 97251	Withdrawn June 1981, reinstated August 1982
D7656		
D7657		
D7658	BREL Swindon	
D7659		
D7660	BR Inverness depot	
D7661		
D7662	BREL Derby	

BR 1957 No	TOPS No	Built by	Works No	Period* Date introduced	Date withdrawn	Disposal code
D7663	25 313	BR Derby	—	12/66*		
D7664	25 314	BR Derby	—	12/66*	March 1983	D
D7665	25 315	BR Derby	—	13/66*		
D7666	25 316	BR Derby	—	13/66*		
D7667	25 317	BR Derby	—	1/67*	April 1983	A
D7668	25 318	BR Derby	—	1/67*	July 1982	D
D7669	25 319	BR Derby	—	3/67*	March 1983	A
D7670	25 320	BR Derby	—	1/67*	December 1983	A
D7671	25 321	BR Derby	—	2/67*		
D7672	25 322	BR Derby	—	2/67*		
D7673	25 323	BR Derby	—	3/67*		
D7674	25 324	BR Derby	—	3/67*		
D7675	25 325	BR Derby	—	4/67*		
D7676	25 326	BR Derby	—	4/67*		
D7677	25 327	BR Derby	—	5/67*	February 1984	A

Class 20

The ultimate Type 1 fleet ordered under the BTC Modernisation Scheme was this sizeable fleet of EE designed and built, single-cab units for LMR/ER, and ScR operation. Locomotives normally operated in pairs.

BR 1957 No	TOPS No	Built by	Works No	Period* Date introduced	Date withdrawn	Disposal code
D8000	20 050	EE(VF)	E2347/D375	7/57*	November 1980	P
D8001	20 001	EE(VF)	E2348/D376	7/57*		
D8002	20 002	EE(VF)	E2349/D377	8/57*		
D8003	20 003	EE(VF)	E2350/D378	9/57*	December 1982	C
D8004	20 004	EE(VF)	E2351/D379	8/57*		
D8005	20 005	EE(VF)	E2352/D380	10/57*		
D8006	20 006	EE(VF)	E2353/D381	10/57*		
D8007	20 007	EE(VF)	E2354/D382	10/57*		
D8008	20 008	EE(VF)	E2355/D383	10/57*		
D8009	20 009	EE(VF)	E2356/D384	11/57*		
D8010	20 010	EE(VF)	E2357/D385	11/57*		
D8011	20 011	EE(VF)	E2358/D386	11/57*		
D8012	20 012	EE(VF)	E2359/D387	12/57*	March 1976	C
D8013	20 013	EE(VF)	E2360/D388	12/57*		
D8014	20 014	EE(VF)	E2361/D389	12/57*	March 1976	C
D8015	20 015	EE(VF)	E2362/D390	13/57*		
D8016	20 016	EE(VF)	E2363/D391	1/58*		
D8017	20 017	EE(VF)	E2364/D392	1/58*	December 1982	C
D8018	20 018	EE(VF)	E2365/D393	2/58*	December 1976	C
D8019	20 019	EE(VF)	E2366/D394	3/58*		
D8020	20 020	RSH	E2742/8052	October 1959		
D8021	20 021	RSH	E2743/8053	October 1959		
D8022	20 022	RSH	E2744/8054	October 1959		
D8023	20 023	RSH	E2745/8055	November 1959		
D8024	20 024	RSH	E2746/8056	November 1959	May 1977	C

BR 1957 No	*Disposal details*	*Notes*
D7663		
D7664	Departmental Stock — 97252	
D7665		
D7666		Withdrawn February 1984, reinstated April 1984
D7667	BREL Derby	
D7668	Departmental Stock — 97250	
D7669	BREL Derby	
D7670	BREL Derby	
D7671		
D7672		Withdrawn February 1984, reinstated May 1984
D7673		
D7674		
D7675		
D7676		
D7677	BR Crewe depot	

Engine: EE 8SVT of 1,000hp
Weight: 72 ton
Bogie type: Bo-Bo
Max speed: 75mph
Class code: D10/3, later 10/3 and BR Class 20

Tractive effort: 42,000lb
Length: 46ft 9½in
Height: 12ft 7⅝in
Width: 8ft 9in

BR 1957 No	*Disposal details*	*Notes*
D8000	National Railway Museum, York	
D8001		
D8002		
D8003	BREL Crewe January 1984	Stored August 1981, reinstated September 1982
D8004		Stored October 1983, reinstated December 1983
D8005		Stored September 1983, reinstated November 1983, stored January 1984, reinstated April 1984
D8006		Stored October 1982, reinstated July 1984
D8007		Stored February 1983, reinstated May 1984
D8008		
D8009		
D8010		
D8011		
D8012	BREL Glasgow January 1977	
D8013		Stored May 1983, reinstated May 1984
D8014	BREL Glasgow January 1977	
D8015		
D8016		Stored January 1983, reinstated January 1984
D8017	BREL Crewe January 1984	Previously in store
D8018	BREL Glasgow May 1978	
D8019		Stored November 1983, reinstated January 1984
D8020		
D8021		
D8022		Stored December 1982, reinstated February 1983
D8023		
D8024	BREL Glasgow March 1978	

BR 1957 No	*TOPS No*	*Built by*	*Works No*	*Period* Date introduced*	*Date withdrawn*	*Disposal code*
D8025	20 025	RSH	E2747/8057	November 1959		
D8026	20 026	RSH	E2748/8058	December 1959		
D8027	20 027	RSH	E2749/8059	December 1959		
D8028	20 028	RSH	E2750/8060	13/59*		
D8029	20 029	RSH	E2751/8061	13/59*		
D8030	20 030	RSH	E2752/8062	13/59*		
D8031	20 031	RSH	E2753/8063	1/60*		
D8032	20 032	RSH	E2754/8064	1/60*		
D8033	20 033	RSH	E2755/8065	2/60*	November 1977	C
D8034	20 034	RSH	E2756/8066	3/60*		
D8035	20 035	EE(VF)	E2757/D482	9/59*		
D8036	20 036	EE(VF)	E2758/D483	10/59*	June 1984	
D8037	20 037	EE(VF)	E2759/D484	10/59*		
D8038	20 038	EE(VF)	E2760/D485	10/59*	March 1976	C
D8039	20 039	EE(VF)	E2761/D486	10/59*		
D8040	20 040	EE(VF)	E2762/D487	10/59*		
D8041	20 041	EE(VF)	E2763/D488	11/59*		
D8042	20 042	EE(VF)	E2764/D489	11/59*		
D8043	20 043	EE(VF)	E2765/D490	11/59*		
D8044	20 044	EE(VF)	E2766/D491	11/59*		
D8045	20 045	EE(VF)	E2767/D492	December 1959		
D8046	20 046	EE(VF)	E2768/D493	December 1959		
D8047	20 047	EE(VF)	E2769/D494	December 1959		
D8048	20 048	EE(VF)	E2770/D495	December 1959		
D8049	20 049	EE(VF)	E2771/D496	December 1959		
D8050	20 128	RSH	E2956/8208	March 1961		
D8051	20 051	RSH	E2957/8209	March 1961		
D8052	20 052	RSH	E2958/8210	March 1961		
D8053	20 053	RSH	E2959/8211	April 1961		
D8054	20 054	RSH	E2960/8212	June 1961		
D8055	20 055	RSH	E2961/8213	April 1961		
D8056	20 056	RSH	E2962/8214	April 1961		
D8057	20 057	RSH	E2963/8215	May 1961		
D8058	20 058	RSH	E2964/8216	May 1961		
D8059	20 059	RSH	E2965/8217	May 1961		
D8060	20 060	RSH	E2966/8218	May 1961		
D8061	20 061	RSH	E2967/8219	May 1961		
D8062	20 062	RSH	E2968/8220	May 1961	September 1976	C
D8063	20 063	RSH	E2969/8221	June 1961		
D8064	20 064	RSH	E2970/8222	June 1961		
D8065	20 065	RSH	E2971/8223	June 1961		
D8066	20 066	RSH	E2972/8224	June 1961		
D8067	20 067	RSH	E2973/8225	June 1961		
D8068	20 068	RSH	E2974/8226	June 1961		
D8069	20 069	RSH	E2975/8227	June 1961		
D8070	20 070	RSH	E2976/8228	7/61*		
D8071	20 071	RSH	E2977/8229	7/61*		
D8072	20 072	RSH	E2978/8230	7/61*		

BR 1957 No	Disposal details	Notes
D8025		Stored December 1982, reinstated April 1983
D8026		Stored August 1983, reinstated December 1983
D8027		
D8028		Stored March 1983, reinstated April 1984
D8029		Stored August 1981, reinstated September 1982
D8030		Stored February 1981, reinstated September 1982, stored January 1983, reinstated July 1983
D8031		Stored December 1982, reinstated September 1983
D8032		
D8033	BREL Crewe January 1980	
D8034		
D8035		
D8036		
D8037		
D8038	BREL Glasgow June 1977	
D8039		
D8040		Stored February 1983, reinstated May 1984
D8041		
D8042		Withdrawn February 1981, reinstated May 1981, stored October 1981, reinstated March 1983
D8043		Stored August 1982, reinstated January 1983
D8044		Stored October 1982, reinstated January 1983
D8045		Stored April 1983, reinstated August 1983
D8046		Stored November 1982, reinstated October 1983
D8047		
D8048		Stored February 1981, reinstated September 1982
D8049		Stored March 1983, reinstated January 1984
D8050		
D8051		
D8052		
D8053		
D8054		Stored December 1982, reinstated May 1983
D8055		
D8056		
D8057		
D8058		
D8059		
D8060		
D8061		Stored June 1981, reinstated September 1982
D8062	BREL Derby August 1979	
D8063		Stored October 1982, reinstated December 1982
D8064		
D8065		
D8066		
D8067		
D8068		Stored November 1982, reinstated September 1983
D8069		Stored February 1981, reinstated June 1982
D8070		
D8071		
D8072		

BR 1957 No	TOPS No	Built by	Works No	Period* Date introduced	Date withdrawn	Disposal code
D8073	20 073	RSH	E2979/8231	8/61*		
D8074	20 074	RSH	E2980/8232	8/61*	January 1976	C
D8075	20 075	RSH	E2981/8233	8/61*		
D8076	20 076	RSH	E2982/8234	8/61*		
D8077	20 077	RSH	E2983/8235	8/61*		
D8078	20 078	RSH	E2984/8236	8/61*		
D8079	20 079	RSH	E2985/8237	9/61*	April 1977	C
D8080	20 080	RSH	E2986/8238	9/61*		
D8081	20 081	RSH	E2987/8239	9/61*		
D8082	20 082	RSH	E2988/8240	9/61*		
D8083	20 083	RSH	E2989/8241	10/61*		
D8084	20 084	RSH	E2990/8242	10/61*		
D8085	20 085	RSH	E2991/8243	10/61*		
D8086	20 086	RSH	E2992/8244	10/61*		
D8087	20 087	RSH	E2993/8245	10/61*		
D8088	20 088	RSH	E2994/8246	10/61*		
D8089	20 089	RSH	E2995/8247	10/61*		
D8090	20 090	RSH	E2996/8248	10/61*		
D8091	20 091	RSH	E2997/8249	11/61*	September 1978	C
D8092	20 092	RSH	E2998/8250	11/61*		
D8093	20 093	RSH	E2999/8251	11/61*		
D8094	20 094	RSH	E3000/8252	11/61*		
D8095	20 095	RSH	E3001/8253	11/61*		
D8096	20 096	RSH	E3002/8254	11/61*		
D8097	20 097	RSH	E3004/8256	12/61*		
D8098	20 098	RSH	E3003/8255	12/61*		
D8099	20 099	RSH	E3005/8257	12/61*		
D8100	20 100	RSH	E3006/8258	12/61*		
D8101	20 101	RSH	E3007/8259	12/61*		
D8102	20 102	RSH	E3008/8260	12/61*		
D8103	20 103	RSH	E3009/8261	12/61*		
D8104	20 104	RSH	E3010/8262	13/61*		
D8105	20 105	RSH	E3011/8263	13/61*		
D8106	20 106	RSH	E3012/8264	13/61*		
D8107	20 107	RSH	E3013/8265	13/61*		
D8108	20 108	RSH	E3014/8266	13/61*		
D8109	20 109	RSH	E3015/8267	12/61*	February 1982	C
D8110	20 110	RSH	E3016/8268	1/62*		
D8111	20 111	RSH	E3017/8269	1/62*		
D8112	20 112	RSH	E3018/8270	1/62*		
D8113	20 113	RSH	E3019/8271	2/62*		
D8114	20 114	RSH	E3020/8272	2/62*		
D8115	20 115	RSH	E3021/8273	2/62*		
D8116	20 116	RSH	E3022/8274	2/62*		
D8117	20 117	RSH	E3023/8275	2/62*		
D8118	20 118	RSH	E3024/8276	3/62*		
D8119	20 119	RSH	E3025/8277	3/62*		
D8120	20 120	RSH	E3026/8278	3/62*		
D8121	20 121	RSH	E3027/8279	3/62*		
D8122	20 122	RSH	E3028/8280	3/62*		

BR 1957 No	Disposal details	Notes
D8073		
D8074	BREL Glasgow November 1976	
D8075		
D8076		
D8077		
D8078		Stored October 1980, withdrawn December 1980, reinstated March 1981, stored November 1982
D8079	BREL Derby November 1978	
D8080		Stored August 1982, reinstated June 1984
D8081		
D8082		
D8083		
D8084		
D8085		Stored October 1983, reinstated April 1984
D8086		
D8087		Stored February 1983, reinstated April 1984
D8088		
D8089		
D8090		Stored April 1983
D8091	BREL Glasgow November 1978	
D8092		Stored December 1982, reinstated April 1983
D8093		Stored December 1982, reinstated April 1983
D8094		Stored December 1982, reinstated November 1983
D8095		Stored December 1982, reinstated March 1983
D8096		Stored December 1982, reinstated February 1983
D8097		Stored February 1981, reinstated June 1982
D8098		Stored December 1982, reinstated August 1983
D8099		Stored October 1983, reinstated May 1984
D8100		
D8101		Stored October 1983
D8102		
D8103		Stored December 1982, reinstated February 1984
D8104		Stored October 1982
D8105		Stored December 1983, reinstated February 1984
D8106		Stored December 1982, reinstated May 1984
D8107		Stored December 1982, reinstated June 1983
D8108		Stored February 1983, reinstated January 1984
D8109	BREL Glasgow December 1982	
D8110		
D8111		
D8112		Stored November 1982, reinstated June 1983
D8113		
D8114		
D8115		
D8116		
D8117		Stored October 1982, reinstated May 1984
D8118		
D8119		
D8120		Stored July 1983
D8121		Stored October 1982, reinstated January 1984
D8122		

BR 1957 No	TOPS No	Built by	Works No	Period* Date introduced	Date withdrawn	Disposal code
D8123	20 123	RSH	E3029/8281	4/62*		
D8124	20 124	RSH	E3030/8282	4/62*		
D8125	20 125	RSH	E3031/8283	5/62*		
D8126	20 126	RSH	E3032/8243	5/62*		
D8127	20 127	RSH	E3033/8244	8/62*		
D8128	20 228	EE(VF)	E3599/D998	January 1966		
D8129	20 129	EE(VF)	E3600/D999	February 1966		
D8130	20 130	EE(VF)	E3601/D1000	February 1966		
D8131	20 131	EE(VF)	E3602/D1001	February 1966		
D8132	20 132	EE(VF)	E3603/D1002	March 1966		
D8133	20 133	EE(VF)	E3604/D1003	March 1966		
D8134	20 134	EE(VF)	E3605/D1004	3/66*		
D8135	20 135	EE(VF)	E3606/D1005	3/66*		
D8136	20 136	EE(VF)	E3607/D1006	4/66*		
D8137	20 137	EE(VF)	E3608/D1007	4/66*		
D8138	20 138	EE(VF)	E3609/D1008	4/66*		
D8139	20 139	EE(VF)	E3610/D1009	5/66*		
D8140	20 140	EE(VF)	E3611/D1010	5/66*		
D8141	20 141	EE(VF)	E3612/D1011	5/66*		
D8142	20 142	EE(VF)	E3614/D1013	5/66*		
D8143	20 143	EE(VF)	E3613/D1012	7/66*		
D8144	20 144	EE(VF)	E3615/D1014	7/66*		
D8145	20 145	EE(VF)	E3616/D1015	6/66*		
D8146	20 146	EE(VF)	E3617/D1016	6/66*		
D8147	20 147	EE(VF)	E3618/D1017	7/66*		
D8148	20 148	EE(VF)	E3619/D1018	7/66*		
D8149	20 149	EE(VF)	E3620/D1019	7/66*		
D8150	20 150	EE(VF)	E3621/D1020	7/66*		
D8151	20 151	EE(VF)	E3622/D1021	7/66*		
D8152	20 152	EE(VF)	E3623/D1022	8/66*		
D8153	20 153	EE(VF)	E3624/D1023	8/66*		
D8154	20 154	EE(VF)	E3625/D1024	8/66*		
D8155	20 155	EE(VF)	E3626/D1025	8/66*		
D8156	20 156	EE(VF)	E3627/D1026	8/66*		
D8157	20 157	EE(VF)	E3628/D1027	8/66*		
D8158	20 158	EE(VF)	E3629/D1028	8/66*		
D8159	20 159	EE(VF)	E3630/D1029	9/66*		
D8160	20 160	EE(VF)	E3631/D1030	12/66*		
D8161	20 161	EE(VF)	E3632/D1031	10/66*		
D8162	20 162	EE(VF)	E3633/D1032	10/66*		
D8163	20 163	EE(VF)	E3634/D1033	10/66*		
D8164	20 164	EE(VF)	E3635/D1034	10/66*		
D8165	20 165	EE(VF)	E3636/D1035	10/66*		
D8166	20 166	EE(VF)	E3637/D1036	11/66*		
D8167	20 167	EE(VF)	E3638/D1037	11/66*		
D8168	20 168	EE(VF)	E3639/D1038	11/66*		
D8169	20 169	EE(VF)	E3640/D1039	11/66*		
D8170	20 170	EE(VF)	E3641/D1040	11/66*		
D8171	20 171	EE(VF)	E3642/D1041	11/66*		
D8172	20 172	EE(VF)	E3643/D1042	11/66*		
D8173	20 173	EE(VF)	E3644/D1043	12/66*		
D8174	20 174	EE(VF)	E3645/D1044	11/66*		

BR 1957 No	*Disposal details*	*Notes*
D8123		
D8124		
D8125		
D8126		Stored December 1982, reinstated April 1983
D8127		Stored June 1981, reinstated June 1982
D8128		Stored November 1982, reinstated January 1983
D8129		Stored October 1982, reinstated August 1983 stored September 1983, reinstated December 1983
D8130		Stored December 1982, reinstated April 1984
D8131		Stored August 1983, reinstated April 1984
D8132		Stored August 1983, reinstated April 1984
D8133		Stored August 1983, reinstated February 1984
D8134		
D8135		
D8136		
D8137		
D8138		
D8139		
D8140		Stored December 1982, reinstated January 1984
D8141		
D8142		Stored February 1983, reinstated January 1984
D8143		
D8144		
D8145		
D8146		
D8147		
D8148		
D8149		
D8150		
D8151		Stored February 1983, reinstated January 1984
D8152		
D8153		
D8154		
D8155		
D8156		
D8157		
D8158		
D8159		
D8160		
D8161		
D8162		
D8163		
D8164		
D8165		
D8166		Stored February 1983, reinstated January 1984
D8167		
D8168		
D8169		
D8170		
D8171		
D8172		
D8173		
D8174		

BR 1957 No	TOPS No	Built by	Works No	Period* Date introduced	Date withdrawn	Disposal code
D8175	20 175	EE(VF)	E3646/D1045	12/66*		
D8176	20 176	EE(VF)	E3647/D1046	12/66*		
D8177	20 177	EE(VF)	E3648/D1047	12/66*		
D8178	20 178	EE(VF)	E3649/D1048	13/66*		
D8179	20 179	EE(VF)	E3660/D1055	13/66*		
D8180	20 180	EE(VF)	E3661/D1056	13/66*		
D8181	20 181	EE(VF)	E3662/D1057	13/66*		
D8182	20 182	EE(VF)	E3663/D1058	13/66*		
D8183	20 183	EE(VF)	E3664/D1059	13/66*		
D8184	20 184	EE(VF)	E3665/D1060	13/66*		
D8185	20 185	EE(VF)	E3666/D1061	2/67*		
D8186	20 186	EE(VF)	E3667/D1062	1/67*		
D8187	20 187	EE(VF)	E3668/D1063	1/67*		
D8188	20 188	EE(VF)	E3669/D1064	1/67*		
D8189	20 189	EE(VF)	E3670/D1065	1/67*		
D8190	20 190	EE(VF)	E3671/D1066	1/67*		
D8191	20 191	EE(VF)	E3672/D1067	2/67*		
D8192	20 192	EE(VF)	E3673/D1068	2/67*		
D8193	20 193	EE(VF)	E3674/D1069	2/67*		
D8194	20 194	EE(VF)	E3675/D1070	2/67*		
D8195	20 195	EE(VF)	E3676/D1071	2/67*		
D8196	20 196	EE(VF)	E3677/D1072	2/67*		
D8197	20 197	EE(VF)	E3678/D1073	2/67*		
D8198	20 198	EE(VF)	E3679/D1074	4/67*		
D8199	20 199	EE(VF)	E3680/D1075	4/67*		

Class continued with D8300

Class 15

One of the original modernisation orders was placed with BTH in 1955 for an off centre cab Type 1 loco for local passenger and freight traffic in the London area.

BR 1957 No	Built by	Works No	Date introduced	Date withdrawn	Disposal code
D8200	BTH-Clayton	1031	November 1957	March 1971	C
D8201	BTH-Clayton	1032	February 1958	March 1971	C
D8202	BTH-Clayton	1033	February 1958	June 1968	C
D8203	BTH-Clayton	1034	March 1958	March 1968	D
D8204	BTH-Clayton	1035	April 1958	March 1971	C
D8205	BTH-Clayton	1036	May 1958	September 1968	C
D8206	BTH-Clayton	1037	June 1958	September 1968	C
D8207	BTH-Clayton	1038	July 1958	March 1971	C
D8208	BTH-Clayton	1039	July 1958	September 1968	C
D8209	BTH-Clayton	1040	November 1958	March 1971	C
D8210	BTH-Clayton	1108	October 1959	March 1971	C
D8211	BTH-Clayton	1109	November 1959	March 1971	C
D8212	BTH-Clayton	1110	November 1959	September 1968	C
D8213	BTH-Clayton	1111	December 1959	December 1968	C
D8214	BTH-Clayton	1112	December 1959	December 1970	C
D8215	BTH-Clayton	1113	January 1960	December 1970	C
D8216	BTH-Clayton	1114	January 1960	March 1971	C

BR 1957 No	*Disposal details*	*Notes*
D8175		
D8176		Stored January 1983, reinstated March 1983
D8177		
D8178		
D8179		
D8180		
D8181		
D8182		Stored February 1983, reinstated January 1984
D8183		
D8184		
D8185		
D8186		
D8187		
D8188		
D8189		Stored February 1983, reinstated April 1983
D8190		
D8191		
D8192		
D8193		
D8194		Stored February 1983, reinstated April 1984
D8195		
D8196		Stored April 1983, reinstatd April 1984
D8197		
D8198		
D8199		

Engine: Paxman 16YXHL of 800hp
Weight: 68 ton
Bogie type: Bo-Bo
Max speed: 60mph
Class code: D8/1, later 8/5 and BR Class 15

Tractive effort: 37,500lb
Length: 42ft 0in
Height: 12ft 6in
Width: 9ft 2in

BR 1957 No	*Disposal details*	*Notes*
D8200	BREL Crewe March 1972	
D8201	BREL Crewe February 1972	
D8202	G. Cohen, Kettering, Northamptonshire October 1969	
D8203	Departmental Stock — 968003	
D8204	BREL Crewe April 1972	
D8205	G. Cohen, Kettering, Northamptonshire May 1969	
D8206	D. Woodham, Barry March 1970	
D8207	BREL Crewe April 1972	
D8208	G. Cohen, Kettering, Northamptonshire April 1969	
D8209	BREL Crewe April 1972	
D8210	BREL Crewe March 1972	
D8211	BREL Crewe December 1971	
D8212	G. Cohen, Kettering, Northamptonshire April 1969	
D8213	G. Cohen, Kettering, Northamptonshire May 1969	
D8214	BREL Crewe December 1971	
D8215	BREL Crewe November 1971	
D8216	BREL Crewe January 1972	

BR 1957 No	Built by	Works No	Date introduced	Date withdrawn	Disposal code
D8217	BTH-Clayton	1115	January 1960	March 1968	C
D8218	BTH-Clayton	1116	February 1960	March 1971	C
D8219	BTH-Clayton	1117	February 1960	September 1968	C
D8220	BTH-Clayton	1118	March 1960	March 1971	C
D8221	BTH-Clayton	1119	March 1960	March 1971	C
D8222	BTH-Clayton	1120	March 1960	March 1971	C
D8223	BTH-Clayton	1121	April 1960	December 1968	C
D8224	BTH-Clayton	1122	April 1960	March 1971	C
D8225	BTH-Clayton	1123	May 1960	March 1971	C
D8226	BTH-Clayton	1124	May 1960	March 1971	C
D8227	BTH-Clayton	1125	May 1960	September 1968	C
D8228	BTH-Clayton	1126	June 1960	March 1971	C
D8229	BTH-Clayton	1127	June 1960	March 1971	C
D8230	BTH-Clayton	1128	July 1960	March 1971	C
D8231	BTH-Clayton	1129	July 1960	March 1971	C
D8232	BTH-Clayton	1130	August 1960	March 1971	C
D8233	BTH-Clayton	1131	August 1960	February 1969	D
D8234	BTH-Clayton	1132	September 1960	March 1971	C
D8235	BTH-Clayton	1133	September 1960	October 1968	C
D8236	BTH-Clayton	1134	October 1960	October 1968	C
D8237	BTH-Clayton	—	November 1960	March 1969	D
D8238	BTH-Clayton	—	December 1960	September 1968	C
D8239	BTH-Clayton	—	January 1961	March 1971	C
D8240	BTH-Clayton	—	January 1961	October 1968	C
D8241	BTH-Clayton	—	February 1961	April 1968	C
D8242	BTH-Clayton	—	February 1961	March 1971	C
D8243	BTH-Clayton	—	February 1961	February 1969	D

Class 20 — Continued from D8199

BR 1957 No	TOPS No	Built by	Works No	Date introduced	Date withdrawn	Disposal code
D8300	20 200	EE(VF)	E3681/D1076	March 1967	August 1979	C
D8301	20 201	EE(VF)	E3682/D1077	March 1967		
D8302	20 202	EE(VF)	—	March 1967		
D8303	20 203	EE(VF)	E3684/D1079	March 1967		
D8304	20 204	EE(VF)	—	March 1967		
D8305	20 205	EE(VF)	E3686/D1081	March 1967		
D8306	20 206	EE(VF)	E3687/D1082	April 1967		
D8307	20 207	EE(VF)	E3688/D1083	April 1967	July 1983	A
D8308	20 208	EE(VF)	E3689/D1084	April 1967		
D8309	20 209	EE(VF)	E3690/D1085	April 1967		
D8310	20 210	EE(VF)	E3691/D1086	April 1967		
D8311	20 211	EE(VF)	E3692/D1087	April 1967		
D8312	20 212	EE(VF)	E3693/D1088	April 1967		
D8313	20 213	EE(VF)	E3694/D1089	May 1967		
D8314	20 214	EE(VF)	E3695/D1090	May 1967		
D8315	20 215	EE(VF)	E3696/D1091	May 1967		

BR 1957 No	*Disposal details*	*Notes*
D8217	G. Cohen, Kettering, Northamptonshire March 1969	
D8218	BREL Crewe November 1971	
D8219	G. Cohen, Kettering, Northamptonshire April 1969	
D8220	BREL Crewe November 1971	
D8221	BREL Crewe December 1971	
D8222	BREL Crewe December 1971	
D8223	G. Cohen, Kettering, Northamptonshire October 1969	
D8224	BREL Crewe December 1971	
D8225	BREL Crewe December 1971	
D8226	BREL Crewe December 1971	
D8227	G. Cohen, Kettering, Northamptonshire November 1969	
D8228	BREL Crewe December 1971	
D8229	BREL Crewe January 1972	
D8230	BREL Crewe November 1971	
D8231	BREL Crewe January 1972	
D8232	BREL Crewe November 1971	Withdrawn October 1968, reinstated October 1968
D8233	Departmental Stock — 968001	
D8234	BREL Crewe November 1971	
D8235	G. Cohen, Kettering, Northamptonshire July 1969	
D8236	G. Cohen, Kettering, Northamptonshire July 1969	
D8237	Departmental Stock — 968002	
D8238	G. Cohen, Kettering, Northamptonshire June 1969	
D8239	BREL Crewe January 1972	
D8240	G. Cohen, Kettering, Northamptonshire July 1969	
D8241	J. Cashmore, Great Bridge, Tipton December 1968	
D8242	BREL Crewe November 1971	
D8243	Departmental Stock — 968000	

BR 1957 No	*Disposal details*	*Notes*
D8300	BREL Glasgow September 1979	
D8301		
D8302		
D8303		
D8304		
D8305		
D8306		
D8307	BREL Glasgow	
D8308		
D8309		
D8310		
D8311		Stored December 1982, reinstated August 1983
D8312		
D8313		Stored December 1981, reinstated September 1982
D8314		
D8315		Stored July 1983

BR 1957 No	TOPS No	Built by	Works No	Period* Date introduced	Date withdrawn	Disposal code
D8316	20 216	EE(VF)	E3697/D1092	6/67*		
D8317	20 217	EE(VF)	E3698/D1093	November 1967		
D8318	20 218	EE(VF)	E3699/D1094	November 1967		
D8319	20 219	EE(VF)	E3700/D1095	January 1968		
D8320	20 220	EE(VF)	E3701/D1096	November 1967		
D8321	20 221	EE(VF)	E3702/D1097	December 1967		
D8322	20 222	EE(VF)	E3703/D1098	December 1967		
D8323	20 223	EE(VF)	E3704/D1099	October 1967		
D8324	20 224	EE(VF)	E3705/D1100	November 1967		
D8325	20 225	EE(VF)	E3706/D1101	November 1967		
D8326	20 226	EE(VF)	E3683/D1078	February 1968		
D8327	20 227	EE(VF)	E3685/D1080	February 1968		

Class 16

Another fleet of Type 1 locomotives ordered under the 1955 Modernisation Scheme was this fleet of 10 NBL units powered by a Paxman engine for ER operation.

BR 1957 No	Built by	Works No	Date introduced	Date withdrawn	Disposal code
D8400	NBL	27671	May 1958	July 1968	C
D8401	NBL	27672	June 1958	September 1968	C
D8402	NBL	27673	July 1958	July 1968	C
D8403	NBL	27674	July 1958	July 1968	C
D8404	NBL	27675	August 1958	February 1968	C
D8405	NBL	27676	September 1958	September 1968	C
D8406	NBL	27677	September 1958	September 1968	C
D8407	NBL	27678	September 1958	September 1968	C
D8408	NBL	27679	September 1958	September 1968	C
D8409	NBL	27680	September 1958	September 1968	C

Class 17

Ordered in 1961, this fleet was announced as the new standard Type 1 unit, with a central cab, providing good all round visibility for the staff — however the design was not totally satisfactory and it was dropped.

BR 1957 No	Built by	Works No	Date introduced	Date withdrawn	Disposal code
D8500	Clayton	4365U1	September 1962	March 1971	C
D8501	Clayton	4365U2	October 1962	October 1968	C
D8502	Clayton	4365U3	October 1962	October 1971	C
D8503	Clayton	4365U4	October 1962	October 1971	C
D8504	Clayton	4365U5	October 1962	November 1971	C

BR 1957 No	*Disposal details*	*Notes*
D8316		
D8317		
D8318		
D8319		
D8320		
D8321		
D8322		
D8323		
D8324		
D8325		
D8326		
D8327		

Engine: Paxman 16YHXL of 800hp
Weight: 68 ton
Bogie type: Bo-Bo
Max speed: 60mph
Class code: D8/2, later 8/4, and BR Class 16

Tractive effort: 42,000lb
Length: 42ft 6in
Height: 12ft 6in
Width: 8ft 8½in

BR 1957 No	*Disposal details*	*Notes*
D8400	G. Cohen, Kettering, Northamptonshire November 1969	
D8401	G. Cohen, Kettering, Northamptonshire September 1969	
D8402	G. Cohen, Kettering, Northamptonshire November 1969	
D8403	G. Cohen, Kettering, Northamptonshire April 1969	
D8404	Cox & Danks, Park Royal, London July 1968	
D8405	G. Cohen, Kettering, Northamptonshire December 1969	
D8406	Birds Ltd, Long Marston July 1969	
D8407	G. Cohen, Kettering, Northamptonshire December 1969	
D8408	G. Cohen, Kettering, Northamptonshire May 1969	
D8409	G. Cohen, Kettering, Northamptonshire May 1969	

Engine: (2) Paxman 6ZHXL, giving 900hp*
Weight: 68 ton
Bogie type: Bo-Bo
Max speed: 60mph
Class code: 9/18 or 9/19 (depending on equipment), BR Class 17
*D8586/7 had Rolls-Royce power units

Tractive effort: 40,000lb
Length: 50ft 7½in
Height: 12ft 8in
Width: 8ft 9½in

BR 1957 No	*Disposal details*	*Notes*
D8500	BREL Glasgow November 1971	Withdrawn October 1968, reinstated May 1969
D8501	BREL Glasgow January 1972	
D8502	BREL Glasgow January 1973	
D8503	BREL Glasgow June 1972	Withdrawn October 1968, reinstated November 1969
D8504	J. Cashmore, Great Bridge, Tipton December 1975	Withdrawn October 1968, reinstated May 1969

BR 1957 No	*Built by*	*Works No*	*Date introduced*	*Date withdrawn*	*Disposal code*
D8505	Clayton	4365U6	October 1962	October 1971	C
D8506	Clayton	4365U7	October 1962	September 1971	C
D8507	Clayton	4365U8	October 1962	December 1971	C
D8508	Clayton	4365U9	October 1962	December 1971	C
D8509	Clayton	4365U10	November 1962	October 1968	C
D8510	Clayton	4365U11	November 1962	March 1971	C
D8511	Clayton	4365U14	November 1962	October 1968	C
D8512	Clayton	4365U16	December 1962	December 1968	D
D8513	Clayton	4365U13	December 1962	September 1971	C
D8514	Clayton	4365U12	July 1963	October 1968	C
D8515	Clayton	4365U20	August 1963	October 1971	C
D8516	Clayton	4365U19	April 1963	October 1971	C
D8517	Clayton	4365U18	June 1963	October 1968	C
D8518	Clayton	4365U15	April 1963	October 1968	C
D8519	Clayton	4365U22	July 1963	October 1968	C
D8520	Clayton	4365U23	May 1963	October 1968	C
D8521	Clayton	4365U17	July 1963	October 1968	D
D8522	Clayton	4365U24	June 1963	October 1968	C
D8523	Clayton	4365U25	July 1963	October 1968	C
D8524	Clayton	4365U26	July 1963	October 1968	C
D8525	Clayton	4365U27	August 1963	October 1971	C
D8526	Clayton	4365U28	August 1963	October 1968	C
D8527	Clayton	4365U29	August 1963	December 1968	C
D8528	Clayton	4365U30	July 1963	October 1971	C
D8529	Clayton	4365U31	May 1963	December 1971	C
D8530	Clayton	4365U32	April 1963	March 1971	C
D8531	Clayton	4365U33	May 1963	September 1971	C
D8532	Clayton	4365U34	July 1963	December 1968	C
D8533	Clayton	4365U35	August 1963	October 1968	C
D8534	Clayton	4365U36	June 1963	October 1968	C
D8535	Clayton	4365U21	July 1963	March 1971	C
D8536	Clayton	4365U37	August 1963	December 1971	C
D8537	Clayton	4365U40	June 1963	July 1968	C
D8538	Clayton	4365U41	June 1963	October 1971	C
D8539	Clayton	4365U38	June 1963	October 1971	C
D8540	Clayton	4365U39	August 1963	October 1971	C
D8541	Clayton	4365U42	June 1963	October 1971	C
D8542	Clayton	4365U43	August 1963	October 1971	C
D8543	Clayton	4365U44	September 1963	September 1971	C
D8544	Clayton	4365U45	September 1963	October 1971	C
D8545	Clayton	4365U46	May 1964	October 1971	C

BR 1957 No	*Disposal details*	*Notes*
D8505	BREL Glasgow April 1974	Withdrawn October 1968, reinstated May 1969
D8506	BREL Glasgow December 1971	Withdrawn October 1968, reinstated November 1969
D8507	A. King, Norwich c1976	Withdrawn October 1968, reinstated November 1969
D8508	A. King, Norwich December 1975	Withdrawn October 1968, reinstated May 1969
D8509	BREL Glasgow January 1972	
D8510	BREL Glasgow November 1971	Withdrawn December 1968, reinstated November 1969
D8511	J. McWilliam, Shettleston, Glasgow August 1970	
D8512	Departmental Stock — 8512	Withdrawn October 1968, reinstated November 1968
D8513	BREL Glasgow December 1971	Withdrawn October 1968, reinstated May 1969
D8514	BREL Glasgow January 1972	
D8515	BREL Glasgow November 1972	
D8516	A. King, Norwich January 1976	Withdrawn October 1968, reinstated November 1969
D8517	J. McWilliam, Shettleston, Glasgow September 1970	
D8518	BREL Glasgow February 1972	
D8519	BREL Glasgow May 1972	
D8520	BREL Glasgow May 1972	
D8521	Departmental Stock — 8521	
D8522	BREL Glasgow May 1972	
D8523	BREL Glasgow June 1972	
D8524	J. McWilliam, Shettleston, Glasgow September 1970	
D8525	A. King, Norwich February 1976	
D8526	BREL Glasgow May 1972	
D8527	BREL Glasgow June 1972	
D8528	BREL Glasgow July 1973	Withdrawn October 1968, reinstated November 1969
D8529	A. King, Norwich February 1976	Withdrawn October 1968, reinstated November 1968, withdrawn December 1968, reinstated November 1969, withdrawn October 1971, reinstated November 1971
D8530	BREL Glasgow October 1971	Withdrawn October 1968, reinstated May 1969, withdrawn June 1969, reinstated October 1969
D8531	A. King, Norwich c1975	Withdrawn October 1968, reinstated November 1969
D8532	BREL Glasgow June 1972	
D8533	BREL Glasgow January 1972	
D8534	BREL Glasgow February 1973	
D8535	BREL Glasgow November 1971	
D8536	A. King, Norwich December 1975	
D8537	J. McWilliam, Shettleston, Glasgow February 1969	
D8538	BREL Glasgow December 1972	
D8539	A. King, Norwich c1976	
D8540	BREL Glasgow November 1972	
D8541	BREL Glasgow February 1973	
D8542	J. Cashmore, Great Bridge, Tipton c1976	
D8543	BREL Glasgow June 1972	
D8544	J. McWilliam, Shettleston, Glasgow c1971	
D8545	BREL Glasgow November 1973	Built during 1963

BR 1957 No	Built by	Works No	Date introduced	Date withdrawn	Disposal code
D8546	Clayton	4365U47	September 1963	October 1971	C
D8547	Clayton	4365U48	September 1963	February 1969	C
D8548	Clayton	4365U49	September 1963	December 1971	C
D8549	Clayton	4365U50	October 1963	September 1971	C
D8550	Clayton	4365U51	November 1963	October 1971	C
D8551	Clayton	4365U52	October 1963	October 1971	C
D8552	Clayton	4365U53	October 1963	December 1971	C
D8553	Clayton	4365U54	October 1963	October 1968	C
D8554	Clayton	4365U55	October 1963	June 1969	C
D8555	Clayton	4365U56	October 1963	September 1971	C
D8556	Clayton	4365U57	October 1963	February 1969	C
D8557	Clayton	4365U58	November 1963	September 1971	C
D8558	Clayton	4365U59	November 1963	December 1971	C
D8559	Clayton	4365U60	November 1963	October 1971	C
D8560	Clayton	4365U61	November 1963	February 1969	C
D8561	Clayton	4365U62	November 1963	November 1971	C
D8562	Clayton	4365U63	November 1963	October 1971	C
D8563	Clayton	4365U64	December 1963	December 1971	C
D8564	Clayton	4365U65	December 1963	February 1969	C
D8565	Clayton	4365U66	December 1963	November 1971	C
D8566	Clayton	4365U67	December 1963	December 1968	C
D8567	Clayton	4365U68	January 1964	October 1971	C
D8568	Clayton	4365U69	January 1964	October 1971	P
D8569	Clayton	4365U70	January 1964	December 1968	C
D8570	Clayton	4365U71	January 1964	November 1968	C
D8571	Clayton	4365U72	January 1964	June 1969	C
D8572	Clayton	4365U73	January 1964	June 1969	C
D8573	Clayton	4365U74	January 1964	October 1971	C
D8574	Clayton	4365U75	January 1964	December 1971	C
D8575	Clayton	4365U76	February 1964	October 1968	C
D8576	Clayton	4365U77	February 1964	February 1969	C
D8577	Clayton	4365U78	February 1964	February 1969	C
D8578	Clayton	4365U79	March 1964	June 1969	C
D8579	Clayton	4365U80	March 1964	October 1971	C
D8580	Clayton	4365U81	March 1964	October 1971	C
D8581	Clayton	4365U82	March 1964	October 1971	C
D8582	Clayton	4365U83	March 1964	January 1969	C
D8583	Clayton	4365U84	April 1964	September 1971	C
D8584	Clayton	4365U85	April 1964	October 1968	C
D8585	Clayton	4365U86	May 1964	October 1968	C
D8586	Clayton	4365U87	December 1964	September 1971	C
D8587	Clayton	4365U88	February 1965	October 1971	C
D8588	B/Peacock	8005	March 1964	October 1971	C
D8589	B/Peacock	8006	May 1964	July 1970	C
D8590	B/Peacock	8007	May 1964	March 1971	C
D8591	B/Peacock	8008	June 1964	December 1968	C
D8592	B/Peacock	8009	May 1964	September 1971	C

BR 1957 No	*Disposal details*	*Notes*
D8546	J. Cashmore, Great Bridge, Tipton December 1975	
D8547	Birds Ltd, Cardiff April 1970	After withdrawal to Birds at Long Marston
D8548	J. Cashmore, Great Bridge, Tipton October 1975	
D8549	BREL Glasgow June 1972	
D8550	J. Cashmore, Great Bridge, Tipton September 1975	
D8551	J. Cashmore, Great Bridge, Tipton September 1975	
D8552	A. King, Norwich c1975	
D8553	J. McWilliam, Shettleston, Glasgow February 1969	
D8554	J. McWilliam, Shettleston, Glasgow c1971	
D8555	BREL Glasgow May 1972	
D8556	Birds Ltd, Long Marston April 1970	
D8557	J. McWilliam, Shettleston, Glasgow c1975	
D8558	BREL Glasgow February 1973	
D8559	BREL Glasgow April 1974	
D8560	Birds Ltd, Long Marston December 1969	
D8561	BREL Glasgow July 1973	
D8562	BREL Glasgow May 1973	
D8563	J. Cashmore, Great Bridge, Tipton December 1975	
D8564	Birds Ltd, Long Marston April 1970	
D8565	BREL Glasgow May 1973	
D8566	J. McWilliam, Shettleston, Glasgow c1969	
D8567	BREL Glasgow January 1973	
D8568	DTG on North York Moors Railway	After withdrawal used by Hemelite and later Ribblesdale Cement
D8569	J. McWilliam, Shettleston, Glasgow May 1969	
D8570	Birds Ltd, Long Marston July 1969	
D8571	J. McWilliam, Shettleston, Glasgow July 1971	
D8572	J. Cashmore, Great Bridge, Tipton August 1970	After withdrawal to Birds at Long Marston site — then resold
D8573	J. McWilliam, Shettleston, Glasgow c1975	
D8574	A. King, Norwich c1975	Withdrawn October 1971, reinstated November 1971
D8575	J. McWilliam, Shettleston, Glasgow April 1969	
D8576	Birds Ltd, Long Marston March 1970	
D8577	Birds Ltd, Long Marston April 1970	
D8578	BREL Glasgow November 1972	
D8579	BREL Glasgow November 1973	
D8580	A. King, Norwich c1975	
D8581	BREL Glasgow October 1973	
D8582	J. McWilliam, Shettleston, Glasgow June 1969	
D8583	BREL Glasgow August 1973	
D8584	J. McWilliam, Shettleston, Glasgow c1969	
D8585	J. McWilliam, Shettleston, Glasgow June 1969	
D8586	BREL Glasgow July 1973	
D8587	BREL Glasgow February 1974	
D8588	BREL Glasgow July 1973	
D8589	BR Gateshead depot December 1970	
D8590	BREL Glasgow May 1972	
D8591	J. McWilliam, Shettleston, Glasgow c1969	
D8592	BREL Glasgow March 1972	

BR 1957 No	Built by	Works No	Date introduced	Date withdrawn	Disposal code
D8593	B/Peacock	8010	May 1964	October 1971	C
D8594	B/Peacock	8011	June 1964	September 1971	C
D8595	B/Peacock	8012	June 1964	December 1968	C
D8596	B/Peacock	8013	July 1964	December 1968	C
D8597	B/Peacock	8014	June 1964	October 1971	C
D8598	B/Peacock	8015	August 1964	December 1971	D
D8599	B/Peacock	8016	August 1964	October 1971	C
D8600	B/Peacock	8017	August 1964	October 1971	C
D8601	B/Peacock	8018	September 1964	October 1971	C
D8602	B/Peacock	8019	September 1964	October 1971	C
D8603	B/Peacock	8020	September 1964	October 1971	C
D8604	B/Peacock	8021	September 1964	October 1971	C
D8605	B/Peacock	8022	October 1964	November 1968	C
D8606	B/Peacock	8023	October 1964	March 1971	C
D8607	B/Peacock	8024	October 1964	October 1971	C
D8608	B/Peacock	8025	October 1964	October 1971	C
D8609	B/Peacock	8026	November 1964	October 1968	C
D8610	B/Peacock	8027	December 1964	October 1971	C
D8611	B/Peacock	8028	December 1964	October 1968	C
D8612	B/Peacock	8029	January 1965	October 1971	C
D8613	B/Peacock	8030	January 1965	October 1971	C
D8614	B/Peacock	8031	February 1965	October 1971	C
D8615	B/Peacock	8032	March 1965	October 1971	C
D8616	B/Peacock	8033	April 1965	September 1971	C

Class 55

This fleet of 22 twin-engined units was constructed as a direct result of the 'Deltic' prototype tried out on BR in the late 1950s. These locomotives designed and built by English Electric were for use on express passenger services on the ER Anglo-Scottish route.

BR 1957 No	TOPS No	Name	Built by	Works No	Period* Date introduced
D9000	55 022	*Royal Scots Grey*, June 1962	EE(VF)	E2905/D557	3/61*
D9001	55 001	*St Paddy*	EE(VF)	E2906/D558	February 1961
D9002	55 002	*The King's Own Yorkshire Light Infantry*, April 1963	EE(VF)	E2907/D559	February 1961
D9003	55 003	*Meld*	EE(VF)	E2908/D560	March 1961
D9004	55 004	*Queen's Own Highlander*, May 1964	EE(VF)	E2909/D561	4/61*
D9005	55 005	*The Prince of Wales's Own Regiment of Yorkshire*, October 1963	EE(VF)	E2910/D562	May 1961
D9006	55 006	*The Fife and Forfar Yeomanry*, December 1964	EE(VF)	E2911/D563	7/61*
D9007	55 007	*Pinza*	EE(VF)	E2912/D564	June 1961
D9008	55 008	*The Green Howards*, September 1963	EE(VF)	E2913/D565	July 1961

BR 1957 No	Disposal details	Notes
D8593	BREL Glasgow September 1973	
D8594	BREL Glasgow March 1972	
D8595	J. McWilliam, Shettleston, Glasgow c1969	
D8596	J. McWilliam, Shettleston, Glasgow c1969	
D8597	BREL Glasgow July 1973	
D8598	Departmental Stock — 8598	Withdrawn October 1971, reinstated November 1971
D8599	BREL Glasgow November 1971	
D8600	BREL Glasgow April 1973	
D8601	BREL Glasgow February 1974	
D8602	BREL Glasgow April 1972	
D8603	BREL Glasgow April 1972	
D8604	BREL Glasgow April 1972	
D8605	A. Draper, Hull June 1970	
D8606	BREL Glasgow April 1972	
D8607	J. McWilliam, Shettleston, Glasgow c1975	
D8608	J. McWilliam, Shettleston, Glasgow c1975	
D8609	J. McWilliam, Shettleston, Glasgow c1969	
D8610	BREL Glasgow August 1973	
D8611	J. McWilliam, Shettleston, Glasgow c1969	
D8612	J. McWilliam, Shettleston, Glasgow c1975	
D8613	J. McWilliam, Shettleston, Glasgow c1975	
D8614	BREL Glasgow December 1972	
D8615	BREL Glasgow December 1973	
D8616	J. McWilliam, Shettleston, Glasgow c1975	

Engine: (2) Napier D18.25s giving 3,300hp
Weight: 100 ton
Bogie type: Co-Co
Max speed: 100mph
Class code: D33/1, later 33/3 and BR Class 55

Tractive effort: 50,000lb
Length: 69ft 6in
Height: 12ft 10in
Width: 8ft $9\frac{1}{2}$in

BR 1957 No	Date withdrawn	Disposal code	Disposal details	Notes
D9000	January 1982	P	Privately on Nene Valley Railway	
D9001	January 1980	C	BREL Doncaster February 1980	
D9002	January 1982	P	National Railway Museum, York	
D9003	December 1980	C	BREL Doncaster March 1981	
D9004	November 1981	C	BREL Doncaster August 1983	
D9005	February 1981	C	BREL Doncaster February 1983	
D9006	February 1981	C	BREL Doncaster July 1981	
D9007	December 1981	C	BREL Doncaster August 1982	
D9008	December 1981	C	BREL Doncaster August 1982	

BR 1957 No	TOPS No	Name	Built by	Works No	Period* Date introduced
D9009	55 009	*Alycidon*	EE(VF)	E2914/D566	July 1961
D9010	55 010	*The King's Own Scottish Borderer* May 1965	EE(VF)	E2915/D567	8/61*
D9011	55 011	*The Royal Northumberland Fusiliers* May 1963	EE(VF)	E2916/D568	August 1961
D9012	55 012	*Crepello*	EE(VF)	E2917/D569	September 1961
D9013	55 013	*The Black Watch*	EE(VF)	E2918/D570	10/61*
D9014	55 014	*The Duke of Wellington's Regiment* October 1963	EE(VF)	E2919/D571	September 1961
D9015	55 015	*Tulyar*	EE(VF)	E2920/D572	October 1961
D9016	55 016	*Gordon Highlander,* July 1964	EE(VF)	E2921/D573	11/61*
D9017	55 017	*The Durham Light Infantry,* October 1963	EE(VF)	E2922/D574	November 1961
D9018	55 018	*Ballymoss*	EE(VF)	E2923/D575	November 1961
D9019	55 019	*Royal Highland Fusilier,* September 1965	EE(VF)	E2924/D576	13/61*
D9020	55 020	*Nimbus*	EE(VF)	E2925/D577	April 1962
D9021	55 021	*Argyll and Sutherland Highlander,* November 1963	EE(VF)	E2926/D578	5/62*

Class 14

This Class could well be described as the least successful of any type. Built from 1964 for WR trip, local freight and shunting duties, these Type 1 diesel-hydraulic units were phased out after only three-four years' operation; the majority going to industrial service.

BR 1957 No	Built by	Works No	Date introduced	Date withdrawn	Disposal code
D9500	BR Swindon	—	July 1964	April 1969	S
D9501	BR Swindon	—	July 1964	March 1968	C
D9502	BR Swindon	—	July 1964	April 1969	S
D9503	BR Swindon	—	July 1964	April 1968	C
D9504	BR Swindon	—	July 1964	April 1968	S
D9505	BR Swindon	—	July 1964	April 1968	E
D9506	BR Swindon	—	August 1964	March 1968	C
D9507	BR Swindon	—	August 1964	April 1968	C
D9508	BR Swindon	—	September 1964	October 1968	C
D9509	BR Swindon	—	September 1964	October 1968	C
D9510	BR Swindon	—	September 1964	April 1968	C
D9511	BR Swindon	—	September 1964	April 1968	C
D9512	BR Swindon	—	September 1964	April 1968	C
D9513	BR Swindon	—	October 1964	March 1968	S

BR 1957 No	*Date withdrawn*	*Disposal code*	*Disposal details*	*Notes*
D9009	January 1982	P	Deltic Preservation Society, North York Moors Railway	
D9010	December 1981	C	BREL Doncaster May 1982	
D9011	November 1981	C	BREL Doncaster November 1982	
D9012	May 1981	C	BREL Doncaster September 1981	
D9013	December 1981	C	BREL Doncaster December 1982	
D9014	November 1981	C	BREL Doncaster February 1982	
D9015	January 1982	P	Midland Railway Trust, Butterley	
D9016	December 1981	P	Privately on Nene Valley Railway	As spares loco
D9017	December 1981	C	BREL Doncaster January 1983	
D9018	October 1981	C	BREL Doncaster January 1982	
D9019	December 1981	P	Deltic Preservation Society, North York Moors Railway	
D9020	January 1980	C	BREL Doncaster January 1980	
D9021	December 1981	C	BREL Doncaster August 1982	

Engine: Paxman 6YJX of 650hp
Weight: 50 ton
Wheel dia: 48in
Max speed: 40mph
Class code: 6/1 later BR Class 14

Tractive effort: 30,910lb
Length: 34ft 7in
Height: 13ft 0in
Width: 8ft $7\frac{1}{2}$in

BR 1957 No	*Disposal details*	*Notes*
D9500	NCB Ashington Colliery as 9312/92	
D9501	C. F. Booth, Rotherham, South Yorkshire June 1968	
D9502	NCB Ashington Colliery as 9312/97	
D9503	BSC Corby Works September 1980	Previously used by BSC
D9504	NCB Ashington Colliery as 506/2233	Used at various NCB (NE) sites out of use
D9505	Exported to Belgium May 1975	First used by Earles Cement, at Hope, then to Hunslet before export
D9506	Arnott Young Ltd, Rawmarsh December 1968	
D9507	BSC Corby Works December 1982	Withdrawn December 1980 — stored
D9508	NCB Ashington Colliery, as 9312/99 March 1984	
D9509	G. Cohen, Kettering, Northamptonshire February 1971	
D9510	BSC Corby Works c1981	Previously used by BSC
D9511	NCB Ashington Colliery c1974	
D9512	BSC Corby Works February 1982	Previously used by BSC
D9513	NCB Ashington Colliery as D1/9513	Used at Arnott Young, Rawmarsh, and then sold to NCB, used at various sites

BR 1957 No	Built by	Works No	Date introduced	Date withdrawn	Disposal code
D9514	BR Swindon	—	October 1964	April 1969	S
D9515	BR Swindon	—	October 1964	April 1968	E
D9516	BR Swindon	—	October 1964	April 1968	P
D9517	BR Swindon	—	October 1964	October 1968	C
D9518	BR Swindon	—	October 1964	April 1969	S
D9519	BR Swindon	—	November 1964	October 1968	C
D9520	BR Swindon	—	November 1964	April 1968	P
D9521	BR Swindon	—	November 1964	April 1969	S
D9522	BR Swindon	—	November 1964	December 1967	C
D9523	BR Swindon	—	December 1964	April 1968	P
D9524	BR Swindon	—	December 1964	April 1969	P
D9525	BR Swindon	—	January 1965	April 1968	S
D9526	BR Swindon	—	January 1965	November 1968	P
D9527	BR Swindon	—	January 1965	April 1969	C
D9528	BR Swindon	—	January 1965	March 1969	C
D9529	BR Swindon	—	January 1965	April 1968	P
D9530	BR Swindon	—	February 1965	October 1968	C
D9531	BR Swindon	—	February 1965	December 1967	S
D9532	BR Swindon	—	February 1965	April 1968	C
D9533	BR Swindon	—	February 1965	April 1968	C
D9534	BR Swindon	—	March 1965	April 1968	E
D9535	BR Swindon	—	March 1965	December 1968	C
D9536	BR Swindon	—	March 1965	April 1969	S
D9537	BR Swindon	—	March 1965	April 1968	P
D9538	BR Swindon	—	March 1965	April 1969	C
D9539	BR Swindon	—	April 1965	April 1968	P
D9540	BR Swindon	—	April 1965	April 1968	S
D9541	BR Swindon	—	April 1965	April 1968	C
D9542	BR Swindon	—	May 1965	April 1968	C
D9543	BR Swindon	—	May 1965	April 1968	C
D9544	BR Swindon	—	May 1965	April 1968	C
D9545	BR Swindon	—	June 1965	April 1968	C
D9546	BR Swindon	—	June 1965	April 1968	C
D9547	BR Swindon	—	July 1965	April 1968	C
D9548	BR Swindon	—	July 1965	April 1968	E
D9549	BR Swindon	—	August 1965	April 1968	E
D9550	BR Swindon	—	August 1965	April 1968	C
D9551	BR Swindon	—	September 1965	April 1968	P
D9552	BR Swindon	—	September 1965	April 1968	C
D9553	BR Swindon	—	September 1965	April 1968	P
D9554	BR Swindon	—	October 1965	April 1968	C
D9555	BR Swindon	—	October 1965	April 1969	S

BR 1947 No	*Disposal details*	*Notes*
D9514	NCB Ashington Colliery as 9312/96	
D9515	Exported to Spain 1981	Previously used by BSC Corby — then to Hunslet before export
D9516	Great Central Railway, Loughborough	Previously used by BSC Corby until 1978
D9517	NCB Ashington Colliery as 9312/93 March 1984	
D9518	NCB Ashington Colliery as 9312/95	
D9519	G. Cohen, Kettering, Northamptonshire January 1971	
D9520	Rutland Railway Museum at Cottesmore	Previously used by BSC Corby — until December 1980, then at NYMR
D9521	NCB Ashington Colliery as 9312/90	
D9522	Arnott Young Ltd, Rawmarsh August 1968	
D9523	Great Central Railway, Loughborough	Previously used by BSC at Corby until 1980
D9524	Scottish RPS, Falkirk	Previously used by BP Ltd at Grangemouth
D9525	NCB Lambton Colliery as 507	Used at various NCB (NE) area sites
D9526	Diesel & Electric Group, West Somerset Railway, Minehead	Previously used by APCM at Westbury works
D9527	NCB Ashington Colliery, as 9312/94 March 1984	
D9528	NCB Ashington Colliery c1979	Withdrawn September 1968, reinstated December 1968 used as spares loco
D9529	North York Moors Railway	Previously used by BSC Corby until 1980
D9530	NCB Mardy Colliery c1979 (previously in use)	Previously used by Gulf Oil at Milford Haven until October 1975
D9531	NCB Ashington Colliery as 9312/92	Previously used by Arnott Young at Rawmarsh until December 1968
D9532	BSC Corby Works c1983	Previously used by BSC
D9533	BSC Corby Works c1983	Previously used by BSC
D9534	Exported to Italy c1976	Previously used by Earles Cement at Hope
D9535	NCB Ashington Colliery as 9312/59 March 1984	Used at various NCB (NE) area sites
D9536	NCB Ashington Colliery as 9312/91	
D9537	Gloucestershire & Warwickshire Railway	Previously used by BSC Corby until 1981
D9538	BSC Corby Works December 1982	Previously used by Shell-BP at Stanford-le-Hope until 1970
D9539	Gloucestershire & Warwickshire Railway	Previously used by BSC Corby
D9540	NCB Ashington Colliery as 2233/508	Used at various NCB (NE) area sites. Now out of use
D9541	BSC Corby Works c1983	Previously used by BSC Corby
D9542	BSC Corby Works c1983	Previously used by BSC Corby
D9543	C. F. Booth, Rotherham, South Yorkshire c1969	
D9544	BSC Corby Works September 1980	Used as spares loco
D9545	NCB Ashington Colliery c1971	Used as spares loco
D9546	C. F. Booth, Rotherham, South Yorkshire c1969	
D9547	BSC Corby Works December 1982	Previously used by BSC
D9548	Exported to Spain c1981	Previously used by BSC Corby, then to Hunslet before export
D9549	Exported to Spain c1981	Previously used by BSC Corby, then to Hunslet before export
D9550	C. F. Booth, Rotherham, South Yorkshire c1969	
D9551	Privately at West Somerset Railway	Previously used by BSC Corby until December 1980
D9552	BSC Corby Works September 1980	Previously used by BSC
D9553	Gloucestershire & Warwickshire Railway	Previously used by BSC Corby
D9554	BSC Corby Works December 1982	Previously used by BSC Corby until December 1980
D9555	NCB Ashington Colliery as 9107/57	Used at various NCB (NE) area sites

Section 5
British Railways TOPS Numbers

Class 01 (01 001-01 002) *see* D2954-D2955

Class 02 (02 001-02 004) *see* D2850-D2869

Class 03 (03 001-03 371) *see* D2000-D2199, D2370-D2399

Class 04 *see* D2200-D2341

Class 05 (05 001) *see* D2500-D2618

Class 06 (06 001-06 010) *see* D2410-D2444

Class 07 (07 001-07 014) *see* D2985-D2998

Class 08 (08 001-08 958) *see* D3000-D4192

Class 09 (09 001-09 026) *see* D3665-D3671, D3719-D3721, D4099-D4114

Class 10 *see* D3137-D3151, D3439-D3453, D3473-D3502, D3612-D3651, D4049-D4094

Class 11 *see* 12033-12138

Class 12 *see* 15 211-15 236

Class 13 (13 001-13 003) *see* D4500-D4502

Class 14 *see* D9500-D9555

Class 15 *see* D8200-D8243

Class 16 *see* D8400-D8409

Class 17 *see* D8500-D8616

Class 20 (20 001-20 228) *see* D8000-D8199, D8300-D8327

Class 21 *see* D6100-D6157

Class 22 *see* D6300-D6357

Class 56

Introduced for freight operation from the mid-1970s, due to projected increase in freight traffic. First 30 built by Electroputere in Romania, others by BREL. Based on proven Class 47 designs.

TOPS No	*Built by*	*Works No*	*Name*	*Date introduced*	*Date withdrawn*
56 001	Electroputere	—	—	February 1977	
56 002	Electroputere	—	—	February 1977	
56 003	Electroputere	—	—	February 1977	
56 004	Electroputere	—	—	February 1977	
56 005	Electroputere	—	—	March 1977	
56 006	Electroputere	—	—	February 1977	
56 007	Electroputere	—	—	April 1977	

Class 23 *see* D5900-D5909
Class 24 (24 001-24 150) *see* D5000-D5150
Class 25 (25 001-25 327) *see* D5151-D5299, D7500-D7677
Class 26 (26 001-26 046) *see* D5300-D5346
Class 27 (27 001-27 212) *see* D5347-D5415
Class 28 *see* D5700-D5719
Class 29 *see* D6100-D6157
Class 30/31 (31 001-31 447) *see* D5500-D5699, D5800-D5862
Class 33 (33 001-33 212) *see* D6500-D6597
Class 35 *see* D7000-D7100
Class 37 (37 001-37 308) *see* D6600-D6999
Class 40 (40 001-40 199) *see* D200-D399
Class 41 *see* D600-D604
Class 42 *see* D800-D832, D866-D870
Class 43 *see* D833-D865
Class 44 (44 001-44 010) *see* D1-D10
Class 45 (45 001-45 150) *see* D11-D137
Class 46 (46 001-46 056) *see* D138-D193
Class 47 (47 001-47 901) *see* D1100-D1999
Class 48 *see* D1702-D1706
Class 50 (50 001-50 050) *see* D400-D449
Class 52 *see* D1000-D1073
Class 53 *see* D0280/D1200
Class 55 (55 001-55 022) *see* D9000-D9022

Engine: Ruston 16RK3CT of 3,250hp
Weight: 125 ton
Bogie type: Co-Co
Max speed: 80mph
Class code: BR Class 56

Tractive effort: 60,750hp
Length: 63ft 6in
Height: 13ft 0in
Width: 9ft 2in

TOPS No	*Disposal Code*	*Disposal details*	*Notes*
56 001			
56 002			
56 003			
56 004			
56 005			
56 006			
56 007			

TOPS No	Built by	Works No	Name	Date introduced	Date withdrawn
56 008	Electroputere	—	—	April 1977	
56 009	Electroputere	—	—	May 1977	
56 010	Electroputere	—	—	July 1977	
56 011	Electroputere	—	—	June 1977	
56 012	Electroputere	—	—	April 1977	
56 013	Electroputere	—	—	August 1977	
56 014	Electroputere	—	—	March 1977	
56 015	Electroputere	—	—	February 1977	
56 016	Electroputere	—	—	May 1977	
56 017	Electroputere	—	—	May 1977	
56 018	Electroputere	—	—	August 1977	
56 019	Electroputere	—	—	May 1977	
56 020	Electroputere	—	—	May 1977	
56 021	Electroputere	—	—	June 1977	
56 022	Electroputere	—	—	May 1977	
56 023	Electroputere	—	—	July 1977	
56 024	Electroputere	—	—	June 1977	
56 025	Electroputere	—	—	July 1977	
56 026	Electroputere	—	—	July 1977	
56 027	Electroputere	—	—	September 1977	
56 028	Electroputere	—	—	September 1977	
56 029	Electroputere	—	—	September 1977	
56 030	Electroputere	—	—	October 1977	
56 031	BREL Doncaster	—	*Merehead,* September 1983	May 1977	
56 032	BREL Doncaster	—	*Sir Demorannwy/ County of South Glamorgan*	July 1977	
56 033	BREL Doncaster	—	—	August 1977	
56 034	BREL Doncaster	—	—	August 1977	
56 035	BREL Doncaster	—	*Taff Merthyr,* July 1981	October 1977	
56 036	BREL Doncaster	—	—	January 1978	
56 037	BREL Doncaster	—	*Richard Trevithick,* July 1981	January 1978	
56 038	BREL Doncaster	—	*Western Mail,* June 1981	February 1978	
56 039	BREL Doncaster	—	—	January 1978	
56 040	BREL Doncaster	—	*Oystermouth,* March 1982	February 1978	
56 041	BREL Doncaster	—	—	February 1978	
56 042	BREL Doncaster	—	—	May 1979	
56 043	BREL Doncaster	—	—	March 1978	
56 044	BREL Doncaster	—	—	May 1978	
56 045	BREL Doncaster	—	—	June 1978	
56 046	BREL Doncaster	—	—	July 1978	
56 047	BREL Doncaster	—	—	July 1978	
56 048	BREL Doncaster	—	—	September 1978	
56 049	BREL Doncaster	—	—	October 1978	
56 050	BREL Doncaster	—	—	October 1978	
56 051	BREL Doncaster	—	—	November 1978	
56 052	BREL Doncaster	—	—	December 1978	
56 053	BREL Doncaster	—	—	December 1978	
56 054	BREL Doncaster	—	—	January 1979	
56 055	BREL Doncaster	—	—	February 1979	
56 056	BREL Doncaster	—	—	March 1979	
56 057	BREL Doncaster	—	—	March 1979	
56 058	BREL Doncaster	—	—	April 1979	
56 059	BREL Doncaster	—	—	May 1979	
56 060	BREL Doncaster	—	—	June 1979	

TOPS No	*Disposal Code*	*Disposal details*	*Notes*
56 008			
56 009			
56 010			
56 011			
56 012			
56 013			
56 014			
56 015			
56 016			
56 017			
56 018			
56 019			
56 020			
56 021			
56 022			
56 023			
56 024			
56 025			
56 026			
56 027			
56 028			
56 029			
56 030			
56 031			
56 032			
56 033			
56 034			
56 035			
56 036			
56 037			
56 038			
56 039			
56 040			
56 041			
56 042			Constructed February 1978. Fitted with experimental bogies
56 043			
56 044			
56 045			
56 046			
56 047			
56 048			
56 049			
56 050			
56 051			
56 052			
56 053			
56 054			
56 055			
56 056			
56 057			
56 058			
56 059			
56 060			

TOPS No	Built by	Works No	Name	Date introduced	Date withdrawn
56 061	BREL Doncaster	—	—	July 1979	
56 062	BREL Doncaster	—	—	August 1979	
56 063	BREL Doncaster	—	—	August 1979	
56 064	BREL Doncaster	—	—	September 1979	
56 065	BREL Doncaster	—	—	October 1979	
56 066	BREL Doncaster	—	—	October 1979	
56 067	BREL Doncaster	—	—	November 1979	
56 068	BREL Doncaster	—	—	November 1979	
56 069	BREL Doncaster	—	—	December 1979	
56 070	BREL Doncaster	—	—	December 1979	
56 071	BREL Doncaster	—	—	December 1979	
56 072	BREL Doncaster	—	—	January 1980	
56 073	BREL Doncaster	—	—	February 1980	
56 074	BREL Doncaster	—	*Kellingley Colliery,* June 1982	March 1980	
56 075	BREL Doncaster	—	—	April 1980	
56 076	BREL Doncaster	—	*Blyth Power,* September 1982	April 1980	
56 077	BREL Doncaster	—	—	May 1980	
56 078	BREL Doncaster	—	—	May 1980	
56 079	BREL Doncaster	—	—	June 1980	
56 080	BREL Doncaster	—	—	July 1980	
56 081	BREL Doncaster	—	—	July 1980	
56 082	BREL Doncaster	—	—	August 1980	
56 083	BREL Doncaster	—	—	September 1980	
56 084	BREL Doncaster	—	—	October 1980	
56 085	BREL Doncaster	—	—	November 1980	
56 086	BREL Doncaster	—	—	December 1980	
56 087	BREL Doncaster	—	—	December 1980	
56 088	BREL Doncaster	—	—	January 1981	
56 089	BREL Doncaster	—	—	January 1981	
56 090	BREL Doncaster	—	—	February 1981	
56 091	BREL Doncaster	—	—	May 1981	
56 092	BREL Doncaster	—	—	June 1981	
56 093	BREL Doncaster	—	—	June 1981	
56 094	BREL Doncaster	—	—	July 1981	
56 095	BREL Doncaster	—	—	August 1981	
56 096	BREL Doncaster	—	—	August 1981	
56 097	BREL Doncaster	—	—	September 1981	
56 098	BREL Doncaster	—	—	September 1981	
56 099	BREL Doncaster	—	—	October 1981	
56 100	BREL Doncaster	—	—	November 1981	
56 101	BREL Doncaster	—	—	November 1981	
56 102	BREL Doncaster	—	—	December 1981	
56 103	BREL Doncaster	—	—	December 1981	
56 104	BREL Doncaster	—	—	February 1982	
56 105	BREL Doncaster	—	—	March 1982	
56 106	BREL Doncaster	—	—	April 1982	
56 107	BREL Doncaster	—	—	May 1982	
56 108	BREL Doncaster	—	—	June 1982	
56 109	BREL Doncaster	—	—	August 1982	
56 110	BREL Doncaster	—	—	September 1982	
56 111	BREL Doncaster	—	—	October 1982	
56 112	BREL Doncaster	—	—	November 1982	
56 113	BREL Doncaster	—	—	December 1982	
56 114	BREL Doncaster	—	—	January 1983	
56 115	BREL Doncaster	—	—	January 1983	
56 116	BREL Crewe	—	—	March 1983	
56 117	BREL Crewe	—	—	March 1983	
56 118	BREL Crewe	—	—	April 1983	

TOPS No	*Disposal Code*	*Disposal details*	*Notes*
56 061			
56 062			
56 063			
56 064			
56 065			
56 066			
56 067			
56 068			
56 069			
56 070			
56 071			
56 072			
56 073			
56 074			
56 075			
56 076			
56 077			
56 078			
56 079			
56 080			
56 081			
56 082			
56 083			
56 084			
56 085			
56 086			
56 087			
56 088			
56 089			
56 090			
56 091			
56 092			
56 093			
56 094			
56 095			
56 096			
56 097			
56 098			
56 099			
56 100			
56 101			
56 102			
56 103			
56 104			
56 105			
56 106			
56 107			
56 108			
56 109			
56 110			
56 111			
56 112			
56 113			
56 114			
56 115			
56 116			
56 117			
56 118			

TOPS No	Built by	Works No	Name	Date introduced	Date withdrawn
56 119	BREL Crewe	—	—	May 1983	
56 120	BREL Crewe	—	—	May 1983	
56 121	BREL Crewe	—	—	June 1983	
56 122	BREL Crewe	—	—	July 1983	
56 123	BREL Crewe	—	—	July 1983	
56 124	BREL Crewe	—	*Blue Circle Cement,* October 1983	September 1983	
56 125	BREL Crewe	—	—	October 1983	
56 126	BREL Crewe	—	—	November 1983	
56 127	BREL Crewe	—	—	December 1983	
56 128	BREL Crewe	—	—	December 1983	
56 129	BREL Crewe	—	—	January 1984	
56 130	BREL Crewe	—	—	April 1984	
56 131	BREL Crewe	—	—	April 1984	
56 132	BREL Crewe	—	—	June 1984	
56 133	BREL Crewe	—	*Crewe Locomotive Works,* June 1984	July 1984	
56 134	BREL Crewe	—	—	September 1984	
56 135	BREL Crewe	—	—		

Class 58

Designated as BR's purpose designed and built freight locomotive, the Class 58 is a direct descendant of the Class 56 design, using revised equipment, and cheaper constructional methods.

TOPS No	Built by	Works No	Date introduced	Date withdrawn	Disposal code
58 001	BREL Doncaster	—	May 1983		
58 002	BREL Doncaster	—	May 1983		
58 003	BREL Doncaster	—	July 1983		
58 004	BREL Doncaster	—	September 1983		
58 005	BREL Doncaster	—	October 1983		
58 006	BREL Doncaster	—	October 1983		
58 007	BREL Doncaster	—	November 1983		
58 008	BREL Doncaster	—	December 1983		
58 009	BREL Doncaster	—	January 1984		
58 010	BREL Doncaster	—	February 1984		
58 011	BREL Doncaster	—	March 1984		
58 012	BREL Doncaster	—	March 1984		
58 013	BREL Doncaster	—	March 1984		
58 014	BREL Doncaster	—	April 1984		
58 015	BREL Doncaster	—	July 1984		
58 016	BREL Doncaster	—			
58 017	BREL Doncaster	—			
58 018	BREL Doncaster	—			
58 019	BREL Doncaster	—			
58 020	BREL Doncaster	—			
58 021	BREL Doncaster	—			
58 022	BREL Doncaster	—			
58 023	BREL Doncaster	—			
58 024	BREL Doncaster	—			
58 025	BREL Doncaster	—			
58 026	BREL Doncaster	—			
58 027	BREL Doncaster	—			
58 028	BREL Doncaster	—			
58 029	BREL Doncaster	—			
58 030	BREL Doncaster	—			
58 031	BREL Doncaster	—			
58 032	BREL Doncaster	—			

TOPS No	*Disposal Code*	*Disposal details*	*Notes*
56 119			
56 120			
56 121			
56 122			
56 123			
56 124			
56 125			
56 126			
56 127			
56 128			
56 129			
56 130			
56 131			
56 132			
56 133			
56 134			
56 135			

Engine: Ruston 12RK3ACT of 3,300hp
Weight: 130 ton
Bogie type: Co-Co
Max speed: 80mph
Class code: BR Class 58
Tractive effort: 60,000lb
Length: 62ft 9½in
Height: 12ft 10in
Width: 8ft 10½in

TOPS No	*Disposal details*	*Notes*
58 001		Completed during December 1982
58 002		
58 003		
58 004		
58 005		
58 006		
58 007		
58 008		
58 009		
58 010		
58 011		
58 012		
58 013		
58 014		
58 015		
58 016		
58 017		
58 018		
58 019		
58 020		
58 021		
58 022		
58 023		
58 024		
58 025		
58 026		
58 027		
58 028		
58 029		
58 030		
58 031		
58 032		

TOPS No	Built by	Works No	Date introduced	Date withdrawn	Disposal Code
58 033	BREL Doncaster	—			
58 034	BREL Doncaster	—			
58 035	BREL Doncaster	—			
58 036	BREL Doncaster	—			
58 037	BREL Doncaster	—			
58 038	BREL Doncaster	—			
58 039	BREL Doncaster	—			
58 040	BREL Doncaster	—			
58 041	BREL Doncaster	—			
58 042	BREL Doncaster	—			
58 043	BREL Doncaster	—			
58 044	BREL Doncaster	—			
58 045	BREL Doncaster	—			
58 046	BREL Doncaster	—			
58 047	BREL Doncaster	—			
58 048	BREL Doncaster	—			
58 049	BREL Doncaster	—			
58 050	BREL Doncaster	—			

ELECTRIC TRACTION PART 2

Section 1
Pre-Nationalisation Numbers

Southern Railway

SR design electric locomotives for third rail or 660/750V overhead operation, operated on all three SR divisions, and could be described as the prototypes for the later E5000 type.

Original SR No	BR 1948 No	Built by	Works No	Date introduced	Date withdrawn
CC1	20001	SR Ashford/Brighton	—	— 1941	January 1969
CC2	20002	SR Ashford/Brighton	—	— 1945	December 1968
CC3*	20003	BR Ashford	—	— 1948	October 1968

*Number allocated but never carried.

North Eastern Railway

6000 *see* E26000

6480-1 *see* NER 1-2

6490-9 *see* NER 3-12

6999 *see* NER 13

ES1

Built specially for the Newcastle Quayside branch of the NER where steam traction was impractical due to tunnel sections where steam blow-back was common. One example now preserved.

Original NER No	LNER No	BR 1948 No	Built by	Works No	Date introduced	Date withdrawn
1	6480	26500	Brush	—	— 1905	September 1964
2	6481	26501	Brush	—	— 1905	September 1964

TOPS No	*Disposal details*	*Notes*
58 033		
58 034		
58 035		
58 036		
58 037		
58 038		
58 039		
58 040		
58 041		
58 042		
58 043		
58 044		
58 045		
58 046		
58 047		
58 048		
58 049		
58 050		

20001-20002

Type: 660-750V dc
Weight: 99 ton
Bogie type: Co-Co
Max speed: 75mph
Class code: 7P5F (SR Class CC), BR Class 70
Tractive effort: 40,000lb
Length: 56ft 9in
Height: 12ft 6in
Width: 8ft $7\frac{1}{4}$in

20003

Type: 660-750V dc
Weight: 104 ton
Bogie type: Co-Co
Max speed: 75mph
Class code: 7P5F, BR Class 70
Tractive effort: 45,000lb
Length: 58ft 3in
Height: 12ft 8in
Width: 8ft $7\frac{1}{4}$in

Original SR No	*Disposal code*	*Disposal details*	*Notes*
CC1	C	J. Cashmore, Newport, Gwent August 1969	Withdrawn December 1968, reinstated January 1969
CC2	C	J. Cashmore, Newport, Gwent September 1969	
CC3	C	G. Cohen, Kettering, Northamptonshire November 1969	

Type: 600V dc
Weight: 46 ton
Bogie type: Bo-Bo
Max speed: 25mph
Class code: ES1
Tractive effort: 25,000lb
Length:
Height:
Width:

Original NER No	*Disposal code*	*Disposal details*	*Notes*
1	P	National Railway Museum, York	Previously preserved at Leicester Museum of Technology
2	C	T. W. Ward, Choppington c1966	

The English Electric 'Deltic' Class 55 Type 5 locomotives, introduced to replace steam power on ECML duties, were one of the most followed diesel classes of our time. Now all have been withdrawn and the majority cut up. However six have been saved from the cutter's torch by preservation societies. No 55 014, formerly D9014 introduced in September 1961, is shown here at the head of the 08.05 King's Cross-Hull on 16 May 1980 near Biggleswade.
Colin J. Marsden

D9531 after withdrawal was sold to Arnott Young at Rawmarsh and later to the NCB, northeast area, where the locomotive is currently used at Ashington Colliery with the number 9312/92. *Colin J. Marsden*

The first diesel locomotives built carrying the TOPS five-figure numbers were the Class 56s introduced from 1977. No 56 068 built by BREL Doncaster passes Trowell Junction during September 1981. *Colin J. Marsden*

No E1000 rebuilt from gas turbine No 18100 by Metropolitan Vickers at Trafford Park was the pioneer of the 25kV electric locomotive fleet, designed for driver/crew training in readiness for production classes. This locomotive was later renumbered E2001. *BR*

EB1

Built by the NER in association with English Electric, these 10 Bo-Bo, 1,100hp locomotives were for use on the Shildon-Newport line; line reverted to steam traction from early 1935 and locos stored. No 11 going to departmental stock.

Original NER No	*LNER No*	*BR 1948 No*	*Built by*	*Works No*	*Date introduced*	*Date withdrawn*
3	6490	26502	NER Darlington	999	— 1914	August 1950
4	6491	26503	NER Darlington	1000	— 1914	August 1950
5	6492	26504	NER Darlington	1001	— 1914	August 1950
6	6493	26505	NER Darlington	1002	— 1914	August 1950
7	6494	26506	NER Darlington	1003	— 1914	August 1950
8	6495	26507	NER Darlington	1004	— 1914	August 1950
9	6496	26508	NER Darlington	1005	— 1914	August 1950
10	6497	26509	NER Darlington	1006	— 1914	August 1950
11	6498	26510	NER Darlington	1007	— 1914	December 1942
12	6499	26511	NER Darlington	1008	— 1918	August 1950

6700 *see* E26000

EE1

Built as the locomotive for an ambitious electrification scheme by the NER of the York-Newcastle main-line, however the loco only operated a few trial runs on the Shildon section before being stored.

Original NER No	*LNER No*	*BR 1948 No*	*Built by*	*Works No*	*Date introduced*	*Date withdrawn*
13	6999	26600	NER Darlington	1169	— 1922	August 1950

Section 2

British Railways 1948 Numbers

20001-3 *see* CC1-CC3

Class 76

Built for use as mixed traffic locomotives for the Manchester-Sheffield-Wath dc electrification scheme, based on the LNER prototype No 6000/6701.

BR 1948 No	*TOPS No*	*TOPS re-No*	*Name*	*Built by*	*Works No when built*	*Amended Works No*	*Date introduced*
E26000	—	—	*Tommy*, June 1952	LNER Doncaster	—	—	March 1941
E26001	76 001	—	—	BR Gorton	1004	1008	October 1950
E26002	76 002	—	—	BR Gorton	1005	1009	October 1950
E26003	76 003	76 036	—	BR Gorton	1006	1010	November 1950
E26004	76 004	—	—	BR Gorton	1007	1011	February 1951
E26005	—	—	—	BR Gorton	1008	1012	January 1951
E26006	76 006	—	—	BR Gorton	1009	1013	January 1951
E26007	76 007	—	—	BR Gorton	1010	1014	February 1951
E26008	76 008	—	—	BR Gorton	1011	1015	March 1951

Type: 1,500V dc
Weight: 74½ ton
Bogie type: Bo-Bo
Max speed: 45mph
Class code: EB1

Tractive effort: 28,000lb
Length: 39ft 4in
Height: 11ft 6¼in
Width: 8ft 4in

Original NER No	*Disposal code*	*Disposal details*	*Notes*
3	C	Wanty & Co, Catcliffe, Sheffield c1950	
4	C	Wanty & Co, Catcliffe, Sheffield c1950	
5	C	BR Darlington c1950	
6	C	Wanty & Co, Catcliffe, Sheffield c1950	
7	C	Wanty & Co, Catcliffe, Sheffield c1950	
8	C	Wanty & Co, Catcliffe, Sheffield c1950	
9	C	Wanty & Co, Catcliffe, Sheffield c1950	
10	C	Wanty & Co, Catcliffe, Sheffield c1950	
11	D	Departmental Stock — No 100	
12	C	Wanty & Co, Catcliffe, Sheffield c1950	

Type: 1,500V dc
Weight: 110 ton
Bogie type: 2-Co-2
Max speed: 90mph
Class code: EE1

Tractive effort: 28,000lb
Length: 53ft 6in
Height: 13ft 0in
Width: 8ft 10in

Original NER No	*Disposal code*	*Disposal details*	*Notes*
13	C	Wanty & Co, Catcliffe, Sheffield c1950	Also carried number 26699

Type: 1,500V dc
Weight: 87¾ ton
Bogie type: Bo-Bo
Max speed: 65mph
Class code: 7P8F, EM1, BR Class 76

Tractive effort: 45,000lb
Length: 50ft 4in
Height: 13ft 0in
Width: 9ft 0in

BR 1948 No	*Date withdrawn*	*Disposal code*	*Disposal details*	*Notes*
E26000	March 1970	C	BREL Crewe October 1972	Formerly LNER 6000, and 6701
E26001	November 1980	C	C. F. Booth, Rotherham May 1983	
E26002	June 1978	C	C. F. Booth, Rotherham	
E26003	July 1981	C	C. F. Booth, Rotherham May 1983	Stored from August 1980
E26004	June 1978	C	C. F. Booth, Rotherham	Withdrawn February 1977, reinstated August 1977
E26005	March 1970	C	BREL Crewe March 1971	
E26006	July 1981	C	C. F. Booth, Rotherham May 1983	
E26007	July 1981	C	C. F. Booth, Rotherham June 1983	
E26008	July 1981	C	C. F. Booth, Rotherham June 1983	

BR 1948 No	*TOPS No*	*TOPS re-No*	*Name*	*Built by*	*Works No when built*	*Amended Works No*	*Date introduced*
E26009	76 009	—	—	BR Gorton	1012	1016	March 1951
E26010	76 010	—	—	BR Gorton	1013	1017	March 1951
E26011	76 011	—	—	BR Gorton	1014	1018	May 1951
E26012	76 012	—	—	BR Gorton	1015	1019	May 1951
E26013	76 013	—	—	BR Gorton	1016	1020	May 1951
E26014	76 014	—	—	BR Gorton	1017	1021	May 1951
E26015	76 015	—	—	BR Gorton	1018	1022	July 1951
E26016	76 016	—	—	BR Gorton	1019	1023	July 1951
E26017	—	—	—	BR Gorton	1020	1024	July 1951
E26018	76 018	76 035	—	BR Gorton	1021	1025	September 1951
E26019	—	—	—	BR Gorton	1022	1026	September 1951
E26020	76 020	—	—	BR Gorton	1023	1027	October 1951
E26021	76 021	—	—	BR Gorton	1024	1028	October 1951
E26022	76 022	—	—	BR Gorton	1025	1029	September 1951
E26023	76 023	—	—	BR Gorton	1026	1030	September 1951
E26024	76 024	—	—	BR Gorton	1027	1031	September 1951
E26025	76 025	—	—	BR Gorton	1032	—	January 1952
E26026	76 026	—	—	BR Gorton	1033	—	January 1962
E26027	76 027	—	—	BR Gorton	1034	—	January 1952
E26028	76 028	—	—	BR Gorton	1035	—	January 1952
E26029	76 029	—	—	BR Gorton	1036	1032	December 1951
E26030	76 030	—	—	BR Gorton	1037	1033	December 1951
E26031	—	—	—	BR Gorton	1038	—	January 1952
E26032	76 032	—	—	BR Gorton	1039	—	January 1952
E26033	76 033	—	—	BR Gorton	1040	—	January 1952
E26034	76 034	—	—	BR Gorton	1041	—	January 1952
E26035	—	—	—	BR Gorton	1042	—	January 1952
E26036	76 036	76 003	—	BR Gorton	1043	—	February 1952
E26037	76 037	—	—	BR Gorton	1044	—	February 1952
E26038	76 038	76 050	—	BR Gorton	1045	—	April 1952
E26039	76 039	76 048	—	BR Gorton	1046	—	April 1952
E26040	76 040	—	—	BR Gorton	1047	—	April 1952

BR 1948 No	*Date withdrawn*	*Disposal code*	*Disposal details*	*Notes*
E26009	July 1981	C	C. F. Booth, Rotherham July 1983	
E26010	July 1981	C	C. F. Booth, Rotherham June 1983	
E26011	July 1981	C	C. F. Booth, Rotherham June 1983	
E26012	July 1981	C	C. F. Booth, Rotherham July 1983	
E26013	July 1981	C	C. F. Booth, Rotherham May 1983	
E26014	July 1981	C	C. F. Booth, Rotherham May 1983	
E26015	July 1981	C	C. F. Booth, Rotherham March 1983	
E26016	July 1981	C	C. F. Booth, Rotherham April 1983	
E26017	March 1970	C	BR Reddish depot, by Cashmores October 1971	
E26018	July 1981	C	C. F. Booth, Rotherham June 1983	
E26019	October 1971	C	BREL Crewe May 1972	
E26020	August 1977	P	National Railway Museum, York as No 26020	
E26021	July 1981	C	C. F. Booth, Rotherham May 1983	
E26022	July 1981	C	C. F. Booth, Rotherham May 1983	
E26023	July 1981	C	C. F. Booth, Rotherham July 1983	
E26024	July 1981	C	C. F. Booth, Rotherham June 1983	
E26025	July 1981	C	C. F. Booth, Rotherham March 1983	
E26026	July 1981	C	C. F. Booth, Rotherham July 1983	
E26027	July 1981	C	C. F. Booth, Rotherham March 1983	
E26028	July 1981	C	C. F. Booth, Rotherham June 1983	
E26029	July 1981	C	Coopers, Brightside, Sheffield March 1983	
E26030	July 1981	C	C. F. Booth, Rotherham April 1983	
E26031	October 1971	C	BREL Crewe May 1972	
E26032	July 1981	C	Coopers, Brightside, Sheffield March 1983	
E26033	July 1981	C	Coopers, Brightside, Sheffield March 1983	Stored June 1980, reinstated September 1980
E26034	July 1981	C	C. F. Booth, Rotherham March 1983	
E26035	March 1970	C	BR Reddish depot, by Cashmores October 1971	
E26036	July 1981	C	F. Berry, Leicester May 1983	Stored August 1980
E26037	July 1981	C	F. Berry, Leicester May 1983	Withdrawn October 1971, reinstated November 1971
E26038	February 1977	C	C. F. Booth, Rotherham	
E26039	February 1977	C	C. F. Booth, Rotherham	
E26040	July 1981	C	F. Berry, Leicester May 1983	

BR 1948 No	TOPS No	TOPS re-No	Name	Built by	Works No when built	Amended Works No	Date introduced
E26041	76 041	—	—	BR Gorton	1048	—	April 1952
E26042	—	—	—	BR Gorton	1049	—	May 1952
E26043	76 043	—	—	BR Gorton	1050	—	May 1952
E26044	76 044	76 031	—	BR Gorton	1051	—	June 1952
E26045	—	—	—	BR Gorton	1052	—	June 1952
E26046	76 046	—	*Archimedes,* May 1959	BR Gorton	1053	—	August 1952
E26047	76 047	—	*Diomedes,* September 1960	BR Gorton	1054	—	August 1952
E26048	76 048	76 039	*Hector,* March 1960	BR Gorton	1055	—	September 1952
E26049	76 049	—	*Jason,* August 1960	BR Gorton	1056	—	October 1952
E26050	76 050	76 038	*Stentor,* August 1960	BR Gorton	1057	—	November 1952
E26051	76 051	—	*Mentor,* June 1959	BR Gorton	1058	—	January 1953
E26052	76 052	—	*Nestor,* August 1961	BR Gorton	1059	—	January 1953
E26053	76 053	—	*Perseus,* October 1960	BR Gorton	1060	—	March 1953
E26054	76 054	—	*Pluto,* April 1961	BR Gorton	1061	—	April 1953
E26055	76 055	—	*Prometheus,* June 1959	BR Gorton	1062	—	June 1953
E26056	76 056	—	*Triton,* July 1959	BR Gorton	1063	—	July 1953
E26057	76 057	—	*Ulysses,* April 1960	BR Gorton	1064	—	August 1953

26500-1 *see* NER 1-2
26502-12 *see* NER 3-12
26600 *see* NER 13

Class 77

After a short period of operation of EM1 locos on passenger duties, it was decided to build seven Co-Co high power passenger machines, capable of 90mph. Built by BR at Gorton, Manchester.

BR 1948 No	Name	Built by	Works No	Date introduced	Date withdrawn
E27000	*Electra,* August 1959	BR Gorton	1065	December 1953	September 1968
E27001	*Ariadne,* October 1959	BR Gorton	1066	March 1954	September 1968
E27002	*Aurora,* June 1959	BR Gorton	1067	May 1954	September 1968
E27003	*Diana,* January 1961	BR Gorton	1068	August 1954	September 1968
E27004	*Juno,* June 1959	BR Gorton	1069	September 1954	September 1968
E27005	*Minerva,* May 1959	BR Gorton	1070	December 1954	September 1968
E27006	*Pandora,* May 1959	BR Gorton	1071	December 1954	September 1968

BR 1948 No	Date withdrawn	Disposal code	Disposal details	Notes
E26041	November 1980	C	C. F. Booth, Rotherham March 1983	Stored from April 1980
E26042	March 1970	C	BR Reddish depot, by Cashmores October 1971	
E26043	June 1978	C	C. F. Booth, Rotherham	
E26044	July 1981	C	Coopers, Brightside, Sheffield February 1984	Stored June 1980, reinstated September 1980
E26045	November 1971	C	BREL Crewe April 1972	
E26046	November 1980	C	C. F. Booth, Rotherham March 1983	Stored from August 1980
E26047	November 1980	C	C. F. Booth, Rotherham May 1983	Stored from September 1980
E26048	July 1981	C	C. F. Booth, Rotherham June 1983	Cab preserved at Liverpool Road, Manchester
E26049	November 1980	C	C. F. Booth, Rotherham March 1983	Stored from August 1980
E26050	July 1981	C	C. F. Booth, Rotherham May 1983	Stored June 1980, reinstated September 1980
E26051	July 1981	C	C. F. Booth, Rotherham March 1983	Stored June 1980, reinstated August 1980
E26052	June 1978	C	C. F. Booth, Rotherham	
E26053	November 1980	C	C. F. Booth, Rotherham March 1983	Stored June 1980, reinstated September 1980
E26054	July 1981	C	C. F. Booth, Rotherham May 1983	Stored July 1980, reinstated September 1980
E26055	February 1977	C	C. F. Booth, Rotherham	
E26056	June 1978	C	BR Reddish depot, by C. F. Booth March 1983	
E26057	February 1977	C	BR Reddish depot, by C. F. Booth March 1983	

Type: 1,500V dc
Weight: 102 ton
Bogie type: Co-Co
Max speed: 90mph
Class code: EM2 BR Class 77

Tractive effort: 45,000lb
Length: 59ft 0in
Height: 13ft 0in
Width: 8ft 10in

BR 1948 No	Disposal code	Disposal details	New NS No	Notes
E27000	E	Exported to Netherlands State Railways September 1969	1502	
E27001	E	Exported to Netherlands State Railways September 1969	1505	
E27002	E	Exported to Netherlands State Railways September 1969	1506	Scheduled for preservation
E27003	E	Exported to Netherlands State Railways September 1969	1501	
E27004	E	Exported to Netherlands State Railways September 1969	1503	
E27005	E	Exported to Netherlands State Railways September 1969	—	Dismantled for spares
E27006	E	Exported to Netherlands State Railways September 1969	1504	

Section 3
British Railways 1957 Numbers

Class 80

Before any of the new ac classes of electric locomotive could take up operations on the LMR, staff training had to take place, and for this former gas turbine No 18100 was rebuilt by Metro-Vickers into a 25kV electric. Major rebuilding took place inside, but little alteration was carried out to the body.

BR 1957 No	*Revised 1957 No*	*Built by*	*Works No*	*Date introduced*	*Date withdrawn*	*Disposal code*
E1000	E2001	M/Vickers	—	— 1958	April 1968	C

E2001 *see* E1000

Class 81

For the electrification of the LMR, 100 prototype locomotives were ordered from various builders. The first type AL1 were ordered from AEI(BTH)/BRCW, and the first locomotive for the 'new railway' was handed over on 27 November 1959.

BR 1957 No	*TOPS No*	*Built by*	*Works No*	*Period introduced*	*Date withdrawn*	*Disposal code*
E3001	81 001	BRCW	1083	12/59		
E3002	—	BRCW	1084	1/60	November 1968	C
E3003	81 002	BRCW	1085	2/60		
E3004	81 003	BRCW	1086	4/60		
E3005	81 004	BRCW	1087	5/60		
E3006	81 005	BRCW	1088	7/60		
E3007	81 006	BRCW	1089	8/60		
E3008	81 007	BRCW	1090	10/60		
E3009	—	BRCW	1091	10/60	August 1968	C
E3010	81 008	BRCW	1092	11/60		
E3011	81 009	BRCW	1093	12/60		
E3012	81 010	BRCW	1094	12/60		
E3013	81 011	BRCW	1095	12/60		
E3014	81 012	BRCW	1096	13/60		
E3015	81 013	BRCW	1097	13/60		
E3016	81 014	BRCW	1098	3/61		
E3017	81 015	BRCW	1099	5/61		
E3018	81 016	BRCW	1100	3/61	July 1983	A
E3019	—	BRCW	1101	4/61	July 1971	C
E3020	81 017	BRCW	1102	5/61		
E3021	81 018	BRCW	1103	6/61		
E3022	81 019	BRCW	1104	10/61		
E3023	81 020	BRCW	1105	2/62		

Class continued with E3096

Class 83

The first of the ac classes to be built by English Electric were these 12 (15) AL3 locomotives introduced from 1960 conforming to the same basic design as the previous AL1s but with detail differences. The final three locos of build designated as freight (Type B) units (lower gearing). Later rebuilt as standard.

BR 1957 No	*TOPS No*	*Built by*	*Works No*	*Period introduced*	*Date withdrawn*	*Disposal code*
E3024	83 001	EE(VF)	E2928/E264	7/60	August 1983	A
E3025	83 002	EE(VF)	E2929/E265	7/60	August 1983	A
E3026	83 003	EE(VF)	E2930/E266	8/60	May 1975	C
E3027	83 004	EE(VF)	E2931/E267	9/60	January 1978	C

Type: 25kV ac
Weight: 109 ton
Bogie type: A1A-A1A
Max speed: 90mph
Class code: BR Class 80

Tractive effort: 40,000lb
Length: 66ft 9¼in
Height: 12ft 10in
Width: 9ft 0in

BR 1957 No	*Disposal details*	*Notes*
E1000	J. Cashmore, Great Bridge, Tipton c1973	Rebuilt from Gas Turbine No 18100

Type: 25kV ac
Weight: 79½ ton
Bogie type: Bo-Bo
Max speed: 100mph
Class code: AL1 BR Class 81

Tractive effort: 48,000lb
Length: 56ft 6in
Height: 12ft 4½in
Width: 8ft 8¼in

BR 1957 No	*Disposal details*	*Notes*
E3001		Stored November 1983
E3002	BR Workshops, Crewe January 1969	
E3003		
E3004		
E3005		
E3006		
E3007		
E3008		
E3009	BR Workshops, Crewe August 1968	
E3010		
E3011		
E3012		
E3013		
E3014		
E3015		
E3016		
E3017		
E3018	BREL Crewe	Stored March 1983
E3019	BREL Crewe October 1971	
E3020		
E3021		
E3022		
E3023		

Type: 25kV ac
Weight: 76½ ton
Bogie type: Bo-Bo
Max speed: 100mph
Class code: AL3 BR Class 83

Tractive effort: 40,000lb
Length: 52ft 6in
Height: 13ft 0½in
Width: 8ft 8¾in

BR 1957 No	*Disposal details*	*Notes*
E3024	BR Crewe depot	Stored October 1982
E3025	BR Stoke depot	Stored October 1981
E3026	BREL Crewe July 1975	
E3027	BR Willesden depot February 1978	

BR 1957 No	TOPS No	Built by	Works No	Period introduced	Date withdrawn	Disposal code
E3028	83 005	EE(VF)	E2932/E268	10/60	August 1983	A
E3029	83 006	EE(VF)	E2933/E269	10/60	August 1983	A
E3030	83 007	EE(VF)	E2934/E270	11/60	August 1983	A
E3031	83 008	EE(VF)	E2935/E271	12/60	August 1983	A
E3032	83 009	EE(VF)	E2936/E272	12/60	August 1983	A
E3033	83 010	EE(VF)	E2937/E273	13/60	August 1983	A
E3034	83 011	EE(VF)	E2938/E274	2/61	August 1983	A
E3035	83 012	EE(VF)	E2941/E277	7/61		

Class continued with E3098

Class 84

GEC sub-contracted the design and building of one of the ac fleets, later designated AL4 to the NBL Co of Glasgow. Their design again followed the previous types, except that drop light style side windows and oval buffers were fitted.

BR 1957 No	TOPS No	Built by	Works No	Period introduced	Date withdrawn	Disposal code
E3036	84 001	NBL	27793	3/60	January 1979	P
E3037	84 002	NBL	27794	5/60	September 1980	C
E3038	84 003	NBL	27795	6/60	November 1980	A
E3039	84 004	NBL	27796	7/60	November 1977	A
E3040	84 005	NBL	27797	8/60	April 1977	A
E3041	84 006	NBL	27798	10/60	January 1978	C
E3042	84 007	NBL	27799	10/60	April 1977	C
E3043	84 008	NBL	27800	12/60	October 1979	A
E3044	84 009	NBL	27801	13/60	August 1978	D
E3045	84 010	NBL	27802	3/61	November 1980	C

Class 82

The second fleet of prototype ac locomotives designated Class AL2 was constructed by Beyer Peacock in association with AEI (Metro Vickers).

BR 1957 No	TOPS No	Built by	Works No	Period introduced	Date withdrawn	Disposal code
E3046	—	B/Peacock	1021/7884	5/60	January 1971	C
E3047	82 001	B/Peacock	1022/7885	7/60	August 1983	A
E3048	82 002	B/Peacock	1023/7886	8/60	August 1983	A
E3049	82 003	B/Peacock	1024/7887	9/60	August 1983	A
E3050	82 004	B/Peacock	1025/7888	10/60	October 1983	A
E3051	82 005	B/Peacock	1026/7889	11/60		
E3052	82 006	B/Peacock	1027/7890	12/60	August 1983	A
E3053	82 007	B/Peacock	1028/7891	1/62	August 1983	A
E3054	82 008	B/Peacock	1029/7892	11/61		
E3055	—	B/Peacock	1030/7893	4/62	September 1969	C

Class 85

Forty of the 100 prototype ac locomotives were built by BR themselves, and are basically the same as all other types. Much of the equipment fitted to this fleet was with experience gained from the previous Class 81-84 units.

BR 1957 No	TOPS No	Built by	Works No	Period introduced	Date withdrawn	Disposal code
E3056	85 001	BR Doncaster	—	9/61		
E3057	85 002	BR Doncaster	—	6/61		
E3058	85 003	BR Doncaster	—	6/61		
E3059	85 004	BR Doncaster	—	8/61		
E3060	85 005	BR Doncaster	—	8/61		

BR 1957 No	Disposal details	Notes
E3028	BR Stoke depot	Stored October 1982
E3029	BR Crewe depot	Stored October 1982
E3030	BR Stoke depot	Stored October 1982
E3031	BR Stoke depot	Stored December 1981
E3032	BR Longsight depot	Stored October 1982
E3033	BR Longsight depot	Stored October 1982
E3034	BR Crewe depot	Stored October 1982
E3035		Stored November 1982, reinstated May 1983

Type: 25kV ac
Weight: 76½ ton
Bogie type: Bo-Bo
Max speed: 100mph
Class code: AL4 BR Class 84
Tractive effort: 50,000lb
Length: 53ft 6½in
Height: 13ft 0½in
Width: 8ft 8¼in

BR 1957 No	Disposal details	Notes
E3036	National Railway Museum, York	
E3037	Texas Metals, Hyde, Cheshire February 1983	First sold to GEC at Trafford Park
E3038	Railway Technical Centre, Derby	Proposed for future Departmental use
E3039	BR Crewe electric depot	
E3040	BR Crewe electric depot	
E3041	Crewe Basford Hall by Cashmore	
E3042	Crewe Basford Hall by Cashmore	
E3043	BREL Crewe	
E3044	Departmental stock — 968021	
E3045	Texas Metals, Hyde, Cheshire February 1983	First sold to GEC at Trafford Park

Type: 25kV ac
Weight: 79½ ton
Bogie type: Bo-Bo
Max speed: 100mph
Class code: AL2 BR Class 82
Tractive effort: 50,000lb
Length: 56ft 0in
Height: 13ft 0¾in
Width: 8ft 9in

BR 1957 No	Disposal details	Notes
E3046	BREL Crewe June 1971	
E3047	BR Crewe depot	Stored May 1982
E3048	BR Crewe depot	Stored October 1981
E3049	BR Willesden depot	Stored August 1982
E3050	BR Stoke depot	Stored September 1982, reinstated August 1983
E3051		Stored November 1982, reinstated April 1983
E3052	BR Stoke depot	Stored June 1982
E3053	BR Crewe depot	Stored September 1982
E3054		Stored November 1982, reinstated April 1983
E3055	BREL Crewe August 1970	Out of service from 1966

Type: 25kV ac
Weight: 80 ton
Bogie type: Bo-Bo
Max speed: 100mph
Class code: AL5 BR Class 85
Tractive effort: 50,000lb
Length: 56ft 6in
Height: 13ft 0½in
Width: 8ft 8¼in

BR 1957 No	Disposal details	Notes
E3056		
E3057		
E3058		
E3059		
E3060		

BR 1957 No	TOPS No	Built by	Works No	Period introduced	Date withdrawn	Disposal code
E3061	85 006	BR Doncaster	—	13/61		
E3062	85 007	BR Doncaster	—	13/61		
E3063	85 008	BR Doncaster	—	11/61		
E3064	85 009	BR Doncaster	—	12/61		
E3065	85 010	BR Doncaster	—	12/61		
E3066	85 011	BR Doncaster	—	4/62		
E3067	85 012	BR Doncaster	—	1/62		
E3068	85 013	BR Doncaster	—	5/62		
E3069	85 014	BR Doncaster	—	5/62		
E3070	85 015	BR Doncaster	—	8/62		
E3071	85 016	BR Doncaster	—	11/62		
E3072	85 017	BR Doncaster	—	12/62		
E3073	85 018	BR Doncaster	—	2/63		
E3074	85 019	BR Doncaster	—	13/62		
E3075	85 020	BR Doncaster	—	1/63		
E3076	85 021	BR Doncaster	—	4/63		
E3077	85 022	BR Doncaster	—	3/63		
E3078	85 023	BR Doncaster	—	3/63		
E3079	85 024	BR Doncaster	—	10/63		
E3080	85 025	BR Doncaster	—	4/63		
E3081	85 026	BR Doncaster	—	7/63		
E3082	85 027	BR Doncaster	—	6/63	May 1983	A
E3083	85 028	BR Doncaster	—	9/63		
E3084	85 029	BR Doncaster	—	5/64		
E3085	85 030	BR Doncaster	—	7/64		
E3086	85 031	BR Doncaster	—	3/62		
E3087	85 032	BR Doncaster	—	11/62		
E3088	85 033	BR Doncaster	—	2/63		
E3089	85 034	BR Doncaster	—	7/63		
E3090	85 035	BR Doncaster	—	11/63		
E3091	85 036	BR Doncaster	—	10/63		
E3092	85 037	BR Doncaster	—	2/64		
E3093	85 038	BR Doncaster	—	11/63		
E3094	85 039	BR Doncaster	—	2/64		
E3095	85 040	BR Doncaster	—	13/64		

Class 81 continued from E3023

The final two Class AL1s were to be fitted with freight gear ratios and classified as Type B locomotives, however this equipment was not fitted and the locomotives emerged as standard Type A locomotives.

Technical description: See E3001-E3023 Section

BR 1957 No	Original BR 1957 No	TOPS No	Built by	Works No	Period introduced	Date withdrawn
E3096	E3301	81 021	BRCW	1106	6/62	
E3097	E3302	81 022	BRCW	1107	2/64	

Class 83 continued from E3035

Two of the AL3 build were constructed as Type B freight locomotives and numbered accordingly, later converted to the standard type, while the last of the build was a test bed for electronic equipment.

Technical description: See E3024-E3035 section

BR 1957 No	Original BR 1957 No	TOPS No	Built by	Works No	Period introduced	Date withdrawn
E3098	E3303	83 013	EE(VF)	EE2939/E275	3/61	August 1983
E3099	E3304	83 014	EE(VF)	EE2940/E276	5/61	August 1983
E3100	E3305*	83 015	EE(VF)	EE2942/E278	7/62	

*Not carried

BR 1957 No	Disposal details	Notes
E3061		
E3062		Stored March 1983, reinstated September 1983
E3063		
E3064		
E3065		
E3066		
E3067		
E3068		
E3069		
E3070		
E3071		
E3072		
E3073		
E3074		
E3075		
E3076		
E3077		Stored April 1984
E3078		
E3079		
E3080		
E3081		
E3082	BREL Crewe	Stored May 1983
E3083		
E3084		
E3085		
E3086		
E3087		
E3088		Stored April 1983, reinstated September 1983
E3089		
E3090		
E3091		
E3092		
E3093		
E3094		
E3095		

BR 1957 No	Disposal code	Disposal details	Notes
E3096			
E3097			

BR 1957 No	Disposal code	Disposal details	Notes
E3098	A	BR Stoke depot	Stored October 1981
E3099	A	BR Crewe depot	Stored March 1981
E3100			Stored December 1981, withdrawn August 1983, reinstated November 1983

Class 86

This class of 100 BR/EE designed and built Class AL6 (86) locomotives were produced from the vast experience gained from the five prototype classes. Today five sub classes operate: 86/0 standard 80mph locos, 86/1 prototype Class 87 locos, 86/2 standard 100mph locos, 86/3, 86/0s fitted with SAB wheels, and 86/4 locomotives modified with SAB wheels and reused suspension.

BR 1957 No	*TOPS No*	*Revised TOPS No*	*Name*	*Built by*	*Works No*	*Period introduced*
E3101	86 252	—	*The Liverpool Daily Post,* February 1980	BR Doncaster	—	9/65
E3102	86 009	—	—	BR Doncaster	—	9/65
E3103	86 004	—	—	BR Doncaster	—	9/65
E3104	86 010	—	—	BR Doncaster	—	10/65
E3105	86 030	—	—	BR Doncaster	—	7/65
E3106	86 214	—	*Sans Pareil,* April 1980	BR Doncaster	—	7/65
E3107	86 248	—	*Sir Clwyd/County of Clwyd,* March 1981	BR Doncaster	—	10/65
E3108	86 038	—	—	BR Doncaster	—	7/65
E3109	86 016	86 316	*Wigan Pier,* September 1984	BR Doncaster	—	7/65
E3110	86 027	86 327	—	BR Doncaster	—	7/65
E3111	86 024	86 324	—	BR Doncaster	—	7/65
E3112	86 006	—	—	BR Doncaster	—	9/65
E3113	86 232	—	*Harold MacMillan,* October 1979	BR Doncaster	—	9/65
E3114	86 020	86 320	—	BR Doncaster	—	10/65
E3115	86 003	—	—	BR Doncaster	—	10/65
E3116	86 238	—	—	BR Doncaster	—	10/65
E3117	86 227	—	*Sir Henry Johnson,* March 1981	BR Doncaster	—	10/65
E3118	86 041	86 261	*Driver John Axon GC,* February 1981	BR Doncaster	—	10/65
E3119	86 229	—	*Sir John Betjeman,* June 1983	BR Doncaster	—	10/65
E3120	86 019	86 319	—	BR Doncaster	—	10/65
E3121	86 241	—	*Glenfiddich,* March 1979	BR Doncaster	—	10/65
E3122	86 012	86 312	*Elizabeth Garrett Anderson,*October 1983	BR Doncaster	—	10/65
E3123	86 015	86 315	*Rotary International,* June 1984	BR Doncaster	—	11/65
E3124	86 035	—	—	BR Doncaster	—	11/65
E3125	86 209	—	*City of Coventry,* February 1979	BR Doncaster	—	12/65
E3126	86 231	—	*Lady of the Lake* (N/F)	BR Doncaster	—	11/65
E3127	86 240	—	*Bishop Eric Treacy,* April 1979	BR Doncaster	—	11/65
E3128	86 013	86 313	—	BR Doncaster	—	12/65
E3129	86 205	—	*City of Lancaster,* October 1979	BR Doncaster	—	12/65
E3130	86 037	—	—	BR Doncaster	—	13/65
E3131	86 222	—	*Fury,* April 1979	BR Doncaster	—	13/65
E3132	86 221	—	*Vesta,* April 1979	BR Doncaster	—	13/65
E3133	86 236	—	*Josiah Wedgwood,* November 1980	BR Doncaster	—	13/65
E3134	86 224	—	*Caledonian,* June 1979	BR Doncaster	—	13/65
E3135	86 040	86 256	*Pebble Mill,* November 1981	BR Doncaster	—	1/66
E3136	86 044	86 253	*The Manchester Guardian* November 1980	BR Doncaster	—	13/65
E3137	86 045	86 259	*Peter Pan,* October 1979	BR Doncaster	—	1/66
E3138	86 242	—	*James Kennedy GC,* November 1981	BR Doncaster	—	1/66
E3139	86 043	86 257	*Snowdon,* January 1981	BR Doncaster	—	1/66

Type: 25kV ac
Weight: 82¾ ton†
Bogie type: Bo-Bo
Max speed: 80-100mph
Class code: AL6 BR Class 86

Tractive effort: 58,000lb
Length: 58ft 6in
Height: 13ft 0$^9/_{16}$in
Width: 8ft 8¼in
†Various upon type

BR 1957 No	*Date withdrawn*	*Disposal code*	*Disposal details*	*Notes*
E3101				
E3102				
E3103				
E3104				
E3105				
E3106				
E3107				
E3108				
E3109				
E3110				
E3111				
E3112				
E3113				
E3114				
E3115				
E3116				
E3117				
E3118				
E3119				
E3120				
E3121				
E3122				
E3123				
E3124				
E3125				
E3126				
E3127				
E3128				
E3129				
E3130				
E3131				
E3132				
E3133				
E3134				
E3135				
E3136				
E3137				
E3138				
E3139				

BR 1957 No	TOPS No	Revised TOPS No	Name	Built by	Works No	Period introduced
E3140	86 046	86 258	*Talyllyn* April 1984	BR Doncaster	—	3/66
E3141	86 208	—	*City of Chester,* March 1979	EE(VF)	E3722/E382	2/66
E3142	86 047	86 254	*William Webb Ellis,* October 1980	EE(VF)	E3723/E283	2/66
E3143	86 203	86 103	*André Chapelon,* January 1981	EE(VF)	E3724/E384	3/66
E3144	86 048	86 260	*Driver Wallace Oakes GC,* February 1981	EE(VF)	E3725/E385	3/66
E3145	86 014	86 314	—	EE(VF)	E3726/E386	3/66
E3146	86 017	86 317	—	EE(VF)	E3727/E387	4/66
E3147	86 211	—	*City of Milton Keynes,* May 1982	EE(VF)	E3728/E388	4/66
E3148	86 032	86 432	—	EE(VF)	E3729/E389	4/66
E3149	86 246	—	*Scafell Pike* (N/F)	EE(VF)	E3730/E390	4/66
E3150	86 202	86 102	*Robert A. Riddles,* May 1981	EE(VF)	E3731/E391	4/66
E3151	86 212	—	*Preston Guild,* April 1979	EE(VF)	E3732/E392	4/66
E3152	86 023	86 323	—	EE(VF)	E3733/E393	5/66
E3153	86 039	—	—	EE(VF)	E3734/E394	5/66
E3154	86 042	86 255	*Penrith Beacon,* November 1980	EE(VF)	E3735/E395	5/66
E3155	86 234	—	*J. B. Priestley OM,* December 1980	EE(VF)	E3736/E396	6/66
E3156	86 220	—	*Goliath,* — 1979	EE(VF)	E3737/E397	7/66
E3157	86 021	86 321	—	EE(VF)	E3738/E398	7/66
E3158	86 223	—	*Hector,* June 1979	EE(VF)	E3739/E399	7/66
E3159	86 028	86 328	*Aldeniti,* March 1984	EE(VF)	E3740/E400	7/66
E3160	86 036	—	—	EE(VF)	E3741/E401	11/66
E3161	86 249	—	*County of Merseyside,* September 1981	EE(VF)	E3453/E299	10/65
E3162	86 226	—	*Mail,* — 1979	EE(VF)	E3454/E300	9/65
E3163	86 018	86 318	—	EE(VF)	E3455/E301	9/65
E3164	86 225	—	*Hardwicke,* October 1980	EE(VF)	E3456/E302	9/65
E3165	86 215	—	*Joseph Chamberlain,* April 1981	EE(VF)	E3457/E303	9/65
E3166	86 216	—	*Meteor,* — 1979	EE(VF)	E3458/E304	10/65
E3167	86 228	—	*Vulcan Heritage,* March 1980	EE(VF)	E3459/E305	9/65
E3168	86 230	—	*The Duke of Wellington,* June 1981	EE(VF)	E3460/E306	7/65
E3169	86 239	—	*L. S. Lowry,* November 1980	EE(VF)	E3461/E307	7/65
E3170	86 002	—	—	EE(VF)	E3462/E308	7/65
E3171	86 011	86 311	*Airey Neave,* April 1983	EE(VF)	E3463/E309	10/65
E3172	86 233	—	*Sir Lawrence Olivier,* June 1980	EE(VF)	E3464/E310	7/65
E3173	86 204	—	*City of Carlisle,* December 1978	EE(VF)	E3465/E311	9/65
E3174	86 022	86 322	—	EE(VF)	E3466/E312	9/65
E3175	86 218	—	*Planet,* June 1979	EE(VF)	E3467/E313	10/65
E3176	86 007	—	—	EE(VF)	E3468/E314	9/65
E3177	86 217	—	*Comet,* October 1980	EE(VF)	E3469/E315	9/65
E3178	86 244	—	*The Royal British Legion,* November 1981	EE(VF)	E3470/E316	9/65
E3179	86 207	—	*City of Lichfield,* March 1981	EE(VF)	E3471/E317	10/65
E3180	86 008	—	—	EE(VF)	E3472/E318	10/65

BR 1957 No	Date withdrawn	Disposal code	Disposal details	Notes
E3140				
E3141				
E3142				
E3143				
E3144				
E3145				
E3146				
E3147				
E3148				
E3149				
E3150				
E3151				
E3152				
E3153				
E3154				
E3155				
E3156				
E3157				
E3158				
E3159				
E3160				
E3161				
E3162				
E3163				
E3164				
E3165				
E3166				
E3167				
E3168				
E3169				
E3170				
E3171				
E3172				
E3173				
E3174				
E3175				
E3176				
E3177				
E3178				
E3179				
E3180				

BR 1957 No	TOPS No	Revised TOPS No	Name	Built by	Works No	Period introduced
E3181	86 243	—	*The Boys Brigade,* April 1983	EE(VF)	E3473/E319	11/65
E3182	86 245	—	*Dudley Castle,* May 1984	EE(VF)	E3474/E320	10/65
E3183	86 251	—	*The Birmingham Post,* February 1980	EE(VF)	E3475/E321	11/65
E3184	86 206	—	*City of Stoke on Trent,* December 1978	EE(VF)	E3476/E322	10/65
E3185	86 005	—	—	EE(VF)	E3477/E323	10/65
E3186	86 025	86 325	—	EE(VF)	E3478/E324	11/65
E3187	86 034	—	—	EE(VF)	E3479/E325	11/65
E3188	86 031	—	—	EE(VF)	E3480/E326	11/65
E3189	86 250	—	*The Glasgow Herald,* September 1980	EE(VF)	E3481/E327	12/65
E3190	86 210	—	*City of Edinburgh,* February 1979	EE(VF)	E3482/E328	11/65
E3191	86 201	86 101	*Sir William A. Stanier,* October 1978	EE(VF)	E3483/E329	12/65
E3192	86 247	—	*Abraham Darby,* October 1981	EE(VF)	E3484/E330	12/65
E3193	86 213	—	*Lancashire Witch,* March 1981	EE(VF)	E3485/E331	12/65
E3194	86 235	—	*Novelty,* June 1979	EE(VF)	E3486/E332	13/65
E3195	86 026	86 326	—	EE(VF)	E3487/E333	13/65
E3196	86 219	—	*Phoenix,* — 1979	EE(VF)	E3488/E334	13/65
E3197	86 237	—	*Sir Charles Hallé,* November 1983	EE(VF)	E3489/E335	13/65
E3198	86 033	—	—	EE(VF)	E3490/E336	1/66
E3199	86 001	—	—	EE(VF)	E3491/E337	2/66
E3200	86 029	86 329	—	EE/VF)	E3492/E388	2/66

E3301-E3302 *see* E3096-E3097

E3303-E3305 *see* E3098-E3100

Class 71

Following the decision to electrify the Kent Coast route under the 1955 Modernisation Plan this fleet of 24 booster electric locomotives were constructed, normally being used on such trains as the 'Golden Arrow' and 'Night Ferry'.

BR 1957 No	BR 1967 re-No	TOPS No	Built by	Works No	Date introduced	Date withdrawn
E5000	E5024	—	BR Doncaster	—	February 1959	November 1966
E5001	—	71 001	BR Doncaster	—	February 1959	November 1977
E5002	—	71 002	BR Doncaster	—	February 1959	November 1977
E5003	—	—	BR Doncaster	—	March 1959	January 1967
E5004	—	71 004	BR Doncaster	—	April 1959	November 1977
E5005	—	—	BR Doncaster	—	May 1959	January 1967
E5006	—	—	BR Doncaster	—	May 1959	October 1966
E5007	—	71 007	BR Doncaster	—	June 1959	November 1977
E5008	—	71 008	BR Doncaster	—	July 1959	November 1977
E5009	—	71 009	BR Doncaster	—	August 1959	November 1977
E5010	—	71 010	BR Doncaster	—	October 1959	November 1977
E5011	—	71 011	BR Doncaster	—	October 1959	November 1977
E5012	—	71 012	BR Doncaster	—	November 1959	November 1977
E5013	—	71 013	BR Doncaster	—	December 1959	November 1977
E5014	—	71 014	BR Doncaster	—	February 1960	November 1977

BR 1957 No	Date withdrawn	Disposal code	Disposal details	Notes
E3181				
E3182				
E3183				
E3184				
E3185				
E3186				
E3187				
E3188				
E3189				
E3190				
E3191				
E3192				
E3193				
E3194				
E3195				
E3196				
E3197				
E3198				
E3199				
E3200				

Type: 750V dc (O/H and 3rd rail)
Weight: 77 ton
Bogie type: Bo-Bo
Max speed: 90mph
Class code: BR Class 71

Tractive effort: 43,800lb
Length: 50ft 7in
Height: 13ft 1in
Width: 9ft $3\frac{1}{16}$in

BR 1957 No	Disposal code	Disposal details	Notes
E5000	R	To Class 74	
E5001	P	National Railway Museum, York	Stored from October 1976
E5002	C	J. Cashmore, Newport, Gwent December 1978	Stored from October 1976
E5003	R	To Class 74	
E5004	C	BREL Doncaster December 1979	Stored from October 1976
E5005	R	To Class 74	
E5006	R	To Class 74	
E5007	C	J. Cashmore, Newport, Gwent c1978	Stored from October 1976
E5008	C	J. Cashmore, Newport, Gwent c1978	Stored from October 1976
E5009	C	BREL Doncaster September 1979	Stored from October 1976
E5010	C	BREL Doncaster August 1979	Stored from October 1976
E5011	C	BREL Doncaster November 1979	Stored from October 1976
E5012	C	J. Cashmore, Newport, Gwent c1978	Stored from October 1976
E5013	C	BREL Doncaster November 1979	Stored from October 1976
E5014	C	BREL Doncaster September 1979	Stored from October 1976

BR 1957 No	BR 1967 Re-No	TOPS No	Built by	Works No	Date introduced	Date withdrawn
E5015	—	—	BR Doncaster	—	February 1960	February 1966
E5016	—	—	BR Doncaster	—	April 1960	November 1966
E5017	—	—	BR Doncaster	—	March 1960	January 1967
E5018	E5003	71 003	BR Doncaster	—	April 1960	November 1977
E5019	—	—	BR Doncaster	—	June 1960	November 1966
E5020	E5005	71 005	BR Doncaster	—	June 1960	November 1977
E5021	—	—	BR Doncaster	—	August 1960	January 1967
E5022	E5006	71 006	BR Doncaster	—	September 1960	November 1977
E5023	—	—	BR Doncaster	—	November 1960	January 1967
E5024 — see E5000						

Class 73

The dual power 'electro-diesel' concept was designed by and for the Southern Region. Within one shell a loco combining a straight dc locomotive, with its own self-contained diesel-electric powerplant. First six were SR prototypes — remainder built to a revised design by English Electric.

BR 1957 No	*TOPS No*	*Name*	*Built by*	*Works No*	*Date introduced*
E6001	73 001	—	BR Eastleigh	—	February 1962
E6002	73 002	—	BR Eastleigh	—	March 1962
E6003	73 003	—	BR Eastleigh	—	April 1962
E6004	73 004	—	BR Eastleigh	—	July 1962
E6005	73 005	—	BR Eastleigh	—	August 1962
E6006	73 006	—	BR Eastleigh	—	November 1962
E6007	73 101	*Brighton Evening Argus,* December 1980	EE(VF)	E3569/E339	October 1965
E6008	73 102	—	EE(VF)	E3570/E340	October 1965
E6009	73 103	—	EE(VF)	E3571/E341	November 1965
E6010	73 104	—	EE(VF)	E3572/E342	November 1965
E6011	73 105	—	EE(VF)	E3573/E343	December 1965
E6012	73 106	—	EE(VF)	E3574/E344	December 1965
E6013	73 107	—	EE(VF)	E3575/E345	December 1965
E6014	73 108	—	EE(VF)	E3576/E346	January 1966
E6015	73 109	—	EE(VF)	E3577/E347	January 1966
E6016	73 110	—	EE(VF)	E3578/E348	January 1966
E6017	73 111	—	EE(VF)	E3579/E349	January 1966
E6018	73 112	—	EE(VF)	E3580/E350	February 1966
E6019	73 113	—	EE(VF)	E3581/E351	February 1966
E6020	73 114	—	EE(VF)	E3582/E352	February 1966
E6021	73 115	—	EE(VF)	E3583/E353	February 1966
E6022	73 116	—	EE(VF)	E3584/E354	March 1966
E6023	73 117	—	EE(VF)	E3585/E355	March 1966
E6024	73 118	—	EE(VF)	E3586/E356	March 1966
E6025	73 119	—	EE(VF)	E3587/E357	March 1966
E6026	73 120	—	EE(VF)	E3588/E358	April 1966
E6027	—	—	EE(VF)	E3589/E359	April 1966
E6028	73 121	*Croydon 1883-1983*	EE(VF)	E3590/E360	April 1966
E6029	73 122	—	EE(VF)	E3591/E361	April 1966
E6030	73 123	*Gatwick Express,* May 1984	EE(VF)	E3592/E362	May 1966
E6031	73 124	—	EE(VF)	E3593/E363	May 1966
E6032	73 125	—	EE(VF)	E3594/E364	May 1966
E6033	73 126	—	EE(VF)	E3595/E365	May 1966
E6034	73 127	—	EE(VF)	E3596/E366	May 1966
E6035	73 128	—	EE(VF)	E3597/E367	June 1966

BR 1957 No	*Disposal code*	*Disposal details*	*Notes*
E5015	R	To Class 74	
E5016	R	To Class 74	
E5017	R	To Class 74	
E5018	C	BREL Doncaster March 1980	Stored from October 1976
E5019	R	To Class 74	
E5020	C	J. Cashmore, Newport, Gwent September 1978	Stored from October 1976
E5021	R	To Class 74	
E5022	C	J. Cashmore, Newport, Gwent c1978	Stored from October 1976
E5023	R	To Class 74	

Type: 750V dc or D/E EE6K of 600hp
Weight: 76½ ton
Bogie type: Bo-Bo
Max speed: 80*/90mph
Class code: 72*, later 73, BR Class 73
Tractive effort: 42,000lb (elec)*, 34,000lb (diesel)*
40,000lb (elec), 36,000lb (diesel)
Length: 53ft 8in (buffers extended)
Height: 12ft $5\frac{7}{16}$in
Width: 8ft 8in
*E6001-6

BR 1957 No	*Date withdrawn*	*Disposal code*	*Disposal details*	*Notes*
E6001				
E6002				
E6003				
E6004				
E6005				
E6006				
E6007				Carried No 73 100 December 1980-January 1981
E6008				
E6009				
E6010				
E6011				
E6012				
E6013				
E6014				
E6015				
E6016				
E6017				
E6018				
E6019				
E6020				
E6021	April 1982	C	BR Selhurst depot August 1982	
E6022				
E6023				
E6024				
E6025				
E6026				
E6027	July 1972	C	BR Slade Green depot February 1973	
E6028				
E6029				
E6030				
E3031				
E6032				
E6033				
E6034				
E6035				

BR 1957 No	*TOPS No*	*Name*	*Built by*	*Works No*	*Date introduced*
E6036	73 129	*City of Winchester,* December 1982	EE(VF)	E3598/E368	June 1966
E6037	73 130	—	EE(VF)	E3709/E369	July 1966
E6038	73 131	—	EE(VF)	E3710/E370	July 1966
E6039	73 132	—	EE(VF)	E3711/E371	July 1966
E6040	73 133	—	EE(VF)	E3712/E372	August 1966
E6041	73 134	—	EE(VF)	E3713/E373	August 1966
E6042	73 135	—	EE(VF)	E3714/E374	August 1966
E6043	73 136	—	EE(VF)	E3715/E375	September 1966
E6044	73 137	—	EE(VF)	E3716/E376	September 1966
E6045	73 138	—	EE(VF)	E3717/E377	October 1966
E6046	73 139	—	EE(VF)	E3718/E378	October 1966
E6047	73 140	—	EE(VF)	E3719/E379	October 1966
E6048	73 141	—	EE(VF)	E3720/E380	December 1966
E6049	73 142	*Broadlands,* September 1980	EE(VF)	E3721/E381	January 1967

Class 74

Rebuilt from SR Class 71 electric locomotives, these machines were introduced for the Bournemouth line electrification scheme of the mid-1960s, for use with passenger and freight trains, especially those operating to and from Southampton docks.

BR 1957 No	*TOPS No*	*Former Class 71 No*	*Rebuilt by*	*Works No*	*Date introduced*	*Date withdrawn*
E6101	74 001	E5015	BR Crewe	—	March 1968	December 1977
E6102	74 002	E5016	BR Crewe	—	November 1967	June 1977
E6103	74 003	E5006	BR Crewe	—	January 1968	December 1977
E6104	74 004	E5024	BR Crewe	—	March 1968	December 1977
E6105	74 005	E5019	BR Crewe	—	March 1968	December 1977
E6106	74 006	E5023	BR Crewe	—	April 1968	June 1976
E6107	74 007	E5003	BR Crewe	—	April 1968	December 1977
E6108	74 008	E5005	BR Crewe	—	May 1968	December 1977
E6109	74 009	E5017	BR Crewe	—	May 1968	December 1977
E6110	74 010	E5021	BR Crewe	—	June 1968	December 1977

Section 4
British Railways TOPS Numbers

Class 70 (20001-20003) *see* CC1-CC3

Class 71 (71 001-71 014) *see* E5000-E5024

Class 73 (73 001-73 142) *see* E6001-E6049

Class 74 (74 001-74 010) *see* E6101-E6110

Class 76 (76 001-76 057) *see* E26000-E26057

Class 77 *see* E27000-E27006

BR 1957 No	*Date withdrawn*	*Disposal code*	*Disposal details*	*Notes*
E6036				
E3037				
E6038				
E6039				
E6040				
E6041				
E6042				
E6043				
E6044				
E6045				
E6046				
E6047				
E6048				
E6049				

Type: 750V dc or D/E Paxman 6YJXL of 650hp
Weight: 86$\frac{1}{4}$ ton
Bogie type: Bo-Bo
Max speed: 90mph
Class code: BR Class 74

Tractive effort: 47,500lb (elec), 40,000lb (diesel)
Length: 50ft 5$\frac{3}{4}$in (buffers extended)
Height: 13ft 0$^{5}/_{8}$in
Width: 9ft 3$^{1}/_{16}$in

BR 1957 No	*Disposal code*	*Disposal details*	*Notes*
E6101	C	Birds Ltd, Long Marston c1979	
E6102	C	J. Cashmore, Newport, Gwent December 1977	
E6103	C	J. Cashmore, Newport, Gwent December 1980	
E6104	C	Birds Ltd, Long Marston c1979	
E6105	C	BR Fratton depot by Pounds Ltd January 1981	
E6106	C	G. Cohen, Kettering, Northamptonshire July 1977	
E6107	C	Birds Ltd, Long Marston c1979	
E6108	C	Birds Ltd, Long Marston c1979	
E6109	C	Birds Ltd, Long Marston c1979	
E6110	C	BREL Doncaster October 1979	After withdrawal to Derby for possible departmental use

Class 80 *see* E1000
Class 81 (81 001-81 022) *see* E3001-E3023, E3096-E3097
Class 82 (82 001-82 008) *see* E3046-E3055
Class 83 (83 001-83 015) *see* E3024-E3035, E3098-E3100
Class 84 (84 001-84 010) *see* E3036-E3045
Class 85 (85 001-85 040) *see* E3056-E3095
Class 86 (86 001-86 401) *see* E3101-E3200

Class 87

Introduced for the 'new' electric railway between Crewe and Glasgow, these Class 87s were the ultimate design in ac traction, based on the previous AL1-AL6 classes.

TOPS No	*Name*	*Built by*	*Works No*	*Date introduced*	*Date withdrawn*
87 001	*Royal Scot,* July 1977	BREL Crewe	—	June 1973	
87 002	*Royal Sovereign,* July 1978	BREL Crewe	—	June 1973	
87 003	*Patriot,* June 1978	BREL Crewe	—	July 1973	
87 004	*Britannia,* April 1978	BREL Crewe	—	July 1973	
87 005	*City of London,* November 1977	BREL Crewe	—	August 1973	
87 006	*City of Glasgow,* December 1977	BREL Crewe	—	November 1973	
87 007	*City of Manchester,* October 1977	BREL Crewe	—	October 1973	
87 008	*City of Liverpool,* November 1977	BREL Crewe	—	November 1973	
87 009	*City of Birmingham,* November 1977	BREL Crewe	—	November 1973	
87 010	*King Arthur,* June 1978	BREL Crewe	—	December 1973	
87 011	*The Black Prince,* May 1978	BREL Crewe	—	January 1974	
87 012	*Coeur-de-Lion,* May 1978	BREL Crewe	—	January 1974	
87 013	*John o' Gaunt,* March 1978	BREL Crewe	—	February 1974	
87 014	*Knight of the Thistle,* May 1978	BREL Crewe	—	January 1974	
87 015	*Howard of Effingham,* May 1978	BREL Crewe	—	February 1974	
87 016	*Sir Francis Drake,* April 1978	BREL Crewe	—	March 1974	
87 017	*Iron Duke,* May 1978	BREL Crewe	—	March 1974	
87 018	*Lord Nelson,* March 1978	BREL Crewe	—	May 1974	
87 019	*Sir Winston Churchill,* May 1978	BREL Crewe	—	March 1974	
87 020	*North Briton,* May 1978	BREL Crewe	—	March 1974	
87 021	*Robert the Bruce,* June 1978	BREL Crewe	—	April 1974	
87 022	*Cock o' The North,* June 1978	BREL Crewe	—	April 1974	
87 023	—	BREL Crewe	—	April 1974	
87 024	*Lord of the Isles,* May 1978	BREL Crewe	—	April 1974	
87 025	*County of Cheshire,* November 1982	BREL Crewe	—	April 1974	
87 026	*Sir Richard Arkwright,* October 1982	BREL Crewe	—	May 1974	
87 027	*Wolf of Badenoch,* May 1978	BREL Crewe	—	May 1974	
87 028	*Lord President,* May 1978	BREL Crewe	—	May 1974	
87 029	*Earl Marischal,* June 1978	BREL Crewe	—	June 1974	
87 030	*Black Douglas,* July 1978	BREL Crewe	—	June 1974	
87 031	*Hal o' The Wynd,* June 1978	BREL Crewe	—	July 1974	
87 032	*Kenilworth,* May 1978	BREL Crewe	—	July 1974	
87 033	*Thane of Fife,* May 1978	BREL Crewe	—	August 1974	

Type: 25kV ac
Weight: $83\frac{1}{4}$ ton
Bogie type: Bo-Bo
Max speed: 110mph
Class code: BR Class 87

Tractive effort: 58,000lb
Length: 56ft 6in
Height: 13ft $1\frac{1}{4}$in
Width: 8ft $8\frac{1}{4}$in

TOPS No	*Disposal code*	*Disposal details*	*Notes*
87 001			Named *Stephenson* from January 1976-July 1977
87 002			
87 003			
87 004			
87 005			
87 006			
87 007			
87 008			
87 009			
87 010			
87 011			
87 012			
87 013			
87 014			
87 015			
87 016			
87 017			
87 018			
87 019			
87 020			
87 021			
87 022			
87 023			Named *Highland Chieftain* from June 1978-May 1984
87 024			
87 025			Named *Borderer* from June 1978-November 1982
87 026			Named *Redgauntlet* from May 1978-October 1982
87 027			
87 028			
87 029			
87 030			
87 031			
87 032			
87 033			

TOPS No	Name	Built by	Works No	Date introduced	Date withdrawn
87 034	*William Shakespeare,* May 1978	BREL Crewe	—	September 1974	
87 035	*Robert Burns,* April 1978	BREL Crewe	—	October 1974	
87 101	*Stephenson,* October 1977	BREL Crewe	—	January 1977*	

Departmental Traction: Part 3 Section 1 Diesel (including Petrol)

Pre-Nationalisation Stock

Southern Railway

SR No	BR No	Description	Type	Built by and Works No	Date introduced
49S	DS49*	Petrol Shunter	0-4-0	Exmouth Jn Shops	June 1940
343S	DS343*	Petrol Shunter	0-4-0	AEC Southall	— 1930
346S	DS346*	Petrol Inspection Car	0-4-0	LBSCR/Drewry 615	— 1915
400S	DS400	Diesel Mech Shunter	0-4-0	Fowler JF 22934	— 1941
600S	DS600	Diesel Mech Shunter	0-4-0	Fowler JF 22997	— 1943
499S	DS499*	Petrol Shunter	0-4-0	Lancing Carriage Works	— 1935

*Number not carried

Great Western Railway

GWR No	BR No	Description	Type	Built by and Works No	Date introduced
15	—	Petrol Shunter	0-4-0	Simplex 2138	— 1923
22	—	Petrol Shunter	0-4-0	Simplex 5031	— 1930
23	—	Petrol Shunter	0-4-0	Simplex 3731	— 1925
24	—	Petrol Shunter	0-4-0	Simplex 3821	— 1926
25	—	Petrol Shunter	0-4-0	Simplex 5074	— 1930
26	—	Petrol Shunter	0-4-0	Simplex 4178	— 1927
27	—	Petrol Shunter	0-4-0	Simplex 3820	— 1926
No 1	—	Mechanical Shunter	0-4-0	Fowler 19451	— 1933

London Midland Scottish Railway

LMSR No	BR No	Description	Type	Built by and Works No	Date introduced
5519	ZM9	Mechanical Shunter	0-4-0	H/Clarke D563	— 1930
2	ED1	Mechanical Shunter	0-4-0	Fowler JF21048	— 1935
MPU1	953	Mobile Power Unit	0-6-0		May 1939*
MPU2	954	Mobile Power Unit	0-6-0		May 1939*
MPU3	—	Mobile Power Unit	0-6-0		Sept 1939*

*Rebuilt

TOPS No	*Disposal code*	*Disposal details*	*Notes*
87 034			
87 035			
87 101			Numbered 87 036 when built

*Constructed during late 1974 and used as test loco. Into Capital Stock January 1977

SR No	*Date withdrawn*	*Disposal code*	*Disposal details*	*Notes*
49S	September 1959	C	T. W. Ward, Briton Ferry	
343S	October 1952	C	BR Workshops, Eastleigh	
346S	June 1949		—	
400S	June 1957		—	First used by WD. Sold to SR in 1946
600S	January 1963	C	Birds Ltd, Long Marston	First used by WD. Sold to SR in 1947
499S	March 1965	C	BR Workshops, Lancing	

GWR No	*Date withdrawn*	*Disposal code*	*Disposal details*	*Notes*
15	February 1951	C	BR Workshops, Swindon March 1951	
22	— 1952		—	2ft gauge
23	July 1960	C	BR Workshops, Swindon October 1960	
24	November 1960	C	BR Workshops, Swindon November 1960	
25	— 1951		—	2ft gauge
26	July 1960	C	BR Workshops, Swindon October 1960	
27	July 1960	C	BR Workshops, Swindon October 1960	
No 1	March 1940	S	Ministry of Supply	

LMSR No	*Date withdrawn*	*Disposal code*	*Disposal details*	*Notes*
5519	October 1957	C	BR Workshops, Horwich c1958	1ft 6in gauge loco
2	June 1962	C	BR Workshops, Derby June 1962	
MPU1		C		Ex-LMS No 7056
MPU2		C		Ex-LMS No 7055
MPU3		C		Ex-LMS No 1831

London North Eastern Railway

LNER No	BR No	Built by	Works No	Introduced to Departmental fleet	Date Withdrawn from stock
100	26510*	NER Darlington	1007	December 1942	April 1963

Other Companies' Stock (including battery and electric)

Owning company	Original No	Subsequent re-No	Description	Type	Date introduced
Midland Railway	1550	BEL1	Battery Shunter	4-wheel	— 1914
North Staffs Railway	—	BEL2	Battery Shunter	4-wheel	— 1917
Lancs & Yorks Railway	2	—	Battery Shunter	4-wheel	— 1916
Lancs & Yorks Railway	1	—	Electric Loco	2-4-2	— 1912
L&SWR	75S	DS75	Electric Loco	Bo	— 1898
L&SWR	74S	DS74*	Electric Loco	Bo-Bo	— 1899
Lancs & Yorks Railway	1	—	Petrol Shunter	4-wheel	— 1919
Lancs & Yorks Railway	2	—	Petrol Shunter	4-wheel	— 1920
Lancs & Yorks Railway	3	—	Petrol Shunter	4-wheel	— 1920

*Number not carried

British Railways (diesel and electric)

In Numerical order

BR No	Former No	Built by	Works No	Introduced or date taken into Dept stock	Date withdrawn
ED1	See LMSR No 2				
ED2	—	Fowler	4200041	— 1949	June 1965
ED3	—	Fowler	4200042	— 1949	September 1967
ED4	—	Fowler	4200043	— 1949	February 1964
ED5	—	Fowler	4200044	— 1949	June 1965
ED6	—	Fowler	4200045	— 1949	September 1967
ED7	—	Fowler	22891	— 1955	February 1964
ZM9	See LMSR No 5519				
ED10	—	R/Hornsby	411322	— 1958	February 1965
15	See GWR No 15				
20	See BR No 97020				
22	See GWR No 22				
23	See GWR No 23				
24	See GWR No 24				
25	See GWR No 25				
26	See GWR No 26				
27	See GWR No 27				
ZM32	—	R/Hornsby	416214	— 1957	March 1964
DS49	See SR No 49S				
52	11104	Hibberd	3466	— 1950	March 1967
56	—	R/Hornsby	338424	— 1955	May 1970
DS74	See LSWR 74S				
DS75	See LSWR 75S				

LNER No	Disposal code	Disposal details	Notes
100	C	BR Workshops, Doncaster	

*BR number not carried until January 1959

Date withdrawn	Disposal code	Disposal details	Notes
September 1964	C	A. King, Norwich c1964	Built at Derby
June 1963	P	Staffordshire Industrial Museum	Built at Stoke
May 1946	C	Railway Works, Derby c1946	
— 1920	C	Railway Works, Horwich	Based on 2-4-2T steam
October 1968	P	National Railway Museum, York	
July 1965	C	Cox & Danks, Park Royal c1965	
November 1930	P	Chasewater RPS	Used at various industrial sites prior to preservation
November 1930	C	Arnott Young 1963	Used at various industrial sites
November 1930	C	Synthetite Mold 1965	

Use	Disposal code	Disposal details	Notes
CCE Shunter	C	BR Workshops, Derby September 1967	
CCE Shunter	C	G. Cohen, Kettering, Northamptonshire March 1968	
CCE Shunter	C	J. Cashmore, Great Bridge, Tipton c1968	
CCE Shunter	C	J. Cashmore, Great Bridge, Tipton c1968	
CCE Shunter	C	G. Cohen, Kettering, Northamptonshire c1966	
CCE Shunter	—	—	Built 1940
CCE Shunter	S	Church Farm, Fen Stanton, Cambridgeshire	3ft 0in gauge
Works Shunter	P	Narrow Gauge Railway Centre, Blaenau Ffestiniog	1ft 6in gauge
CCE Shunter	C	J. Cashmore, Newport, Gwent c1967	
CCE Shunter	C	T. J. Thomson, Stockton-on-Tees c1976	

BR No	Former No	Built by	Works No	Introduced or date taken into Dept stock	Date withdrawn
81	—	A/Barclay	424	— 1958	July 1967
82	—	R/Hornsby	425485	— 1958	May 1970
83	—	R/Hornsby	432477	— 1959	May 1970
84	—	R/Hornsby	432478	— 1959	May 1970
85	—	R/Hornsby	432489	— 1959	May 1970
86	—	R/Hornsby	463151	— 1961	May 1970
87	—	R/Hornsby	463152	— 1961	May 1970
88	D2612	Hunslet	5661	February 1961	December 1967
89	D2615	Hunslet	5664	January 1964	November 1977†
91	—	BR Swindon	—	— 1958	— 1967†
92	—	BR Swindon	—	— 1958	— 1967†
100	See LNER No 100				
DS209*	—	Secmafer	—	— 1965	Returned to France 1968
DS343	See SR No 343S				
DS346	See SR No 346S				
DS400	See SR No 400S				
DS600	See SR No 600S				
PWM650	See 97650				
PWM651	See 97651				
PWM652	See 97652				
PWM653	See 97653				
PWM654	See 97654				
DS1169	—	R/Hornsby	237923	— 1946	October 1972
DS1173	—	Drewry	2217/D46	July 1947	March 1967†
D2554 (05 001)	See 97803				
D2991	—	R/Hornsby	480692	May 1973	—
D5705	See No 15705				
D5901	—	EE(VF)	E2378/D418	December 1969	November 1975
D7076	—	B/Peacock	7980	August 1974	November 1982
D7096	—	B/Peacock	8000	August 1974	November 1982
D8512	—	Clayton	4365U16	July 1969	January 1972
D8521	—	Clayton	4365U17	July 1969	October 1978
D8598	—	B/Peacock	8015	March 1972	October 1978
15705	D5705	M/Vickers	—	December 1968	September 1977
97020	20	R/Hornsby	408493	— 1957	April 1981
97201	24061	BR Crewe	—	November 1975	—
97202	25131	BR Derby	—	September 1983	January 1984
97250	25318	BR Derby	—	May 1983	—
97251	25305	B/Peacock	—	August 1983	—
97252	25314	BR Derby	—	September 1983	—
97401*	46009	BR Derby	—	October 1983	July 1984
97402*	46023	BR Derby	—	December 1983	—
97650	PWM650	R/Hornsby	312990	— 1953	—
97651	PWM651	R/Hornsby	431758	— 1959	—
97652	PWM652	R/Hornsby	431759	— 1959	—
97653	PWM653	R/Hornsby	431760	— 1959	—
97654	PWM654	R/Hornsby	431761	— 1959	—
97800	08600	BR Derby	—	January 1979	—
97801	08267	BR Derby	—	March 1978	—
97802*	08070	BR Derby	—	February 1978	January 1980
97803	05001	Hunslet	4870	January 1981	September 1983

BR No	*Use*	*code*	*Disposal details*	*Notes*
81	CCE/PW Shunter	I	Capital Stock as 2nd No D2956	
82	CCE Shunter	C	T. J. Thomson, Stockton-on-Tees c1976	
83	CCE Shunter	C	W. Heselwood, Attercliffe, Sheffield c1971	
84	CCE Shunter	C	Arnott Young, Parkgate, Rawmarsh c1970	
85	CCE Shunter	C	Arnott Young, Parkgate, Rawmarsh c1970	
86	CCE Shunter	C	Arnott Young, Parkgate, Rawmarsh c1970	
87	CCE Shunter	C	T. J. Thomson, Stockton-on-Tees c1976	
88	Works Shunter	C	Argosy Salvage, Shettleston, Glasgow	
89	Works Shunter	I	Capital Stock — D2615	
91	CCE Shunter	I	Capital Stock — D2370	
92	CCE Shunter	I	Capital Stock — D2371	
100				
DS209*	CCE Shunter	E	Trial loco returned to France	Carried French No 233.S.2
DS343				
DS346				
DS400				
DS600				
PWM650				
PWM651				
PWM652				
PWM653				
PWM654				
DS1169	CCE Shunter	C	G. Cohen, Kettering, Northamptonshire July 1973	
DS1173	CCE Shunter	I	Capital Stock — D2341	
D2554				
D2991	Generator loco			
D5705				
D5901	Test loco	C	BREL Doncaster February 1977	
D7076	Dead load loco	P	Bury Transport Museum December 1982	
D7096	Dead load loco	A	BR Test Track Old Dalby	
D8512	Test loco	C	BREL Glasgow January 1973	
D8521	Generator loco	C	BREL Glasgow April 1979	
D8598	Test loco	C	BREL Glasgow March 1979	
15705	Test loco/carriage heating vehicle	P	Privately at Swindon	Also carried No TDB968006
97020	S&T Shunter	C	RG Signal Works by Cartwrights of Tipton August 1982	
97201	Test loco at RTC			Also carried No TDB968007
97202	CM&EE test loco	A	BREL Toton depot	Returned to No 25131
97250	ETHEL			
97251	ETHEL			
97252	ETHEL			
97401*	Test loco	C	BR at Old Dalby	Used by CEGB in train crash
97402*	Test loco			
97650	CCE Shunter			
97651	CCE Shunter			
97652	CCE Shunter			
97653	CCE Shunter			
97654	CCE Shunter			
97800	CM&EE Shunter			Was No 97880. Named *Ivor*
97801	CM&EE test loco			Was No 968020. Named *Pluto*
97802*	Battery charger	C	BREL Glasgow February 1980	
97803	IoW Shunter	P	Wight Loco Soc Haven Street	Departmental use since 1966

BR No	Former No	Built by	Works No	Introduced or date taken into Dept stock	Date withdrawn
97804	06003	A/Barclay	435	March 1981	—
97805	03079	BR Doncaster	—	April 1984	—
97880	See No 97800				
ADB966506	D3078	BR Darlington	—	September 1973	December 1978
ADB966507	D3006	BR Derby	—	October 1973	June 1979
ADB966508	D3035	BR Derby	—	January 1974	January 1979
ADB966509	D3069	BR Darlington	—	January 1975	June 1979
ADB966510	D3037	BR Derby	—	November 1974	December 1978
ADB966511	See No 968011				
ADB966512	See No 968012				
ADB966513	See No 968010				
ADB968000	D8243	BTH-Clayton	—	September 1969	—
ADB968001	D8233	BTH-Clayton	1131	December 1969	September 1982
ADB968002	D8237	BTH-Clayton	—	August 1969	September 1982
ADB968003	D8203	BTH-Clayton	1034	January 1970	June 1978
TDB968004	Number allocated for conversion of D7055 to Heating unit				
TDB968005	D7089	B/Peacock	7993	October 1974	November 1975
TDB968006	See No 15705				
RDB968007	See No 97201				
TDB968008	24054	BR Crewe	—	August 1976	October 1982
TDB968009	24142	BR Derby	—	August 1976	September 1982
ADB968010	08117	BR Derby	—	September 1977	November 1978
ADB968011	08119	BR Derby	—	September 1977	April 1979
ADB968012	08111	BR Derby	—	September 1977	April 1979
ADB968013	31013	Brush	84	March 1979	October 1982
ADB968014	31002	Brush	73	July 1980	October 1982
ADB968015	31014	Brush	85	July 1977	October 1982
ADB968016	31008	Brush	79	February 1981	October 1982
RDB968020	See 97801				
ADB968021	84009	NBL	27801	August 1978	—
ADB975812	43000	BR Crewe	—	October 1979	January 1982
ADB975813	43001	BR Crewe	—	October 1979	January 1982

*Number not carried
†To Capital Stock

High Speed Train Power Cars

Prototype Unit. Class 41 (252 DMU)

Class 41

Prototype High Speed Train set formed of 10 cars, including two power cars, for new generation of high speed rail travel, unit operated on ER and WR. Later classified as DMU Class 252.

Original No	Revised No	Set No	Built by	Works No	Date introduced	Date withdrawn
41 001	43 000	252 001	BREL Crewe	—	June 1972	November 1976
41 002	43 001	252 001	BREL Crewe	—	August 1972	November 1976

Use	Disposal code	Disposal details	Notes
S&T Shunter			
IoW Shunter			
Snowplough	C	BREL Doncaster February 1979	
Snowplough	C	BREL Doncaster November 1979	
Snowplough	C	BREL Doncaster May 1979	
Snowplough	C	BREL Doncaster April 1980	
Snowplough	C	BREL Doncaster March 1979	
Heating unit			
Heating unit	P	Class 15 Preservation Society	
Heating unit	A	BR Toton depot	
Heating unit	C	F. Berry, Leicester at BR Colchester depot July 1981	
Cancelled			
Heating unit	C	T. J. Thomson, Stockton-on-Tees December 1975	
Heating unit	P	Bury Transport Museum as D5054	
Heating unit	A	Coopers Metals, Sheffield	
Snowplough	C	BREL Doncaster March 1979	Also allocated No ADB966513
Snowplough	C	BREL Doncaster April 1980	Also allocated No ADB966511
Snowplough	C	BREL Doncaster April 1979	Also allocated No ADB966512
Heating unit	C	BREL Doncaster August 1983	
Heating unit	C	BREL Crewe May 1984	
Heating unit	C	BREL Doncaster June 1983	
Heating unit	A	BREL Crewe	
Mobile load bank			
Test motive power	A	BREL Derby	
Test motive power	A	BREL Derby	

Engine: Paxman 12RP200L of 2,500hp
Weight: 66 ton
Bogie type: Bo-Bo
Max speed: 125mph
Class code: 41, later Class 252

Tractive effort: 17,980lb
Length: 56ft 3in
Height: 12ft 10in
Width: 9ft 0in

Original No	*Disposal code*	*Disposal details*	*Notes*
41 001	D	Departmental Stock — 975812	
41 002	D	Departmental Stock — 975813	

Class 253, 254

Production series High Speed Train sets, differing largely from prototype set. Power cars conform to unit stock with trailer vehicles, but could also be classified as locomotives. Two power cars per unit set (trailer vehicles not listed).

Power Car No	*Set No**	*Built by*	*Works No*	*Name*	*Date introduced*
43 002	253 001	BREL Crewe	—	*Top of the Pops*	February 1976
43 003	253 001	BREL Crewe	—	—	February 1976
43 004	253 002	BREL Crewe	—	—	March 1976
43 005	253 002	BREL Crewe	—	—	March 1976
43 006	253 003	BREL Crewe	—	—	May 1976
43 007	253 003	BREL Crewe	—	—	March 1976
43 008	253 004	BREL Crewe	—	—	March 1976
43 009	253 004	BREL Crewe	—	—	April 1976
43 010	253 005	BREL Crewe	—	—	April 1976
43 011	253 005	BREL Crewe	—	—	April 1976
43 012	253 006	BREL Crewe	—	—	May 1976
43 013	253 006	BREL Crewe	—	—	May 1976
43 014	253 007	BREL Crewe	—	—	May 1976
43 015	253 007	BREL Crewe	—	—	May 1976
43 016	253 008	BREL Crewe	—	—	June 1976
43 017	253 008	BREL Crewe	—	—	June 1976
43 018	253 009	BREL Crewe	—	—	June 1976
43 019	253 009	BREL Crewe	—	—	July 1976
43 020	253 010	BREL Crewe	—	—	July 1976
43 021	253 010	BREL Crewe	—	—	July 1976
43 022	253 011	BREL Crewe	—	—	July 1976
43 023	253 011	BREL Crewe	—	—	August 1976
43 024	253 012	BREL Crewe	—	—	July 1976
43 025	253 012	BREL Crewe	—	—	August 1976
43 026	253 013	BREL Crewe	—	—	August 1976
43 027	253 013	BREL Crewe	—	—	September 1976
43 028	253 014	BREL Crewe	—	—	August 1976
43 029	253 014	BREL Crewe	—	—	September 1976
43 030	253 015	BREL Crewe	—	—	September 1976
43 031	253 015	BREL Crewe	—	—	September 1976
43 032	253 016	BREL Crewe	—	—	October 1976
43 033	253 016	BREL Crewe	—	—	October 1976
43 034	253 017	BREL Crewe	—	—	November 1976
43 035	253 017	BREL Crewe	—	—	November 1976
43 036	253 018	BREL Crewe	—	—	November 1976
43 037	253 018	BREL Crewe	—	—	November 1976
43 038	253 019	BREL Crewe	—	—	December 1976
43 039	253 019	BREL Crewe	—	—	December 1976
43 040	253 020	BREL Crewe	—	—	December 1976
43 041	253 020	BREL Crewe	—	—	December 1976
43 042	253 021	BREL Crewe	—	—	February 1977
43 043	253 021	BREL Crewe	—	—	February 1977
43 044	253 022	BREL Crewe	—	—	March 1977
43 045	253 022	BREL Crewe	—	*The Grammar School, Doncaster AD1350*	March 1977
43 046	253 023	BREL Crewe	—	—	March 1977
43 047	253 023	BREL Crewe	—	*Rotherham Enterprise*	March 1977
43 048	253 024	BREL Crewe	—	—	March 1977
43 049	253 024	BREL Crewe	—	*Neville Hill*	April 1977
43 050	253 025	BREL Crewe	—	—	May 1977
43 051	253 025	BREL Crewe	—	—	April 1977
43 052	253 026	BREL Crewe	—	*City of Peterborough*	April 1977
43 053	253 026	BREL Crewe	—	*County of Humberside*	May 1977
43 054	253 027	BREL Crewe	—	—	May 1977
43 055	253 027	BREL Crewe	—	—	June 1977
43 056	254 001	BREL Crewe	—	*University of Bradford*	July 1977

Engine: Paxman 12RP200L of 2,250hp
Weight: 69 ton
Bogie type: Bo-Bo
Max speed: 125mph
Class code: 253, 254

Tractive effort: 17,980lb
Length: 58ft 5in
Height: 12ft 9in
Width: 8ft 11in

Power Car No	*Date withdrawn*	*Disposal code*	*Disposal details*	*Notes*
43 002				
43 003				
43 004				
43 005				
43 006				
43 007				
43 008				
43 009				
43 010				
43 011				
43 012				
43 013				
43 014				
43 015				
43 016				
43 017				
43 018				
43 019				
43 020				
43 021				
43 022				
43 023				
43 024				
43 025				
43 026				
43 027				
43 028				
43 029				
43 030				
43 031				
43 032				
43 033				
43 034				
43 035				
43 036				
43 037				
43 038				
43 039				
43 040				
43 041				
43 042				
43 043				
43 044				
43 045				
43 046				
43 047				
43 048				
43 049				
43 050				
43 051				
43 052				
43 053				
43 054				
43 055				
43 056				

Power Car No	Set No*	Built by	Works No	Name	Date introduced
43 057	254 001	BREL Crewe	—	*Bounds Green*	July 1977
43 058	254 002	BREL Crewe	—	—	July 1977
43 059	254 002	BREL Crewe	—	—	August 1977
43 060	254 003	BREL Crewe	—	—	August 1977
43 061	254 003	BREL Crewe	—	*City of Lincoln*	August 1977
43 062	254 004	BREL Crewe	—	—	September 1977
43 063	254 004	BREL Crewe	—	—	September 1977
43 064	254 005	BREL Crewe	—	*City of York*	October 1977
43 065	254 005	BREL Crewe	—	—	October 1977
43 066	254 006	BREL Crewe	—	—	October 1977
43 067	254 006	BREL Crewe	—	—	October 1977
43 068	254 007	BREL Crewe	—	—	November 1977
43 069	254 007	BREL Crewe	—	—	November 1977
43 070	254 008	BREL Crewe	—	—	November 1977
43 071	254 008	BREL Crewe	—	—	November 1977
43 072	254 009	BREL Crewe	—	—	December 1977
43 073	254 009	BREL Crewe	—	—	December 1977
43 074	254 010	BREL Crewe	—	—	December 1977
43 075	254 010	BREL Crewe	—	—	December 1977
43 076	254 011	BREL Crewe	—	—	December 1977
43 077	254 011	BREL Crewe	—	*County of Nottingham*	December 1977
43 078	254 012	BREL Crewe	—	*Shildon — County Durham*	January 1978
43 079	254 012	BREL Crewe	—	—	January 1978
43 080	254 013	BREL Crewe	—	—	January 1978
43 081	254 013	BREL Crewe	—	—	February 1978
43 082	254 014	BREL Crewe	—	—	February 1978
43 083	254 014	BREL Crewe	—	—	February 1978
43 084	254 015	BREL Crewe	—	—	February 1978
43 085	254 015	BREL Crewe	—	*City of Bradford*	March 1978
43 086	254 016	BREL Crewe	—	—	April 1978
43 087	254 016	BREL Crewe	—	—	May 1978
43 088	254 017	BREL Crewe	—	—	May 1978
43 089	254 017	BREL Crewe	—	—	May 1978
43 090	254 018	BREL Crewe	—	—	May 1978
43 091	254 018	BREL Crewe	—	—	May 1978
43 092	254 019	BREL Crewe	—	*Highland Chieftain*	June 1978
43 093	254 019	BREL Crewe	—	—	June 1978
43 094	254 020	BREL Crewe	—	—	June 1978
43 095	254 020	BREL Crewe	—	*Heaton*	June 1978
43 096	254 021	BREL Crewe	—	—	July 1978
43 097	254 021	BREL Crewe	—	*The Light Infantry*	July 1978
43 098	254 022	BREL Crewe	—	—	July 1978
43 099	254 022	BREL Crewe	—	—	August 1978
43 100	254 023	BREL Crewe	—	*Craigentinny*	August 1978
43 101	254 023	BREL Crewe	—	*Edinburgh International Festival*	October 1978
43 102	254 024	BREL Crewe	—	*City of Wakefield*	October 1978
43 103	254 024	BREL Crewe	—	—	October 1978
43 104	254 025	BREL Crewe	—	—	October 1978
43 105	254 025	BREL Crewe	—	*Hartlepool*	October 1978
43 106	254 026	BREL Crewe	—	—	October 1978
43 107	254 026	BREL Crewe	—	—	November 1978
43 108	254 027	BREL Crewe	—	—	November 1978
43 109	254 027	BREL Crewe	—	—	January 1979
43 110	254 028	BREL Crewe	—	*Darlington*	January 1979
43 111	254 028	BREL Crewe	—	—	February 1979
43 112	254 029	BREL Crewe	—	—	February 1979
43 113	254 029	BREL Crewe	—	*City of Newcastle upon Tyne*	February 1979
43 114	254 030	BREL Crewe	—	—	March 1979
43 115	254 030	BREL Crewe	—	—	March 1979
43 116	254 031	BREL Crewe	—	*City of Kingston upon Hull*	March 1979
43 117	254 031	BREL Crewe	—	—	March 1979

Power Car No	*Date withdrawn*	*Disposal code*	*Disposal details*	*Notes*
43 057				
43 058				
43 059				
43 060				
43 061				
43 062				
43 063				
43 064				
43 065				
43 066				
43 067				
43 068				
43 069				
43 070				
43 071				
43 072				
43 073				
43 074				
43 075				
43 076				
43 077				
43 078				
43 079				
43 080				
43 081				
43 082				
43 083				
43 084				
43 085				
43 086				
43 087				
43 088				
43 089				
43 090				
43 091				
43 092				
43 093				
43 094				
43 095				
43 096				
43 097				
43 098				
43 099				
43 100				
43 101				
43 102				
43 103				
43 104				
43 105				
43 106				
43 107				
43 108				
43 109				
43 110				
43 111				
43 112				
43 113				
43 114				
43 115				
43 116				
43 117				

Power Car No	Set No*	Built by	Works No	Name	Date introduced
43 118	254 032	BREL Crewe	—	—	March 1979
43 119	254 032	BREL Crewe	—	—	April 1979
43 120	S	BREL Crewe	—	—	September 1977
43 121	S	BREL Crewe	—	—	September 1977
43 122	S	BREL Crewe	—	—	April 1979
43 123	S	BREL Crewe	—	—	April 1979
43 124	S	BREL Crewe	—	—	June 1981
43 125	253 028	BREL Crewe	—	—	April 1979
43 126	253 028	BREL Crewe	—	—	May 1979
43 127	253 029	BREL Crewe	—	—	May 1979
43 128	253 029	BREL Crewe	—	—	June 1979
43 129	253 030	BREL Crewe	—	—	June 1979
43 130	253 030	BREL Crewe	—	—	July 1979
43 131	253 031	BREL Crewe	—	—	July 1979
43 132	253 031	BREL Crewe	—	—	July 1979
43 133	253 032	BREL Crewe	—	—	July 1979
43 134	253 032	BREL Crewe	—	—	August 1979
43 135	253 033	BREL Crewe	—	—	August 1979
43 136	253 033	BREL Crewe	—	—	August 1979
43 137	253 034	BREL Crewe	—	—	September 1979
43 138	253 034	BREL Crewe	—	—	September 1979
43 139	253 035	BREL Crewe	—	—	March 1980
43 140	253 035	BREL Crewe	—	—	March 1980
43 141	253 036	BREL Crewe	—	—	April 1980
43 142	253 036	BREL Crewe	—	—	May 1980
43 143	253 037	BREL Crewe	—	—	February 1981
43 144	253 037	BREL Crewe	—	—	February 1981
43 145	253 038	BREL Crewe	—	—	March 1981
43 146	253 038	BREL Crewe	—	—	March 1981
43 147	253 039	BREL Crewe	—	—	May 1981
43 148	253 039	BREL Crewe	—	—	May 1981
43 149	253 040	BREL Crewe	—	—	June 1981
43 150	253 040	BREL Crewe	—	—	June 1981
43 151	253 041	BREL Crewe	—	—	June 1981
43 152	253 041	BREL Crewe	—	—	June 1981
43 153	254 033	BREL Crewe	—	*University of Durham*	January 1981
43 154	254 033	BREL Crewe	—	—	January 1981
43 155	254 034	BREL Crewe	—	—	January 1981
43 156	254 034	BREL Crewe	—	—	January 1981
43 157	254 035	BREL Crewe	—	*Yorkshire Evening Post*	April 1981
43 158	254 035	BREL Crewe	—	—	April 1981
43 159	254 036	BREL Crewe	—	—	April 1981
43 160	254 036	BREL Crewe	—	—	April 1981
43 161	254 037	BREL Crewe	—	—	June 1981
43 162	254 037	BREL Crewe	—	*Borough of Stevenage*	June 1981
43 163	253 041	BREL Crewe	—	—	July 1981
43 164	253 041	BREL Crewe	—	—	July 1981
43 165	253 042	BREL Crewe	—	—	September 1981
43 166	253 042	BREL Crewe	—	—	September 1981
43 167	253 043	BREL Crewe	—	—	September 1981
43 168	253 043	BREL Crewe	—	—	September 1981
43 169	253 044	BREL Crewe	—	—	September 1981
43 170	253 044	BREL Crewe	—	—	September 1981
43 171	253 045	BREL Crewe	—	—	September 1981
43 172	253 045	BREL Crewe	—	—	September 1981
43 173	253 046	BREL Crewe	—	—	September 1981
43 174	253 046	BREL Crewe	—	—	September 1981
43 175	253 047	BREL Crewe	—	—	October 1981
43 176	253 047	BREL Crewe	—	—	October 1981
43 177	253 048	BREL Crewe	—	—	November 1981
43 178	253 048	BREL Crewe	—	—	November 1981

Power Car No	*Date withdrawn*	*Disposal code*	*Disposal details*	*Notes*
43 118				
43 119				
43 120				
43 121				
43 122				
43 123				
43 124				
43 125				
43 126				
43 127				
43 128				
43 129				
43 130				
43 131				
43 132				
43 133				
43 134				
43 135				
43 136				
43 137				
43 138				
43 139				
43 140				
43 141				
43 142				
43 143				
43 144				
43 145				
43 146				
43 147				
43 148				
43 149				
43 150				
43 151				
43 152				
43 153				
43 154				
43 155				
43 156				
43 157				
43 158				
43 159				
43 160				
43 161				
43 162				
43 163				
43 164				
43 165				
43 166				
43 167				
43 168				
43 169				
43 170				
43 171				
43 172				
43 173				
43 174				
43 175				
43 176				
43 177				
43 178				

Power Car No	Set No*	Built by	Works No	Name	Date introduced
43 179	253 049	BREL Crewe	—	—	November 1981
43 180	253 049	BREL Crewe	—	—	November 1981
43 181	253 050	BREL Crewe	—	—	November 1981
43 182	253 050	BREL Crewe	—	—	November 1981
43 183	253 051	BREL Crewe	—	—	February 1982
43 184	253 051	BREL Crewe	—	—	February 1982
43 185	253 052	BREL Crewe	—	—	March 1982
43 186	253 052	BREL Crewe	—	—	March 1982
43 187	253 053	BREL Crewe	—	—	April 1982
43 188	253 053	BREL Crewe	—	—	April 1982
43 189	253 054	BREL Crewe	—	—	April 1982
43 190	253 054	BREL Crewe	—	—	April 1982
43 191	253 055	BREL Crewe	—	—	May 1982
43 192	253 055	BREL Crewe	—	—	May 1982
43 193	253 056	BREL Crewe	—	*Yorkshire Post*	June 1982
43 194	253 056	BREL Crewe	—	—	June 1982
43 195	253 057	BREL Crewe	—	—	July 1982
43 196	253 057	BREL Crewe	—	—	July 1982
43 197	253 058	BREL Crewe	—	—	August 1982
43 198	253 058	BREL Crewe	—	—	August 1982

*Set numbers no longer used

Miscellaneous Stock

EMU conversions to locomotives

BR TOPS No	Departmental No	Former No	Rebuilt by	Date introduced	Date withdrawn
97701	DB975178	M61136	BREL Wolverton	— 1973	
97702	DB975179	M61139	BREL Wolverton	— 1973	
97703	—	M61182	BREL Doncaster	— 1980	
97704	—	M61185	BREL Doncaster	— 1980	
97705	—	M61184	BREL Doncaster	— 1980	
97706	—	M61189	BREL Doncaster	— 1980	
97707	LDB975407	M61166	BREL Doncaster	— 1975	
97708	LDB975408	M61173	BREL Doncaster	— 1975	
97709	LDB975409	M61172	BREL Doncaster	— 1975	
97710	LDB975410	M61175	BREL Doncaster	— 1975	

Internal User Locomotives

No	Former No	Built by	Works No	Date into internal fleet	Date withdrawn
PO1	08173	BR Darlington	—	May 1978	
PO1	08247	BR Darlington	—	August 1977	May 1978

Power Car No	Date withdrawn	Disposal code	Disposal details	Notes
43 179				
43 180				
43 181				
43 182				
43 183				
43 184				
43 185				
43 186				
43 187				
43 188				
43 189				
43 190				
43 191				
43 192				
43 193				
43 194				
43 195				
43 196				
43 197				
43 198				

BR TOPS No	Use	Disposal code	Disposal details	Notes
97701	Battery/electric loco			
97702	Battery/electric loco			
97703	Battery/electric loco			
97704	Battery/electric loco			
97705	Battery/electric loco			
97706	Battery/electric loco			
97707	Battery/electric loco			
97708	Battery/electric loco			
97709	Battery/electric loco			
97710	Battery/electric loco			

No	Disposal code	Disposal details	Notes
PO1			
PO1	—	—	Returned to Capital Stock May 1978

A fleet of 24 660–750V dc third rail/overhead locomotives were built for the SR in the late-1950s, later classified as Class 71. No E5009, later 71 009 is shown here. Ten of this class were rebuilt in 1966/67 as Class 74 electro-diesels. *BR*

Ten redundant Class 501 EMU motor cars have been rebuilt into battery-electric departmental locomotives for electrification project work. Two of these Class 97 locomotives are illustrated at Cricklewood. *BR*